Writing for College and Career

FOURTH EDITION

FOURTH EDITION

Writing for College and Career

(formerly *Writing for Career-Education Students*)

Andrew W. Hart

James A. Reinking

St. Martin's Press   New York

Senior Editor: Mark Gallaher
Developmental editor: Cathy Pusateri
Project editor: Elise Bauman
Production supervisor: Chris Pearson
Graphics: G&H Soho
Cover design: Ben Santora, Darby Downey

For information, write:
St. Martin's Press, Inc.
175 Fifth Avenue
New York, NY 10010

ISBN: 0–312–02078–3

Previous editions of this book, published by St. Martin's Press, were titled
Writing for Career-Education Students.

Acknowledgments

Allstate Life Insurance Company. "What Kind of Life Insurance Will Work Best for You?"
   From *Life Insurance: Some Facts You Should Know*, 1979. Reprinted by permission.
American Cancer Society, Inc. "What is Chemotherapy?" Reprinted by permission of the
   American Cancer Society, Inc.
Barnes & Noble Bookstores, Inc. Excerpts from *Webster's Dictionary* sales letter. Re-
   printed by permission of Barnes & Noble Bookstores, Inc.

Acknowledgments and copyrights are continued at the back of the book on page
523, which constitutes an extension of the copyright page.

For Andrea, Paul, Bruce, and Helen

To the Instructor

Writing for College and Career is a clear, step-by-step introduction to the essentials of practical writing. It is designed for students in vocational and technical programs or for courses enrolling a mixture of vocational and liberal arts students in which a strong emphasis on job-related writing is desired. It may be used for teaching first-year English composition. It is also suitable for a one-term course in technical communication.

This fourth edition offers many improvements over its predecessors, including these most significant ones:

- The style of the text has been streamlined to make it even more readable.
- Chapter 3, "The Theme," has been expanded to include discussion of headings and subheadings as well as the value of word processing in the planning, drafting, and revising stages of the writing process.
- Chapter 7, "Description," now features detailed discussions and sample papers on both objective and impressionistic description.
- Coverage of the memorandum has been expanded and now appears in a separate chapter, Chapter 10.
- Chapter 14, "The Library Research Paper," has been revised to include information on periodical indexes that provide students with references to articles unavailable in their own libraries.
- Chapter 16, "Tables, Graphs, and Drawings," now discusses the computer-assisted preparation of graphs.
- The usage errors section of the Handbook has an added unit on avoiding sexist language.
- The *Instructor's Manual* includes assignment sheets for the different kinds of writing discussed in the text. These can be duplicated and distributed to students for use in planning their papers.

Together, these improvements and others greatly enhance the usefulness of the text.

While incorporating these changes, the fourth edition retains the same straightforward organization as its predecessors. Following the basic discussion of purpose and audience in Chapter 1, Chapter 2 introduces students to the elements of a paragraph and the ways of developing it. Chapter 3 takes students step by step through the process typically followed in preparing a composition—planning, writing, and revising. These introductory chapters are followed by five chapters on expository writing—process, comparison, classification, description, and definition—each illustrated by several examples of student and professional writing. Chapter 9 considers the chief kinds of business letters, and Chapter 10 discusses memorandums. Chapters 11 through 13 take up more specialized types of communication: proposals, progress reports, investigation reports, and abstracts. Next, Chapter 14 offers detailed coverage of the steps involved in completing library research papers: choosing a suitable topic, using the library, taking notes, preparing an outline, and writing and documenting the paper. Chapters 15 and 16 treat two supplemental topics: oral presentations and the preparation of tables, graphs, and drawings. Finally, Chapter 17 discusses the job search, including letters of application, resumes, interview techniques, and four kinds of post-interview letters. Throughout, the text proceeds from a general to a specialized emphasis and from the classroom to the career.

The Handbook that concludes the text consists of three sections. The first, "Sentence Elements," discusses syntax and the eight parts of speech, offering a "crash course" in traditional grammar but avoiding the excessive complexity and the emphasis on terminology that often merely confuse students. The second section, "Avoiding Common Errors of Usage," is designed to train students' eyes and ears to catch the most common grammatical errors. The final section, "Punctuation and Mechanics," takes up the different marks of punctuation as well as capitalization, abbreviations, numbers, and italics.

The exercises in the first section of the Handbook ask students to identify grammatical elements; those in the second section ask them to correct faulty sentences; and those in the third ask them to supply missing punctuation and other mechanical features. A chart inside the back cover of the book lists correction symbols for the instructor's use in marking student papers. The symbols are keyed for student reference to the pertinent discussions in the book.

To a greater degree than comparable texts with which we are familiar, *Writing for College and Career* keeps its sights on what students need to know and *why* they need to know it. In introducing each type of writing, we point out its importance both on the job and in the students' college courses. Directions are presented in an easy-to-follow, step-by-step format—the mode of presentation students encounter most frequently in their technical or vocational courses. The students' writing examples offer realistic, achievable goals and, when compared with the professionally written examples, demonstrate that students can indeed produce first-rate work. The examples represent a range of vocational and general interests, and clearly and consistently conform to the patterns of development discussed in the text. The questions accompanying the examples have been designed to underscore important points in the chapter and to reinforce the principles of good writing in general. The suggested writing assignments at the end of each chapter ask students to put these principles into practice in writing of their own.

These features provide a number of benefits. Students readily understand and follow the directions, relate closely to the models, show increased confidence in their own ability, and perceive the value of what they are doing. As a result, they participate more actively in class, put more effort into their assignments, and produce better papers and talks.

Another feature of *Writing for College and Career* is flexibility. We strongly recommend that Chapters 1 through 3 (on audience and purpose, the paragraph, and the theme) be read first, if only as a general review. Beyond these chapters, however, the materials in this book can be "mixed and matched" in a number of ways, depending on the makeup of the class and the course objectives. For example, one instructor might elect to begin with the chapters on expository writing and then proceed to more technical materials, such as business letters, memorandums, reports, and proposals. Another instructor might start with business letters and memorandums, job application letters and resumes, and selected technical reports, then consider types of expository writing, and conclude the course with the library research paper and an oral report based on the paper.

In addition to being suited to the conventional classroom, *Writing for College and Career* is also appropriate for individual study programs in the "open" classroom. The step-by-step approach allows students to proceed at their own pace. When they feel they have mastered a step, they may check with the instructor and then move on to the next step. The variety of writing examples and the large number of suggestions for writing make it possible for the instructor to tailor assignments to the career interests of individual students.

Once again, we are indebted to many people for their encouragement and assistance. First, we would like to thank our colleagues at Ferris State, as well as others who have criticized portions of the manuscript, furnished us with writing models, and helped us in many different ways. These individuals include John Belanger, Arthur Bennett, Thomas Brownell, Mary Braun, Ann Breitenwischer, Emma Crystal, Hugh Griffith, Jane Hart, Anita Hicks, Barbara Johnson, Elaine Nienhouse, and Elliott Smith. Special thanks go to Norma Reinking for her careful proofreading of the entire manuscript during the drafting stage and to Paul Hart for providing the initial word-processing writeup.

In addition, we gratefully acknowledge the perceptive recommendations of the following colleagues who reviewed this edition in manuscript and greatly influenced its final shape: Nancy Adams, St. Louis Community College at Florissant Valley; Nancy Engemann, Western Michigan University; Gloria Isles, Greenville Technical College; Karen Hess, Normandale Community College; Mike Matthews, Tarrant County Junior College; Marilyn C. Terreault, Macomb Community College; and John Ullmer, San Antonio College. We also wish to express our appreciation to the thoroughly professional staff of St. Martin's Press, and especially to Mark Gallaher, Cathy Pusateri, and Elise Bauman. Finally, our greatest debt is to the many students and organizations whose writing examples and other illustrative materials appear in these pages. Without their help this book would not have been possible.

Andrew W. Hart
James A. Reinking

To the Student

No matter what career you choose, your ability to communicate clearly and effectively will directly affect your success. In the classroom, your instructor will often evaluate your mastery of a subject by the papers and examinations you write. Prospective employers will make judgments about your qualifications and decide whether to offer you an interview on the basis of your application letter and resume. Once you are on the job, you must be prepared to write clear, accurate reports, instructions, memorandums, and letters and to give effective oral presentations.

There is nothing mysterious about successful on-the-job communication. It does not require a special talent, nor does it depend on inspiration. It is simply a skill, and, like any other skill, it involves a series of steps or procedures that can be learned. Once you are familiar with the steps, the more you practice the easier the task becomes.

Writing for College and Career will acquaint you with the steps involved in successful communication and show you how to apply them to the specific kinds of situations you can expect to face as you pursue your career. The first three chapters—on purpose and audience, paragraphs, and themes—deal with matters basic to all successful writing. Chapters 4 through 8 explain the most frequently used types of exposition: process, comparison, classification, description, and definition. Chapter 9 discusses business letters, and Chapter 10 covers memorandums. Chapters 11 through 13 deal with four specialized types of on-the-job writing: proposals, progress reports, investigation reports, and abstracts. Chapters 14 through 16 take up library research papers, oral presentations, and the preparation of tables, graphs, and drawings. Chapter 17, the final chapter, presents detailed suggestions for finding a job: locating job openings, preparing application letters and resumes, handling employment interviews, and writing follow-up letters.

The Handbook reviews the basic elements of grammar, the most common writing errors, and punctuation and mechanics, including capitalization, abbreviations, numbers, and italics. A chart inside the back cover lists the correction symbols that your instructor may use in marking your papers. For your convenience, the symbols are keyed to the specific pages in the book where you can find help in correcting the problems your instructor has pointed out.

From time to time, you have probably had the unpleasant experience of using textbooks that seemed to be designed more for instructors than for students. In preparing this book, we have tried never to forget that *you* are buying, reading, and using it. Accordingly, we have written the text with your needs in mind. The book uses simple, everyday language and presents directions in an easy-to-follow, step-by-step format. Most of the writing examples are by students, rather than professionals, and they reflect realistic levels of performance. By comparing the student examples with the professional ones, you will see dramatic evidence that students can produce excellent written work. We believe that if you apply the principles of writing presented in this text, you will write well too. Here's wishing you success!

Andrew W. Hart
James A. Reinking

Contents

3 The Theme   33

4 Explanation of a Process   70

5 Comparison   87

6 Classification   105

10   Memorandums   215

11   Proposals   228

12 Other Professional Reports   250

13 Abstracts   272

14 The Library Research Paper   288

15 Oral Presentations 341

16   Tables, Graphs, and Drawings   353

17   Finding a Job   366

HANDBOOK: Grammar, Usage, Punctuation, and Mechanics   399

Sentence Elements   400

Avoiding Common Errors of Usage　434

Punctuation and Mechanics　486

1

Writing: Purpose and Audience

Human growth, perhaps even survival, requires that we impose order on experience. We need to know how things relate to one another and to sense that our observations and feelings make up some purposeful and meaningful whole. Accordingly, writers order and voice their ideas so that readers can understand and respond to them.

Written communication differs significantly from a conversation. When talking with someone, you can organize your thoughts as the discussion proceeds and clarify your meaning as the other person responds. When you write, however, you have no opportunity for give-and-take. Once a written work has left your hands, it stands alone. Your reader will assume that you have organized and presented your thoughts as clearly as possible.

When you first sit down to write, you will probably concentrate on some limited, practical purpose, rather than on imposing order on the experience. College, for instance, requires many essay examinations, reports, and term papers that present different types of information in various formats. Whether you write for an English instructor or someone else, invariably a well-organized, effectively expressed paper will receive a better grade than a vague, disorganized one, even though both may contain similar ideas. In the first, your ideas stand out. In the second, they are difficult or impossible to grasp.

The ability to write well is also an asset in most careers. The search for a job usually requires a letter of application and a résumé which, if poorly written, invite rejection. Once you are hired, your writing ability will help you to prepare letters, memos, and reports that will impress your superiors and clients and advance your career. The following excerpt underscores the importance of on-the-job writing and speaking.

> As soon as you move one step up from the bottom, your effectiveness depends on your ability to reach others through the spoken or written word. And the further away your job is from manual work, the larger the organization of which you are an employee, the more important it will be that you know how to convey your thoughts in writing or speaking. In the very large organizations, whether it is the government, the large business corporation, or the Army, this ability to express oneself is perhaps the most important of all the skills a person can possess.
> *Peter Drucker, "How to Be an Employer"*

Effective writing involves hard work. Even so, you can learn to write clearly and convincingly by practicing basic writing skills. This text offers you a chance to learn and practice these skills. In addition to teaching the general writing process, it can help you to prepare specialized papers as well. Despite the frustration you may sometimes feel, your best efforts will be worthwhile.

Determining Your Purpose

Anything you write must have a clear *purpose*; otherwise, your readers may misinterpret or not grasp your point. Having a definite purpose also helps to sharpen your awareness of your own thoughts and feelings about a topic. In addition, purpose helps you to identify and define your readers, since their needs and interests will influence what you say and how you say it. Finally, purpose helps you to organize your writing. A pattern of development that works well for one purpose may not be effective for another.

GENERAL PURPOSES OF WRITING

Although there are other writing purposes (for example, to entertain or to express oneself), most of the writing you do will be to *inform* or to *persuade.*

To Inform. Often, your primary aim in writing will be to provide information on a topic about which your reader presumably knows little or nothing. The student who tells classmates how to tile a basement or build a duck-hunting blind provides information, as does the employee who reports on the progress of a project.

To Persuade. Persuasive writing attempts to convince the reader to adopt a position, take an action, or do both. If you write to your local newspaper and oppose plans to build a shopping mall near your neighborhood, your purpose is persuasion. Some on-the-job examples include a sales letter urging readers to sign up for a health-insurance plan and a proposal recommending a particular landscaper for a city's parks and recreation areas.

SPECIAL PURPOSES OF WRITING

Each piece of writing must have a *specific purpose* in addition to one or more general purposes. You might, for example, want to compare two videocassette recorders, classify the chemical contaminants in a lake or stream, give directions for taking photographs with a certain type of camera, or define the term *certified public accountant.*

In the following example, the purpose is specific and clear.

Psychological Impact of the Nuclear Threat on Children and Adolescents: 1965 to 1984

While the physical and ecological effects of nuclear weapons have been studied at great length, relatively little research has been done in this country on the psychological impact of the nuclear arms race on our children.

This lack of interest may reflect the "denial" which adults often feel in trying to cope with our overwhelming fear and seeming helplessness in the face of nuclear war. There is evidence, however, of a growing and pervasive nuclear fear among our children. . . .

The first studies on the nuclear fears of children were published in 1965. They were conducted by psychologists Sibyl Escalona and Milton Schwebel, and were begun in response to the Cuban Missile Crisis. Escalona examined 311 children from widely different socio-economic groups and ranging in age from 10 to 17. Though her survey *did not* refer to the bomb or nuclear war, she hoped to determine the impact of the nuclear threat on aspects of personality development in children. Strikingly, more than 70% of the children sampled spontaneously mentioned that their future would include nuclear weapons and destructive war.

The Schwebel survey of 3,000 junior and senior high school students asked more directly about nuclear confrontation. Schwebel convincingly showed that children do know and care about the threat of thermonuclear war and that they know and *fear* the dangers of nuclear disaster. Even in students who had naive concepts about nuclear weapons, their words conveyed the terror these children associated with all things nuclear. Both Escalona and Schwebel found a greater degree of fear and uncertainty about the future than they had anticipated. As Escalona observed, "The profound uncertainty about whether or not mankind has a foreseeable future exerts a corrosive and malignant influence upon important development processes in normal and well-functioning children."

Few studies were undertaken between 1963 and 1977. But a significant study was conducted by Harvard psychiatrists and PSR members Dr. William Beardslee and Dr. John Mack between 1978 and 1980. Working as part of the Task Force on Psychosocial Aspects of Nuclear Developments, supported by the American Psychiatric Association, they formulated a questionnaire which produced a detailed analysis of children's attitudes on nuclear energy and war. Their sample of over 1,000 students from Boston, Los Angeles, Baltimore and Philadelphia strongly suggests that children are *deeply disturbed* about the threat of nuclear war. Most were aware of the nuclear bomb before they were twelve. The majority believed that nuclear war was either possible or likely, resulting in the devastation of our country. The nuclear issue has even negatively affected their thoughts about marriage and childbearing. The most pervasive finding was a general disquiet or uneasiness about the future and uncertainty about nuclear war.

In the last two years there have been several additional studies, all with similar results. In the most recent, family practitioner Stephen D. Hanna administered the APA questionnaire to 700 students, eleven to nineteen years old, in the Akron, Ohio, area. The expression of fear, helplessness and anger toward the adult generation showed a significant *increase* over the Beardslee/Mack study four years ago.

In all, studies over a twenty-year period clearly indicate the high level of awareness that children have regarding nuclear war. In spite of the reluctance on the part of our adult society to acknowledge its impact on children, the nuclear threat appears very real to children.

Published by Physicians for Social Responsibility

The author of this passage signals the purpose of the writing in the title, which suggests that the nuclear threat is having a psychological impact on young people. The last sentence in paragraph two clarifies this point, which is supported by the results of several studies cited in subsequent paragraphs. The final sentence of the essay offers a rephrased version of the point made in the second paragraph. Everything in this piece of writing relates to its purpose.

In contrast, consider the following paragraph.

Every night before going to bed I clean my teeth with dental floss. Regular flossing keeps teeth free of plaque and also helps maintain healthy gums. I remember when my brother got careless while using floss and gouged a slit in the corner of his lip. The area was sore for a couple of weeks. My lips always seem to be chapped in the wintertime. Maybe I lick them too much. Anyhow, I always carry a tube of lip ice in my pocket. This remedy doesn't always work out for the best, however. Sometimes my body heat causes the ice to become mushy. I guess the answer is to stop licking my lips.

The first two sentences in the paragraph suggest that it will explain the benefits of flossing. However, in the third sentence the writer shifts to a mishap his brother suffered while flossing, and by sentence five, flossing has been abandoned in favor of chapped lips. Obviously, no clear sense of purpose underlies this writing.

Analyzing Your Audience

All good writing is directed toward an audience—one or more persons with whom the writer wishes to communicate. What you say and how you say it depend largely on your audience. For example, you would probably describe your newly purchased used car very differently in letters to your best friend and to your parents, who supplied the down payment. The letter to your friend might focus on the car's slick paint job, customized interior, and powerful engine. The letter to your parents, however, might concentrate on the car's dent- and rust-free body, clean interior, and high gas mileage. Although the topic is the same, the different audiences dictate different treatments.

Often your audience will be made up of people you know well—classmates, members of your social group, or those who share an activity or interest with you. Communicating with this type of audience usually poses few problems because you already know what to say and how to say it. However, when your audience is made up of people you know only slightly or not at all—such as employers, fellow workers, or customers—you must analyze the members of your audience carefully, noting their backgrounds, interests and needs, and your relationship to them.

GENERAL AND SPECIALIZED AUDIENCES

Sometimes you will write for a *general audience*—people who have limited knowledge about your topic. At other times your audience will be a *specialized* one—engineers, chemists, sales personnel, and others with expertise in your topic. General and specialized audiences dictate different approaches to writing.

General Audience. When you write for a general audience, strive for an informal, conversational style by using short, uncomplicated sentences, without resorting to slang. Make your writing smooth and precise and provide whatever background information your reader may need to follow your discussion. Minimize your use of technical terms and define any that your reader might not know. For instance, in a paper on avoiding heart attacks, avoid the word *fibrillation* unless you note that it means "weak and irregular heartbeats."

As a general rule, you should avoid using formulas and equations, although graphs and illustrations geared to the reader's level of understanding are acceptable. Try to add interest and drama to your writing by providing illustrative examples. For instance, in classifying the major kinds of mental illness for an audience of first-year college students, you might describe how typical victims of schizophrenia, paranoia, and manic-depression think and act. Try also to relate your topic to your reader's life. A proposal for installing a new kitchen in someone's home stands a better chance of acceptance if it notes the special features that enhance convenience. Whenever possible, use comparisons to acquaint your readers with unfamiliar devices and processes. To show how the human brain handles messages, for example, you might liken it to a telephone switchboard.

Give careful thought to the *tone* of your writing. Tone reveals the writer's attitude toward a topic and an audience, and it may be matter-of-fact, grim, humorous, chatty, nostalgic, angry—anything you wish to make it. An effective tone takes into account your audience and purpose. A matter-of-fact tone would probably work well in a paper defining inflation, but in a sales letter it might suggest a lack of warmth and friendliness.

Specialized Audience. Writing for a specialized audience involves fewer constraints than writing for a general audience, allowing you to use longer, more complicated sentences, to include many technical terms, and to make use of equations, formulas, and complex graphs and tables. This does not mean, however, that anything is acceptable; rather, you must gear your contents to your audience's level of expertise. If, for instance, you are writing for technicians enrolled in a training program, you should not include a mathematical formula that only a research scientist would understand. Rather, this information should be presented in some other form, such as in a simple graph or written explanation.

Although drama and how information affects your reader's life do not play key roles in writing for a specialized audience, the writing still must interest your readers and satisfy their needs. In on-the-job writing, these needs will depend to a considerable extent on the reader's level of expertise and duties within the organization. For example, the executive reading a report on a new insecticide will want to know such things as the cost of building a new plant to manufacture the product, the probable sales volume and profits, and the potential health and safety hazards for employees, customers, and the general public. In contrast, the engineer in charge of building the plant will be concerned with the chemical reactions involved in the manufacturing process, the conditions necessary for the process to proceed, possible hazards (such as the danger of fire or explosion), and the steps researchers took to avoid them.

A neutral, matter-of-fact tone, suggesting the writer's unbiased but knowledgeable approach to the topic, usually works best for specialized audiences. Before deviating from an impersonal tone, make sure you can justify the shift. For instance, if the insecticide just mentioned promises exceptionally high profits, low manufacturing costs, and a high degree of safety, the report to the executive might well have an enthusiastic tone. However, the same tone would be inappropriate in the engineer's report, as it would fail to convey a sense of objectivity.

TAILORING TOPIC TO AUDIENCE: AN EXAMPLE

Suppose your composition instructor asks you to write a paper explaining a process, and you elect to explain how to take a certain kind of X ray. If you write for a patient who has never had X rays, you might compare the procedure to taking a photograph, then explain what the patient would need or want to know, including the positioning of the body and equipment, the safety and reliability of the procedure, and the time involved. You would use few technical terms and define those necessary to your explanation. Because the patient might be nervous as well as curious, your tone should be reassuring and professional.

If, on the other hand, you write for fellow radiology technicians, you might emphasize exposure factors, film size, and different views that might be required. Quite possibly, you might also present some information in graphs and tables. The audience would understand technical terms and know the details of the procedure, so these details could be omitted. You could speak to these readers as colleagues who appreciate clear and precise information presented in a straightforward, objective tone.

Just as you cannot dial a telephone number at random and then expect to carry on a meaningful conversation, so you cannot communicate effectively without an audience in mind. When you set out to write something, your audience should determine what you say and how you say it. Carefully evaluate their knowledge, interests, and level of sophistication before you start to write.

Exercise

1. Read each of the following examples and then answer these questions:

   What is the writer's purpose, to inform or to persuade?
   Toward what audiences is the writing directed? How do you know?

   a. Hunting is an important part of the lives of many Americans, and its roots go back to the beginning of this country. Hunting is a necessary part of the ecological system that keeps animal populations healthy and under control. Animals have very sharp senses and are far from being defenseless. . . . Contrary to the opinion of many uninformed people, the great majority of hunters are not violent, bloodthirsty killers. Rather, they are gentle, compassionate people who enjoy the outdoors and the challenges it presents. . . .

   Thomas Stuits

   b. Another early illustration of a vehicle vaguely resembling a bicycle appears on a medieval stained-glass window in the church of Stoke Poges, in Buckinghamshire, England. This window, reports Roger St. Pierre in *The Book of the Bicycle*, depicts a cherub astride two wheels in tandem, joined by a wooden backbone. No one knows whether such a vehicle actually existed. But some people believe that the artist would have worked from a model rather than relying strictly on his imagination.

   Douglas Richards

   c. Paper and wood are also damaged by sulfur dioxide. However, in the case of wood, the damage caused by the weathering process is much greater than that which is caused by sulfur dioxide. Paper is affected by sulfur dioxide because of metal impurities in the paper. The metal impurities catalyze the oxidation of sulfur dioxide to sulfur trioxide, which then undergoes hydrolysis to form sulfuric acid. The sulfuric acid that is formed then hydrolizes the cellulose.

Henry Baier

2. Rewrite the passage on page 5 so that it has a firmly established specific purpose.

Conclusion

Writing is a process that yields a product with a definite purpose and audience. Your writing must meet not only your own standards but also those of your readers. The remaining chapters of this book can help you to accomplish these goals.

2

Paragraphs

Writing builds larger units from smaller ones; that is, writers use words to make sentences, sentences to make paragraphs, and paragraphs to make such compositions as letters, reports, and college themes. A *paragraph* consists of one or more related sentences and usually has an indented first line. Some paragraphs, often only a sentence in length, record the words of a single speaker or introduce examples, lists, or items for discussion. Others consolidate several briefly developed ideas into a single unit. However, most paragraphs consist of several sentences that develop a single idea. Paragraphs can stand by themselves as miniature essays or make up multiparagraph compositions.

This chapter focuses on single-idea paragraphs. Learning to write them before you tackle longer compositions benefits you in two ways. First, you learn about the basic writing structures that are shared by paragraphs and longer pieces of writing. Second, you gain confidence in your ability to handle larger writing assignments. The essentials of an effective paragraph include a central idea, a topic sentence, sufficient specific details, a clear pattern of development, and appropriate linking devices.

11

One Central Idea

A paragraph that develops just *one central idea* is said to have unity. Select carefully the material you include in each paragraph so you do not stray from its central idea and possibly confuse your reader. For example, consider the following *faulty* paragraph.

> As he crosses the parking lot, Dave notices two young men shouting and scuffling. When he opens the door to the athletic complex, he can smell the various refreshments. Once inside the gymnasium, he hears the familiar loud noises of the junior varsity basketball game. While undressing in the varsity locker room, he hears different noises.

What exactly is the writer trying to convey? One can only guess. Each of the four sentences expresses a different, unrelated idea.

1. young men shouting and scuffling
2. smells of the refreshments in the athletic complex
3. noises of the junior varsity basketball game
4. noises in the varsity locker room

For meaningful communication, each of these ideas needs to be developed in a separate paragraph.

Each of the following paragraphs *does* develop and clarify one central idea.

> As he opens the door to the crowded gymnasium, Dave is blasted by the familiar noises of the junior varsity basketball game. Hundreds of voices blend together to form one huge roar, which reaches a peak whenever the home team makes a basket. Suddenly a shrill whistle silences the crowd, and then a stabbing buzzer signals a time out. With a break in the action, the pep band strikes up the school fight song. Trumpets blare to the thumping beat of a bass drum.
>
> While the band is playing, Dave turns and walks toward the locker room, where he is greeted by different noises. The mumbling and joking of the players mix with the muffled voices of the coaches discussing the game plan in the closed office. The clanging of steel lockers as they are opened and closed blends in. Aerosol cans of skin toughener hiss as the spray is applied to ten-

der feet. Mouse-like squeaks are heard as the nervous players pace the floor. Finally the coaches come out to give their last words of advice and encouragement.

Mike Hogan

All the sentences in the first paragraph point toward one idea—the noises in the gym during the basketball game. No unrelated details, such as the "smell of the various refreshments," are included. Similarly, everything in the second paragraph points toward a single, but *different*, idea—the noises of the locker room. The writer signals this shift with a new paragraph.

Exercise

Identify which of the following paragraphs is unified and which is not. Give reasons for your answer.

1. Every occupation has drawbacks that spark worker complaints. Industrial workers complain about heat and noise. Waiters and hotel clerks mention that they are always on their feet. Loneliness is the interstate trucker's companion. Working for long hours or during odd hours is part of the "glamour" job of professional athletes. But one complaint is more frequent than any other. The employee is treated like a machine or number.
2. Advertisers know that they can slip their messages through to us by making us laugh. The skits in Alka-Seltzer commercials are good examples of a humorous approach. Bathroom tissue commercials are ridiculous but not really intended to be funny. We may laugh at people who get excited about those familiar plastic-covered rolls, but we are supposed to take their joy in the product seriously. I for one cannot. As a matter of fact, I become very angry whenever I think about the constant interruption of programs so that sponsors can show commercials. It's high time the government stepped in to curb this abuse of the airwaves.

Topic Sentence

The *topic sentence* states the central idea of the paragraph. The central idea is the controlling inference, a conclusion the writer has drawn and wishes to discuss. All other sentences develop the central idea, thus ensuring unity. Certain key words in the topic sentence pinpoint the central idea and may reveal a strongly marked attitude toward the topic. Read this topic sentence.

> Riding the roller coaster at Grant Amusement Park is very exciting.

The phrase *riding the roller coaster* signals what the paragraph will discuss, while the word *exciting* signals the writer's attitude. Sentences built on this topic sentence should focus on the excitement of riding the roller coaster.

A topic sentence helps the writer choose what to include in the paragraph and what to leave out. Only information that supports the paragraph's central idea and attitude should be included. The topic sentence also helps prevent the reader from misinterpreting the writer's intentions.

OVERLY BROAD TOPIC SENTENCE

Your topic sentence should not be too broad. The following sentence, for example, embraces far too much territory. To develop it properly, the writer would need to write a long article or perhaps even a book.

> Technology has made great strides in the twentieth century.

Here are two adequate topic sentences.

> The pocket calculator offers three advantages over the adding machine.

> Frequent headaches can be a warning sign of high blood pressure.

You could develop the first idea by citing the pocket calculator's low cost, portability, and versatility; the second idea by indicating the frequency, location, and time of headaches triggered by high blood pressure.

POSITION OF THE TOPIC SENTENCE

Topic sentences most often appear at the beginning or the end of the paragraph, but they can be positioned elsewhere as well.

Topic Sentence First. Experienced writers often lead with the topic sentence, and you may find it helpful to do the same. Placing the topic sentence first makes the paragraph easier to write and informs the reader right away of what it will discuss. The topic sentence in the following example is italicized.

> *The nursing station is a hubbub of activity.* Doctors write new orders at desks cluttered with patients' charts. Laboratory and X-ray technicians explain the results of tests. The pharmacist brings medications and inquires about any new orders for drugs. Inhalation and physical therapists check charts for their new orders. The dietician asks why a certain patient is not eating properly. Telephones ring and patients' signal lights flash continually. The members of the nursing team, all with their own duties, try desperately to keep up with everything that is going on. This pace continues through most of the morning shift.
>
> *Clare Mutter*

Each sentence following the topic sentence supports it with another example of frenzied activity.

Topic Sentence Last. To emphasize the support for the main idea and build gradually to a conclusion, writers sometimes end paragraphs with the topic sentence. This arrangement can also create suspense as the reader anticipates the summarizing remark. Here is a well-developed paragraph with the topic sentence placed at the end.

> Most people know that our upper atmosphere has a layer of ozone, a highly reactive special form of oxygen that filters the sun's ultraviolet radiation. This filtering provides important protection against skin cancer. Harvard scientists have estimated that depleting the ozone layer by 16 percent could result in more

than 100,000 additional cases of skin cancer each year. Furthermore, such depletion could seriously reduce the number of phytoplanktons, one-celled organisms that live in the sea and produce most of the world's oxygen. Some scientists even believe that increased ultraviolet radiation might raise the temperature of our lower atmosphere and cause catastrophic weather. *Clearly the ozone layer is important, perhaps vital, to the protection of life on earth.*

Ted VandenHeuvel

The sentences leading up to the topic sentence establish clearly that the ozone layer is indeed "important, perhaps vital" to life on earth.

Implied Topic Sentence. The experienced writer occasionally constructs a paragraph in which the central idea is implied rather than stated directly. Although the paragraph lacks a topic sentence, all its sentences, taken together, suggest a single idea that the reader can easily grasp. Here is an example.

Parents who are concerned that their children get enough to eat during the growing years often not only overfeed their children but also cause them to establish lifelong habits of overeating. The person who is constantly praised for cleaning up his or her plate as a child later on experiences a sort of gratification while cleaning up all too many plates. The easy availability of so much food is a constant temptation for many people, particularly the types of foods served in fast-food restaurants and the snack foods advertised on television. Such foods, because they are laced with salt and sugar, tend to be more tempting than other sorts. But many people don't need temptation from the outside; their overeating is a result of such psychological factors as nervousness, loneliness, insecurity, or an indisposition to be active or to exercise.

Kenneth Reichow

Collectively, these details suggest a clear central idea: that overeating is caused by several factors. However, effective paragraphs without stated topic sentences are difficult to write and demand more from the reader. When you write in college and on the job, it is best to include clearly expressed topic sentences.

Exercise

Identify which of the following sentences are suitable topic sentences and which are not. Give reasons for your answers.

1. The trip to the Blair Chemical Company was a real disappointment.
2. The oddest thing happened on my way to English class.
3. Rock music has had a fascinating history.
4. For a New Yorker, Raymond certainly has provincial ideas about marriage.
5. The group leader gave several reasons for the project's falling behind schedule.
6. The development of nuclear power plants required engineers to cope with many complex problems.
7. I had a strange dream the other night.
8. Advertising has had a tremendous impact on American life in the last quarter century.

Specific Details

Most successful paragraphs contain a generous supply of specific details that develop and clarify the idea expressed in the topic sentence. These details may include facts, figures, thoughts, observations, steps, listings, illustrative examples, and personal experiences. Each detail is one piece of a larger picture and by itself may mean very little. However, when enough details are grouped together properly, the total picture emerges. Read the paragraph that follows.

American tourists are regularly amazed at how easy it is to get around London, a metropolis with a population in excess of ten million people. This mobility is possible because the British have built and maintained multiple systems of public transportation. First, there is the subway, called the underground by Londoners. Actually, there are seven subways, and each has its own distinctive color on the easily read subway maps and signs. The tracks extend everywhere under the city, the coaches are as comfortable as they are safe, and the fares begin at about seventy-five cents. Second, above ground are those big red double-decker buses we've all seen in movies and on TV. Third, for longer trips into the immediate suburbs and nearby towns, there are the Green Line coaches, which can be boarded throughout the city. Finally, there are the famous London taxicabs. Most are black, specially built vehicles with comfortable leg room. The fares are comparable to what they are in such American cities as New York and Boston.

Mark Grozdon

The first added detail—that the British have multiple systems of transportation—means little by itself. But as detail follows detail, and you learn about the subways, buses, Green Line coaches, and taxicabs, you gain a total picture of the transportation systems and understand why getting around London is easy.

Now read the following paragraph, which lacks sufficient details.

There are two reasons why prices at McDonald's are low. One is that the selection of food is limited. Also the franchise makes a deliberate effort to hold down operating costs.

The problem here is determining what the writer means. This short selection begins with an adequate topic sentence, but the writer doesn't develop it sufficiently. Instead of clarifying the main idea, the remaining sentences only raise questions. For example, what does the writer mean by a "limited" selection? Are the hamburgers served only with mustard? Are deli sandwiches and tacos unavailable? And what does "a deliberate effort to hold down operating costs" mean? Are workers paid rock-bottom wages? Are disposable utensils and napkins used? Is inferior meat served? Are portion sizes controlled? Although the writer may know the answers to these questions, the reader, left with a vague impression rather than a clear picture, can only guess at them.

The preceding examples suggest three noteworthy benefits of providing ample specific details. First, the reader receives the message you intend to send—there is no misunderstanding or confusion. Second, specific details make your message more vivid and interesting (consider how dull the paragraph about London transportation would be if it merely named the four types of transportation without describing them). Finally, sufficient details eliminate any concern about "getting enough words." When you strive to give your reader a complete picture, the length of your paper will usually take care of itself. Students often ask,

"How many details should my paragraphs include?" This question defies easy answer. Occasionally, one or two sentences will provide enough support. Usually, though, more are needed. Readability also plays a role in setting paragraph length. Paragraphs signal natural dividing points, allowing the reader to pause and absorb the material presented up to that point. Too little paragraphing can overwhelm the reader with long blocks of material. Too much can create an undesirable choppy effect. To prevent such problems, writers occasionally use two or more paragraphs to develop a single idea, or they combine several short paragraphs into one.

Exercise

Choose two of the following topic sentences and prepare for each a list of specific details that could be used to write a well-developed paragraph.

1. Homecoming day was exceptionally dreary.
2. My dog is well trained.
3. Working as a _____ can be very boring.
4. To get the most from their classes, students should do three things.
5. Making your own _____ is both easy and enjoyable.
6. My _____ instructor knows how to motivate students to learn.
7. The working conditions at my last job left much to be desired.

Pattern of Development

The details that you include in your paragraphs cannot be presented in whatever order they happen to come to mind. Such a helter-skelter approach would make it difficult if not impossible for the reader to grasp your meaning. Rather, writers use several common *patterns of development* for their paragraphs. The pattern you choose for a particular paragraph depends on your subject and purpose in writing.

There are eight common patterns of development. The first and second are basic; the others, although described here as separate patterns, are actually special forms of the first or second. In the examples that follow, the topic sentences are italicized.

PATTERN ONE: GENERAL TO SPECIFIC

The *general-to-specific pattern*, sometimes called the *deductive* method, is the most common pattern of paragraph development. The writer begins with a general statement, the topic sentence, then follows it with sentences that explain or support it. Here is an example.

> *My roommate Leonard is the most high-strung person I've ever met.* Spending one evening with him is about all that most people can take. At the supper table Leonard constantly drums his fingers on the table top in a staccato beat. Occasionally he stops long enough to gulp down some hunks of food. Those hunks are no doubt well-churned in the most active stomach east of Pocatello. Later, when it's time for a few hands of cards before cracking the books, you'd swear Leonard is shuffling the spots right off the cards. Nobody ever asks to cut the deck when he deals. If I happen to discard casually, Leonard pounces on the card, meticulously arranging it and the whole pile into a neat stack. These nervous mannerisms carry over into his studying. It's a unique experience to watch Leonard pace the floor, abruptly turn, and mumble something like "suburb located right outside city limits, exurb located further out." I can imagine what he's like during an exam. Only when this bundle of nerves winds down and goes to bed does peace come to our room.
>
> *Steve Lintemuth*

Leonard's mannerisms while eating, playing cards, and studying clearly show that he is extremely high-strung.

PATTERN TWO: SPECIFIC TO GENERAL

The *specific-to-general pattern* of development, sometimes called the *inductive* method, presents specific statements first and then concludes with a general statement, the topic sentence. The following paragraph illustrates this pattern.

> When we opened the door to Thad's apartment, an unpleasant smell of mold and overripe garbage assailed our noses. Old newspapers littered the floors in every room. On the living room wall, amidst curling posters of rock stars, someone had painted a giant dart board, the wavering outer circle measuring at least four feet in diameter. Two large, battered trash cans sat

just inside the kitchen door, their contents overflowing onto the floor. The kitchen sink and drain board were piled high with empty milk containers, crusted plastic dishes, and paper carry-out boxes from Pizza King and Colonel Sanders. In the bedroom, two stained mattresses, stripped of bedding, rested on the splintered, grimy floor. *The whole apartment was such a catastrophe that we felt sickened by it.*

Donna Gilbert

The writer prepares for the topic sentence with details that show the state of the living room, kitchen, and bedroom.

PATTERN THREE: TIME SEQUENCE

The *time-sequence pattern* arranges events according to the order in which they happen in time. The topic sentence may come first or last, or it may be implied. Following is a paragraph that illustrates this pattern.

On April 16, 1947, the French freighter *Grandcamp* exploded, setting off a fiery chain reaction that almost wiped Texas City, Texas, off the map. Already carrying a cargo of peanuts, cotton, oil-well machinery, and sisal twine, the vessel was in port to take on an additional 1,400 tons of ammonium nitrate fertilizer. The evening after the highly flammable fertilizer had been loaded, a small fire started in the hold of the ship. Apparently afraid that using water would damage their other cargo, the ship's officers made only limited attempts to put out the fire. By morning a large black cloud of smoke hung over the ship, causing the port authorities to order it towed out of the harbor. Then, as the tugboats began this risky task, the ship exploded, dissolving in a flash of fire and steel fragments. The force of the explosion rattled windows 150 miles away and registered on a seismograph in Denver, Colorado. Nearby warehouses collapsed, and only minutes later a local chemical plant exploded, virtually destroying the city's business district. As a finale, another freighter—also carrying nitrates—exploded in the harbor shortly after midnight. By this time, most people had fled the city, leaving the widespread fires to burn themselves out. In all, almost 500 people were killed, another 1,000 were seriously injured, and property losses exceeded $100 million. *It was the worst industrial disaster in this country's history.*

David A. Phillips

The size of the *Grandcamp*'s ammonium nitrate cargo, the force of the initial explosion, and the resulting damages, injuries, and deaths lend weight to the writer's conclusion.

PATTERN FOUR: SPACE SEQUENCE

The *space-sequence pattern* arranges specific statements so as to show how objects or their parts relate to one another in space. For example, in describing a building you might start at the top and work down to the bottom, noting what you see in that order, or you might start at the bottom and work up. This pattern offers many possibilities: left to right, right to left, nearby to faraway, faraway to nearby, and so on. A paragraph arranged by space sequence may begin or end with the topic sentence or have an implied topic sentence. Read this example.

> *The ceramic elf in our family room is quite a sight.* The toes of his reddish-brown slippers hang over the mantel. Pudgy, yellow-stockinged legs rise from the slippers and disappear into an olive-green tunic. This jacket, gathered at the waist with a thick brown belt that fits snugly around his roly-poly belly, looks wrinkled and slept in. His short, meaty arms hang comfortably, one hand resting on the knapsack at his side and the other clutching the bowl of an old black pipe. An unkempt, snow-white beard, dotted by occasional snarls, extends from his belt to his lower lip. A button nose, capped with a smudge of gold dust, mischievous black eyes, and an unruly snatch of hair peeking out from under his burnt-orange stocking cap complete Bartholomew's appearance.
>
> *Maria Sanchez*

Note the bottom-to-top sequence, beginning with the toes of the elf's slippers and ending with his "unruly snatch of hair."

PATTERN FIVE: ORDER OF CLIMAX

The *order-of-climax pattern* presents a series of points in a logical progression with the main point coming last. The progression may, for example, be from the least important to the most important, least complex to most complex, or least characteristic to most characteristic. This approach encourages the reader to continue until the end. Once again, the topic sentence may precede or follow the supporting details, or be implied. Here is an example.

> My wardrobe includes three pairs of Levi's straight-leg jeans. Their tough polyester-cotton fabric, strong stitching, and rivet-reinforced front pockets add up to a garment that easily outlasts any slacks I've ever worn. More important, Levi's are all the rage among young people these days. I can wear them to classes, cookouts, roller skating parties, or any informal occasion at all and be right in style. But above all, it's the look and feel of Levi's that attract me. Trim-legged, snug in the seat, they offer comfort without drooping or bagginess. *I'll spend my money on Levi's straight-leg jeans every time.*
>
> *Marc O'Leary*

The phrases "more important" and "above all" clearly signal that O'Leary has arranged his reasons in order of their importance to him.

PATTERN SIX: ENUMERATION

A paragraph developed by *enumeration* presents supporting details in the form of a list. Sometimes the items are numbered, as in the following example. At other times, numbers are only suggested.

> *Although cancer shows no symptoms in its earliest stages, symptoms often do appear before the disease starts to spread.* Because early detection increases a person's chances of survival, a knowledge of the disease's seven warning signals is very important. These signals are (1) any change in bowel or bladder habits, (2) a sore that does not heal, (3) any unusual bleeding or discharge, (4) a thickening or lump in the breast or elsewhere, (5) indigestion or difficulty in swallowing, (6) any marked change in a mole or wart, and (7) a nagging cough or hoarseness. Anyone experiencing any of these symptoms for more than two weeks should see a physician promptly.
>
> *Janet Cheyney*

As in this example, the topic sentence generally identifies the items being listed.

PATTERN SEVEN: ILLUSTRATION

Illustration uses specific examples or instances to support the point made by the topic sentence. This example typifies the pattern.

> *Cats are often quite successful at training their owners.* For example, my sister and her husband have a tabby who refuses to use his hatch in the basement. Instead, he will go to one of the doors in the house and meow to have it opened. Like well-trained owners, either my sister or her husband will stop whatever she or he is doing and let the cat out. Similarly, my next-door neighbor's longhair doesn't like cat food and has trained his owners to cook for him. Over the years, I have noticed how the meals in that house are prepared with the cat's preferences in mind as much as those of anyone else. Finally, my own cat, Ripple, has trained me to dispose of his nightly killings. Each morning, I go out onto the cement patio behind the kitchen, collect the dead prey, and dutifully put it in the garbage can. Then, after he has rubbed up against my leg for all of four or five seconds, I take him into the house and feed him a nice breakfast.
>
> *Allen Franklin*

Each of the examples in this passage points out a different kind of training. In other cases, writers may use an extended single example.

PATTERN EIGHT: CAUSE AND EFFECT

The *cause* pattern explains why an event, attitude, or condition occurs; the *effect* pattern explores its consequences. The first passage that follows shows causes; the second examines effects.

> *Over the last few years, three factors have brought about a drastic decrease in the production of American zinc.* First of all, zinc is a nonrecyclable resource and as a result has become less attractive to potential users than is a recyclable metal such as aluminum. Second, the low quality of American zinc renders it uncompetitive. American slab zinc must first be purified, then blended to meet a particular industry's standards. Purification is a very expensive two-step process; many foreign producers, who have a much higher grade of ore to work with, do not have to use

this process. Third, because of the increased use of plastics and magnesium in the automobile industry, zinc, a heavy and dense metal, has lost one of its major customers. Government-mandated mileage for automobiles requires lighter vehicles, thus stripping zinc of its appeal.

John Emery

Poor language skills can be the source of much grief for college students. Students who came from high school without having learned to read and understand substantial amounts of written material on their own soon find themselves in trouble in a variety of classes: history, psychology, literature, political science, business, and so on. They simply cannot keep up the basic reading and as a consequence fall further and further behind. Lectures can be a problem all their own. If students have not acquired note-taking skills in high school, much of what their professors say is lost to them. And once they are faced with an essay examination, they are unable to analyze and relay much of what they have heard or supposedly read, let alone to comment on it. Frustrated and angry, they look around for someone to blame for their problems and usually pick the professor, thus making a bad situation even worse.

Kerry Briske

The topic sentence of the first paragraph includes the phrase *three factors have brought about*, which signals that the remaining sentences will discuss causes. The topic sentence of the second contains the phrase *the source of much grief*, which suggests a focus on effects. When you write a cause or an effect paragraph, always suggest your pattern of choice in the topic sentence.

OTHER PATTERNS OF DEVELOPMENT

The preceding patterns of development are not the only ones available to writers. *Comparison* and *classification*, also common methods of development, are discussed in detail in Chapters 5 and 6, which focus on multiparagraph essays.

Exercise

Identify the pattern of development—time sequence, space sequence, order of climax, enumeration, illustration, or cause-effect—that would best develop each of the following topic sentences.

1. There are several good reasons for getting a vocational education degree.
2. I'll never forget my flight to New York last January.
3. Experience has taught me that in stressful situations friends sometimes behave in unpleasant ways.
4. Alcoholism, a problem for several million Americans, can have several causes.
5. The lobby of the Piltdown Building is an impressive sight.
6. The agenda for the meeting listed seven items for discussion.
7. Alcoholism can lead to a number of serious health problems.

Linking Devices

Now you are familiar with some patterns of development that give order to your paragraphs. *Next* you must make sure that the sentences within the paragraphs are linked to one another so that they flow smoothly and allow your reader to follow your train of thought without difficulty. *After all*, you arranged your sentences in a particular sequence to develop one continuous idea. *That is*, the idea expressed by each sentence is in some way related to the ideas in the preceding and following sentences, and all of them are related, directly or indirectly, to the central idea expressed in the topic sentence. *Of course*, these relationships are clear to you because you wrote the paragraph. *However*, you must also make them clear to your reader. The job is accomplished with linking devices. The resulting paragraph is said to have coherence.

LINKING DEVICE ONE:
CONNECTING (TRANSITIONAL) EXPRESSIONS

Certain items in the preceding paragraph are italicized, and each is an example of a connecting, or transitional, word or phrase. Read the paragraph again. Notice how *now, next, after all, that is, of course,* and *however* connect the sentences and relate their ideas to one another. To see this clearly, try reading the paragraph aloud with, and then again without, the italicized items.

Here are some of the most commonly used connecting words and phrases, grouped according to the relationships they show.

SIMILARITY: likewise, similarly

CONTRAST: on the other hand, on the contrary, at the same time, otherwise, however, nevertheless, but, yet, still, although, whereas

RESULT OR EFFECT: since, consequently, accordingly, hence, thus, as a result, therefore, because, if, for this reason

ADDING IDEAS TOGETHER: first, in the first place, second, furthermore, moreover, too, also, in addition, finally, in conclusion

PROVIDING EMPHASIS OR CLARITY: that is, in other words, again, as a matter of fact, in fact, indeed, nonetheless, besides, after all, above all

INDICATING TIME RELATIONSHIP: later, until, while, meanwhile, now, from now on, after, next, afterwards, at times, once, when, then, subsequently

INTRODUCING AN EXAMPLE: for example, for instance, to illustrate

CONCEDING A POINT: of course, granted that, to be sure

Note how the italicized words and phrases in the following example link the sentences together.

> *Psychiatric nurses deserve a medal for courage.* They deal with severely depressed patients, as well as pathological personalities who have no sense of right or wrong. *For this reason*, they must be on guard at all times; they must, in effect, have eyes at the back of their heads. They must also have a great deal of self-control. When their patients display anger and violence, these nurses cannot respond in kind. *On the contrary*, they must be tolerant and understanding. *Furthermore*, they must be able to recognize attempts at deception. Sometimes a depressed person, just prior to suicide, will act in a completely normal way because he or she has made the decision to die. The nurses must understand this behavior and be alert for any possible attempt.
>
> *Peg Feltman*

The connecting words and phrases used in this paragraph make the relationships among sentences clear and the writing easy to follow.

LINKING DEVICE TWO:
REPETITION OF KEY WORDS AND PHRASES

Repetition of key words and phrases also helps the reader follow the writer's train of thought. As you read the following paragraph, note how the repetition of the phrase *college policy* and variations thereon aid in linking the sentences together.

I'm fed up with college policy. Many of the rules seem to be roadblocks designed to inconvenience me. For example, I live nineteen miles from campus. When I tried to get a commuter sticker for my car, I was told that *college policy* requires that I live twenty or more miles away in order to qualify for one. To make matters worse, *college policy* prohibits noncommuter students from parking anywhere on campus except in one special lot, which is always full. More than once I've been frantically searching for a parking spot when I should have been in class. And then there's the *school's* tuition *policy*. At our school, students register for the coming term five weeks before it starts. The deadline for paying tuition is exactly three weeks before the term begins. If payment isn't made by then, it's the *policy of the college* to cancel the registration. Last term the tuition check from my parents was delayed in the mail and arrived one day late. As a result, I had to spend three and a half hours reregistering at the start of the term and couldn't get one of my required courses. I think it's high time for the *college* to reexamine some of its *policies*. After all, shouldn't the main *policy* of any *college* be to help, not hinder, its students' efforts to get an education?

Alex Malinowski

LINKING DEVICE THREE:
PRONOUNS AND DEMONSTRATIVE ADJECTIVES

Pronouns and demonstrative adjectives help produce a smooth, easily followed flow of ideas. Pronouns (*I, you, he, she, him, her, they, them, who, whom*, and so on) point back to nouns or pronouns that appear earlier in the sentence or in previous sentences. Thus they pull the sentences closer together and help guide the reader along a continuous path. The four demonstrative adjectives—*this, that, these,* and *those*—usually precede nouns and refer to nouns that were mentioned earlier. Pronouns should be used carefully so there is no doubt about what they refer to. The information given in the Handbook at the end of the text will help you avoid pronoun problems.

Here are two paragraphs illustrating the use of pronouns and demonstrative adjectives.

Pronouns

I was waiting for the bus, half asleep, when a wizened old man, a total stranger, walked up to *me* and began to talk. Almost immediately, something made *me* want to hear what *he* had to say. First, the old man talked about *his* children. *He* had four, three sons and a daughter. All of *them* were married and had families, but none of *them* treated *him* with respect, especially since *he* had retired and *his* wife had died of cancer. *His* grandchildren, all of *whom* were teen-agers or older, hardly knew *him*. *They* didn't even send *him* Christmas cards. The old man had worked for forty years in a steel mill. *He* suffered from emphysema but didn't like to go for treatment because the young doctors treated *him* like a beggar. Worst of all, *he* lived alone in a single room at the YMCA. As the bus moved away, I looked back at *him* standing pitifully in a cloud of diesel exhaust. *What a shame, I thought, that older people are often forgotten members of our society.*

Gwendolyn Putalik

Demonstrative Adjectives

There are two kinds of dental mouth mirrors. The first is made of ordinary glass and has a flat reflecting surface. With *this* mirror the dentist sees the patient's teeth just the way the patient sees them in a regular looking glass. The second, the magnifying mirror, has a concave surface that makes everything look larger. *This* mirror gives the dentist a better view of the mouth. Both of *these* mirrors are about the same diameter as a 25-cent piece. They are securely mounted in circular stainless-steel holders, with the rims equal in depth to the thickness of the mirrors.

Lisa Hines

In the first paragraph, the pronouns *I* and *me* refer unmistakably to the narrator; *he*, *him*, and *his* refer to the old man; and *whom* and *they* refer to the grandchildren. In the second paragraph, the first use of *this mirror* clearly means the flat one, the second refers to the concave one, and *these mirrors* refers to both types.

COMBINATIONS OF LINKING DEVICES

Often, two or three types of linking devices join forces in a single paragraph. The following example includes all three types.

> A few weeks ago, *I* spent the weekend with some friends *who* own a big Victorian *house* on the shore of Lake Michigan. Upon arriving, *I* was struck by how much *it* resembled the *house* *I* had lived in as a little girl. That night, *I* was awakened by the growling of *my dog*, *who* seemed to be just outside the bedroom door. *I* put on a robe and stepped into the hall. In the shadows, *I* saw the *dog* disappear down the *stairs*. *Then*, *I* heard a series of growls that faded into silence. *I* tiptoed across the cold floor to the *staircase* and peered down into the darkness but could see nothing. *Then*, in an instant of lucid thought, *I* realized where *I* was—in *my* old childhood *home*. But more important, *I* also remembered that *my dog* had died fifteen years before. Shocked and trembling with fear, *I* spun around, rushed back to bed, and buried *myself* in the blankets, waiting in silence for morning.
>
> *Catherine Ruhn*

This paragraph repeats the words *house* and *dog* as well as makes use of the transitional expression *then* and the pronouns *I*, *who*, *it*, *my*, and *myself*. Note also the variant expressions *home*, *stairs*, and *staircase*.

Exercise

Select three paragraphs from the first four sections of this chapter and list the linking devices in each according to type. Note the relationship that each connecting expression shows and the person, place, or thing to which each pronoun and demonstrative adjective refers.

Conclusion

To test your understanding of how to write paragraphs and to review points that may have slipped to the back of your mind, reexamine several of the sample paragraphs in this chapter, and see whether you can answer the following questions.

1. What is the central idea?
2. How do the specific details help form a complete picture in the reader's mind?
3. Which pattern of development is used?
4. Which linking devices are used?

Suggestions for Writing

Write a well-organized paragraph that develops one of the following ideas. Use the pattern of development you think most appropriate and include enough specific details for adequate development.

1. The one quality most necessary for success in my chosen field is _____.
2. One example of Americans' tendency to waste is _____.
3. Proper inflation pressure prolongs tire life.
4. To me, the most attractive career would be _____.
5. The best (or worst) thing about fast-food restaurants is _____.
6. The most difficult part of being an X-ray technician (or substitute another occupation) is _____.
7. The college course I find most useful is _____.
8. One reason licensing of auto mechanics is a good (or bad) idea is _____.
9. Last night, I had a very disturbing dream.
10. Concentration (or substitute another term) is an important part of a successful golf game (or substitute another sport).
11. The view from the top of _____ proved breathtaking.
12. Although I knew college would be different from high school, the differences are not what I had expected.
13. What I most enjoy doing in my spare time is _____.
14. When you first view _____, you feel as though you have stepped out of a time machine.
15. Sometimes a college student can't help feeling that he or she is regarded as a number, not a person.

16. Apart from physical attractiveness, the most desirable attribute a spouse can have is _____.

17. For healthful exercise, nothing can beat _____.

18. A friend's recent experience has completely changed his attitude toward the police.

19. My next-door neighbor has a cliché for every occasion.

20. Women's basketball (or substitute another sport) is a sport whose time has come.

21. Government figures show that the problem of _____ is growing more serious each year.

22. Transplanting a tree (or substitute another task) must be carried out with great care.

3

The Theme

Your course instructor will probably ask you to write a number of *themes*, also known as essays, compositions, and papers. Writing themes is good training for many kinds of college and on-the-job writing.

Many students dread theme assignments. Much of the anxiety stems from the mistaken idea that good themes are dashed off in a burst of inspiration by "born writers." Students themselves sometimes promote this notion by boasting that their best papers were cranked out in an hour or so of spare time. Occasionally, these claims may be true—and natural ability and even "inspiration" may help. Yet most successful themes are produced by following a careful procedure while writing. When you read the well-written papers of your classmates or colleagues, you see only the final product, not the *process* the writers followed along the way.

The basic writing process includes three stages. In the first, *choosing your topic*, you select an appropriate topic and determine your audience. In stage two, *developing and organizing your information*, you accumulate ideas and information, arrange them suitably, and develop a thesis statement. Finally, in the *writing and revising* stage, you prepare and then polish a first draft.

Although this three-stage scheme appears simple and straightforward, writing is a flexible process. Rather than proceeding systematically through the three stages, writers often reverse direction or skip forward temporarily. For example, before you determine your audience, some of the points you wish to develop in the paper may occur to you. As you prepare the first draft, you might expand the scope of the paper and backtrack to stage two to develop these additional points. Moreover, specialized types of writing require special procedures. Nonetheless, this basic three-stage writing process works well not only for themes but also for most other types of writing.

Before tackling any paper, be sure you know exactly what your instructor expects. Some instructors assign a single topic; others allow their students to choose one of several topics or give students free choice. Similarly, your instructor may or may not specify the length of your paper. In any case, if you have questions about the assignment, clear them up before you begin work. Your instructor will likely admire your determination to "get it right" from the start.

Stage One: Choosing Your Topic

A *subject* is a broad area for discussion, such as chemistry, business, or education. A *topic* is one small segment of a subject, such as the commercial preparation of ammonia, the impact of computers on small banks, or the use of teaching assistants in high schools. To produce an effective essay, you must first choose a topic that can be developed properly within any assigned word limit.

FACTORS IN CHOOSING A TOPIC

If your instructor assigns a specific topic, you are ready to consider your audience and purpose. If you are asked to choose a topic, careful thinking is required. Often, an instructor encourages the entire class to explore a general subject and then asks students to choose a topic related to it.

Suppose, for example, that your class has been discussing the trend toward shorter work weeks and increased leisure time. The class discussion then turns to profitable, enjoyable ways of using this time, and several students suggest participation in hobbies and sports. Your instructor asks you to choose a topic related to one of these subjects and to write a two- or three-page paper. You select some aspect of participation in sports. Obviously, sports is too broad a subject, as is a single sport such as tennis. Further narrowing is therefore necessary. To be successful, your topic must meet these requirements.

1. It must clearly *relate* to, or be part of, the general subject.
2. It must be *limited* enough so that adequate development is possible within any assigned word range.
3. It must *interest* you and your reader. If the topic bores you, you will produce a dull paper that will be a chore for you to write and for others to read.
4. It must be something you *know* about or can *learn* enough about in the limited time you have to write it.

You can draw on three basic sources of information when writing a paper. The first—and often the most useful—is *personal experience*. When you write about your own experiences, you have a vast fund of beliefs, feelings, and facts to tap. For example, if you played on the high school tennis team for three years, you would have many possibilities. On the other hand, if you do not know a birdie from a bogie and lack the time and interest to learn about them, you should not write about golf. *Something you have seen and heard*, even though you have not actually participated in it, often works well too. Think about what you have observed at home, work, and school or learned from movies, classroom discussions, plays, concerts, and athletic events.

Finally, consider *what you have learned through reading*. Trade publications, shop manuals, magazines, technical journals, newspapers, novels, or textbooks often provide interesting material for a paper. Of course, you must identify the sources of any facts or ideas that you borrow from others. For short papers, most instructors ask that you name only the author and the publication in which the information appears. For library research papers, follow the documentation guidelines in Chapter 14.

Note well: The most important person in your life is *you*. Topics you know about and take an interest in will yield your most effective writing.

Exercise

1. Select three of the following subjects. Using your personal experience as a source, list three points you could make about each subject. Briefly outline the experience that illustrates or supports each point.

   a. business ethics

   b. a particular field of science

   c. concern for public health

   d. the two-income family

   e. the federal bureaucracy

   f. vocational education

   g. occupational hazards

   h. a particular occupation

   i. money

2. For each of the preceding subjects, list three questions that you could answer by doing some reading.

WAYS OF FOCUSING ON A TOPIC

With some luck, a suitable topic will occur to you almost immediately. However, most writers experience difficulty in choosing a topic. If you do, try discussing the general subject with your classmates, friends, family members, or instructor. Such discussion can expose a variety of aspects that might have escaped you. Furthermore, knowing how others feel about a subject can sharpen your own awareness and help develop a sense of audience.

If discussions with others do not prove fruitful, other strategies are available.

Brainstorming. Brainstorming involves listing anything you can think of that might help you arrive at a suitable topic. Jot down items and ideas as soon as they occur to you, without evaluating them or worrying about grammar, punctuation, or spelling. Do not bypass anything that seems silly or irrelevant, for it may suggest other, more valuable ideas as you write it down. Continue listing your ideas until no more come to mind.

Suppose, for example, that your experience on the high school tennis team prompts you to write your sports theme about tennis. Already you have started to focus, since tennis is only one of many possible sports topics. However, since more focusing is needed, you turn to brainstorming, which yields the following list:

1. its increasing popularity
2. major tournaments
3. different court surfaces
4. equipment needed
5. tennis scoring
6. tennis terminology
7. different rackets
8. different grips
9. tennis strategy (singles)
10. tennis strategy (doubles)
11. playing the net
12. topspin strokes
13. backspin strokes
14. different serves
15. return of serve
16. proper body position
17. importance of footwork
18. special shots: the lob
19. special shots: the drop volley
20. special shots: the over-head
21. today's "bad boys"

Although this is only a partial list of topics related to tennis, it shows the importance of narrowing a subject. Of course, it would be impossible to cover all these aspects in a short paper—you could write only one or two sentences about each, and no clear picture of anything would emerge. Also, the problem of organization would be enormous. On the other hand, if you focused on *one* aspect of tennis—such as playing better singles—you could develop each main point in a paragraph or more. This is what focus is all about. Above all, it involves saying more about less, concentrating on a single aspect of a subject and then developing it properly.

How narrowly and in what direction you focus depends on two factors. First, you must consider the length of your paper: *the shorter it is, the narrower your focus must be.* For a three-hundred-word theme, you might focus on some conditioning exercises for a singles player and, for a five- to six-hundred-word theme, on conditioning exercises, concentration, and consistency. The other factor to consider in narrowing your focus is this: *evaluate your audience.* For the beginning tennis player, you might focus on equipment or scoring; for the intermediate player, on conditioning, concentration, and consistency; and for the advanced player, on special shots. As noted earlier, your audience should dictate your approach.

Free Writing. *Free writing* is similar to brainstorming but produces a set of sentences rather than words, phrases, and clauses. It yields fewer ideas in a given time span than does brainstorming, but you are less likely to forget the meaning of some items.

Free writing on tennis might produce something like this:

> Sports. If that's what my instructor wants me to write on, tennis is my best bet. After all, I've done a lot of playing. But just what should I say? Should I write about Wimbledon or the Davis Cup? That might be a good bet. After all, lots of people follow these matches on TV. . . . What about a paper on the different court surfaces? Well, serious players might like it, but not beginners. I could write about equipment, clothing, or scoring. Any of these should appeal to people who are thinking about tennis lessons. . . . What about tennis strategy? I could say something about playing the net, using a topspin, or backspin strokes, or using different serves. . . . Here's an idea. Why not a paper on playing a better game of tennis singles? What could I put in it? Something about conditioning exercises, concentration, and playing a consistent game should fill the bill. Should I also write about special shots like lobs, volleys, and overheads? Maybe, but I don't think so. If I tried it, the paper would probably be way too long. Anyway, that stuff is for real pros.

This example of free writing offers the same possibilities for a paper on some aspect of tennis as does the brainstorming list.

Asking Questions. Asking the following series of *basic questions* can also help to narrow a subject to a suitable and workable topic.

1. What is a good definition of my subject?
2. What categories make it up?
3. How do these categories compare with one another?

4. What are my subject's parts and how does it work?
5. What uses does it have?
6. What are its causes or origins?
7. What are some important instances of it?
8. What impact has it had?

To begin, turn these general questions into more specific ones about your subject. The questions on tennis might be as follows:

1. What is tennis?
2. What are the different kinds of tennis?
3. How are these different kinds similar and different?
4. What does a tennis match consist of, and how is it scored? What equipment is required?
5. What are the benefits of playing tennis?
6. How did tennis originate?
7. What are some noteworthy matches? Who are some noteworthy players?
8. What significance can be attached to the game? How does it affect players, spectators, and the public?

Some of these questions provide leads to suitable topics. For example, the third question might lead to a paper comparing tennis singles and doubles, the fourth to a paper showing how a match is structured and scored, and the eighth to a paper exploring the impact of amateur tennis on the sporting-goods industry.

You can also formulate additional questions directly or indirectly related to one of the questions about your general subject. Here, for instance, are three questions suggested by those in the preceding list.

1. What surfaces do tennis courts have, and how do the surfaces affect the game?
2. What should the beginner know about selecting and maintaining tennis equipment?
3. How can players improve their game?

Any of these questions would lead to a suitable topic for a paper. The second question might lead to a paper on equipment. The third question might lead to a paper on conditioning, concentration, and consistency or to one on special shots.

Exercise

Choose one of the three subjects you selected for the exercise on page 36. Use one of the focusing techniques discussed in the text to narrow the subject to a topic suitable for a two- or three-page paper.

Stage Two: Developing and Organizing Your Information

Once you choose and narrow your topic, you must *generate information* about it, *organize* that information properly, and *develop a thesis statement*.

GENERATING YOUR INFORMATION

Brainstorming is useful for generating the information needed to develop a topic as well as for finding a topic. To brainstorm a topic, jot down everything you might possibly use in your paper: facts, ideas, illustrations, examples—all the details you need to communicate fully and clearly with your reader. (You may wish to review the discussion of specific details on pages 17–19.) Jot down the details as they occur to you; do not be concerned with arranging them in any special order at this stage.

Suppose you have elected to write for intermediate tennis players and to discuss conditioning, concentration, and consistency. Your list of details might look like this:

1. always keep ball in play
2. don't try foolish shots
3. place the ball so opponent runs
4. stay in good condition yourself
5. running
6. jogging
7. skipping rope
8. keeps you on your toes
9. keep your mind only on the game

10. personal distractions
11. courtside distractions
12. temper distractions
13. don't continually drive ball with power
14. two-on-one drill
15. lob ball over their heads
16. return a down-the-line passing shot
17. don't try spectacular overhead
18. chance for opponent to make mistake
19. game of percentages
20. most games are lost, not won

Note that the items listed are not necessarily expressed in complete sentences. Some may not even make sense to anyone but you. That is sufficient. Only you must understand their meaning at this point. Notice, too, how some of the ideas lead to others. For example, the first item "keeping the ball in play"—leads naturally to the second—"avoiding foolish shots." Likewise, the third item—"place the ball so the opponent runs"—leads to the fourth—"staying in good condition yourself"—which, in turn, leads to the subsequent items. As you organize and write your paper, you will probably combine, modify, and omit some ideas as well as add others. For now, though, you have a good start on the supporting material.

One final note: If you have trouble preparing your brainstorming list, perhaps your topic is not as promising as you originally thought. Sometimes all you need to do is take a break and then try again. But if your trouble continues, switch to another topic and start a new list of details. Now—not later—is the time to redirect your efforts.

Exercise

Using the brainstorming technique, prepare a list of details for the topic you developed for the exercise on page 40.

ORGANIZING YOUR INFORMATION

Now you are ready to organize your details and ideas in some meaningful pattern that will guide your writing and help your reader grasp your ideas. If you have ever listened to a disorganized speaker spill out ideas helter-skelter, you probably found it difficult to pay attention, let alone to comprehend the speech. The same holds true for writing. A garbled list of ideas serves no one; an orderly presentation helps communication succeed.

Papers can be organized by means of flexible notes or a formal outline. Either will produce a pattern for your paper—that is, show how your ideas will be grouped and presented. Following that pattern in your writing ensures that you will not overlook any part of it. Use whichever system your instructor specifies.

Flexible Notes. To prepare a set of *flexible notes*, list the major points you wish to make at the top of separate sheets of paper. Following are the three points, or headings, for the tennis paper:

1. conditioning
2. concentration
3. consistency

Under each heading, record the details from your brainstorming list that will develop that point. The three lists might resemble the following.

Conditioning

stay in good condition yourself
running
jogging
skipping rope
keeps you on your toes
two-on-one drill
lob ball over their heads
return a down-the-line passing shot

Concentration

keep your mind only on the game
personal distractions
courtside distractions
temper distractions

Consistency

always keep ball in play
don't try foolish shots
place the ball so opponent runs
don't continually drive ball with power
don't try spectacular overhead
chance for opponent to make mistake
games of percentages
most games are lost, not won

At this stage, think about how you will arrange your three main headings. Which one will come first? Second? Third? Your decision will depend largely on your topic and your audience. In this case, since conditioning, concentration, and consistency are concurrent activities for a tennis player, the obvious choice is order of climax—moving from the least important to the most important idea. Following this order, you might choose the following sequence.

1. conditioning (important)
2. concentration (more important)
3. consistency (most important)

Now you are ready to prepare a plan covering each of your paragraphs. Such a plan is not as yet definite. Until you are actually writing, you cannot know for sure how many paragraphs each of the three main headings will require. A quick glance at the number of items under each heading, however, suggests two paragraphs for conditioning, one for concentration, and two for consistency. Here is the plan for the tennis paper.

FIRST PARAGRAPH: introduction and thesis statement
SECOND PARAGRAPH: discuss conditioning
THIRD PARAGRAPH: continue to discuss conditioning
FOURTH PARAGRAPH: discuss concentration
FIFTH PARAGRAPH: discuss consistency
SIXTH PARAGRAPH: discuss consistency
SEVENTH PARAGRAPH: conclusion

(Thesis statements are discussed on pages 46–48 and introductions and conclusions on pages 54–58.)

Formal Outline.   There are two different systems of notation for *formal outlines*: the letter-number system and the number-decimal system.

The *letter-number* system of outlining arranges the main divisions by roman numerals and the various subdivisions by capital letters, arabic numbers, and lowercase letters in decreasing order of importance.

I.
   A.
   B.
      1.
      2.
         a.
         b.
II.

The *number-decimal* system of outlining, used mostly by engineers and scientists, relies entirely on numbers and decimal points arranged according to the following scheme.

1.0
  1.1
  1.2
    1.2.1
    1.2.2
      1.2.2.1
      1.2.2.2
2.0

There are two types of formal outlines—the *topic outline* and the *sentence outline*—and both may follow either system of notation. The topic outline presents entries in the form of words or sentence fragments. The sentence outline uses complete sentences. Although sentence outlines allow the inclusion of more details as well as the writer's attitude toward each entry, they are time-consuming to prepare. For this reason, topic outlines are more commonly used, particularly in technical writing.

Following are topic and sentence outlines for the tennis paper. Both outlines use the letter-number system of notation. Notice that periods follow the items in the sentence outline but do not follow those in the topic outline. Also, the items at each level are grammatically parallel in both outlines.

Topic Outline

I. Introduction. Establishes context for discussion to come and presents thesis statement
II. Conditioning
   A. Conditioning off the court
     1. Ways of keeping in condition
     2. Benefits of conditioning
   B. Conditioning on the court
     1. Ways of preparing for a match
     2. Benefits of conditioning
III. Concentration
   A. Types of distractions
   B. Effects of distractions
IV. Consistency
   A. Examples of inconsistent play
   B. Effects of inconsistent play
   C. Benefits of consistent play
V. Conclusion. Ends paper smoothly

Sentence Outline

I. Introduction. The introduction establishes the background for the discussion and presents the thesis statement.
II. To have endurance, you must keep in good physical condition.
   A. Off-the-court exercises help build your endurance.
     1. Jogging, running in place, and jumping rope are good exercises.
     2. These exercises will increase your stamina and accustom you to staying on your toes.
   B. On-the-court exercises also build your endurance.
     1. The two-on-one drill is a good exercise.
     2. This drill will keep you running by simulating the conditions of a game.

III. To play well, you must concentrate on the game.
   A. Courtside and personal distractions can destroy concentration.
   B. These distractions result in poorly hit balls and cost you points.
IV. To win, you must play a consistent game.
   A. Spectacular shots and power strokes ruin consistency.
   B. These shots cost you more points than you will gain.
   C. If you play consistently, your opponent is more likely to make a mistake.
 V. The conclusion ends the paper smoothly.

As the sample outlines indicate, the writer has not yet decided on what information to include in the introduction and conclusion. These decisions can be made later on, most likely at the first-draft stage.

Exercise

Using flexible notes or a formal outline, organize the list of specific details you prepared for the exercise on page 41. Organize the details in the order that is most appropriate for your topic and audience.

WRITING YOUR THESIS STATEMENT

If your instructor assigns a specific topic, you may think of your thesis statement before you begin to outline. If you do not, prepare it now. The thesis statement tells what the paper will contend, describe, define, or illustrate. Think carefully about the following questions.

What is my purpose in writing?
For what audience am I writing?
How will I organize my information?
What is my position or attitude?

Your thesis statement should reflect your answers to these questions. Ordinarily, it is a single sentence. Sometimes, though, two or more sentences are needed, especially for longer papers or when a single sentence would be too lengthy or clumsy.

As noted earlier, the topic sentence clearly states the central idea of a paragraph. It also helps you decide what information to include and what to exclude. *What the topic sentence does for a single paragraph, the thesis statement does for an entire theme.*

There are two types of thesis statements—*specific* and *general*. The specific type clearly spells out the main points the theme will discuss. Read this example, which could serve as the thesis statement for the tennis paper.

SPECIFIC STATEMENT: Three keys to playing better tennis singles are conditioning, concentration, and consistency.

The purpose and scope of the essay, the three areas of emphasis, and the order of presentation are readily apparent. Positioned in your opening paragraph, this statement would clearly inform the reader of your paper's content and organization.

A general thesis statement presents the writer's topic and purpose but not the points to be discussed. For the tennis paper, such a statement might read as follows.

GENERAL STATEMENT: If you wish to improve your tennis singles game, you can go about it in several ways.

Note that in this case, the reader has no clues to identify the "several ways." Certain kinds of writing, such as process explanations and descriptions of objects, commonly use general thesis statements.

PROCESS EXPLANATION STATEMENT: Caulking a bathtub is a process that involves a few simple steps.

OBJECT DESCRIPTION STATEMENT: A videotape is a magnetic strip on which the sound and picture parts of a telecast are recorded for future broadcast.

Once you have crafted your thesis statement, add it to the introduction part of your outline, as in the following examples.

FLEXIBLE NOTES OUTLINE: First Paragraph. Introduction and thesis statement: "Three keys to playing better tennis singles are conditioning, concentration, and consistency."

TOPIC OUTLINE: I. Introduction. Establishes context for discussion to come and presents thesis statement: "Three keys to better tennis singles are conditioning, concentration, and consistency."

SENTENCE OUTLINE: I. Introduction. The introduction establishes the background for the main discussion and presents the thesis statement: "Three keys to better tennis singles are conditioning, concentration, and consistency."

This addition helps remind you that each segment of the paper develops some segment of the thesis and thus keeps your writing on track. If the outline accompanies the paper, the reader can grasp your central idea with even greater ease.

As you write, you may need to alter your thesis statement somewhat or even change it completely. In this case, prepare the new version right away. Otherwise, your thesis statement may point in one direction and the rest of your theme in another.

Exercise

Write a specific thesis statement for the list of details you organized for the exercise on page 46. Add the thesis statement to the introduction of your outline.

Stage Three: Writing and Revising Your Paper

Writing and revising require the same systematic, careful approach as the earlier stages of the writing process. Producing a first draft generally does not present serious problems. All too often, though, students view revision as no more than a little light retouching—fixing the spelling here, adding a comma there—before the paper is submitted. The result in this case is almost always an inadequate paper.

WRITING YOUR FIRST DRAFT

Writing the first draft should be relatively easy. After all, you have a suitable topic, a thesis statement that indicates your purpose and tells your reader what to expect, enough supporting details, and a written plan to follow. Even so, you still may find it hard to get started: the words may not come to mind, and all you can do is doodle or stare at the blank page. Perhaps the delay occurs when you try to write the introduction. For many writers, this is the most difficult part of a theme to write. *If you cannot determine how to begin, skip the introduction for the time being. Do the less difficult parts first; show yourself some progress.* Once you have developed your main points, an effective opening should be easier to write.

With your thesis statement and written plan in hand, turn to the first main heading. For the tennis theme, it is *conditioning.* Evaluate the items under this heading, and then prepare a suitable topic sentence for what will be your second paragraph. (The first paragraph, of course, will be your introduction.) Such a sentence might take this form: *Since you will be running continually, conditioning is necessary.* Now you are ready to develop this section with the details listed in your plan. Here are some suggestions.

1. Write on every other line of ruled 8½ × 11-inch paper, leaving wide margins. You will then have room to revise.

2. Write quickly, capturing the drift of your thoughts. Concentrate on content and organization, discussing your main points and supporting details in the proper sequence.

3. Do *not* spend a lot of time trying to write complete or smooth sentences. Do *not* pause to polish each sentence after you write it. These delays could break your train of thought and start you doodling or staring again. Fragments, loosely worded sentences, or other errors can be corrected later.

4. Do *not* worry about messy work. Cross out and insert above or below the line or in the margin as necessary.

Sometimes one sentence will adequately explain a specific point; other times more information is needed. Writing may help you think of other related details, facts, or examples not on your original list. Include them now, and if they later prove unnecessary, just cross them out.

Once you finish the first main section of your paper (*conditioning,* in our example), move on to the other sections (*concentration* and *consistency*). When you have completed these sections and start to write the conclusion, you may experience the same difficulty you had with the introduction. *If you do, skip the conclusion too until later*.

Here is how the rough draft of the tennis paper, including an introduction and conclusion, might look.

Introduction: Thesis statement shows organization	As tennis becomes more popular, more 1 people are working to improve their game. *Three keys to playing better tennis singles are conditioning, concentration, and consistency.*
Conditioning paragraphs, topic sentences italicized	*Since you will be running continually,* 2 *conditioning is necessary.* This must start before you get to center court. A lot of running in place or jogging 5 miles a day will help build up your endurance for a 3- or 5-set match. Remember, there's no one out there to help you, and there will be very little rest time. Jumping rope is also excellent. It teaches you to stay on your toes and not be flat-footed.
	That's not the whole story on conditioning. Later, when you're ready to take to the 3 court, some tennis drills will help you. These include the two-on-one drill and the shadow drill. All these movements help prepare you for the actual conditions of a game. If you practice them now, they'll come naturally during a game.
Concentration paragraph, topic sentence italicized	*During a game, remember the second* 4 *thing that will help your tennis game: concentration.* Pay attention to the game you are playing and nothing else. You can be distracted by players in the next court. Learn to ignore their presence. Avoid joking with your opponent and talking with friends on the sidelines. Get rid of such personal distractions as worrying about a test or personal problem. And don't think about what you will do after the game. Concentrate only on the game or you'll have problems.

Consistency
paragraphs, topic
sentences italicized

Consistency is another—and perhaps the ₅
most important—key to game improvement.
Go for steady and sure shots. If you try a pro-
style overhead or power drive, you may miss
more often and burn out your energy.

Because tennis is a game of percentages, ₆
it is better to keep the ball in play steadily
than go for brilliance. Hit the ball with average speed and power. Frequently, you don't
win a match, but your opponent loses it.

Conclusion

You probably will not become a tennis ₇
celebrity just by following these suggestions,
however you will improve your game.

When you have finished the first draft, put it aside for at
least a day before you start revising. Unless you do, you will not
see your writing with a fresh eye and will read what you *think*
you have written, not what you actually have written. Taking a
break also allows you to catch errors that you would otherwise
overlook.

Exercise

Write a first draft based on the organizational plan and the thesis statement that you prepared for the exercises on pages 46 and 48.

REVISING YOUR FIRST DRAFT

The last major step in the writing process—*revision*—requires you to examine your draft word by word, sentence by
sentence, paragraph by paragraph, and to make any needed improvements. To catch any problems you might otherwise overlook, it is useful to read your paper aloud. This is especially helpful for noticing such errors as word omissions, clumsy sentences,
and sentence fragments.

To revise your paper thoroughly, read it several times, once
for each of the following reasons.

Check on your audience and purpose.
Check on the content and arrangement of ideas.

Strengthen paragraph structure and development.
Clarify sentences and words.
Correct misuse of English.

In addition, read your draft for any problems or errors that recur frequently in your writing. Finally, if you have not yet titled your paper, you need to do so now.

Checking Your Audience and Purpose. A successful paper is tailored to its audience and marked by a clearly defined purpose. Answering the following questions will help you achieve these ends.

1. What is my goal—to provide information, change my reader's mind, or prompt some action?
2. Am I addressing a general reader or one with technical expertise?
3. If it is a general reader, are technical terms used sparingly and clearly explained? Have I provided sufficient background for the reader?
4. If it is a reader with technical knowledge, is appropriate technical language used?
5. Is the tone appropriate throughout, or should I modify it to improve the reader's response?

Checking the Content and Arrangement of Ideas. As you re-read your paper to check the content and arrangement of ideas, make sure you have said everything you want to say, and fill in any gaps where a reader might need more information. Think about these questions as you read.

1. Have I fulfilled my purpose?
2. Where is more information needed?
3. What kind of information is needed? Details? Examples? Statements by authorities?
4. Where can I obtain the information? From my own experience? By talking to others? By reading?
5. Is any information unnecessary?
6. Is my paper properly organized, or do I need to reorganize any part of it?

If the organization of your paper seems less than clear, compose a list of all major and minor supporting points. Then check this outline for logic and completeness and, if necessary, add new points, delete excess information, rearrange existing parts, or rewrite weak sentences.

Strengthening Paragraph Structure and Development. Examine your paragraphs one by one. Ask yourself these basic questions about each one, and correct any shortcomings you find.

1. Does each paragraph have only one central idea?
2. Is there a topic sentence that states this central idea?
3. Does this topic sentence help to develop the thesis statement?
4. Does each of the other sentences help to develop the topic sentence?
5. Does each paragraph follow an appropriate pattern of development?
6. Are the sentences within the paragraphs connected by appropriate linking devices so each leads smoothly to the next?
7. Does each paragraph contain enough supporting detail?

Clarifying Sentences and Words. Reevaluate your words and sentences to determine if they make your reader's job easier. At the same time, ask the following questions.

1. Are my sentences written in clear, simple language?
2. Am I sure of the meanings of the words I use?
3. Have I carelessly omitted any necessary words?
4. Have I became "windy," cluttering the paper with excess words?
5. Have I punctuated properly to prevent confusion or misreading?

Correcting Misuse of English. Finally, check your writing for correct use of English. Common errors include improper punctuation, faulty pronoun references, dangling modifiers, misplaced modifiers, nonparallelism, faulty comparisons, sentence fragments, comma splices, and run-on sentences. Because the correct use of the English language defies brief explanation, punctuation guidelines and usage errors are discussed in detail in the Handbook at the end of the book.

Spelling deserves special mention because errors suggest that you are careless in your thinking and your work. You can check spelling most effectively by reading your theme backward, from the last word to the first. This approach allows you to concentrate only on the spelling of individual words and not on content. Whenever you are uncertain of a spelling or find a misspelled word, check the dictionary. Keep a list of your own hard-to-spell words so you can watch for them in your writing.

Finally, before preparing your final draft, you might find it helpful to ask a trusted friend or classmate to critique your writing. The questions and suggestions posed by others often provide a valuable perspective that can improve your writing.

WRITING YOUR INTRODUCTION

If you have delayed writing your introduction, you should do so now. Generally, a single paragraph that includes the thesis statement suffices for a short theme, but longer papers often use two or more introductory paragraphs. The introduction frequently begins with a broad statement that directly relates to the thesis and is followed by one or more sentences that progressively narrow the scope of the discussion and lead the reader smoothly to the thesis statement, which ends the introduction.

The introduction acquaints the reader with you and your topic. A well-written introduction arouses interest and signals clearly what lies ahead, thus enticing the reader forward. On the other hand, a dull or confusing opening creates an unfavorable impression and slows the reader's understanding. To attract the reader's attention, one of the following approaches can be implemented.

Make one or more arresting statements.
Cite a personal experience.
Present a case history.
Note specific details related to your topic.

The sample introductions that follow demonstrate these approaches. In each example, the thesis statement is italicized.

Arresting Statements. The following opening uses arresting statements to gain the reader's interest.

> Today, as in the past, humans continue to infringe upon the basic right of nature's species to survive. Through ignorance, oversight, and technological changes, we are threatening the survival of some 130 species of animals. Until their natural environments are properly maintained, the last chance of survival for these species may depend upon captive breeding in the nation's zoos. But captive breeding is a complex undertaking fraught with many difficulties. *Each species presents special psychological, social, and physical problems which must be solved if breeding is to succeed.*
>
> DeWayne Lubbers

Note the narrowing technique used in this passage. The first sentence suggests that humans threaten the existence of other creatures, a point clearly though not directly related to the problems of captive breeding. The following three sentences point out the number of animal species that humans are threatening, offer a solution to the threat, and indicate that the solution itself presents problems. All of the sentences in the passage lead, by clear stages, to the thesis statement, which identifies the types of problems encountered by breeders.

Personal Experience. The writer of the following opening describes a personal experience that leads into his thesis statement.

> In July 1979, I and 1,600 fellow employees of a large furniture company gathered for the company's annual picnic. Eating began about noon. By 2 P.M., several people started complaining of stomach distress, and by 5 P.M., over 800 had been stricken. *All of us were victims of food poisoning, an illness that results from eating food that contains certain bacteria or their toxins.*
>
> Alan Helwig

Case History. In the following opening, the writer gives the details of a case history, which leads into her thesis statement.

Jane and Dick Smith were proud, new parents of an eight-pound, ten-ounce baby girl named Jenny. One summer night, Jane put Jenny to bed at 8:00. Five hours later, Jane found Jenny dead. The baby had given no cry of pain, shown no sign of trouble. Even the doctor did not know why she had died, for she was healthy and strong. The autopsy report confirmed the doctor's suspicion—the infant was a victim of the "sudden infant death syndrome," also known as SIDS or "crib death." *SIDS is the sudden and unexplainable death of an apparently healthy sleeping infant.* It is the number one cause of death in infants after the first week of life and as a result has been the subject of numerous research studies.

Trudy Stelter

Specific Details. Following a general thesis statement, this paragraph catalogs specific details that support the statement.

Analyzing furnace-flue gas for carbon dioxide (CO_2) is a process that every furnace serviceman needs to know. When a furnace is operating normally, the CO_2 content of the flue gas will be 8 to 10 percent. A lower reading may denote an air leak in the furnace, the wrong type of fuel oil, a defective nozzle, an air shutter that is open too far, a flame with the wrong shape, or any of several other undesirable conditions.

Charles Finnie

Attention-getting devices are not always necessary in introductions. Technical papers often follow relatively rigid patterns in which such devices play no role. (Chapters 4 through 8 discuss in detail many of these patterns.) Your readers, their degree of interest in the subject, and the type of paper you write dictate the type of introduction you should use.

WRITING YOUR CONCLUSION

A conclusion rounds out your paper and signals the end of the discussion. A short paragraph usually suffices, but longer papers may require two or more concluding paragraphs. An adequate conclusion summarizes or supports the main ideas developed by the theme and signals that the discussion is complete. Since it is your last chance to communicate to your reader, try to make your conclusion effective.

There are several common kinds of effective conclusions. You may, for example, end your essay in one of the following ways.

Summarize your discussion.
Offer a recommendation.
Present a challenge.
Make a prediction.

Summary. The following paragraph summarizes the steps involved in grilling chicken.

> Grilling chickens, then, is quite simple if you use quality meat, select a high-grade cooking oil, and baste and turn the meat regularly. Anyone who can follow directions can do a first-rate job.
>
> *Joe Fowler*

Recommendation. The following passage uses a recommendation-type conclusion.

> TV advertisers rely mainly upon subtle exploitation of the viewers' egos and senses, and only in a small way upon facts. Viewers should therefore become aware of what commercials are doing and be critical of their message.
>
> *Sherry Forrest*

Challenge. The writer of a paper about physical fitness concludes with a challenge.

> And therein lies the challenge. You can't merely puff hard for a few days and then revert to your recliner. You must sweat and strain and puff regularly, week in and week out. They're your muscles, your lungs, your heart. The only caretaker they have is you.
>
> *Monica DuVall*

Prediction. Here is a conclusion that makes a prediction on the basis of ideas developed earlier in the writing.

The factors that cause utopian communities to fail cannot be overcome. Any utopian settlement in the United States is ill-fated: our present society rests on ideals that are totally unlike utopian ideals. Utopia is a dream, a hope, an attempt to find peace and happiness, but in the end it will prove unattainable.

Jimmy Ray Belnap

Several cautions are in order when you write a conclusion. First, do not veer off in an entirely new direction or introduce an entirely new topic. Imagine the effect if the writer of a carefully developed paper on playing tennis ended by saying, "Some of these suggestions can also help improve your handball game." Suddenly the reader is asked to consider an entirely new topic, which is then left totally undeveloped. Further, do not add a sentence or two in desperation when the hour is late and the paper is due the next day. Such last-minute additions are usually ineffective. For example, "Thus you can see the value of good study habits" is too weak to reinforce what comes before it and thus leaves the reader with no strong impression. Also, never apologize for your handling of the topic. Saying you could have discussed your points in more detail only calls your approach into question.

Some specialized kinds of writing use specialized types of conclusions. These conclusions are discussed at the appropriate points in the text. Some technical papers have no conclusion at all. Sets of instructions and descriptions of objects, for instance, may simply end when the last step has been presented or the last part described. The purpose and content lend a sense of completeness and make a conclusion unnecessary.

USING HEADINGS

Although headings are not often used in most nontechnical writing, they are a common feature of on-the-job reports and technical publications. A set of headings functions as a kind of map, showing the divisions and subdivisions of the writer's "territory." Headings serve to pinpoint the reader's position in the paper and allow those who want to explore one part of the paper to proceed directly to it. They also make the reader's job easier by breaking the text into smaller, more easily dealt with blocks of print.

Like the examples in Chapters 11 and 12, most short on-the-job reports require only one level of heading. With some longer reports, however, you may need to supply two or three levels. Unless your instructor or employer specifies differently, use the following format for typing and positioning the three levels of headings.

FIRST-LEVEL HEADING

As shown, the first-level heading is typed in capital letters and is centered on the page.

Second-Level Heading

The second-level heading is typed in upper- and lowercase letters and is positioned at the left margin of the page.

Third-Level Heading.   The third-level heading begins with a paragraph indent, is followed by a period, and runs into the text discussion.

CHOOSING YOUR TITLE

Unless a title pops into your head as you are writing, choose one after you have completed your paper. The title you select should focus narrowly on your topic, rather than reflect the general subject area. For our tennis paper, "The Three C's of Better Tennis Singles" would be more effective than simply "Tennis," which suggests a general discussion of the sport. In addition, your reader must be able to see the connection between what the title promises and what the paper delivers. For example, "Tennis Singles: Moving to the Top" misleads by indicating that the paper will explain how to become a professional player or champion, a matter it does not discuss. To avoid unwieldy titles, try to use eight words or less.

The title of a nontechnical paper can be either common or catchy. A common title simply tells the reader what to expect, whereas a catchy one attempts to arouse the reader's curiosity. Here are some examples of each kind.

COMMON: "Is a Hairpiece for You?"
CATCHY: "Toupee or Not Toupee?"
COMMON: "Buying Your Home with Other People's Money"
CATCHY: "Home Free"

However, *technical papers rarely have catchy titles.* Instead, they use one that gives a direct and straightforward indication of the paper's content. Such a title is in keeping with the purpose and audience of the writing. Here are two examples of technical titles.

Computers in the Medical Laboratory
Arsenic and the Environment

As the examples show, the title should be a sentence fragment, not a complete sentence.

The Finished Product

If you followed the steps discussed in this chapter, your tennis paper would look something like the following theme. As you read it, pay careful attention to the marginal notes, which point out some of the key writing elements. (The thesis statement, topic sentences, and some of the linking devices are printed in italics.)

Title: specific, accurate, catchy	***The Three C's of Better Tennis Singles***
Introduction: arresting statement	*In the last few years tennis has enjoyed a* 1 *rise in popularity unequaled by any other*
Linking device	*sport. As a result,* many players are trying to
Thesis statement and statement of organization	improve their game. *Three keys to playing better tennis singles are conditioning, concentration, and consistency.*
Topic sentence, with links to preceding paragraph	*Since a singles match requires endur-* 2 *ance, proper conditioning is necessary.* This conditioning should begin before you arrive

at the court. Jogging three to five miles a day and running in place are both excellent exercises for increasing your stamina. *These* exercises help ensure that, in a deciding third set, you will not lose the match because of exhaustion. Jumping rope, *another good exercise,* conditions you to stay on your toes rather than play flat-footed. You'll have a much better chance of reaching and returning your opponent's shots if you start toward them from your toes.

When you arrive at the court, a good conditioning exercise is the two-on-one drill. Have two of your friends stand at the net and hit the ball to you in the opposite backcourt. Ideally *their* shots should be just out of your reach so that you are continually chasing the ball. On your return shots, alternately try to lob the ball over their heads, drive it between them down the middle of the court, send a passing shot down the line, or drill the ball low and hard directly at the net players. With *this continual running* and *these four types of returns,* you will be preparing for the actual conditions of your next match.

As you play that match, you should work on developing the ability to concentrate—the second key to improving your game. Concentration involves focusing your attention only on the game at hand and not allowing anything else to distract you. Courtside and personal distractions are the two most common among tennis players. Courtside distractions include watching players in the next court, talking to a friend outside the court, and joking with your opponent between points. Personal distractions include such things as worrying about a test, mulling over a personal problem, and thinking about the refreshments after the game. *All of these distractions*

Specific details: jogging, etc.
Linking device
Linking device
Topic sentence, with links to preceding paragraph
Specific details
Linking device
Specific details: types of shots
Linking device
Topic sentence, with links to preceding paragraphs
Term defined
Specific details: distractions
Linking device

result in poorly hit balls and lost points. All good tennis players are able to discipline themselves to concentrate only on the game.

Probably the most important key to improving your game is consistency. Steady placement of your shots is much more effective than occasional brilliance. Many players make the mistake of trying spectacular shots and using power strokes rather than playing a steady, consistent game. For example, don't try to blast a spectacular pro-style overhead or continually overpower your opponent with hard, driving shots. Such efforts will lose more points for you than they will win.

Tennis is a game of percentages. The *consistent* player keeps the ball *steadily* in play so the opponent is more apt to make a mistake. Hitting the ball away from your opponent with average speed is percentage tennis; drilling the ball with power is not. All experienced players realize that very often matches are not won, but lost.

If you follow these suggestions, don't expect to successfully challenge any tennis celebrity.

Do expect, however, to start beating some of the players who used to beat you.

Ferris Finnerty

Margin notes (left column):

Topic sentence, with links to preceding paragraphs

Specific details: spectacular shots, power strokes, blast, overpower, etc.

Topic sentence
Linking device (links to preceding paragraph)

Specific details

Conclusion (prediction)

Line numbers: 5, 6, 7

Comparing the first draft of this paper (pages 50–51) with the final version shows that revising has produced improvements at every point. In the opening paragraph, the second draft smooths the path to the thesis statement and creates greater interest in the topic by expanding on the background information and putting more emphasis on the popularity of tennis. The revised version of paragraph 2 develops a topic sentence that suggests more clearly how off-court exercises, by increasing a player's endurance, can directly affect playing. Paragraph 2 also substitutes spelled-out numbers for numerals.

By limiting discussion to the two-on-one drill, the revision of paragraph 3 is more sharply focused. A new topic sentence replaces the overly vague original and eliminates a number of unnecessary words. The remainder of the paragraph explains how to carry out the two-on-one drill—important information the first draft does not supply. The topic sentence of revised paragraph 4 now includes the word *key*, which links the subject of concentration more closely to the thesis statement. In addition, details have been added to the paragraph that identify particular distractions and the problems they can cause. The rewritten versions of paragraphs 5 and 6 provide a more detailed, forceful, and convincing treatment of why consistency is important. Finally, the new conclusion gains force by suggesting a more specific goal ("beating some of the players who used to beat you"). The rewritten conclusion also eliminates a comma splice in the original.

The marginal notes that accompany the final version point out some of the elements that make this paper effective. However, the most important point to be made could not be noted there: the paper is successful because the writer followed an orderly procedure to arrive at an appropriate topic, to establish a specific focus, to develop and organize the necessary information, and to write and polish the draft.

Exercise

Revise the first draft you prepared for the exercise on page 51, then supply a suitable title. Type or neatly write your essay in final form.

Word Processing and the Writer

Anyone who writes on the job or plans a professional writing career should become acquainted with word processing and its functions in writing. A word-processing program can be enormously helpful and efficient, but it cannot eliminate bad writing, substitute for proper organization, or guarantee correct grammar and sentence structure.

Using a word processor is a straightforward procedure in which documents are entered into the unit with a keyboard, then "saved"—that is, stored—for later editing and reusing. All stored information is called *data*. Using a word processor entails learning the functions of some keys unique to computer keyboards but does not require you to be a "computer whiz" to master the procedure. Ordinarily, the keyboard is used to retrieve material as well as to enter data into the unit. Thus, the greatest asset you can have when approaching word processing for the first time is skill in typing.

Hundreds of word-processing programs are now available. As a result, you do not learn "word processing" per se but rather the word-processing program you are using. Fortunately, once you have learned one program it is much easier to become adept at others because all programs perform essentially the same functions.

FEATURES OF WORD-PROCESSING SYSTEMS

A typical word-processing unit consists of a computer, a video screen, a keyboard, and a printer.

A *computer* is an electronic tool that stores data and programs. A *program* is a means of storing or retrieving the data. It allows you to store a document such as a letter and later to modify it, add to it, or delete parts of it. Most computers use hard disks and floppy disks as means of storage, although some also use tape. Unlike hard disks, floppy disks are removable and portable, much like the LP records and CDs on which music is recorded, and they require the same careful handling.

The data entered into a word processor or retrieved from it are displayed on the video screen, and when copies are required, they are reproduced by means of a *printer*. Printers come in many variations, some producing letters resembling those of a typewriter and others mimicking typeset copy. All are much faster then typing by hand. Once data have been entered into the unit, the word-processing program allows you to manipulate the material in almost unlimited ways by making use of special functions that are activated through the *keyboard*. The more important of these functions are discussed here.

Insert Mode. When you enter words into a paragraph, the insert mode allows you to move the rest of the text over to make room, so that nothing is erased. The *stet complementary* function closes the gap when material is deleted.

Overstrike Mode. The overstrike mode is the reverse of the insert mode, allowing you to type over existing text without moving it to the right.

Delete Commands. The most basic delete command is usually the backspace key, which lets you back up over typed material and erase it. But word-processing programs also have commands that delete a word, a line, or even a large block of type.

Cut and Paste. The cut-and-paste function is the electronic equivalent of scissors and glue. It allows you to mark a section of text and move it to a new location in the document.

Search and Replace. The search-and-replace function allows you to replace a word, a few letters, or a phrase whenever it appears in a document. Suppose that after referring to "Mrs. Smith" throughout your document, you discover that her name is really spelled "Smythe." By using the search-and-replace function, you can automatically change the name throughout. This function also permits you to stop the system each time the target item is found so you can consider the case individually. Thus you can find target items without replacing them.

Spell Check. The spell-check function checks spelling by comparing each word with a long list of known words. Any word not recognized is flagged and a list of possible alternatives given. The spell check may, however, stop on words that are not misspelled (such as uncommon proper names) but are simply not on the computer's list. Also, a spell check cannot indicate when you have typed the wrong word, say *they're* for *their*, or when you have misspelled one word as another word, say *form* for *from*. Some word processors also contain a thesaurus that provides synonyms for particular words.

Boilerplate or Merge. The boilerplate function allows you to create new documents out of stock pieces. It is taken from legal terminology, where "boilerplate" terminology is stock language used in many documents. If you write many business letters, for instance, the boilerplate function lets you save standard paragraphs and call them up for different letters, rather than retype them.

Form Letters. Similar to the preceding function but more automated, the form-letter mode allows you to write a single stock document, usually a letter, and reprint it multiple times with different information, such as recipients' names, inserted. (This explains how "personalized" advertising letters are produced.)

Headers and Footers. The headers and footers function allows you to enter once, at the beginning, a title at the top or bottom of a page. The title will then print out automatically on each subsequent page.

Other Functions. Additional functions can number pages and help with bibliographies, footnotes, and outlines.

Word-processing systems have transformed the writing process. Writers who use them can make instant changes—move paragraphs, experiment with different patterns of organization— and still have a clean document to read and revise. Errors or false starts can be eliminated as if they had never existed.

USEFULNESS OF WORD PROCESSORS

Although most useful for revision, word processors can also help you during the earlier stages of the writing process.

Planning and Drafting. When searching for a topic, you can brainstorm or free write on the word processor, entering whatever words, phrases, or ideas come to mind. For best results, brainstorm for about ten minutes; then stop and comb through your entries for bits and pieces that seem promising. You can copy these onto a new document and use them as the basis for more brainstorming or free writing until you arrive at a suitable topic.

Word processing can also help you when you generate and organize the material needed to develop your topic. Thus, outline-processing programs allow you to create outlines on screen and then easily add, delete, modify, and move divisions and subdivisions. For example, a subhead in one division of the outline can easily be moved to another division with a keystroke or two. A number of programs are particularly adaptable to brainstorming, allowing you to enter items and then present them in the form of an outline. Some programs provide alternative outlines for you to consider.

Word processing is likewise helpful during the drafting stage. Whenever your writing effort stalls, note the spot with an asterisk or other marker. When you have reached the end of the draft, use the automatic "find" function to return to that spot for further work. If your system has a spell-check function, use it to weed out misspellings on the completed draft. Similarly, a thesaurus function lets you call up sets of alternatives to words you consider inexact or overused. Once you have edited your document, you can print it out.

Revising. A word processor makes revision much easier. It allows you to rewrite unwanted sections of your draft, add new material, delete unwanted material, and move parts of the text as desired.

As you revise, keep a backup printed copy after every major stage of the revision. You then have protection if you accidentally erase a file or lose your work to an electrical power surge. It can be quite frustrating if you want to use something from an earlier draft only to find you erased it when you revised. Further, discarded sections sometimes serve as the basis for a new paper. To distinguish the major stages from one another, you can label them "Copy A," "Copy B," and so on. Deleted sections of text can go into a specially labeled file.

During revision, jot down helpful ideas or comments in your text. You can mark them off using a special symbol, such as <   >, and delete them later if you wish. If you are struggling with a troublesome section of text, try writing two or three versions, experimenting with them, and using your favorite version in your draft.

Avoid allowing the program to control how you revise. Because it is easy to back up a few words and rewrite your text, you may be tempted to fiddle endlessly with sentences and words and never develop the essay as a whole. It can also be tempting to move blocks of your draft around without making the proper transitions to fit them into their new positions. Instead of taking the easy path, make the changes that will result in the most effective essay.

Make at least one revision using a printout of your essay. When you revise on the computer, you are limited to one screen at a time, and because a screen shows only about twenty-four lines at a time, it is more difficult to gauge the whole manuscript. A printout allows you to compare several pages at a time so that you can, for example, more easily see whether some paragraph would work better if moved from one page to another. A printout also makes you more conscious of the flow of your writing.

When you finish revising, check the coherence of your draft by reading a printed copy. Where you have added, deleted, or moved text, make sure the transitions are appropriate. Where you have been working at the sentence level, make sure the sentences have not been mangled by your changes. When this corrected version is stored, make a final spelling check. Reread your text and replace inexact words with more exact ones if your system has a thesaurus function.

TEXT EVALUATION PROGRAMS

Computer programs that evaluate and analyze finished documents also have found widespread use. For example, some programs print out the first and last sentences of each paragraph so you can check transitions from one paragraph to the next. These programs usually check sentence length too, warning you when you have written too many excessively long or short sentences and recommending corrective action. Most programs also list any occurrence of *its* and *it's* as well as many other confusing word pairs, enabling you to check whether you have made the right choices. The programs likewise flag vague words and wordy expressions, suggesting alternatives. For example, the expression *at this point in time* would be flagged as wordy and the alternatives *now* and *at this time* suggested as replacements. Often a text evaluation program includes a thesaurus that provides a list of synonyms for many words. Programs are constantly being revamped to provide more functions.

Suggestions for Writing

Select another broad subject from the exercise on page 36 or from the list that follows and narrow it to a topic suitable for a two- or three-page paper. Determine your audience and focus, compile a list of specific details, organize them in an appropriate way, develop a thesis statement, write a first draft, and revise and title the paper.

1. Medicine
2. Politics
3. National defense
4. Organized crime
5. Divorce
6. Investments
7. Popular music
8. News media
9. Movies
10. Computers

4

Explanation of a Process

Process explanation, widely used in college and on the job, presents directions for doing something, tells how a procedure was or is carried out, or explains some natural happening. The following one-paragraph example of process explanation gives directions for filing a metal workpiece. (The thesis statement is printed in italics.)

> *Good flat-filing technique is important to any mechanic and not difficult to acquire.* The procedure requires only one item: a wooden-handled metal file which has been chalked to provide lubrication and prevent a buildup of metal shavings on its filing surfaces. To begin filing, grasp the handle of the file firmly, and lay one filing surface on the metal workpiece. Apply downward and forward pressure on the file, pushing it away from you until the near edge of the filing surface reaches the workpiece. At that point, raise the file up off the workpiece, bring it back, and repeat the procedure. Do not draw the file backward across the part; doing so will dull the file. When most of the chalk has worn off the side you are using, turn the file over and use the second side until most of its chalk has worn off too. If necessary, rechalk the file by applying chalk with a back-and-forth motion. Continue filing until the surface of the workpiece has the desired smoothness. Before putting the file away, clean and chalk it to keep it dry and prevent rusting.
>
> *David Hammis*

Almost all careers require a knowledge of process. For example, process explanation is needed to describe how to test the brakes of an automobile, perform cardiopulmonary resuscitation, give an insulin injection, take fingerprints, program a computer, develop photographs, measure air contaminants, charge a refrigeration unit, or analyze a chemical compound. Because of its many applications, you need to acquire skill in this type of writing.

Choosing Your Topic

On the job, the work situation dictates your writing topic. In the classroom, however, your instructor may ask you to choose a topic. In this case, select one you have personally participated in, read about, or observed. For instance, if you have never grilled hamburgers, do not try to explain the process to someone else. On the other hand, if you do the outdoor cooking for your family in the summer, grilling hamburgers might be an excellent topic choice. Because you would know the steps involved in the procedure, you could explain them clearly and completely to someone who does not.

You will probably have no trouble selecting a topic. If you do, brainstorming, free writing, or asking questions (see Chapter 3) can help you break the barrier. Be sure to avoid topics that are too simple or too complex, especially if the paper has an assigned word or page length. If you explain how to light a match, your explanation will be trivial, and you will soon run out of meaningful things to say. On the other hand, to explain adequately how to overhaul an automobile engine would require several thousand words and be far too complex a topic.

Exercise

Identify which of the following topics are suitable for a 500- to 750-word process explanation and which are not. Give reasons for your answers.

1. finishing an end table
2. planting a vegetable garden
3. constructing an apartment complex

4. sharpening a pencil
5. building a terrarium
6. running a large corporation
7. raising a child
8. washing and waxing a car

Developing and Organizing Your Information

DETERMINING YOUR STEPS

Once you choose a topic, you are ready to list the actions involved in carrying out the process. The brainstorming procedure discussed in Chapter 3 can help you to accomplish this task. By examining the list you create and grouping together related actions to form steps, you can make clear the major subdivisions of the procedure. The following is an example of how the steps involved in grilling hamburgers might be grouped.

Step I. Get the fire going
 1. remove the grill rack
 2. stack the charcoal briquets
 3. light the briquets
 4. spread the burning briquets out

Step II. Make the patties
 1. select the right amount of hamburger
 2. shape the hamburger into a ball
 3. flatten and compress the ball
 4. place the patties on a plate

Step III. Prepare for grilling
 1. check the grill temperature
 2. rub the grill with some hamburger
 3. replace the rack on the grill

Step IV. Do the grilling
 1. place the patties on the grill
 2. sear the patties
 3. grill the patties to taste

After you have listed all the steps, make sure they appear in proper order. Many processes have only one correct order—these are called *fixed-order* processes. When you change a flat tire, for example, you must jack up the car before removing the flat and remove the flat before installing the spare tire. Other processes, however, offer a choice of arrangements—these are called *order-of-choice* processes. When you grill hamburgers, for instance, you can make the patties before or after you light the charcoal. Since some order is needed, however, order-of-choice processes should be presented in the order that has worked best for you.

WRITING YOUR THESIS STATEMENT

If you have not already drafted your thesis statement, do so now. As you know, the thesis statement establishes one specific focus, helping you decide what to include and exclude and telling your reader what to expect. Process explanations most often have general rather than specific thesis statements that do not list the steps covered in the paper.

Note the focus in the following thesis statement:

> Grilling hamburgers on an outdoor charcoal grill is a simple process that almost anyone can master.

Here, *grilling* indicates that the paper does not explain broiling or pan frying, *hamburgers* that it does not discuss pork chops or hot dogs, and *outdoor charcoal grill* that it does not mention gas grills, electric grills, or open campfires.

Exercise

List the steps involved in performing one of the following activities, arrange them in the appropriate order, and draft a suitable thesis statement for a paper explaining the process.

1. studying for an examination
2. performing some common household task
3. assembling or repairing some small household device
4. breaking a bad habit

Writing and Revising Your Paper

WRITING YOUR INTRODUCTION

In addition to presenting your thesis statement, the introduction should list everything needed to carry out the process. If the purpose of any item is not obvious, indicate that purpose briefly. Sometimes additional information must be given as well. Special conditions—such as the minimum temperature required for painting the exterior of a building—or special skills—such as knowing how to perform chemical analyses with an X-ray spectrograph—must be noted.

Following is a sample introductory paragraph for a paper on hamburger-grilling.

> Grilling hamburgers on an outdoor charcoal grill is a simple process that almost anyone can master. Before starting, you will need a clean grill, charcoal briquets, charcoal lighter fluid and matches, hamburger meat, a plate, a spatula, and some water to put out any flame caused by fat drippings. The sizzling, tasty patties you will have when you finish are a treat that almost everyone will enjoy.
>
> *E. M. Przybylo*

Notice that the paragraph begins with the thesis statement, lists the items needed, and briefly explains the water's purpose. Since the process does not require any special conditions or skills, none is mentioned.

THEORY AND LIST OF STEPS

Technical papers often include a *statement of theory*—the basic principle that underlies the process and makes its execution possible. Customarily, the theory follows the introduction in a separate paragraph. Do not confuse the theory with the reason for performing the process. This reason, if mentioned at all, usually appears in the introduction. Nontechnical process explanations, such as our example on grilling hamburgers, do not include statements of theory. Most scientific procedures, however, rest on some underlying principle, which is made clear to the reader in the statement of theory.

If you are explaining a technical process, list its steps in a single sentence positioned immediately after the theory. Nontechnical papers do not have such listings.

The following example of a technical process explanation includes both a theory and a list of steps.

> This process is based upon the fact that potassium chlorate decomposes to form oxygen when heated. The manganese dioxide does not supply oxygen but rather promotes the decomposition of the potassium chlorate at a low temperature. The process consists of six steps: (1) preparing an oxygen mixture, (2) placing the mixture in the test tube, (3) positioning the collection bottles in the trough, (4) collecting the oxygen, (5) removing the collection bottle and delivery tube from the trough, and (6) final cleanup.
>
> *Phyllis Jedele*

DISCUSSING YOUR STEPS

At this point, you are ready to explain the steps of your process in detail. If you have ever experienced trouble while trying to assemble a bicycle, piece of furniture, or some other item by using factory-supplied directions, you know the importance of presenting steps carefully. The following guidelines will help you do just that.

1. Present each step of the process in one or more paragraphs so each is separated clearly for your reader.
2. Develop each step with enough details to make it clear.
3. Do not omit information that is obvious to you but may not be obvious to your reader. Whenever the purpose of something is less than clear, note the purpose. The reader will then be less likely to skip the step or action.
4. If a step or action is especially hard to carry out, warn the reader and explain how to overcome the difficulty.
5. If the reader might perform an action improperly, provide a warning—especially if the improper procedure would be dangerous.
6. If two steps must be performed simultaneously, warn the reader at the start of the first one.

Use time signals as needed to clarify the sequence of actions or to add smoothness to the writing. Common signals include *first, as, during, after, next, now, once, when, then,* and *finally.* However, do not overload your paper with these signals, as this may impede your reader's progress.

Here is how the steps for grilling hamburgers might be developed. (The topic sentences and time signals are italicized.)

The first step is to get the fire going. Remove the grill rack and stack about twenty charcoal briquets in a pyramid shape in the center of the grill so that they can burn off one another and produce a hotter fire. *Next* squirt charcoal lighter fluid over the briquets. Wait about five minutes for the fluid to soak into the charcoal; *then* toss in a lighted match. The flame will burn for a few minutes before it goes out. *When* this happens, let the briquets sit for another fifteen minutes so the charcoal can start to burn. Do not squirt on any more lighter fluid as a flame could follow the stream back into the can, causing it to explode. As the briquets begin to turn ash-white, spread them out with a stick so that they barely touch each other. Air can *then* circulate and produce a hot, even fire—the kind that makes grilling a success.

After spreading out the briquets, start making the hamburger patties. First, however, reserve a small bit of hamburger for treating the grill rack. To make each patty, form about one-fourth pound (about two ice cream scoops) of hamburger into a ball. *Then* flatten the ball and compress the meat tightly to ensure extra firmness and lessen the chance that the patty will fall apart on the grill. To ensure that they cook evenly throughout, do not make the patties too thick. One inch thick by five inches in diameter is recommended; these dimensions allow for shrinkage, and the patties will fit the buns perfectly. As the patties are made, place them side by side on a plate. Stacking would cause them to stick together.

Now prepare for grilling. To check the heat of the briquets, hold the palm of your hand over them at the height the meat will be cooking—about six inches in average. *When* you can barely count "one Mississippi, two Mississippi, three Mississippi" before pulling your hand away, the temperature is right. To prevent the patties from sticking to the rack, rub it with the hamburger you reserved; *then* replace it on the grill.

You are now ready for the actual grilling. To begin, use the spatula to space the patties evenly above the briquets. *After* a minute or two, turn the patties with the spatula and expose the raw sides to the heat. This will sear the meat and lock in the flavor. *When* both sides have been seared, grill the patties to your taste. If you like them rare—juicy and red inside—cook them six to eight minutes per side. If you like them well done—not juicy and brown inside—allow twelve to fifteen minutes per side.

E. M. Pryzbylo

As is customary, the actions are presented as commands (for example, "Remove the grill rack") because this form is the most direct and the easiest to follow. At several points, the writer explains *why* something should be done. The first paragraph indicates that stacking the briquets produces a hotter fire, the second paragraph that compressing the patties makes them less likely to fall apart, and the fourth that searing the meat locks in the flavor. The first paragraph warns against the danger of squirting lighter fluid on the charcoal and calls for a fifteen-minute waiting period after the charcoal is first lighted. Without this warning, the reader might attempt to start grilling immediately.

WRITING YOUR CONCLUSION

Conclude in the manner that will suit your paper best and help your reader most. The conclusion can (1) *summarize* the process, (2) *evaluate* the results, or (3) *discuss* the importance of the process. The paper on grilling hamburgers might conclude in the following way.

Once the patties are cooked the way you like them, place them on buns. *Now* you are ready to enjoy a mouth-watering treat that you will long remember.

E. M. Przybylo

Many on-the-job explanations have no conclusion and end when the last step has been presented.

REVISING YOUR DRAFT

When you revise, follow the guidelines in Chapter 3 (pages 51–54). In addition, ask yourself the following questions.

Have I listed all items necessary to carry out the process?

Have I noted any required special conditions or training?

If appropriate, have I included a theory and list of steps?

Is every necessary step discussed?

Is each step explained sufficiently so that it can be performed properly?

Have I noted the purpose of a step when necessary?

Have I warned the reader about any steps that might be dangerous or performed improperly? That are especially hard to carry out? That must be performed simultaneously?

Are the directions presented in the form of commands?

Exercise

In magazines or newspapers, find examples of process explanations and bring them to class for a discussion of how they illustrate step-by-step directions.

Other Types of Process Papers

Sometimes, instead of writing directions for your reader to follow, you may want to explain, for an audience that will not carry it out, how a process is or was performed. These explanations differ from sets of directions in three ways.

1. The list of materials and equipment is sometimes omitted.
2. The explanation is less detailed.
3. The steps are written in the passive voice, rather than as commands in the active voice.

A sentence written in the active voice has the subject *you*, which may be stated or implied. The subject *performs* the action specified by the verb. A sentence in the passive voice has a subject that *receives* the action specified by the verb. Four examples follow.

Active Voice

Before starting to refinish the chest, remove as much ornamental hardware as possible. (Subject *you* is understod, performs action.)

To prevent contamination of the culture, you must flame the opening of the tube. (Subject *you* is stated, performs action.)

Passive Voice

Before the chest was refinished, as much hardware as possible was removed. (Subject *hardware* receives action.)

The opening of the tube is flamed to prevent contamination of the culture. (Subject *opening* receives action.)

The following examples show how the three types of process explanation differ.

Directions (active voice)

To begin step one, slowly turn the intensity knob clockwise until a spot of light appears on the screen. Adjust the focus control to make the spot as small and sharp as possible. Next, turn up the horizontal gain control until there is a horizontal line about eight divisions long on the screen. Adjust the intensity so the line is bright enough to be seen plainly, and readjust the focus for the finest possible line.

Glenn Jones

How Process Is Performed (passive voice)

The tumbler is loaded with about 500 pounds of rollers. One scoop of abrasive grit is mixed with water until a thin gravylike mixture is obtained. Then the mixture is placed in the tumbler, which is set to rotate at about 40 revolutions per minute. During rotation, the rollers are worn down by the action of the abrasive mixture. Every twenty minutes, the tumbler is stopped and the diameter of a sample roller is checked. When the rollers are the right diameter, they are removed from the tumbler and rinsed free of grit in preparation for the next step.

Barry McGovern

How Process Was Performed (passive voice)

The analyzer was adjusted so the scale read zero and connected to the short sampling tube which had previously been inserted into the smokestack. The sample was taken by depressing the bulb the requisite number of times, and the results were then read and recorded. The procedure was repeated, this time using the long sampling tube and sampling through the fire door.

Charles Finnie

Examples of Process Explanation

Compression Pressure Testing of an Automobile Engine

Thesis statement: indicates significance of test

Compression pressure testing is a process that indicates the compression ratio of an automobile engine. Here is a simple, accurate procedure for determining engine compression. The tools needed to carry out this process include a spark plug wrench, a large screwdriver, a remote-control starter switch, and a compression pressure gauge.

List of items needed for test

Statement of theory

The process is based on the fact that if the head gasket and piston rings are in good condition, the combustion chamber will be tightly sealed during the compression stroke. If a gauge is inserted in place of the spark plug, the amount of compression can be measured. A high gauge reading indicates a good seal, and a low reading indicates a poor seal. The three basic steps in the procedure are: (1) preparing the engine for testing, (2) pressure testing, which includes inserting the gauge into each cylinder and recording the readings, and (3) comparing the pressure readings to one another and to the engine compression specifications.

List of steps in process

Topic Sentence: introduces first step and first action to carry it out

To prepare the engine, first remove the spark plug wire located at the top of each plug. Next, remove the plugs from the block with the spark plug wrench. Connect the

Purpose of steps noted

remote-control starter switch to the starter solenoid terminals. To prevent the car from starting, disconnect and ground the ignition-coil tower wire located at the distributor. Finally, block open the carburetor throttle with the large screwdriver. This will prevent gas from overflowing.

Topic sentence: introduces second step and first action to carry it out

Warning provided

To pressure test the engine, force the end of the gauge into the number one spark plug hole. Make sure the rubber tip of the gauge completely seals the hole, or inaccurate readings will result. Depress the remote-control starter switch until the engine cranks seven complete compression strokes. Observe and record the compression reading, and the number of the cylinder tested. Remove the gauge and test each of the remaining cylinders in the same way.

4

Topic sentence: introduces third step

Significance of readings discussed

In order to interpret the results of the pressure tests, the readings must be compared with one another and with the engine compression specifications. First, compare the individual cylinder readings. They should be within 20 percent of one another. A greater variation indicates that excessive wear has caused an unbalanced engine, which cannot be corrected by mere tuning. The second comparison, between the average of the readings and the known engine compression specification, shows the amount of engine wear. If the average is within 20 percent of the specification, the engine is considered mechanically sound. If the average is more than 20 percent below the specification, the engine is excessively worn and should be rebuilt. If the average is more than 20 percent above the specification, the engine has heavy carbon deposits and needs to be decarbonized. Low pressure readings in two adjacent cylinders may indicate a faulty head gasket.

5

One-sentence
conclusion further
considers significance
of test

Periodic compression tests will indicate   6
the condition of an auto engine and alert the
owner to any needed repairs or adjustments.

Frank Perry

Hand Developing X-Ray Film

X-ray film developing is a procedure whereby the invisible,   1
latent image on exposed film is converted to a visible image by
treating the film with a developer solution. The special equipment needed to perform this process includes an exposed X-ray
film in its cassette, a film hanger, three solution tanks, and a
dryer. The solutions needed are developer, fixer, and water, each
in a separate tank at 68°F. The procedure is carried out in a dark-
room.

The process is based on the fact that an alkaline developer   2
transforms exposed (ionized) silver bromide crystals on the film
into clumps of black metallic silver that form an image. The un-
exposed (nonionized) silver bromide is not affected by this treatment. The complete development process consists of five steps: (1)
developing, (2) rinsing, (3) fixing, (4) rerinsing, and (5) drying the
film.

The exposed film is first removed from the cassette and at-   3
tached to the hanger. The film is then suspended in the developer
solution for about five minutes. This solution softens and swells
the gelatin on the outside of the film, then reacts with the ionized
silver bromide crystals to reduce them to metallic silver.

When the film is developed, it is placed in the rinse water   4
tank, which contains running water, for thirty seconds. Running
water ensures that the film is rinsed properly. It removes the alkaline part of the developer so it will not neutralize the acidic fixer.

Next the film is placed in the fixer solution for ten minutes.   5
This solution clears the film of nonionized silver bromide and
hardens the gelatin emulsion, thus increasing its resistance to
damage.

The film is then returned to the rinse tank. It is allowed to re-   6
main there for twenty-five minutes so that the fixing salts will be

removed, since residual fixer would cause the image to discolor and fade.

Finally, the film is removed from the rinse water tank and 7 the excess water is allowed to run off. The film is then placed in the dryer, generally a type of rack. During the drying process, the film can be easily damaged. Since dirt from the air may become embedded in the film or the film may become scratched, extreme care is taken to protect the film at this stage.

Drying takes approximately fifteen minutes. The dried film 8 is a permanent, finished radiograph that helps diagnose a suspected condition.

Janet Brown

Discussion Questions

1. Point out why this is an appropriate process to explain.
2. What is the purpose of the last sentence in paragraph 1?
3. Where is the theory discussed? Why is it desirable to include the theory for this process?
4. Why has the writer given the purpose for each step? In what way is this information helpful?
5. This chapter discusses three types of process papers: those giving directions, those merely explaining how a process is performed, and those reporting on how a process was performed. Which type does this paper illustrate? How do you know?

Add a Skylight for Light and Air

Whether your home is a ranch, split or colonial type, you can 1 give any room in it additional light and air by installing a skylight. With a skylight you gain reduced lighting costs, maximum air circulation in the summer as the hotter air escapes, some free heat in the winter because the unit acts as a solar collector (especially true for southern exposures) and streaming sunlight, creating the feeling of a Vermeer canvas.

Installing the Paeco 30 × 46-inch Skyliner takes about 4 to 5 2 hours in a cathedral ceiling and, more time, 2 to 3 days for a flat ceiling. . . .

You need a tape, rafter square, hammer, saw, screwdriver 3
(better, a brace and bit snips), utility knife, prybar with a broad
flat end (or a fairly brutish putty knife), drill, stapler, caulking
gun and trowel. Although a portable circular saw may be used to
cut open the roof sheathing, the most efficient combination of
cutters are a jigsaw and reciprocating saw. These give you speed,
control and easy access to rafters and joists, which are awkward
to undercut. Materials needed are enough $2 \times$ stock to box in both
the roof and ceiling (except for cathedrals), plus the light-shaft
framing. You also need drywall, insulation, common, roofing and
drywall nails, perhaps a bit of roofing felt, roof mastic, silicone
caulking, corner bead, tape and jointing compound.

Begin by cutting out a small hole in the ceiling where the sky- 4
light will go, then drilling a reference hole through the roof from
this access point. The hole represents a corner of the roof's rough
opening, so it *should* be right next to the rafter which borders the
skylight. Also, check the weather report before you start opening
the roof unless you really relish working under the gun because
the rains have begun.

Mark the outline of the rough opening on the roof, starting 5
from the drilled reference hole and following the dimensions on
the carton. Don't cut anything yet. Strip back enough shingles
(three tab butts are 12×36 in.) to completely expose the roofing
felt over the opening. To remove the shingles, first separate the
overlapping course from those below them, driving a putty knife
or prybar end underneath before lifting. Be gentle with a brittle,
old roof to avoid cracking it. Work on a real hot day, when the
roofing shingles will be most flexible. After separating the shingles, remove the four roofing nails holding each one and set the
shingles aside for later refitting and installation.

Mark the rough opening outline again and saw it out. Next 6
trim back the rafters, as necessary, at the correct angle to accommodate either plumb or raked end walls. Start the cuts $1\frac{1}{2}$ in.
above and below the opening to provide room for the box heading
to be nailed between the adjacent rafters and to the cut rafter
ends (at the high and low ends of the opening). Make sure that the
top edges of the cut rafters are flush with the header, which is the
drywall, corner bead, tape and joint compound. Sand and prime
and you're ready to paint.

Bernie L. Price, Reprinted from Mechanix Illustrated
Magazine. Copyright © 1981 by CBS Magazines.

Discussion Questions

1. To what kind of audience is the paper directed? How do you know?
2. At what points does the writer provide warnings?
3. Why is this material presented in the form of commands?

Suggestions for Writing

Write a paper explaining one of the following processes or another approved by your instructor. Prepare a complete list of steps, select an appropriate order, and develop each step with sufficient details.

1. Installing a manual throttle
2. Preparing a blood smear for microscopic examination
3. Balancing a cash register till
4. Growing a specific type of fruit or vegetable in your home garden
5. Recording a credit-card purchase
6. Monitoring the atmosphere for contaminants
7. Drawing up an income statement
8. Assembling or repairing some common household device
9. Treating a bite from a poisonous snake
10. Giving a sick patient a bed bath
11. Making a blueprint
12. Regripping a golf club
13. Training a dog (or some other pet)
14. Charging a refrigeration unit
15. Preparing a sales report
16. Taking an inventory
17. Potting a plant
18. Conducting a nitrate test for water potability
19. Changing the oil in an automobile
20. Sewing a zipper in an article of clothing
21. Balancing a checkbook
22. Making up a payroll
23. Grinding a tool bit
24. Repainting a car
25. Cleaning and gapping spark plugs
26. Selling a customer some item or service

27. Cutting internal threads on a workpiece
28. Turning a taper on a lathe
29. Installing, modifying, or overhauling a particular type of air conditioning or refrigeration unit
30. Carrying out a process related to your field

5
Comparison

Hardly a day goes by that you do not use comparison in some way. You may, for example, weigh two different job offers, explain two methods of wallpapering a room, consider three different health-insurance plans or evaluate several different television sets. When you compare, you examine two or more items and note likenesses, differences, or both.

The following brief example notes both likenesses and differences.

> *Although most people know that companies issue both common and preferred stock, few are aware of the key similarities and differences between them.* First, both represent a share in the ownership of a corporation. Also, both types may be either par—that is, a stated value is printed on the certificate—or no-par, in which case no value is printed on the certificate. The corporation issuing the stock has no obligation to pay returns to the owners of either type of stock, but when returns are paid, they may take the form of cash or of additional shares of stock. Perhaps the most important difference between the two kinds of stock is that dividends must be paid on preferred stock before being paid on common stock. Likewise, holders of preferred stock also get first distribution of company assets, as in a bankruptcy. In certain instances, however, preferred stock may be recalled or redeemed by the issuing corporation, or may even be

converted into common stock. Additionally, holders of preferred stock often have more restricted voting rights than holders of common stock, this in exchange for some special benefit—such as a guaranteed rate of return. Holders of common stock, then, carry a greater risk of loss than holders of preferred stock because common stock has no guarantees and no built-in protection.

Donna Stephanoff

You will use comparison both in college and on the job. Your instructor may ask you to write on the basic differences between banks and savings and loan institutions or between preventive dental care and restorative dental care. Your employer may ask you to evaluate two plans for improving working conditions or to report on the performance characteristics of several lathes, computers, or other pieces of equipment. Although comparisons are not necessarily limited to two items, you will have less difficulty if you first master comparing just two.

Choosing Your Topic

If you are asked to choose your topic, make sure the items you select have some clearly evident basis for meaningful comparison. For example, you could compare two golfers' driving ability off the tee, putting ability, and sand play; or two cars in terms of their appearance, gas mileage, and warranties. But you could not very well compare a golfer with a car. Where would you begin? What would you say?

The items must also provide a useful comparison. On the job, the work situation almost always determines your topic, and you can assume that it will interest your reader. But for other writing situations, select items about which you can provide either new information or new ways of thinking. It would be difficult, for example, to write a worthwhile paper comparing a pencil and a ball-point pen. There certainly is a basis for comparison—both are writing instruments—and clearly there are similarities and differences that you could discuss. But these likenesses and contrasts are so obvious and well known that it would be virtually impossible to provide any new information or a fresh way of thinking about the objects. On the other hand, you can write interestingly about commonplace objects. For example, you could draft a useful comparison of two different types of ballpoint pens: Type A is a better buy than Type B because it lasts three times as long. Further, Type A can be refilled when the ink runs out, but Type B must be discarded. Type A writes more sharply and is less likely to skip because it has a magnesium-alloy ball rather than a stainless-steel ball; Type B is inclined to leak and Type A does not. A comparison such as this meets all the requirements for choosing a topic. The similarities and differences are not so obvious that they are uninteresting. On the contrary, the comparison enables readers to learn something or to see the items in a new way.

Exercise

Determine which of the following pairs of items can be meaningfully compared and which cannot. Give reasons for your answers.

1. alligators and crocodiles
2. whole milk and skim milk
3. Social Security benefits and life-insurance benefits
4. an electric typewriter and a pencil
5. Asian elephants and African elephants
6. a table and a chair
7. silk and nylon
8. a roller coaster and a space shuttle
9. a farmer and a clothing salesperson
10. a neurosis and a psychosis
11. Acme aspirin and Aik-kure aspirin
12. a frog and a parakeet

Developing and Organizing Your Information

DETERMINING SPECIFIC POINTS OF COMPARISON

Armed with two suitable items to compare, you are ready to select your points of comparison—that is, your *focus*. This focus depends on your purpose and the desired length of your paper.

Suppose you supervise the record and tape department of a large department store, with two excellent salespeople, Pat Price and Lee Evans, working for you. The store manager has told you of plans to open a branch store in a suburban shopping mall and has asked you to submit a one- to two-page report comparing the qualifications of your two salespeople for managing its record department. Without your purpose to guide you—helping your boss choose between the two salespeople—think about the possible points of comparison you could generate by brainstorming. Here is just a partial list.

1. clothes
2. religion
3. hobbies
4. sense of humor
5. eye color
6. mathematical ability
7. hairstyle
8. sales skills
9. use of tobacco
10. bowling ability
11. musical knowledge
12. social activities
13. attendance habits
14. interest in current affairs
15. cooperativeness
16. food preferences
17. smile
18. political views
19. knowledge of ordering and accounting procedures

Obviously, religion, eye color, and bowling ability have no bearing on one's ability to manage a record and tape department, so these can be omitted from the list. As you continue to evaluate the listed items, you are establishing your focus.

After eliminating all the nonpertinent characteristics, you still may have far too many for a one- or two-page report. If you tried to develop all of them, you could probably write only one or two sentences about each, which would not give your reader a clear impression of the two candidates. For this reason, focus on the few essential points and develop each in a paragraph or two. Because you are trying to help your boss choose between Pat and Lee, it will be wise to focus on their differences rather than their similarities. For instance, if both candidates are cooperative and have excellent attendance habits, you could eliminate these points. However, if both are highly skilled salespeople, you would want to include this similarity because sales skills are so important in this case. Once you have decided on the most significant differences between the two candidates—their musical knowl-

edge and familiarity with ordering and accounting procedures—
you have established your focus.

However, it is not enough merely to state that two items are
similar or different; you must also show your reader *how* this is so
with well-chosen specific details and examples. Specific details
help your reader receive the message you intend to send. For example, if you say only that both Pat and Lee are excellent salespeople, your reader may not know exactly what you mean. On
the other hand, if you also point out that both candidates are
pleasant even with difficult customers, know what is in stock and
where to find it, maintain the stock in good order, and consistently gain sales by encouraging additional purchases, your reader
will easily grasp what you mean by "excellent salespeople."

To obtain enough specific details, conduct another brainstorming session. For each point of comparison, list all the supporting details that come to mind. Make a separate list for each of
the two items to be compared. This procedure may seem cumber-
some now, but later it will prove useful, enabling you to write
your paper more easily.

DETERMINING YOUR ORGANIZATION

Comparison papers can be organized by either the *block
method* or the *alternating method*. In the block method, the
items being compared provide the basic organization. The writer
first presents, in one block, all the information about the first
item and then, in another block, all the information about the
other. The paper comparing Pat and Lee, organized by the *block
method*, would look like this.

    I. Introduction
   II. Body
      A. Specific details about Pat
        1. Sales skills
        2. Musical knowledge
        3. Familiarity with ordering and accounting proce-
          dures
      B. Specific details about Lee
        1. Sales skills
        2. Musical knowledge
        3. Familiarity with ordering and accounting proce-
          dures
  III. Conclusion

Note that section B on Lee includes the same points of comparison as does section A on Pat, and that the points follow the same order in both sections. Your paper should also adhere to these guidelines.

Use the block method only for short papers—that is, for papers that discuss only a few points of comparison. Your reader can then keep the points in the first block clearly in mind while reading the second block.

For more lengthy papers—that is, those that discuss numerous points of comparison—use the alternating method. Here the points of comparison, not the items, provide the basic organization. The writer discusses a single point, comparing the items on that point, then proceeds to the next point. Organized according to the alternating method, the Pat and Lee paper would have this pattern.

    I. Introduction
   II. Body
       A. Sales skills
           1. Pat's skills
           2. Lee's skills
       B. Musical knowledge
           1. Pat's knowledge
           2. Lee's knowledge
       C. Familiarity with ordering and accounting procedures
           1. Pat's knowledge
           2. Lee's knowledge
  III. Conclusion

Generally, readers follow the alternating method more easily than the block method because a specific comparison is completed at each point, making it unnecessary to turn back to grasp a similarity or difference.

WRITING YOUR THESIS STATEMENT

If you have not already formulated your thesis statement, do so now. The thesis statement tells your reader what to expect and helps you stick to your purpose as you write.

Here is a possible thesis statement for the comparison of the two salespeople:

Although Pat and Lee are both excellent salespeople, I believe Pat would be the better choice for manager because of her wider knowledge of music and her greater familiarity with ordering and accounting procedures.

The statement does these three things that all thesis statements for comparison should do.

1. Name the two items under discussion.
2. State the specific points of comparison.
3. Indicate whether the paper will point out similarities, differences, or both.

Exercise

Compare two vacation spots in order to recommend one to a friend. List as many differences and similarities as you can; then, considering your friend's vacation preferences, pick three or four points to discuss. (Differences should predominate, because they will determine your recommendation.) Choose either the block or alternating method of organization, prepare an outline, and then write a suitable thesis statement.

Writing and Revising Your Paper

WRITING YOUR INTRODUCTION

The introduction presents your thesis statement and eases the reader into the main discussion. Chapter 3 (pages 54–56) discusses common kinds of introductions. For a nontechnical paper, you could choose to attract the reader's attention by making an arresting statement, presenting a personal experience, citing a case history, or telling an anecdote. Short on-the-job comparisons customarily open with one or more sentences that establish the reason for the writing and then proceed to the thesis statement. The comparison of Pat and Lee might be introduced in this way.

As you requested, I have compared the qualifications of Pat Price and Lee Evans for the job of managing the record and tape department in our new branch store in the Eastbrook Mall. *Although Pat and Lee are both excellent salespeople, I believe Pat would be the better choice for manager because of her wider knowledge of music and her greater familiarity with ordering and accounting procedures.*

WRITING THE BODY OF YOUR PAPER

As you write the body of your paper, use suitable linking devices to indicate points of similarity and difference. Comparison papers often use the following linking devices:

> TO INDICATE SIMILARITY: also, correspondingly, likewise, in the same manner, in like manner, similarly
>
> TO INDICATE DIFFERENCE: although, but, however, in contrast, nevertheless, on the contrary, on the other hand, whereas
>
> TO INDICATE ADDITION: in addition, besides, furthermore, moreover.

Following is the body of the report on Pat and Lee. The first paragraph discusses their similar sales expertise; the second points out the differences in their musical background. (The topic sentences and linking devices are italicized.)

> *Pat and Lee's sales expertise shows itself in several ways.* Both are unfailingly friendly and courteous with customers, even those who behave discourteously or take up a great deal of time without making purchases. *Similarly*, both know at all times what is in stock, and because they keep the merchandise in good order, they can quickly locate whatever the customer wants. *Moreover*, both consistently get extra sales by calling their customers' attention to other tapes and records of interest and by suggesting purchases of such items as tape-head cleaners and carrying cases for records.
>
> Pat has a solid background in music. She plays several instruments and for two years held the job of concert master in her high-school orchestra. For one summer she sang with a local rock group. *Thus*, she is acquainted with both classical and popular music. *In contrast*, Lee plays just one instrument, the accordion, and her background in popular music comes almost entirely from listening to it. She knows little of classical music. *Pat's background would therefore be a greater asset for the new manager's position than would Lee's.*

WRITING YOUR CONCLUSION

Your conclusion should end the paper effectively. (Pages 56–58 discuss common kinds of conclusions.) The purpose of the paper on Pat and Lee—that is, to recommend one of them for the manager's position—suggests a conclusion that predicts the success of the recommended candidate.

> All things considered, Pat is more highly qualified to manage the new record and tape department. If she is given the job, I am confident that she will handle it successfully.

REVISING YOUR DRAFT

Follow the guidelines on pages 51–54 when you revise your paper. In addition, answer these questions.

Do my items provide a meaningful and interesting comparison?
Do the points of comparison fit my purpose?
Are these points supported by adequate specific details?
Is my organization appropriate?
Are the points of comparison the same and presented in the same order for both items?
Are the introduction and conclusion appropriate and effective?
Are appropriate linking devices used to show likenesses and differences clearly?

Exercise

Choose the most effective type of introduction and conclusion for the paper comparing vacation spots (see the exercise on page 93). Explain your choices.

Examples of Comparison

Downhill Skis vs. Cross-Country Skis

Introduction: begins
with general comment

Winter is a very special season, bringing   1
many fun-filled sports that can be enjoyed at

on winter sports, then narrows focus to skiing

Thesis statement: indicates paper will discuss differences, not similarities

Topic sentence: signals discussion of first point of difference

Linking device showing effect

Linking device showing difference

Topic sentence: signals discussion of second point of difference

First design difference and reason for it

Linking device showing result

Second design difference and reason for it

Third design difference and reason for it

no other time of year. Of these, skiing has long ranked among the most popular. Devotees of skiing have a choice of two kinds: downhill and cross-country. *Despite the similarity of the two sports, the skis used for each have quite different construction features.*

 Because downhill and cross-country skis are used on different terrains, they require different materials of construction. Downhill skis must be constructed to withstand the high stresses generated by sharp turns, lateral movements, and high speeds. *Thus*, they are made of lightweight, durable materials such as fiberglass and graphite fibers. *In contrast*, cross-country skis, being subjected to less severe stresses, may be made of wood.

 These differences in materials are paralleled by differences in design. Downhill skis range from two-and-one-half to three-and-one-quarter inches wide, a width that provides stability at high speeds. With cross-country skis, stability is less important than ease of movement along trails. *Therefore*, cross-country skis are narrower, usually one-and-one-half to two inches wide. A downhill ski has a smooth bottom surface that requires frequent waxing and a metal strip on each edge, running from tip to tail. The smoothness increases the velocity at which the skier can travel, while the iron strips help in stopping and turning. Because high speed and quick turning are less important in cross-country skiing, the bottoms of its skis have a scaly surface except at the tip and tail and lack metal strips. These skis require no waxing. As for bindings, those on downhill skis restrict the skier's ability to move his or her feet so that body motion, rather than the motion of walking, determines the direction of

2

3

<table>
<tr><td>Linking device
showing contrast</td><td>travel. With cross-country skis, *on the other hand*, the heel is left free, allowing a walking movement.</td></tr>
<tr><td>Conclusion echoes
introduction by
noting popularity
of skiing</td><td>Yes, downhill and cross-country skis are different. But despite their differences they share one similarity—providing healthy, fun-filled recreation for hosts of winter sports enthusiasts.</td></tr>
</table>

Linking device
showing contrast

travel. With cross-country skis, *on the other hand*, the heel is left free, allowing a walking movement.

Conclusion echoes
introduction by
noting popularity
of skiing

Yes, downhill and cross-country skis are 4 different. But despite their differences they share one similarity—providing healthy, fun-filled recreation for hosts of winter sports enthusiasts.

Brenda Burns

Two Members of the Team: The Assistant and Hygienist

Because of the spiraling demand for dental care, dentists 1 must employ a dental health team in order to provide efficient service for their patients. The two team members who work directly with the patient are the dental assistant and the dental hygienist. *Although they share some duties, there are marked differences in the schooling they receive and in most of the jobs they perform.*

Both the assistant and the hygienist perform such tasks as an- 2 swering the telephones, scheduling and confirming appointments, accepting payments, and keeping books. In addition, both demonstrate basic oral care techniques—for example, the proper way of brushing and flossing teeth and of utilizing a Water-Pik to care for crowns and bridgework. Furthermore, both team members expose and process dental radiographs, which the dentist uses to diagnose problems and plan treatment. This overlap in duties facilitates patient care.

The dental assistant pursues a two-year program which in- 3 *cludes courses in dental materials, oral anatomy, bio-dental sciences, dental office management, clinical practice, and clinical procedures.* Graduates are eligible to take a Certificate Examination, and, upon passing it, to work under the direct supervision of the dentist.

The primary responsibilities of the assistant include prepar- 4 *ing the patient, assisting the dentist at the chairside, and dismiss-*

ing the patient. Preparation includes seating the patient comfortably in the dental chair, fastening the napkin in place, and adjusting the headrest. The assistant then sets up the instrument tray for the required procedure and, to help reassure the patient, may explain what the dentist is going to do. If the patient has been having problems with a certain tooth, the assistant may examine it in order to obtain information for the dentist. Chairside assisting includes passing instruments to the dentist, suctioning saliva and dental debris from the mouth, and keeping the working area clean and dry with the air and water syringe. In addition, the assistant retracts the tongue and pushes the cheek away from the jaw, holds the mirror near the tooth, and mixes the necessary medication and fillings. When the dentist has finished, the assistant records pertinent information on a chart and dismisses the patient after explaining any special care that the newly restored tooth needs.

In contrast, the two-year curriculum in dental hygiene prepares the student to work under the direction of the dentist but without direct supervision. Graduation requirements are more specialized than those for the dental assistant and include such courses as head and neck anatomy, histology and embryology; general and oral pathology, pharmacology, periodontia, dental health education, and clinical dental hygiene. In the clinic, the hygiene student works with patients on a one-to-one basis. Before starting to work, the new graduate must pass a set of licensing examinations. These exams help ensure that only highly skilled personnel will work in the patient's mouth, and they also allow the dentist to take out malpractice insurance on the hygienist.   5

The hygienist provides clinical services that help prevent and control oral diseases such as inflammation of the soft tissue surrounding the teeth and destruction of the bone that anchors them. Among the most common services are scaling and cleaning the teeth and treating them with fluoride. The hygienist also compiles personal medical and dental history records that include information about past diseases, previous dental care, and present medication. Further, this team member casts plaster study models—impressions of the teeth and surrounding tissues— and charts patients' dental conditions.   6

In summary, the dental assistant and the dental hygienist share some common tasks, but the different duties they perform   7 *enhance their value.* The assistant works more closely with and under direction of the dentist. On the other hand, the hygienist, while still directed by the dentist, works more independently, performing a variety of specialized duties. Together, their contributions increase the efficiency of the dentist's work.

Lynn Schroder

Discussion Questions

1. Explain why the thesis statement is effective.
2. Why is this topic appropriate for a comparison paper?
3. Where does the writer state her purpose?
4. Why has the writer devoted more space to differences than to similarities?
5. Does the writer use the block or alternating method of organization and why?

A Little Disk Music

Scratch the LP. Switch on the CD. That's exactly what more and more music enthusiasts—from the Mozart-crazed to the heavy-metal-dazed—are doing. . . . 1

Why do you want an earful of this joyful noise? Aside from its high-tech status—it's widely considered the greatest advance in the field since Edison recorded sound—the compact disk system offers some practical advances. The disks themselves, introduced in 1983, are only 4¾ inches in diameter and hold up to 74 minutes of play on a single side. That's up to three times as much as a 12-inch LP side. The players can be connected to almost any stereo component system and, with laser technology replacing needles, produce sound that is blessedly free from the pops, crackles and hisses that can plague LPs and tape cassettes. Player operation is so simple and the disks so durable—a night on a radiator will leave a disk unwarped—that they can be used by children and their children. 2

Price is the bad news, but it's getting better. Disks started out at $22 each and have lately sunk to about $14 at many discount 3 stores, but that's still roughly double what you'd pay for an average LP. Prices for disk players were originally in the $1,000 range. New model introductions last fall at the $500 level and below, with generous discounting on some models, made these machines among the hottest sellers last Christmas. Clearly, the compact disk is angling to outclass and replace the LP. It's also likely to cut into the market for prerecorded tape cassettes, because a disk sounds much better and is even more convenient. . . .

At half the thickness, two-fifths the diameter and a tenth the weight of an LP, the disk is a dream to store. Two of them in their hard plastic packages, called jewel boxes, displace about the same volume as one LP in its jacket. While disk players will never be as small as cassette players, Sony has been selling all it can make of the $300 five-inch-square battery-operable D-5 model, the first portable disk player. . . .

It's no wonder compact disks are prized for durability. LPs are made from soft, easily scratched vinyl. Disks are made of tougher acrylic. Whereas an LP is embossed with a spiral groove that is exposed, a disk is embossed with a spiral track of microscopic indentations that are coated with a layer of aluminum and sealed from the outside world by a second layer of plastic.

Disks use a process called digital audio to convert music vibrations into numbers. These numbers are arranged according to a complicated code and spread onto the disk as a pattern of indentations in the spiral track. A finely focused laser beam is bounced off the aluminum layer of the spinning disk and onto a photocell, which generates a signal in accordance with the pattern of indentations. This process causes no degradation of the disk and generates no surface noise. The digital encoding means that a compact disk system can reproduce far greater contrasts of loud and soft than LPs or cassettes can.

Most players can absorb relatively strong mechanical shocks and vibrations. It's hard to force the laser off the track because the code tells the laser pickup where it is so it can fight to stay there—as if the tone arm of a turntable were locked on the LP groove. If the laser is forced off the track, it can remember where it was and pick up where it left off.

As with a cassette deck, this kind of stability is good for parties where dancing can make a tone arm jump. It also allows the disk to make inroads into another domain of the cassette: the car. . . .

Installing a car player is a chore, but connecting one up at   9 home is about as uncomplicated as anything in audio can be: a stereo patchcord coming from the player is plugged into left and right terminals marked AUX for auxiliary on the back of an amplifier.

Spinning a disk is also child's play. Open the loading drawer   10 of the player, drop in a disk and press PLAY. The drawer will close, the disk will spin and the music will start. Setting the volume before the music begins can be tricky: when playing LPs, some people have unconsciously developed a habit of turning the volume up to where background noise is audible. This, of course, won't work on a CD that has no background noise and may just blow your speakers when a CD's truly loud passages come on. One disk release of Tchaikovsky's *1812 Overture* has a yellow label attached to its jewel box that reads CAUTION! DIGITAL CANNONS.

Finding your way around a disk may be the most fun of all.   11 When you want to hear a selection buried deep in an LP, plopping the needle in the groove may be straightforward but it hurts the record. Besides, hitting the exact space between the bands can be maddeningly difficult. Locating the beginning of a selection in the middle of a cassette is usually a trial-and-error process.

On a disk, the same codes that tell the laser where it is let you   12 tell it where to go. On some machines—such as the Hitachi DA-4000 ($400), the JVC XL-V300B ($550) and the Magnavox FD2040SL ($500)—pressing the PLAY or SKIP button three times will cause the player to skip directly to the third band before playing. Others—such as Sony's CDP102 ($450), Radio Shack's CD-1000 ($400) and Magnavox's FD3040SL ($600)—have you press a button marked 3, then push PLAY. If you aren't sure which band you want to hear, an audible search feature lets you scan the laser across the disk and hear quick snatches of the recording.

For even more convenience, the disk is encoded with a   13 wealth of information that can be displayed by the player, such as the number of bands on the disk, the total playing time and the time for each band. Many machines, called programmable, let you use this information to rearrange the order in which selections on the disk are played. Such a player generally can be told to ignore certain bands, play a passage defined by exact time boundaries and automatically pause at the end of a selection.

Many players are available with remote control, a feature that is especially handy because all the disk's music is on one side—the flip side is just the label. This version of most disk players adds at least $50 to the price. Remote control is taken to the max by the Technics SL-P15, which is scheduled for release in July. It has a changer that holds a total of 51 disks. Any portion of any disk can be reached by remote control. It can play 2½ days nonstop without a repeat. The $1,500 list price may be a lot for a record player, but it is quite reasonable for a jukebox.

When you shop for a player, trust your own ears. Buy a disk of piano and orchestra—always an acid test for hi-fi gear—and compare it on various players with your recollection of how the instruments should sound. Try to include the Mission DAD 7000R ($750) in your comparisons: reviews suggest that it has the sound to beat. You may discover, as some new CD owners have, that you just don't like the sound you get with any player. There is a vocal body of dissent among sound experts that finds disk-generated music to have less warmth and color in quiet passages than LPs do. If you find you agree with these persnickety audiophiles, perhaps the compact disk isn't for you—at least until it moves closer to perfection.

Otherwise make your choice based on price and features. Tap the player while it is playing a disk to test its shock resistance. Make sure you understand and like the operating features of a machine you are serious about. Clunky controls can make access to segments of long bands painfully slow. If you are a classical music enthusiast, look especially for the direct access index feature that lets you pinpoint the beginning of a variation deep inside a symphony. Or even an overture. Imagine what a boon that would be for cannon freaks.

Steven J. Forbis, "A Little Disk
Music," *Money*, April, 1985, pp. 128–132.

Discussion Questions

1. Where is the thesis statement located? Is it specific or general? How do you know?
2. What is the purpose of this article?

3. Why do you think the writer devotes more space to CDs than to LPs?
4. Does the writer use the block or alternating method of organization and why?

Suggestions for Writing

Write a comparison paper on one of the following topics or, with your instructor's approval, choose your own topic. Determine your purpose and focus, and formulate a suitable thesis statement. Select your details, choose either the block or alternating method of organization, and then write the paper.

1. Two types of travel accommodations
2. Two types of music or dancing
3. Two techniques of teaching
4. Two auto mechanics (or substitute some other skilled occupation)
5. Single life and married life
6. Television detectives or police officers and real-life detectives or police officers
7. The physical or mental demands of two jobs
8. Two types of parents
9. Two methods of studying
10. Two advertisements for the same or similar products
11. Two athletes
12. Two employers
13. Business, residential, or slum districts of two different cities
14. A favorite social spot during the day and during the evening
15. Two acquaintances who have different political views
16. Two types of leadership
17. Two sportscasters or news commentators
18. Two techniques for doing something in your own field
19. Two devices used in your field
20. The working conditions of two jobs
21. Two makes of computers, VCRs, or stereo systems
22. Two types of investments
23. Two personality types
24. Two computer languages

25. Two brands of a product
26. Medicare and Medicaid
27. Videotape and film
28. Two restaurants
29. Two movies with similar themes or of the same type, such as comedies
30. Floppy and hard disks for computers
31. A day and a night shift in a factory
32. Two kinds of cameras or photographic films
33. Acrylics and oils for painting pictures
34. Two professional or technical magazines in the same field
35. Two kinds of lawn grasses
36. Two kinds of water-filtration systems
37. Two kinds of bacteria or viruses
38. The laser and the surgical scalpel
39. Prefabricated housing and traditional wood-frame construction
40. Yourself as a child and an adult
41. Two towns, neighborhoods, or houses in which you have lived
42. Public and private elementary or secondary schools
43. Two former supervisors
44. Two television sitcoms, game shows, talk shows, or detective shows

6
Classification

Classification breaks a broad topic into separate categories according to some specific principle and then discusses these categories one at a time. Here is an example of classification.

> *Many people who are not diet conscious are surprised to learn that there are actually three types of vegetarian diets.* The first is the diet that consists of fruit and vegetables only. This may be called the true vegetarian diet. The second type, called the lacto-vegetarian diet, includes dairy products along with fruit and vegetables. And the third type, called the ovo-lacto-vegetarian diet, includes both eggs and dairy products as well as vegetables. The lacto-vegetarian uses dairy products because of their high protein content and because they can make vegetable dishes more flavorful but, like the true vegetarian, considers eggs harmful to the digestive and glandular systems. The ovo-lacto vegetarian does not regard eggs as harmful and uses them because of the great variety of ways that they can be prepared and served. But despite their differences, all three types of vegetarians do agree on one dietary prohibition—no meat.
>
> *Connie Merbs*

Like comparison, classification satisfies our instinctive desire to understand how things relate to one another. But do not confuse the two. Comparison shows how individual things or kinds of things are similar or different. Classification shows the relationship among the categories that make up a larger whole. To illustrate, comparison would be used to evaluate two different brands of hair coloring but classification to present the characteristics of temporary, semipermanent, and permanent hair colorings. You will use classification frequently, both in college and on the job. An instructor may assign a paper classifying carburetion systems, computer languages, drawing pens, furnaces, light-measuring instruments, oscilloscopes, respirators, or spectrographs, to name a few possibilities. If you work for a public health organization, you may be asked to classify the microorganisms in a lake to determine the extent, type, and possible sources of contamination. As an agricultural agent, you might classify the soils in some county as part of a soil-mapping project.

Classification is a natural way to approach many topics. It is more difficult to grasp a large or complex topic when it is considered as a whole than when it is separated into categories. Specifically, classification allows both writer and reader to understand two things clearly:

1. the separate categories
2. the way these categories relate to one another

Thus, a paper that classifies cars as subcompacts, compacts, and intermediates might help the reader understand:

1. the size, seating capacity, maneuverability, price, or other distinctive features of typical vehicles in each category
2. how these features vary from category to category

Often, you can divide the categories into subcategories, as Figure 6–1 shows.

Choosing Your Topic

Almost anything that can be divided into categories is a suitable topic for classification. For example, you might classify light-measuring instruments as light-intensity meters, brightness meters, and visibility meters, or secretaries as legal, medical, and

Figure 6–1. Modes of Public Transportation

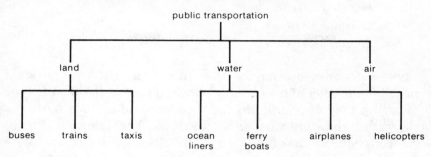

executive. As always, a familiar topic, perhaps one related to your career, yields the best results.

Once you have selected a topic, you should establish your focus. Most topics can be classified in several ways. To write a successful paper, select and develop just one. The one you select depends on your purpose. If you manage a fruit market and want to know whether to stock more exotic, expensive fruits, you might classify your customers according to income—low, medium, and high. To inform new employees about what to expect from undesirable customers, you might group the customers according to the annoying ways they behave. Without a specific purpose to point the way to your focus, classification is a pointless exercise.

Armed with your topic and focus, consider now whether to discuss all possible categories or only selected ones. For example, if you want to provide a comprehensive view of undesirable produce-market customers, you might discuss those who return fruit to the wrong bins, handle the merchandise excessively, continually complain, cheat the market, taste the fruit, or allow their children to run wild in the store. On the other hand, if you want to include only those customers who annoy you the most, you might focus on only three types, such as those who handle the merchandise excessively, complain continually, or cheat the market. Often, writing assignments require you to focus only on selected categories.

Make sure you use just one principle of selection for all the categories. Otherwise, the categories will overlap and cause problems for your readers. Note, for example, the following classification of cars.

1. American small cars
2. British small cars
3. Japanese small cars
4. Sports cars

These categories overlap because they represent two different principles of selection—country of origin for the first three, type of car for the last one. Items can therefore end up in two categories rather than just one, as they should. The Triumph, for instance, could be classified both with British small cars and with sports cars. As you can see, overlapping causes confusion—the very thing classification should clear up.

Exercise

1. Indicate how each of the following individuals would be most likely to classify the families in a particular city.

   a. The local chairperson of the Republican party
   b. A lawn-care professional
   c. The head of the local branch of the Internal Revenue Service
   d. A life insurance agent

2. Identify the overlapping item in each of the following sets of categories.

   a. *Doctors*
      pediatricians
      hospital-staff physicians
      cardiologists
      anesthesiologists
   b. *Bicycles*
      ten-speed
      Fuji
      Schwinn
      Huffy
   c. *Books*
      novel
      paperback
      poetry
      biography

d. *Stores*
   grocery
   drug
   clothing
   chain

Developing and Organizing Your Information

SELECTING SPECIFIC DETAILS

At this point, develop your categories with specific details that provide a clear picture of each one. Not just any details will work; choose only those that relate to your purpose. To illustrate, suppose three people write papers categorizing drinkers as social, heavy, and alcoholics. One may wish to discuss the health concerns of each type; another, the family consequences; and the third, the financial consequences. Without question, each paper would call for markedly different specific details.

List the details for each of your categories on a separate sheet of paper. For instance, after dividing undesirable produce-market customers into those who handle the produce excessively, complain continually, and cheat the market, you might note that squeezers poke their thumbs into the tops of cantaloupes, complainers gripe at having to stand in line, and cheaters add berries to full boxes.

DETERMINING YOUR ORGANIZATION

Organizing a classification paper calls for determining the arrangement of the categories and of the information in each. Order of climax—least important, more important, and most important—may seem most appropriate to your topic, or chronological order may be the clear choice. Your topic, purpose, and categories will help you to choose the best method of organization.

In the undesirable-customers paper, you might first discuss those who create small problems, then those who create larger problems, and finally those who create the greatest problems of all. A topic outline for this organization might look like this.

  I. Introduction
 II. Body
  A. Customers who handle produce excessively
   1. Behavior
   2. Problems caused
  B. Customers who continually complain
   1. Behavior
   2. Problems caused
  C. Customers who cheat the market
   1. Behavior
   2. Problems caused
 III. Conclusion

WRITING YOUR THESIS STATEMENT

The thesis statement for a classification paper should inform the reader of two things.

1. The topic—what you are classifying
2. The focus—the categories you will discuss

In addition, the thesis statement may indicate your central idea—what you want your reader to grasp. Here is a possible thesis statement for the produce-customers paper:

> Undesirable produce-market customers fall into three main categories—those who squeeze the fruit, those who complain constantly, and those who try to cheat the market—and when you meet them all in one day, you have one big headache.

Besides identifying the paper's topic and focus, this statement indicates that the paper will point out the problems caused by these undesirable customers.

Include your thesis statement in the introduction section of your outline to help guide you as you write the paper.

Exercise

Determine a possible purpose for a paper that classifies restaurants as fast food, family, and gourmet. Then prepare a list of details, an outline, and a thesis statement for the paper.

Writing and Revising Your Paper

WRITING YOUR INTRODUCTION

Classification papers can begin in various ways—with an anecdote, a personal experience, an arresting statement, or any other device that leads smoothly to the main discussion. (Chapter 3, pages 54–56, discusses various types of introductions.) The following sample introduction begins broadly, but then the thesis statement focuses on the three categories to be discussed.

> You will find almost as large a variety of customers at a produce market as you will find fruits and vegetables. *Undesirable produce-market customers fall into three main categories— those who squeeze the fruit, those who complain constantly, and those who try to cheat the market—and when you meet them all in one day, you have one big headache.* Perhaps you will recognize these people as I describe them.
>
> *Clarence DeLong*

WRITING THE BODY OF YOUR PAPER

Arrange the material in the body of your classification paper according to your outline, using whatever linking devices you need to make the writing flow smoothly and to show the relationships among ideas. Note that the topic sentences, italicized in the following paragraphs, signal that the produce-customer paper is organized according to order of climax—from the least annoying to the most annoying type of customer.

> *"Sammy Squeezer" is the least annoying of these undesirables.* He wants to make sure that everything he buys is "just right." He pokes his thumbs into the top of a cantaloupe. If they penetrate very deeply, he won't buy that particular specimen, considering it to be overripe. He squeezes the peaches, plums, nectarines, and any other fruit he can get his hands on. *After* ten of these people squeeze one piece of fruit, it will surely be soft, even if it wasn't originally. Moving on to the corn, Sammy carefully peels back the husk to examine the kernels inside. If they don't suit him, he doesn't bother to fold the husk back to protect the kernels; he simply tosses the ear back into the basket. The

problems he creates for the employees are primarily physical—removing the damaged items after he leaves.

   A more annoying customer is "Constance Complainer." She is never satisfied with the quality of the produce: the bananas are too green, the lettuce has brown spots, the berries are too ripe, and the potatoes have green spots. Sometimes you wonder if Constance would have been satisfied with the fruit grown in the Garden of Eden. The produce has no monopoly on her complaints, *however*; Constance also finds fault with the service she receives from the employees. Talking to other customers or directly to the clerks, she can be heard saying such things as "Why is this the only place I ever have to wait in line? They must have trouble getting good help here." Even as she leaves the market, which is none too soon, she must make one last complaint: "You mean I have to carry my own potatoes to the car?" The problems she creates for the employees are primarily mental—she can make your nerves quite active.

   But the most annoying customer of all is "Charlie Cheater." You have to keep your eye on him constantly because he knows all the tricks of cheating. He will add berries onto an already full basket. He will take 6/79¢ oranges and tell you they're the 6/59¢ ones. He will put expensive grapes in the bottom of a sack and add cheaper ones on top. *Then* he'll tell you that they are all the cheaper variety. *Likewise*, he will put expensive nectarines in a sack, place a few cheaper peaches on top, and try to pass them all off as peaches. If caught, he usually says, "I don't know how that happened. My little girl (or boy) must have put them in there." The child usually looks dumbfounded. The problem Charlie creates for the market is twofold: financial and legal. If you don't catch him, your profits suffer. If you do catch him, you almost have to prosecute, usually for amounts of only a dollar or two, or you'll have every Charlie in town at your door.

                                                              Clarence DeLong

For each of its three categories, the paper presents the same kinds of information—details of the customer's behavior and a brief indication of the resulting problems. Notice also the italicized linking devices *after*, *however*, *then*, and *likewise*.

WRITING YOUR CONCLUSION

   The options for writing conclusions are as numerous as those for introductions (see pages 56–58). The conclusion to the produce-market paper establishes the writer's qualifications for dealing with his topic.

> Did you recognize any of these customers? If you didn't and would like to see some of them in action, stop in at Steve's Produce Market. That's where I work, and that's where I meet them.
>
> *Clarence DeLong*

REVISING YOUR DRAFT

As you work through the revision suggestions and questions on pages 51–54, ask yourself these questions as well.

Does my principle of classification suit my purpose?
Have I chosen an appropriate number of categories?
Have I avoided overlapping categories?
Are there enough specific details? Do they relate to my purpose?
Are the categories presented in an appropriate order?

Exercise

Choose the most effective type of introduction or conclusion for the paper classifying restaurants (see the exercise on page 110). Explain your choices.

Examples of Classification

The Classification of Robots

Introduction: provides historical overview

Robots are Johnny-come-latelies in the workplace. Their industrial debut took place in 1968, when General Motors started using them to spot-weld Vega automobiles. By the mid-1980's robots had spread to many industries, finding application in die casting, welding, loading and unloading machine tools, and assembling parts of automobiles and other products. *These operations are carried out by four types of robots: the cylindri-*

Thesis statement names four types of robots but not the writer's point. Note that discussion will

include all types
of robots.

Topic sentence:
indicates types
arranged according
to complexity
Kind of movement
Operating data
Uses

Topic sentence, with
link to preceding
paragraph

Kinds of movement

Operating data

Uses

Topic sentence

Kinds of movement
Linking device
Operating data

Uses

Topic sentence

cal coordinate, rectangular coordinate, spherical coordinate, and jointed spherical types.

The simplest type of robot is the cylindrical coordinate type. This type has three axes of movement: up-and-down, back-and-forth, and rotating. It positions items within ± 0.01 inch of the correct location, has a speed of 36 inches per second, and can handle an 1100-pound load. Because of its relatively low positioning accuracy and high load capacity, it is used mainly to load and unload conveyor belts and fill containers.

The rectangular coordinate type of robot is a notch more complex than the cylindrical coordinate type. This robot also moves up-and-down and back-and-forth, but its third axis of movement is side-to-side rather than rotational. Its positioning accuracy is ± 0.025 inch, its speed is 50 inches per second, and its handling capacity is 350 pounds. Because it has low positioning accuracy— worse than that for the other three types— but is somewhat faster than the cylindrical coordinate type, it is used primarily for spray painting and welding.

Third in order of complexity comes the spherical coordinate type of robot. This robot has the ability to rotate and move up-and-down simultaneously. *As a result*, it can move in any axis. Its positioning accuracy of ± 0.002 inch and speed of 67 inches per second represent a considerable advance over the accuracy and speed of the first two types of robots, but its handling capacity is much lower—just 10 pounds. This set of features suits it especially for loading and unloading small parts from machines and transferring parts from one machine to another.

The jointed spherical type of robot is the most complex of all. It can move up-and-

Kind of movement
Linking device

down, from side-to-side, and rotate, all simultaneously. *Therefore*, it can be made to duplicate the shoulder, elbow, and wrist movements of the human arm. This robot outperforms all of the others in positioning accuracy (± 0.0005 inch) while scoring well in speed (50 inches per second) and load capacity (300 pounds). Because it possesses high accuracy and good mobility, it finds its greatest application in assembly work.

Operating data

Uses

Conclusion: offers
a prediction

Industrial robots are no longer just a product of the science-fiction writer's imagination. They have established themselves firmly in a variety of industries throughout the world. As time passes, we can expect these four types of mechanical servants to take on an even greater array of tasks within our factories.

6

Randy Mashak

Meeting a Special Challenge

Having worked in hospitals as a nurse for several years, I have known nurses in many different specialties who are dedicated and well qualified. *However, the four specialties that I consider the most demanding in the profession are surgical nursing, psychiatric nursing, emergency care, and terminal care.*

1

Surgical nurses are highly skilled in the postoperative care of patients. They know how to run complex equipment such as suction and ventilating machines, as well as how to respond to their patients so that they feel the operation was a success. For example, the surgical nurse helps the patient who has just undergone a radical mastectomy to see that the surgery was for her overall good. In response to obvious anxiety, the nurse reassures the patient that she is just as much a woman as before. Surgical nurses must have a special gift for winning the trust of their patients.

2

Psychiatric nurses deserve a medal for courage. They deal   3
with severely depressed patients as well as pathological personalities who have no sense of right or wrong. For this reason, they
must be on guard at all times; they must, in effect, have eyes at
the back of their heads. They must also have a great deal of self-
control. When their patients display anger and violence, these
nurses cannot respond in kind. On the contrary, they must be tol-
erant and understanding. Furthermore, they must be able to recognize attempts at deception. Sometimes a depressed person, just
prior to suicide, will act in a completely normal way because he
or she has made the decision to die. The nurse must understand
this behavior and be alert for any possible attempt. Perhaps the
most trying part of being a psychiatric nurse is never being able to
relax. For this reason, these nurses often work a few years in a
psychiatric hospital and then take a year off to work in a general
hospital.

Emergency room nurses must have analytical talents and   4
must remain calm in the face of disaster. They have to assess the
patients, determine how serious the situations are, and respond
with the correct treatment. For example, an emergency room
nurse must know that a patient brought in short of breath and cy-
anotic in color probably has congestive heart failure, and immediately establish an airway and administer oxygen, while appear-
ing calm and serene to avoid the snowballing effect of panic. It's
not an easy job to deal with the public when they or one of their
loved ones is in a life-threatening situation. This nurse sees many
horrible sights, such as the victims of motorcycle accidents.
Sometimes the body is brought in first and then a part, such as a
finger, is brought in later. Perhaps the most trying part of being
an ER nurse is the sudden personal identification with a patient.
If a seriously injured five-year-old boy is brought in and the nurse
has a little boy at home, there is bound to be a bond of identification and pity. However, the nurse must suppress this natural emotion because alert actions quite possibly can keep the patient alive
until the doctor arrives. Most nurses don't care for ER duty; but
ER nurses feel that they can do the most good there because someone's tomorrow may depend on it. It's a great feeling when a life
is saved.

Perhaps the nurses I admire most of all are the ones who are   5
able to care for terminally ill patients. To be in constant contact

with someone who is about to die takes a tremendous amount of courage, stamina, and tact. The basic foundation of all nursing is the care and welfare of the patient, but these nurses must face the fact that they can't ultimately help their patients. They can't bring out the element of hope as other nurses do. They must be honest and yet always tactful. When confronted with the horrible question, "Am I going to die?", they can respond by pointing out that everyone will die some day or by engaging the patient in a discussion, saying, for example, "Do you think you're going to die?" If the patient answers, "Yes," the nurse can then ask why he thinks so, and by this discussion help the patient face the inevitable. The nurse must be honest and not promise that he will recover, but must also avoid saying bluntly that he will die. Even though this is the way terminal care nurses "help" their patients, their recognition of inevitability runs counter to the entire nursing philosophy.

Nursing is never easy, and we should all be grateful to the people who choose this demanding profession. But the four types of nurses I have described deserve exceptional praise for meeting a special challenge.   6

Peg Feltman

Discussion Questions

1. Explain why the thesis statement of this paper is effective.
2. What is the purpose of the following phrase in paragraph 1: "Having worked in hospitals as a nurse for several years?"
3. Does this writer focus on all categories of nurses or only selected categories? How do you know?
4. Point out effective details that give the reader a clear picture of the writer's categories.
5. Determine how the paper is organized and then prepare an outline.
6. Identify the linking devices used by the writer.

What Kind of Life Insurance Will Work Best for You?

Allstate Life offers a wide variety of life insurance policies with features to help you meet your particular needs. Every pol-   1 icy is a variation or combination of one or more of three main types of life insurance . . . *whole life insurance, term insurance,* and *endowment insurance.*

What is whole life insurance? Whole life insurance, a form 2 of permanent life insurance, provides a specific protection amount for as long as you live and for as long as your whole life policy remains in force. In the simplest form of whole life insurance, the premiums will be the same every year that the policy remains in force. In addition, your policy will build a cash fund known as the cash value. Once the whole life policy is issued, the company cannot terminate it, but the owner can terminate his policy at any time by not paying the premiums and taking the cash value, if any.

Why is the cash value important? Generally, the cash value 3 of a whole life policy begins to accumulate after the first or second year the policy has been in force. This cash value is yours and you may choose to use it in any of the following ways:

(After the policy has been surrendered, or "cashed in")

- for expenses during retirement years
- for paying off a mortgage early
- for any other purpose you desire

(Without surrendering the policy)

- for obtaining a low interest loan up to nearly the amount of the cash value accumulated
- for continuing a reduced amount of whole life insurance for as long as you live without paying any further premiums
- for continuing your insurance protection for a limited time, without paying any further premiums.

How do whole life policies differ? Whole life policies are cat- 4 egorized either as *straight life insurance* or *limited payment life insurance,* depending upon the way in which premiums are paid. A straight life policy anticipates premiums will be paid as long as you live. A limited payment life policy is completely paid for after a specified number of years. This means you are covered for the original protection amount of your policy as long as you live, after your policy is paid for.

Suppose you wanted to pay premiums only during the years 5 of your highest income or to cease paying premiums at retirement age or at a child's age twenty-one, but did not wish to lose the policy's original amount of protection. Then, limited payment life insurance might be useful to you. However, remember that the premiums on any whole life policy may also be discontinued, and the cash value of the policy can be used to buy a *reduced amount* of paid-up whole life insurance.

What is term insurance? Term insurance is designed to pro- 6 vide temporary protection for a specified number of years. Term policies are either *level*, meaning the protection amount remains constant during the term period, or *decreasing*, meaning the protection amount decreases over the term period.

Some term policies can be used to provide a level amount of 7 protection for the life of the insured. This is made possible through the *renewable* and *convertible* features contained in such term policies.

- At the end of each term period, the policy can be renewed for an annual term period. The premium increases each time the policy is renewed because the insured is older. Such renewals can be continued to an age specified in the policy.
- At or before a specified maximum age, the term policy can be converted to a whole life policy and the protection can be con- tinued in force as long as the premiums are paid when due. If the term policy is not converted to a whole life policy until the specified maximum age, it is quite possible that the premiums on a whole life policy may be more than you will be able to pay. Thus, conversion at an earlier age is often advisable.
- No proof of insurability is necessary at the time you wish to convert or renew either of these types of term policies.

What are some advantages of term insurance? 8

- Term insurance is well suited to provide for your temporary needs.

- The premiums required for term policies are lower than the premiums for permanent life policies providing the same initial protection amount.
- Since all of Allstate Life's term policies are convertible, they may be exchanged for most permanent plans of insurance, regardless of your health at the time you convert.
- Level term insurance may be useful to you if you want a specific amount of insurance protection for a certain number of years (such as when children are young), but have a limited amount of money to spend on life insurance premiums.
- Decreasing term insurance is commonly used by people who want to cover a declining need. For example, many homeowners purchase a decreasing term policy to provide money to pay off their mortgage upon their death.

What are some disadvantages of term insurance?   9

- Because the cost of life insurance rises with increasing age, term insurance will become more expensive each time you wish to renew or purchase a new term policy.
- When your term policy expires (after it is no longer convertible or renewable), you must be in good health in order to acquire a new policy.
- Your term policy will not cover a need that continues beyond the term period.
- Term policies generally do not provide any cash value.

What is endowment insurance? Along with whole life insurance, endowment insurance is another form of permanent life insurance. Endowment policies emphasize your need to build a cash fund. These policies enable you to accumulate an *endowment amount*, or a sum of money, over a specified period of time—with the added guarantee that Allstate Life will complete the plan for you if you do not live to the end of the period.   10

Should you die during those years, your *beneficiary* would receive a death benefit, which could equal or exceed the endowment amount.   11

In order for you to accumulate an endowment amount, higher premiums are required than for other types of life insur-   12 ance providing the same protection amount. So, if you can afford a comprehensive plan that provides for your life insurance needs until maturity and for a cash fund at that time, then endowment insurance may be for you.

Allstate Life Insurance Company, Life Insurance, Some Basic Facts You Should Know

Discussion Questions

1. Two of the three insurance categories are broken down into subcategories. What are these categories and subcategories?
2. What purpose do the headings in this excerpt serve?
3. Using the essay as a guide, create a chart showing the distinctions among the kinds of life insurance.
4. What are the significant differences in format between this example and the classification examples on pages 113–117?

Suggestions for Writing

Prepare a plan for and then write a classification paper based on one of the following subjects or on another approved by your instructor. Make sure that your focus stems from a clear purpose, that your categories do not overlap, that they are arranged in an effective order, and that each is developed by specific details. You may find it helpful to outline the paper before beginning to write.

1. Pocket calculators
2. Nursing degrees
3. Grasses
4. Computer languages
5. Auto mechanics
6. Police work
7. X-ray machines
8. Wines
9. Carburetion systems
10. Sports announcers (or fans)
11. Water-filtration systems
12. Advertising media
13. Financial statements
14. Retail stereo stores
15. Bonds
16. Hair dyes
17. People in line
18. Solar-heating systems
19. Checking accounts
20. Bridges
21. Clouds
22. House designs
23. Sales clerks
24. Offset-printing presses
25. Bacteria
26. Bosses
27. Dates

28. Rock music
29. Moviegoers
30. Types of community government
31. Welding processes
32. Television comedies
33. Churchgoers
34. Assembly-line workers
35. Typewriters
36. Microcomputers
37. Burns
38. Radio stations
39. Supermarket customers
40. College or high-school students
41. Attitudes toward AIDS, drugs, or some other current problem

7

Description

There are two kinds of *description*: objective (scientific) and impressionistic (artistic). Although they differ in purpose, approach, and audience, both form the basis of classroom writing assignments, and both find wide use in the workplace.

Objective Description

Objective Description aims to present factual images by focusing on details that can be measured and verified. Most objective descriptions are written for relatively narrow audiences—people who will design, produce, or use whatever is being described and who require that the information be presented as clearly as possible. The following paragraph is an example of objective description.

> The Emmet racquetball racquet offers players high quality at a reasonable price. It resembles a tennis racquet but is 10 inches shorter, having an overall length of 18½ inches and a maximum width of 8½ inches, and consists of three parts—the handle, neck, and face. The 8-inch long handle is oval in cross-section, with dimensions of 1½ inches by 1¾ inches at the base and tapering to 1 inch by 1¼ inches where it joins the neck. A

123

black cowhide grip begins just below the junction. It is formed of a ½-inch-wide leather strip glued to the handle in a spiral pattern down to the base. The base is covered by a black plastic cap fitted with a wrist cord. The fan-shaped neck joins the handle to the face. It has a length of 2 inches and a height at midwidth of 1¾ inches. The face is oval-shaped with an overall length of 9¾ inches, a minimum width of 6½ inches, and a maximum width of 8½ inches. It consists of a wooden perimeter strung with nylon mesh to form a screen-like pattern of ½-inch squares. The handle, neck, and perimeter of the face are constructed of laminated ash lacquered in a light beige color. Four ¹⁄₁₆-inch-wide red strips run around the outer edge of the face perimeter, adding a decorative note.

Darcy Malone

You can expect to write objective descriptions in a number of your classes. An instructor may ask you to describe a T-square, a surveyor's range pole, a micrometer, or something you have examined under the microscope. On the job, your employer might want you to describe a floor plan, a heating system, a report form, or some newly developed device for the shop. Most objective descriptions follow a similar format.

CHOOSING YOUR TOPIC

As always, when you have a free choice, select something familiar to write about: something you have seen or used at home, in school, on the job, or in connection with some activity. Avoid overly simple or overly complex topics. If you tried to describe a pin or a needle, you would probably exhaust your topic in one short paragraph, whereas the topic *automobile engine* would take you far beyond the typical word range for a student paper.

Ask yourself whether your topic will tell your reader anything new and interesting. For example, you could describe a lead pencil or the American flag, but their features are so well known that writing about either would serve no purpose. However, not all everyday items should be ruled out. Such items as fluorescent light bulbs and hydrometers are commonplace, yet their makeup is unfamiliar to many people. Either would be a suitable topic for a paper directed at laypersons. In objective description, your focus—the major components or functional parts of what you are describing—is predetermined. Once you have selected a topic, you are ready to develop and organize your information.

Exercise

Identify which of the following items would be suitable and unsuitable topics for a 400- to 500-word description paper. Give reasons for your answer.

1. Drafting pen
2. Fuse plug
3. Hedge clippers
4. Nail
5. Paper clip
6. Photocopying machine
7. Television set
8. X-ray tube

DEVELOPING AND ORGANIZING YOUR INFORMATION

Listing the Major Components or Parts. Begin by examining carefully whatever you are describing. If it is a device that can be taken apart and put together, do so—preferably several times. Try to find out the names for the parts, and if you cannot, then use the best terms you can create yourself.

Next, list the item's components or functional parts. For example, if you describe a Sun Vacuum-Pressure Tester for automotive service students, your list would include the following parts: case, indicator dial, damper valve, sensing unit, and rubber-hose connection.

Determining Your Organization. Look over your list and decide the most effective order for discussing the parts. Several logical arrangements are possible. If you describe a television broadcasting tower, for instance, you might start from the top and work down. For a multisection office form, such as an insurance form, you might start with the first section and end with the last. For a device with several parts that operate consecutively, you might list them in their order of operation. If just one part performs the actual function, you might list that part first, and if some parts are concealed, you might first list the external and then the internal parts. The following list for the vacuum-pressure tester begins with the case and follows an external-to-internal order.

External
    case
    pressure-vacuum indicator dial
    rubber hose connection
    damper valve
Internal
    sensing unit

Writing Your Formal Definition. Now you are ready to prepare a one-sentence formal definition, which functions as a thesis statement and identifies what your paper will describe. A formal definition does three things.

1. It names the item being defined.
2. It places the item in a broad category or class.
3. It explains how the item differs from others in the same category.

Here is the formal definition for the vacuum-pressure tester.

> The Sun Vacuum-Pressure Tester, Model VPT-212, is a mechanical device used for checking the manifold vacuum and the fuel pump pressure of automobiles.

For a further discussion of formal definitions, see Chapter 8 (pages 151–153).

Exercise

Choose a device you know well as the topic for an objective description. Then list the item's parts, arrange them in an effective order, and draft a suitable formal definition.

WRITING AND REVISING YOUR PAPER

Writing Your Introduction. Your introduction should contain the formal definition, provide an overall description of the items discussed in the paper, and list the major components or functional parts in the order they are discussed. This list prepares your reader for what follows.

As you write the overall description, consider all important features of the item—such as its dimensions, shape, color, weight, texture, and materials of construction. The importance of a feature depends on the item; for example, weight is probably not important for a diode but should not be ignored when describing a portable humidifier.

Some descriptions are *general* (wire cutters, garden trowels) while others are *specific* (the Snipwell Model R-2 wire cutter, the Digby Model 41 garden trowel). When you describe a specific model of a device, include precise details; for example, you should note the exact length of a specific wire cutter. But for wire cuters in general, a range of lengths would suffice.

To help your reader visualize what you are describing, try comparing its shape to that of something familiar. You might note that a new building has an H-shaped floor plan or that a dental mouth mirror resembles a coin with a rod welded at an angle to the rim. If the shape is too difficult for a comparison to be made, you might include a drawing or photograph of the item (see Chapter 16 for a detailed discussion of illustrations). Mention any illustrations in your introduction.

The introduction that follows uses the typical pattern described here.

The Sun Vacuum-Pressure Tester, Model VPT-212, is a mechanical device used for checking the manifold vacuum and the fuel pump pressure of automobiles. The tester weighs 2.5 pounds, stands 9 inches tall, is 5 inches wide, and is made primarily from stamped steel. It somewhat resembles a small, up-ended box with a handle on the top. The main parts, besides the case, include (1) an indicator dial, (2) a rubber-hose connection, (3) a damper valve, and (4) a sensing unit. The accompanying figure shows a cutaway view of the tester.

Peter Cataldo

Sun Vacuum-Pressure Tester

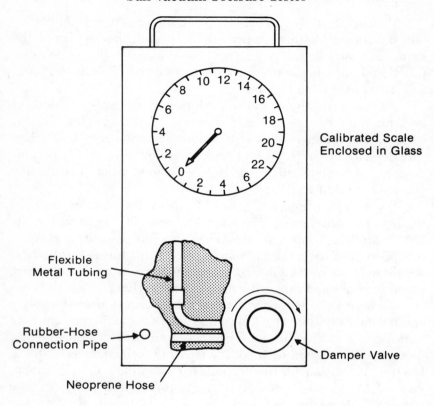

Calibrated Scale
Enclosed in Glass

Flexible
Metal Tubing

Rubber-Hose
Connection Pipe

Damper Valve

Neoprene Hose

Describing the Major Components or Parts. As noted earlier, discuss the major components or parts in the same order that you listed them in the introduction. Unless it is obvious, note the purpose of each part and then any important or interesting features. The amount of detail to include depends on your audience and purpose. A description written to help diemakers construct a die would require detailed discussions of shapes, dimensions, wall thicknesses, and the sizes and locations of openings. However, one familiarizing a supervisor with the die would require much less detail.

As you describe the components or functional parts, pinpoint their positions or locations. Space-indicating words and phrases—such as *above, adjacent to, behind, below, beside, between, next to, under, left of,* and *at the top of*—can help you accomplish this. Often, you also need to describe exactly how the parts are joined together. If you prepare an engineering description of a T-square, for instance, it is not enough to note that the blade is centered on the head at right angles to it. You must also indicate the amount of overlap, whether the blade is set into the head, and—if so—the depth of the inset.

Here is a description of the parts of the vacuum-pressure tester. Note how carefully the writer has described the positions and dimensions of the items that make up each part.

The 3¾-inch indicator dial occupies the upper center part of the front. This dial has two scales. The upper, or vacuum, scale, which is graduated from 0 to 22 inches, records the inches of vacuum. The lower, or pressure, scale, graduated from 0 to 7 inches, records inches of pressure. The dial and its needle are protected by a glass face held securely by a metal rim.

The cylindrical rubber-hose connection is mounted in the lower left-hand corner of the front. This connection, ⅜ inch in diameter and protruding ½ inch, is used to connect the tester to the engine's intake manifold. The 1½-inch damper valve knob extends from the lower right-hand corner and is used to slow the back-and-forth swings of the indicator needle when a pressure reading is taken.

The sensing unit, located inside the case, consists of a vacuum-pressure tube, a pivot device, and a hose. The vacuum-pressure tube is made from thin, flexible metal tubing and resembles the crooked end of a walking cane. One end of the V-shaped pivot device is connected to the top of the vacuum tube and the other to the base of the indicator needle. The accompanying figure illustrates this arrangement. Attached to the lower end of the vacuum tube is a neoprene hose, which is fastened at its other end to the interior opening of the cylindrical hose connection. This hose passes through a clamp arrangement at the rear of the damper valve knob. Turning the knob pinches the hose and slows the swings of the needle.

Peter Cataldo

Arrangement of Vacuum-Pressure Tube and Pivot Device

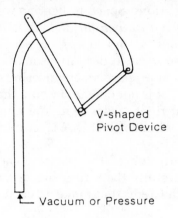

V-shaped
Pivot Device

⌐⌐ Vacuum or Pressure

Writing Your Conclusion. The conclusion of a short paper may range from one sentence to one paragraph in length and can present several kinds of information.

One type of conclusion tells the reader how to use the device being described. The following example, from a description of a device for measuring the amount of solids in sewage, is typical.

> When the cone is filled with one liter of sewage, the settleable solids will sink to the pointed end. The total amount of settleable solids per liter of sewage can be determined by reading the scale. This information allows the sewage treatment operator to determine how effectively the plant is removing solids from sewage.
>
> *Philip Boesenecker*

Another kind of conclusion explains how a device operates. This is especially appropriate for a mechanism with some or all of the functional parts hidden from view. The conclusion of our sample description of the vacuum-pressure tester illustrates this kind of ending.

> Connecting the tester with a rubber hose to the intake manifold of a running engine creates a partial vacuum in the hose and vacuum-pressure tube. This causes the tube to bend in a clockwise direction, activating the pivot device and allowing the

amount of vacuum to be read on the upper scale. When the tester is connected to the fuel line, the tube bends counterclockwise, and pressure is shown on the lower scale. A chart supplied with the tester is used to interpret the readings.

Peter Cataldo

A third type of conclusion emphasizes a particular advantage or feature of the item. For instance, if you describe a new model of some recording device, you might note that it is more accurate and simpler to use than earlier models. Or, if your paper discusses a new kind of record-keeping form, you might discuss its added efficiency.

Revising Your Draft. As you revise, refer to the general guidelines on pages 51–54. Also consider the following questions.

Have I chosen an appropriate item?
Is my formal definition accurate?
Does my overall description include every important feature?
Are the parts discussed in an appropriate order?
Are each part's important features mentioned?
Have I provided comparisons with familiar items when they would be helpful?
Have I used illustrations when appropriate?
Is my conclusion effective? Why did I choose it?

Exercise

Prepare a suitable introduction and conclusion for a paper describing the device you chose for the exercise on page 126. Explain the type of conclusion you use and why.

Examples of Objective Description

Dental Mouth Mirror

Formal definition   *A dental mouth mirror is an instrument* 1
used by dentists, dental hygienists, and den-

Utility of device

Description: includes
materials of
construction and
a comparison

Major parts listing:
alerts reader to the
organization of
what follows

Topic sentence

Description and
purpose, first
type of mirror

Description and
purpose, second
type of mirror

Dimensions and
mounting of mirrors

Topic sentence:
indicates way handle
and mirror are joined

Dimensions of handle

Materials of
construction

Conclusion: tells how
to use mirror,
restates its utility

tal assistants to look inside the mouth and view the patient's teeth. This mirror makes it possible to see tooth surfaces that are beyond the range of direct vision. Besides increasing illumination, it is also a useful retractor of the patient's cheek and tongue. The glass and metal instrument somewhat resembles a coin with a rod welded at an angle to the edge. It consists of two major parts, the mirror and the handle.

The mirror can be one of two kinds. The first of these is made of ordinary glass and has a flat reflecting surface. With the plain mirror, the dentist sees the patient's teeth just the way the patient sees them in a regular looking glass. The second kind, the magnifying mirror, has a concave surface and makes everything look larger, thus giving the dentist a better view of the mouth. The diameter of either mirror is about the same as that of a 25-cent piece. It is securely mounted in a circular, stainless-steel holder with a rim equal in depth to the thickness of the mirror.

The handle is connected to the mirror by a small screw which extends about ½ inch from the edge of the holder and is set at an angle to the plane of the mirror. This screw threads into a socket at the end of the handle. The thick part of the handle is called the shank. It is approximately 2 inches in length, with a diameter of ¼ inch. The thinner portion is 2¾–3 inches long and has a diameter of about ⅛ inch. The handle is made of brushed aluminum or steel.

Held with a modified pen grip and inserted into the mouth, the dental mouth mirror provides immeasurable assistance in the detection of decay and of stains and deposits on the teeth.

Lisa Hines

Human Skin

The skin is the largest organ of the body. It has approxi- 1
mately 20 square feet of surface area for potential contact with
foreign substances in nature and in the industrial environment. It
is a multi-functioning organ whose anatomical and physiologic
properties subserve protection by regulating body heat, receiving
sensations, secreting sweat, manufacturing pigment, and replen-
ishing its own cellular elements. Each of these functions is important in the maintenance of a healthy skin, and any deviation from
the normal can alter the health of the skin and sometimes that of
the entire body.

The structure or anatomical design of the skin is protective 2
because of its thickness, resiliency, and the capacity of certain of
its layers to inhibit the entrance of water and water-soluble chemicals. Its thickness and elasticity protect the underlying muscles,
nerves and blood vessels. Additionally, the thickness and color of
the skin afford protection against the effects of sunlight and other
sources of physical energy.

Structurally, skin is composed of two layers—the epidermis 3
and the dermis. Epidermis has two essential levels—an outermost
stratified layer of horn [keratin] cells called the "stratum corneum" and the inner living cells from which the horn cells arise.
Stratum corneum cells are shed, yet replenished continually because the inner living epidermal layer keeps reproducing cells
which eventually become stratum corneum cells. In short, the
epidermis has its own self-support system. The stratum corneum
layer is essential for protection, being thickest on the palms and
soles. Chemically, it is a complex protein structure which is relatively resistant to mild acids, to water and water-soluble chemicals; but vulnerable to alkaline agents, strong detergents, desic-
cant chemicals, and solvents (see the accompanying figure).

In the lowermost region of the epidermal layer are the basal 4
cells from which all of the epidermal cells arise. Nestled within
the basal cell layer are melanocytes or pigment-producing cells
which furnish protection against ultraviolet radiation. This
comes about through a complex enzyme reaction leading to the
production of pigment or melanin granules which are engulfed
by the epithelial cells which, in turn, migrate to the upper level of
the skin and eventually are shed. Melanin serves as a protective

Diagram of the Skin's Protective Layers

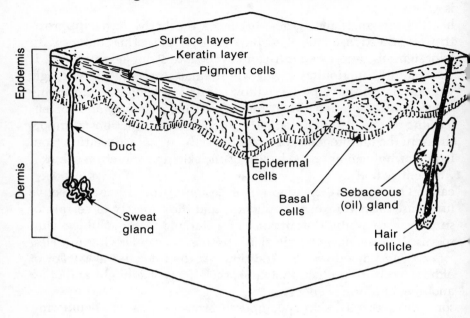

screen against sunlight because the granules absorb photons of light. This mechanism occurs naturally throughout the lifetime of an individual. Sunlight and certain chemicals stimulate pigment formation and, at times, its activity can be inhibited.

Dermis is thicker than epidermis and is composed of elastic and collagen tissue which provide the skin with its resiliency. Invested also in the dermis are sweat glands and ducts which deliver sweat to the surface of the skin; hair follicles in which hairs are encased; sebaceous or oil glands which excrete their products through the hair follicle openings on the skin; blood vessels; and nerves.

Body temperature is regulated by the excretion of sweat, circulation of the blood, and the central nervous system. Blood is maintained at a relatively constant temperature even though the body can be exposed to wide ranges of temperature variations. Sweat facilitates greatly the cooling of the overheated skin surface by evaporation. At the same time, dilation of the blood vessels within the skin also permits heat loss. Conversely, when the body is exposed to severe cold, blood vessels will contract to conserve heat. Nerve endings and fibers present in the skin participate in the receptor and conduction system which allows the individual to differentiate between heat, cold, pain and sense perception. This latter quality allows one to discriminate between dryness or wetness, thickness or thinness, roughness or smoothness, hardness or softness.

Secretory elements within the skin are the sweat glands and   7
the sebaceous glands. Perspiration or sweat contains products from the body's metabolic function, but 99% of sweat is water. . . . Sebaceous or oil glands . . . manufacture an oily substance called "sebum," whose precise physiologic function is not well-understood. Present in normal amounts, it appears to offer some surface protection to the skin. Over-function of these glands is associated with acne.

Coating the outer surface of the keratin layer is a waxy type   8
of mixture composed of sebum, breakdown products of keratin, and sweat. It is believed that the emulsion-like mixture impedes somewhat the entrance of water and water-soluble chemicals, but its actual protective quality is minimal. It does assist in maintaining the surface pH of the skin, which is normally in the range of 4.5 to 6. Its protective capability is minimized because it is easily removed by soaps, solvents and alkalis. Nonetheless, it is continually replenished under normal conditions and does constitute an extra layer of protection which must be removed before keratin cells can be attacked.

Absorption of materials through the skin occurs when the   9
continuity of the skin is disrupted by an abrasion or a laceration or a puncture. Absorption of fat-soluble chemicals, fats and oils can occur via the hair follicle which contains the hair bulb and a portion of the hair shaft. Some substances such as organophosphates are absorbed directly through the intact skin; further, skin permits the ready exchange of gases, except for carbon monoxide. Sweat ducts offer little, if any, avenue for penetration. From the above it is evident that the skin has its own built-in defense mechanism. . . .

Donald J. Birmingham, "Occupational Dermatoses:
Their Recognition, Control and Prevention"

Discussion Questions

1. The introduction—paragraphs 1 and 2—clearly establishes the essay's purpose. What is that purpose?
2. Paragraphs 3–8 discuss the two major components and the subcomponents of the skin. What are they? How does this discussion support the essay's purpose?
3. Identify the organization of the essay and indicate why you think the writer followed it.
4. Who is the audience for this paper? How do you know?

Suggestions for Writing

Write an objective description of one of the following items or another that your instructor approves. Begin with a formal definition and an overall description of the item. Then discuss each of its components or functional parts.

1. Aerosol-spray container
2. Bite-wing X-ray film unit
3. Burette
4. Business form (such as life insurance or job application form)
5. Carpenter's level
6. Clothes pin
7. Cooking tower
8. Crescent wrench
9. Diode
10. Disposable safety razor
11. Drafting compass
12. Egg slicer
13. Hypodermic syringe
14. Meat grinder
15. Needle nose pliers
16. Pizza cutter
17. Pressure cooker
18. Slip lock pliers
19. Smoke detector
20. Soda-acid fire extinguisher
21. Spaghetti tongs

22. Spark plug
23. Spark-plug gapper
24. Surveyor's plumb bob
25. Tire pressure gauge
26. Tire pump
27. T-square
28. X-ray film cassette

Impressionistic Description

Impressionistic description also presents facts, but its primary function is to convey sensory impressions that appeal to the emotions by creating vivid word pictures and arousing moods or feelings. Usually, it is aimed at a more general audience than its objective counterpart. An example follows.

> When the Rib Crib Restaurant first opens on a hot summer day, silence prevails except for the chatter of arriving employees and the occasional click of a refrigerator motor as it turns on and off. Because the kitchen has been closed all night, the air is hot, stuffy, and almost suffocating. Within minutes, however, windows have been thrown open and the ceiling fan turned on, creating a cooling breeze and making the air quite comfortable. Stacks of white paper napkins, brown-rimmed white plates, and grey coffee mugs line the red plastic surface of the counter by the pass-through, awaiting the first customer of the day. Switches snap, gas whooshes as it ignites under the deep fryer, and water splashes into the gleaming coffee maker. Soon the rich aroma of the coffee blends with the smell of the now-sizzling grease. The sound of door chimes and loud, laughing banter from the front of the restaurant signal the arrival of the first customers. Another long work day has begun.
>
> *Barbara Rhodes*

Some impressionistic descriptions merely convey the writer's responses, while others attempt to spur some type of action. For example, to emphasize the dangers posed by unsafe conditions at a hazardous waste dump, a writer might describe the piles of rusty, leaking drums; the puddles of ugly-looking liquids that scar the area; the slimy creek, dotted with dead fish, that flows through the site; and the acrid chemical stench that overhangs the entire area.

SENSORY IMPRESSIONS

Sensory impressions—those that reflect sight, hearing, touch, taste, and smell—are the core of impressionistic description. We experience the world through these five basic senses. To use them effectively in your writing, carefully observe, or draw on your memory of, what you intend to describe: some object, person, scene, event, or situation.

Following are three sample passages using impressionistic description. The first focuses primarily on sight impressions.

> The farm where my aunt and uncle lived when I was a child resembled a painting by a landscape artist. A weathered split-rail fence bordering the winding graveled drive guided the visitor's eye to the white, two-story house. It was a big place with four round pillars across the front, stretching from the floor of the porch to the slate roof. The windows were large and decorated with white lace curtains. I thought the house looked like an antebellum mansion in Mississippi or Alabama. About forty or fifty yards beyond the "big house" stood a long and narrow horse stable, always brilliantly whitewashed. And beyond the stable lay a rolling yellow pasture edged by lines of gray-barked oak trees. I loved that place beyond words, and the unhappiest day of my young life was when my family moved to another state, and it left my life forever.
>
> *Harvey Block*

Sound impressions predominate in the following passage.

> To a perceptive maintenance worker, the health of the systems in an automated car wash can be determined largely by ear. An agonized scream from a moving part forecasts the last days of an overstressed bearing. The snakelike hiss of a high-pressure air leak somewhere in the tangle of air and hydraulic lines signals a coming rupture. With an angry whine, a small hydraulic motor demands attention. The normally contented throb of the powerful hydraulic pump rises in pitch to indicate an overload. The warning these sounds provide allows the main-

tenance worker to head off costly and time-consuming break-downs.

Timothy Nelson

Like most descriptions, the following passage features several sensory impressions rather than focusing on just one, combining sight, sound, touch, taste, and smell.

Over the summer, I took a trip to West Virginia and visited the neighborhood where I had lived until I was twelve years old. To my regret, the house was gone, replaced by a concrete pillar supporting a freeway bridge. The old yard looked like a military depot armed with a force of dirt-moving equipment. Every time a semi growled across the bridge, the ground quivered with insult. Hot, humid air soaked me with sticky sweat; and the whole neighborhood, covered by a filthy layer of dust so thick I could taste it, reeked of diesel fuel. It was hard to remember the green wall of maples, poplars, and oaks that once lined the road passing my house or the spring smells of honeysuckle, lilacs, and violets. Even the old creek that once splashed its way down the valley was gone, and I wondered what engineering arrangement now accommodated the rush of water after a thunderstorm. Only one thing remained: the thirty-foot pole my father had erected to grow morning glories on. Someone had left it—right at the edge of our property—and it was covered with lush vines and lavender and pink blossoms. It seemed to be a small oasis in a barren land.

Wayne Dickens

Exercise

Develop a set of sensory impressions for a favorite outdoor spot, an event you know well, or a place where you have worked. Begin by carefully observing and recording your impressions of sight; then do the same for touch, taste, smell, and sound.

DOMINANT IMPRESSION

A *dominant impression* is the mood or feeling that emerges from the description. Common moods and feelings include fear, anger, horror, frenzy, security, carelessness, happiness, sadness, elegance, and contempt, to name just a few.

The following paragraph conveys a sense of serene elegance.

> The carpeted, wood-paneled elevator is operated by an expressionless woman whose starched white blouse and trim navy uniform enhance her refined appearance. There is no jostling among the elegant passengers as they gaze tranquilly ahead. After flowing upward, the elevator slows to a halt on the fifth floor, its doors glide open, and a tall, elderly gentleman steps into a gap that automatically appears. His impeccably tailored gray suit has a fine herringbone pattern, and the fragrance coming from his pipe suggests one of those small, exclusive shops that sell imported tobaccos. Barely parting his lips, he says, "Nine, please," and then opening the *Wall Street Journal* held under his arm, he begins to scan the day's financial news.
>
> *Beth Buckingham*

Exercise

Select one of the following topics and write a paragraph that evokes a particular dominant impression.

1. Some construction site or shop area
2. A hospital emergency room
3. A view from a hill
4. The interior of a place of worship
5. A storefront
6. A dark street

CHOOSING YOUR TOPIC

For impressionistic descriptions written on the job, the work situation dictates the topic. In class, though, you may have a choice of topic, and when you do, select something familiar. If you have never worked in a machine shop or dined in the Edwardian Room of New York's Plaza Hotel, do not try to describe them. Instead, choose a workplace or a restaurant you know something about. For finding a topic, you may find it helpful to use one of the techniques described on pages 34–36.

DEVELOPING AND ORGANIZING YOUR INFORMATION

Determining Your Vantage Point. You can use either a *fixed* or a *moving vantage point* for impressionistic description.

A fixed observer selects the viewing location and describes only what is apparent from there. To describe an elevator, the writer of the passage on page 140 selected a vantage point inside the elevator and noted only its appearance and the people in it. If she had included details of the building's gray exterior or tinted glass windows, her description would have been unrealistic, for she could not possibly have seen these details from inside the elevator.

A moving observer, on the other hand, can go from one spot to another and describe what is seen at each location, providing that the movements are indicated by appropriate phrases. In the following example, the italicized parts signal the writer's movements.

The wind whistled through the trees as Tricia *waited in line outside* the ice arena. She could hear people blowing into their hands to keep them warm. Slowly the line shuffled forward and finally she *reached the turnstile. Clicking through it*, she *moved into the lobby*. Here were many concession stands. Popcorn machines popped and drink machines gurgled. Children cried, parents yelled at them, and shrill-voiced concessionaires shouted their wares. Wanting none of these, Tricia *proceeded to her seat*.

Georgia Hein

Selecting Your Details. Effective description depends as much on what you exclude as on what you include. Never try to convey every possible detail, as this will lead to a mere catalog of words and be incredibly boring. Instead, select only those details that contribute to your intended impression.

Look back to the elevator paragraph on page 140 and note how the writer omits details that may well have formed part of the scene: tobacco ashes scattered on the floor, chips in the wood paneling, or stains in the carpet. Including such details would detract from the sense of elegance.

Organizing Your Details. Most impressionistic descriptions are organized according to some type of space sequence. You could progress from

top to bottom	front to back
bottom to top	back to front
left to right	nearby to far away
right to left	far away to nearby

Whatever your choice, use appropriate phrasing so that the direction is clear to your reader.

Occasionally you may want to follow a time, rather than a space, sequence. You could, for instance, describe a section of a shopping mall at the start of a business day, during the height of shopping activity, and at closing time. Again, use appropriate phrasing to make your progression clear.

WRITING AND REVISING YOUR PAPER

Writing Your Introduction. Use your introduction to establish a background for what follows (see pages 54–56) and to identify what you will describe. At your option, you may name your dominant impression or allow it to emerge from the description as a whole. Similarly, if one sensory impression predominates, you may or may not elect to point it out.

Read the following introduction.

> The door clicked shut behind me as I arrived at 8:00 a.m. for work at Epstein and Stegman, our city's largest legal firm. I had been hired into the secretarial pool the week before and worked primarily for Mr. Stegman, a prominent tax lawyer. Now all was peaceful, but soon this quiet would vanish under an onslaught of assorted noises.
>
> *Diane Trathen*

The writer indicates that she will describe a law office and concludes with a sentence that names her dominant impression: noisiness. In addition, the 8:00 a.m. arrival time sets up her time-sequence organization.

Writing the Body of Your Paper. As you write the body of your paper, separate the main elements of your description into appropriate paragraphs. Here are the body paragraphs of the law office paper.

> Flicking on the light switch, I stood listening for a moment to the hum of the overhead ventilator, thinking how much it sounded like the buzzing of honey bees on a hot summer day. Heading toward my desk, I paused by the water cooler for a drink. As water gurgled into my cup, I noticed that the cooler was nearly empty and made a mental note to call the custodian for a refill. Within minutes, lawyers and secretaries began crowding into the office, and shortly afterward the furious clackety-clack of typewriters, punctuated by the grinding sound of pencil sharpeners, the squeaking of chairs, and the jangling of telephones filled the room.
>
> At 9:30, Mr. Stegman called me into his office to take my usual morning dictation. But despite the relative absence of turmoil in there, the interlude was hardly restful. Mr. Stegman spoke rapidly in a harsh, nasal voice that grated on my nerves, and I was relieved when he finally stopped talking.
>
> Back at my desk, I started typing Mr. Stegman's work. I rattled away on the electric typewriter, oblivious to the chattering voices of lawyers and secretaries, the incessant drone of the duplicating machine, and the hammerlike banging of file-cabinet drawers being slammed shut. Occasionally, the telephone on my desk rang, and I stopped typing to answer it and buzz Mr. Stegman. Otherwise, nothing interrupted my work.
>
> *Diane Trathen*

Writing Your Conclusion. Conclude your paper in a way that makes it seem finished and unified. If you are describing the unsafe hazardous waste dump, for instance, you might predict the probable consequences of not taking corrective action. When describing a notably attractive view, you might recommend that your reader go see it. Or, like the writer of the law office paper, you might note your feelings when leaving some location.

> The clock on the wall ticked away the morning, and because I was so engrossed in my work I did not hear the secretary

at the next desk tell me it was lunch time. Not until she tapped me on the shoulder did I look up and realize that noon had come. Gratefully, I grabbed my coat and left the now-quieting office for my lunch hour.

Diane Trathen

Revising Your Draft. As you revise, follow the guidelines on pages 51–54. In addition, ask yourself the following questions.

Have I chosen a familiar topic?

Have I described how my topic looks, sounds, smells, feels, or tastes?

Have I created one dominant impression?

Have I described from an effective vantage point?

If the observer is fixed, do I present only what is apparent from that spot? If the observer is moving, do I signal the movements?

Have I selected only the details that contribute to my dominant impression and excluded those that do not?

Have I organized these details effectively?

Are the introduction and conclusion effective, and is the body of the paper separated into appropriate paragraphs?

Examples of Impressionistic Description

Inside a Bodybuilding Gym

Introduction identifies topic and dominant impression

The typical bodybuilding gym offers a mixture of intriguing sensory impressions. Its atmosphere is pure bliss for the hardcore weight lifter and a fascinating treat for the newcomer.

Topic sentence indicates paragraph presents sound impressions

As you enter, a surge of sounds greets your ears. The pulsating beat of music for the aerobics class provides a counterpoint to the squeaks of the cables on the exercise machines and the loud bangs of the weight stacks as they crash onto the bases of the machines. These sounds intermingle with the chanting of the aerobics instructor as she urges her students to greater efforts and the grunts, groans, and occasional screams of the bodybuilders striving to complete yet one more set of exercises.

Topic sentence implied; paragraph presents sight impressions

The room holds an array of exercise machines which, with their pulleys, cables, weight stacks, and handles, appear to the uninitiated like spidery robots or medieval instruments of torture. Black dumbbells, ranging from small hand-held specimens weighing but a few pounds to monsters that would challenge the prowess of an Arnold Schwarzenegger, fill racks along the wall. Long steel bars and the flat platelike weights that fit onto their ends litter the benches and floor. The slick black vinyl seats and handles of the machines glisten under the bright fluorescent lights.

Topic sentence indicates paragraph presents impression of smell

Smells likewise form part of the gym environment. Some are transient and subtle—a whiff of perfume as a woman, released from the aerobics class, passes by on her way to her locker room, or the faint scent of lotion on the face of some nearby exercising bodybuilder. Overlaying these, the pungent odor of liniment laced with acrid sweat hangs everywhere in the air. The smell, honest and earthy, is a fit symbol of the effort expended here.

Topic sentence indicates paragraph discusses exercising, presents impression of touch. Second sentence presents impression of taste.

Easing yourself under a loaded bar to begin lifting, you feel the cold, hard, knurled surface bite into your shoulder and neck. Soon, salty sweat trickles into the corners of your mouth. Oblivious to everything except the desire to complete all your lifts, you raise and lower the weights again and again until your legs burn and tremble. Then, your goal met, you relax with a sigh of satisfaction.

Conclusion reinforces
statement that gym is
blissful for the
weight lifter

To the hardcore lifter, the feeling experi- 6
enced at the end of an exercise session is little short of ecstasy.

Tim van Huisen

Not My Kind of Tire Shop

As I opened the discolored aluminum door of the tire shop 1
and walked across the grime-encrusted green carpet of its show-room, I was hesitant at first about doing business at this place. Nevertheless, I decided to stay.

Directly across from the door stretched a long, battered 2
wooden counter, its top cluttered with piles of papers, books of what appeared to be tire specifications, and a brass cash register that would have been right at home in an antique shop. A tall, red soft drink–dispensing machine flanked the counter on its left, while the grimy wall on its right held a black telephone and a tattered-looking phone book on a tarnished metal chain. Several mismatched chairs, fronted by a coffee table that held two over-flowing ash trays, stood along the left-hand wall. Stacks of dust-covered new tires filled the rest of the showroom, adding to the general impression of grunginess.

Passing through a doorway to the right of the phone, I en- 3
tered the work area, finding myself standing amid a litter of gouged hand tools and muddy jacks. To the left, a set of black-ened, corrugated metal doors screeched protestingly as an em-ployee pulled them along their rusty tracks to admit a customer's car. Their sound almost drowned out the hissing of the hoses that snaked across the floor and supplied high-pressure air to the shop's machines. Just beyond the doors, a scarred-up patching bench stood among discarded patch backs and empty glue tubes. Two mud-caked tire changers occupied the far left corner, to-gether with several piles of nearly bald tires and two lounging em-ployees in greasy coveralls.

Centered on the floor next to the back wall was an old desk 4
holding stacks of paper and a portable radio that blared country music. Behind the desk, another coveralled man sat smoking in a

swivel chair while he rocked back and forth in time with the music. A set of homemade shelves crammed with boxes of tubes, patches, and glue occupied most of the wall space between the desk and the right-hand corner, where sat a computerized tire balancer surrounded by rusty pails that overflowed with tire weights. The floor in front of the right-hand wall was taken up by the front-end alignment pit and a tractor bay crowded with heavy-duty truck and tractor tires. A strong smell of rubber, automobile exhaust, and cigarette smoke permeated the air, leaving an acrid taste in my mouth.

Finishing my look around, I turned quickly before the man   5
at the desk could say anything and walked rapidly out of the service area, through the showroom, and onto the sidewalk. Some other tire shop would definitely get my business.

Scott Smith

Discussion Questions

1. What dominant impression emerges from this description? Does the writer identify the impression or allow readers to grasp it for themselves?
2. What details support the dominant impression?
3. This description focuses primarily on sight impressions. What other impressions does the writer evoke, and where are they found?
4. Does this essay have a fixed or a moving observer? From what vantage point(s) does he view the tire shop?
5. How does the final paragraph relate to what has come before?

Suggestions for Writing

Write an impressionistic description on one of the following topics or one that your instructor approves. Create a dominant impression by using carefully selected, well-organized sensory details observed from an appropriate vantage point or points.

1. Arcade
2. Assembly line
3. Automobile
4. Busy airport
5. Child's messy bedroom

6. City intersection
7. Fast-food establishment
8. Favorite spot to be alone
9. Historical site
10. Holiday gathering (or holiday shopping)
11. Fourth of July fireworks display
12. Laundromat
13. Locker room
14. National, state, or city park
15. Physical fitness center
16. Pizza parlor
17. Professional sporting event
18. Religious ceremony
19. Repair facility (heavy equipment, auto appliance, or the like)
20. Rock concert (or another type of concert)
21. Rundown or wealthy section of a town
22. Scenic spot in your area
23. Segment of an amusement park
24. Segment of a fair
25. Segment of a mall
26. Storm of any type
27. Work area requiring strict safety precautions

8
Definition

Both in college and on the job, you will often use *definition* to explain the meaning of some term. The term may be unfamiliar, abstract, or mean different things to different people. The following example defines *holding company*, a term unfamiliar to many people.

A *holding company is a company organized for the purpose of acquiring enough of the voting stock in other companies to control them.* A holding company, also called a parent company, can raise the funds needed to acquire a subsidiary by selling bonds, preferred stock, or common stock, or some combination of these. The cash raised from such sales is then used to buy voting shares of another company. When a holding company holds anywhere from 20 to 30 percent of a potential subsidiary's shares, it has virtual control of the subsidiary. Before its breakup, American Telephone and Telegraph (AT&T) was the largest holding company in the United States, owning between 16 and 100 percent of twenty-two large companies doing business in forty-eight states. Western Electric, AT&T's manufacturing subsidiary, was wholly owned by the parent company, and Western Electric and AT&T jointly owned Bell Laboratories.

Thomas R. Koning

Occasionally, a brief dictionary-type definition will suffice. For example, in discussing heating systems for a general audience, you might define *furnace plenum* as "an air compartment maintained under pressure and connected to one or more ducts." Frequently, however, brief definitions are inadequate because they fail to capture the complexity of the term. New terms—such as *program trading, gentrification, genetic engineering, yuppie*, and *perestroika*—often require more than a one-sentence definition. The same is true for terms that mean different things to different people—*"basketball superstar"* may mean great defensive player, great offensive player, or team leader to different people. Also, abstract terms—those that stand for an idea, a condition, a quality, something we cannot see, feel, or otherwise experience with our five senses—require extended treatment. *Jealousy, generosity, power, conservatism, love,* and *fear* are abstract terms.

Often an entire paper may be an extended definition. Your instructor may ask you to define a technical or social term such as *weather satellite* or *urban sprawl*. Your employer may ask you to define *corporate responsibility* or *cost-benefit analysis* for new employees. These extended definitions generally combine two or more methods of development; for instance, comparison, process explanation, and description.

Choosing Your Topic

If you choose your own topic, search for a sufficiently complex term that is new, abstract, or means different things to different people. Why, for instance, define *table* when it is completely familiar to anyone who would read your paper? As always, pick a topic that interests you and that you know about or can learn enough about in the time available to you. You can then discuss it in sufficient detail.

Exercise

Identify which of the following would be suitable and unsuitable topics for a 500- to 600-word extended definition. Give reasons for your answers.

1. Automobile
2. Burnout syndrome
3. The British game of cricket
4. Restaurant
5. Evidence
6. Alcoholism
7. Auditing
8. Household scissors

Developing and Organizing Your Information

WRITING YOUR FORMAL DEFINITION

Ordinarily, you will prepare your formal definition soon after you have selected your topic. As noted on page 126 in Chapter 7, a *formal definition* functions as a thesis statement by identifying what the paper will discuss, placing the topic in a broad category or class, and explaining how it differs from other items in that category.

Constructing a formal definition requires careful attention to detail. Suppose, for example, you want to develop a formal definition of *vacuum cleaner*. Determining a broad category poses no serious problem: a vacuum cleaner is a cleaning appliance. A vacuum cleaner's chief purpose is to clean floors, carpets, and upholstery. But brooms and carpet sweepers also clean floors and carpets, and whisk brooms clean upholstery. To distinguish a vacuum cleaner from these other cleaning devices, you could indicate that it operates by electricity and cleans by suction. All these characteristics might yield the following definition.

> A vacuum cleaner is a cleaning appliance that is powered by electricity and cleans floors, carpets, and upholstery by suction.

As you prepare a formal definition, you should avoid common pitfalls.

Overly Broad Definition. A definition should not be too broad, as is the following: "A skunk is a four-legged animal that has black fur with white markings." A cat or dog could also fit this definition. Say instead: "A skunk is a four-legged animal that has a bushy tall and black fur with white markings and that ejects a putrid-smelling secretion when threatened."

Overly Narrow Definition. Also avoid the opposite extreme, an overly narrow definition. The sentence "Motor oil is a liquid petroleum product used to lubricate automobile engines" illustrates this error. After all, motor oil lubricates other engines as well. Correct the definition by adding the missing information: "Motor oil is a liquid petroleum product used to lubricate the engines of automobiles, motorcycles, lawn mowers, and the like."

Circular Definitions. Never define a term by repeating it or using another form of it. Such a definition is circular and clarifies nothing. Saying that a psychiatrist is "a physician who practices psychiatry" will not help someone who does not know what *psychiatry* means. Instead, use words that mean something to your reader—for example, "A psychiatrist is a physician who diagnoses and treats mental disorders."

Omission of Broad Category. Avoid using *is where* or *is when* instead of naming the broad category in which the term belongs. The definitions "A car wash is where automobiles are washed and polished" and "Procrastination is when a person habitually delays taking necessary action" illustrate this error. Notice the improvement when the broad categories are named: "A car wash is an establishment in which automobiles are washed and polished" and "Procrastination is the habit of delaying necessary action."

Unfamiliar Terms. A definition should use terms familiar to the reader. Defining *multiple sclerosis* for a general audience as "a disease characterized by partial demyelination of the brain and spinal cord" would only create puzzlement. A better definition would be, "Multiple sclerosis is a disease characterized by partial destruction of the sheath surrounding certain nerves in the brain and spinal cord."

Technical terms, however, are appropriate for some audiences. *Demyelination*, for example, would be perfectly acceptable in a paper aimed at nursing students, who would understand the term. Your guideline should always be your readers—address them in language they can understand.

Exercise

Identify which of the following formal definitions are satisfactory and which are faulty. Point out the error in each faulty definition.

a. A demijohn is a large glass or earthenware bottle with a narrow neck and a wicker wrapping and handle.
b. A bicycle is a two-wheeled vehicle used for human transportation.
c. A paring knife is a small kitchen knife used to peel vegetables.
d. A "square" is a person who is hopelessly out-of-date, conventional, and stodgy.
e. Anorexia nervosa is when a person persistently refuses to eat.
f. A myelogram is an X-ray examination that uses a special substance to visualize the internal surfaces of the spinal cord.
g. A network is anything reticulated or decussated, at equal distances, with interstices within the intersections.
h. An ichthyologist is a scientist who specializes in ichthyology.

DECIDING HOW TO EXPAND YOUR FORMAL DEFINITION

A formal definition can be expanded by any combination of the following writing methods.

Process Explanation. You can use process explanation to explain how a device operates, a product is made, a procedure is carried out, or a natural event occurs. The following paragraph, taken from a paper defining the term *fingerprint*, tells how to take prints.

> Fingerprinting is carried out by rolling the ball of each finger over a glass or metal inking plate coated with a thin film of special ink. The ink on the finger is then transferred by rolling to the appropriate box on a fingerprint card. Each print consists of a set of clearly defined gray ridges.
>
> *Jimmy Carvel*

Comparison. Comparison can help define an object, device, or process by showing how it resembles or differs from a more familiar one. You might focus on physical properties, construction, mode of operation, size, power, or efficiency, among others. In the following example, defining the air-cooled engine, the writer compares the way it is cooled to the method used for the liquid-cooled engine.

In conventional liquid-cooled engines, the heat from the burning air-fuel mixture passes through the walls of the cylinder and into a coolant in a jacket surrounding the cylinders. The heated coolant is pumped through a radiator, where it is cooled by an air stream blowing past the thin-walled tubes or cells through which it passes. It is then returned to the jacket to absorb more heat.

In air-cooled engines, heat is absorbed directly by a stream of air passing over the outside of the engine. The outside cylinder walls have metal fins to increase the amount of surface from which engine heat is lost, and the cylinders may also have spaces between them for better air circulation. To provide the great volume of air needed for proper cooling, a fan or blower may be utilized. Special cowlings and baffles may also be placed around the engine near the cylinders to increase the flow of air.

Edward Daley

Classification. When you classify, you divide a topic into separate categories and then discuss the categories one at a time. The following excerpt from a paper on air contamination expands the definition of *respirators* by classifying them.

Three major types of respirators—air-supplied devices, self-contained breathing devices, and air-purifying devices—are utilized for protection against air contaminants. Air-supplied devices consist essentially of a mask, hood, or suit connected by a hose to a stationary tank of air. With self-contained breathing devices, air is supplied from a tank carried by the user, or oxygen is generated in a chemical canister. Air-purifying devices are equipped with filters or chemical canisters which remove contaminants from incoming air before the wearer breathes it.

Alice Ludo

Description. Objective description presents a factual image of an object or a device. The following description of a glove box is part of a paper defining *radiation testing*.

> A glove box is a sealed box with one or more transparent sides and a pair of rubber gloves mounted in ports and protruding into the interior. The box is equipped with a blower and filter that maintain a slightly reduced pressure within the unit and also has a double-doored chamber through which radioactive materials are loaded or unloaded.
>
> *William Terry*

Illustration. Illustration by way of examples—using specific incidents, events, or items—works especially well for defining an abstract term or tracing the changes in the meaning of a term. In the following excerpt, the writer uses illustration (in this case, a personal experience) to help develop a paper defining *fear*.

> Once I started school, I developed a great fear of tests, term papers, and speaking in front of the class. Formal speeches were especially hard for me. Heart pounding, cold sweat beading my forehead, I would suffer acute mental agonies as I stammered my way through my talk. This "academic fear syndrome" lasted until my junior year in college.
>
> *Diane Trathen*

Causation. Causation, which probes the reasons behind events, conditions, problems, and attitudes, often helps to define. The following paragraph from a paper defining *glaucoma* shows how the condition develops.

> Glaucoma results when fluid inside the eye fails to drain properly. Pressure builds within the eyeball, damaging or killing the optic nerve, which connects the eye to the brain. Damage can range from impairment of vision to total blindness. The disease is responsible for one out of every eight cases of total blindness.
>
> *Rance Hafner*

Enumeration. Enumeration presents supporting details in a numbered or unnumbered list, as in this example from a paper defining *solar power*.

> Some people are turning to solar power to supply all or part of their energy needs. Solar power has several attractive features: it (1) requires simpler technology than nuclear power, (2) does not pollute the environment, (3) will never become exhausted, and (4) can never be cut off by embargoes. These features point toward a bright future for this form of energy.
>
> *Lisa Brook*

Negation. Negation explains what a term does *not* mean. It is especially useful for defining events and occurrences and for correcting popular misconceptions. Notice its use in the following excerpt.

> Researchers do not know what crib death is, but they do know what it is *not*. They know it cannot be predicted; it strikes like a "thief in the night." Crib deaths occur in seconds, with no sound of pain, and they always happen when the child is sleeping. Suffocation is *not* the cause, nor is aspiration or regurgitation. Investigation has shown no correlation between the incidence of crib death and the mother's use of birth control pills or tobacco or the presence of fluoride in water.
>
> *Trudy Stelter*

The combination of writing methods you choose and the order in which you present your material depends on your topic, purpose, and audience. The following outline shows how you might arrange the material for a paper defining *voiceprints*.

I. Introduction: Includes formal definition "A voiceprint is a graphic record of an individual's voice characteristics."
II. Body
   A. Process of making voiceprint
   B. Uses for voiceprints
      1. Medical uses
         a. Diagnostic uses
         b. Surgical uses
      2. Anticrime uses
III. Conclusion

This outline shows that the writer will use process explanation and classification to develop the paper.

Exercise

Choose a suitable topic for an extended definition paper, prepare a formal definition, choose appropriate methods of development, and arrange them in a suitable order.

Writing and Revising Your Paper

WRITING YOUR INTRODUCTION

Besides presenting the formal definition, the introduction can do several things: attract attention with an arresting statement or question, offer a case history, comment on the importance of the item being defined, or present some pertinent specific details. The introduction to the paper defining *voiceprints* takes the last approach.

> *A voiceprint is a graphic record of an individual's voice characteristics.* The graph consists of a complicated pattern of wavy lines. As is true of fingerprints, no two voiceprints are alike.
>
> Terri Chapman

WRITING THE BODY OF YOUR PAPER

Present the information in the appropriate order and in enough detail to make your message clear. Here is the body of the voiceprint paper, with the material organized according to the outline on page 156.

> *A voiceprint is made by using a sound spectrograph, an instrument that records the energy patterns of the spoken word.* Voice readings are affected by such physiological characteristics as the configuration of the lower respiratory tract and the contours of the vocal cavities, as well as by the movements of the vocal cords, lips, and tongue. *As a result*, each voiceprint is unique.

Making a voiceprint involves having the subject speak into a microphone and recording the voice on a magnetic tape. This tape runs around a cylindrical drum, where an electronic scanning device picks up the information. A pen *then* records the information as a graph.

The medical profession has utilized voiceprints to investigate the characteristics of infant cries and their significance. One study showed that a distress cry is longer, louder, and noisier than a hunger cry and tends to be irregular, with more interruptions and gagging. This same study *also* showed that abnormal cry characteristics appear to be associated with certain physical defects. *For example,* the investigators discovered that an apparently normal infant with an especially shrill cry had no cerebral cortex. Generally, abnormal infants had higher-pitched cries than those with no physical impairment. These findings suggest that voiceprints may have value as a diagnostic tool.

Diagnosing infant problems is not the only medical use of voiceprints. Psychiatrists have used them to determine emotional stress in patients, and they have aided surgeons in repairing cleft palates.

Law enforcement agencies rely heavily on voiceprints to identify bomb hoaxers, individuals making obscene phone calls, and other persons using telephones for illegal purposes. A voiceprint is taken during the phone call, held until a suspect has been apprehended, and then compared with the suspect's voiceprint. This technique has helped the police obtain numerous convictions.

The use of voiceprints in criminal proceedings has not been without controversy and setbacks, however. In a number of instances, appeals courts have reversed convictions obtained through use of voiceprints, holding that prints were unreliable. *Also,* some early studies showed that the percentage of voiceprints mistakenly identified could range as high as 63 percent, thus raising serious doubts about the validity of voiceprints as evidence. Later, *though,* a massive study comparing 34,000 voiceprints led to the conclusion that they do constitute a reliable means of identification.

Terri Chapman

Note that the writer has included a short definition of a sound spectrograph and used the linking expressions *as a result, then, also, for example, however,* and *though.*

WRITING YOUR CONCLUSION

The conclusion generally summarizes the paper's main points, comments on the significance of the information, or—as in the following one-sentence example—makes a prediction.

> With this type of comprehensive evidence, the use of voice-prints in medicine and the courts seems assured for many years to come.
>
> *Terri Chapman*

REVISING YOUR DRAFT

As you revise your paper, refer to the guidelines on pages 51–54 as well as the following questions.

Will my topic interest my reader?

Have I prepared a formal definition that is not too broad, too narrow, or circular? Does it use familiar terms and name a broad category?

Have I developed the paper with an appropriate combination of methods?

Are the methods arranged in an appropriate order?

Have I supplied an appropriate introduction and conclusion?

Exercise

Prepare a suitable introduction and conclusion for a paper defining the topic you chose for the exercise on page 157. Explain your choices.

Examples of Definition

Assertiveness

Formal definition

    Assertiveness is a communication skill that enables individuals to express their feelings and opinions openly in an effective, nonoffensive manner. Programs designed to help minorities and people in lower-level occupations improve their economic lot have shown

Economic consequences of nonassertiveness

1

that such people cannot take full advantage of opportunities for advancement because they lack assertiveness. Since this fact became widely known, many people have enrolled in classes and workshops to learn assertive behavior.

A nonassertive person is probably either passive or aggressive. Passive individuals are generally shy and reluctant to express their opinions, share their feelings, or assume responsibility for their actions. Often, they give in to others' demands, even when doing so runs counter to their best interests. Because of their inability to stand up to others, passive people often harbor strong feelings of resentment, anger, or depression. *In contrast*, aggressive individuals react strongly to even slight criticisms or mild differences of opinion, make harsh judgments, cling stubbornly to their own views however far-fetched or mistaken they are shown to be, and make a practice of fault-finding.

Assertive individuals occupy a middle ground between passive and aggressive individuals. Unlike passive individuals, they express their beliefs and feelings openly. Unlike aggressive individuals, they do not overreact when someone challenges one of their opinions, nor are they dogmatic or judgmental. *As a result*, assertiveness improves communication, reduces antagonisms, and allows differences to be settled in a friendly spirit.

Effective assertive communication depends on three things. To begin with, each participant must let the other know, "I understand what you are saying." *In addition*, each must make his or her opinions clearly known. If this does not happen, meaningful exchange becomes difficult or impossible. *Fi-*

Efforts to overcome nonassertiveness

Topic sentence: indicates paragraph will present a comparison

Characteristics of passive individuals

Linking device: signals switch to second item of comparison

Characteristics of aggressive individuals

Topic sentence with links to preceding paragraph: indicates paragraph will present another comparison

Characteristics of assertive individuals

Linking device: signals switch to discussion of effects of assertiveness

Topic sentence: indicates paragraph will enumerate

Linking device: signals switch to second item of discussion

Linking device:
signals switch to final
item of discussion

nally, each person must tell the other exactly what he or she wants (unless wants do not figure in the matter under discussion). By doing these things, both participants know exactly where they stand and are in a position to deal effectively with any personal differences.

Conclusion: offers
a prediction

Behaving assertively has helped thou- 5
sands of people achieve happier, more rewarding lives. As time passes, we can expect more and more people to recognize the benefits of assertiveness.

Arthur Petry

The Food Chain

It is a truism that we must eat to stay alive and that all the 1
plants and animals upon which we dine must do the same. How many of us, though, ever stop to consider whether or not any pattern underlies all the cross-dining that goes on? There is a pattern, and to understand it we must first familiarize ourselves with the concept of a food chain. *Such a chain can be defined as a hierarchy of organisms in a biological community, or ecosystem, with each member of the chain feeding on the one below it and in turn being fed upon by the one above it.* To put the matter more simply, a food chain starts with a great quantity of plant stuffs which are eaten by a large number of very hungry diners. These are then eaten by a lesser number of other animals, which in turn fall prey to an even smaller number of creatures. With the passage of time, the uneaten organisms die and become part of the soil for the plant to grow in.

To illustrate, let's look for a moment at one particular biolog- 2
ical community, a marshy ecosystem, and a few events that might take place there. First, there are the marsh grasses, with millions of grasshoppers busily feeding upon them. When one grasshopper

isn't looking, a shrew sneaks up and eats it. This process is repeated many times as the day wears on. Later, toward sunset, as
the stuffed and inattentive shrew is crossing an open stretch of
ground, a hawk swoops out of the sky and eats the rodent. The
food chain is completed when the marsh hawk dies and fertilizes
the marsh grasses.

This illustration is not meant to suggest that hawks eat only   3
shrews or shrews eat only grasshoppers; the cycle is much more
complicated than that, involving what biologists call trophic
levels—the different feeding groups in an ecosystem (for example,
some creatures eat green plants and some eat meat). There are
five major trophic levels. The beginning point for any food chain
is green plants, known as producers, which absorb sunlight and
through the process of photosynthesis turn carbon dioxide, water,
and soil nutrients into food, especially carbohydrates, that animals can assimilate.

All of the other life forms subsist either directly or indirectly   4
on the producers. Animals that feed directly on green plants are
the herbivores, called primary consumers. This group includes,
among other creatures, most insects, most rodents, and hooved
animals. The secondary consumers are the carnivores and omnivores. The term "carnivore," meaning an animal that eats only
flesh, is more familiar than the term "omnivore," which desig-
nates an animal that eats both green plants and flesh. Carnivores
include such animals as lions, leopards, eagles, and hawks,
whereas omnivores are represented by foxes, bears, humans, and
so on.

The last feeding group in the food chain consists of the de-   5
composers: bacteria and fungi. These microorganisms recycle the
waste products of living animals and the remains of all dead
things—plants, herbivores, omnivores, and carnivores alike—
into fertilizers that plants, the producers, can use.

Obviously each trophic level must produce more energy than   6
it transfers to the next higher level. With animals, a considerable
part of this energy is lost through body heat. The muscles that
pump the lungs, continually pushing air out of the body and suck-
ing it back in, consume energy. The muscles in the arms and legs
sweat out energy. All of the life-supporting systems of the organism use energy to keep it going. Everything from worms to peo-

ple lives in accordance with this law of energy loss. As long as life's fires burn, energy is lost, never to be regained.

Throughout history we humans have tried to manipulate the food chain so as to provide ever-greater outputs of energy. On the one hand, we have tried, by whatever means we could employ, to rid our fields of harmful birds, insects, and rodents, and our animals of diseases and parasites. On the other, we have constantly striven to produce healthier and more productive strains of plants and animals. Often these attempts have been spectacularly successful. Sometimes, though, the results have proved disastrous, as with the insecticide DDT.

Farmers first began using DDT on a large scale in 1946, right after it had proved its effectiveness in tropical military operations in World War II. As expected, the product proved equally effective as an agricultural pesticide, but there were some unexpected and disastrous side effects. The difficulties were caused by excessive DDT washing off crops, entering irrigation canals, and from there flowing to streams, rivers and lakes. All living creatures in the path of the chemical were contaminated—worms, fish, ducks, indeed all forms of aquatic life. Contaminated worms poisoned songbirds, causing massive dieoffs of birds, and many humans developed serious health problems from eating contaminated aquatic animals. Although Congress has severely restricted the use of DDT in the country, the whole episode stands as a warning of what can happen when humans attempt to manipulate the food chain.

As time continues and the population grows, efforts will be made to further increase the food supply. Let us hope that in doing so we won't act in haste and create catastrophes of even greater magnitude.

Michael Galayda

Discussion Questions

1. Explain why the essay's formal definition is appropriate.
2. What method does the writer use to develop the definition in paragraph 2?
3. How do paragraphs 3–5 develop the definition?
4. Locate three places in the essay where the writer uses brief definitions.

What Is Cancer Chemotherapy?

Chemotherapy means treatment of a disease by the use of   1
drugs. In this case, the disease is cancer. Chemotherapy has been
used in one form or another in the treatment of cancer for the
past twenty-five years. In the last twenty years great strides have
been made in discovering new drugs and new combinations of old
drugs to control or produce a halt in the progression of the disease.

The first type to be controlled, not cured, was leukemia; the   2
knowledge gained there has been applied to many other forms of
cancer.

When a new chemotherapy drug is discovered, it is first used   3
in experiments on animals to discover possible harmful effects. It
is then subjected to a rigid series of tests in highly controlled situations to discover the most effective doses and schedules of administration that will work best for the destruction of cancer cells
without harming normal tissue. The new drug is then approved
by the Food and Drug Administration for general use. From the
time a new drug is discovered until it is in general use may be
from one to four years.

These controls are necessary so that no one will suffer from   4
improper use of a drug. The drug or drugs the doctor prescribes
have gone through all these steps and have been used before with
good results. A doctor would not give them unless he or she felt
there was a good chance of that particular cancer responding to
treatment. A doctor is the best judge of what drug, if any, is best
to use in a particular situation, for only he or she is thoroughly familiar with the patient and his state of health.

Use of Chemotherapy.   As you are probably aware, chemo-   5
therapy is only one method of treating cancer. It may be used
alone, or in conjunction with surgery or radiation. Formerly chemotherapy was used only after all else had failed. This is not true
today. In some cases, chemotherapy is the treatment of choice
and is considered curative in a few less common cancers. In others, chemotherapy may keep the cancer under control for months
or even years. Some may not be benefited at all by chemotherapy.

Again, only the doctor can decide how best to treat the cancer patient.

Effects of Chemotherapy. Many different drugs may be 6 used in chemotherapy. These drugs work by several different methods, but in general they prevent the cells from reproducing. Sometimes a cancer cell may become resistant to one drug, much as a germ can become resistant to penicillin. If this happens, the doctor can switch to a different medication or to a combination of drugs.

Though the drugs are of different composition and may be 7 given differently, they have some possible side effects in common. Some that may occur are loss of appetite, tiredness, nausea, vomiting, diarrhea, temporary loss of hair and suppression of bone marrow function. The bone marrow produces blood cells. Periodic blood tests are given persons receiving chemotherapy to be sure that their blood is being produced in adequate amounts. Occasionally, sores may develop in the mouth or on the lips.

Chemotherapy drugs affect rapidly dividing cells, and the 8 cells of the hair follicles, mouth, skin, stomach, intestines and bone marrow are rapidly dividing cells, so they are also affected. This is why side effects may appear. Nausea and vomiting may be controlled by other drugs. If any symptom becomes too severe, the chemotherapy drugs may be stopped and resumed later, or another drug might be substituted. These symptoms are only temporary and will clear up when the medicine is stopped. Many fortunate patients go through a complete course of treatment with no side effects at all. This does not mean that the drug is not working. The appearance or intensity of side effects has no bearing on how effective the drug will be in treating the cancer. It seems to be a matter of individual tolerance and tumor response.

How Is Chemotherapy Given? Chemotherapy drugs can be 9 given in several ways. They may be applied as an ointment or lotion as in skin cancer, taken by mouth, or given as an injection into the muscle or vein. They are usually given for several days in succession, followed by a period of rest, then given again. This is one way that has been found to be effective against cancer without damaging the normal cells.

Medication is usually given either in the hospital, the doctor's 10 office, or at the outpatient clinic of a hospital. A doctor or a specially trained nurse will administer the medication.

Precautions.   Resistance to infections may be lowered during chemotherapy treatment. Therefore, patients should avoid people with colds or other infections. Unless the treatment is accompanied by severe side effects, patients can usually continue their normal activities, including sexual relations. Unless the doctor states otherwise, there are no special foods that should be eaten, nor are there any to avoid. No medications, including vitamins, aspirins, and birth control pills, should be taken unless approved or prescribed by the doctor.

Chemotherapy is something about which the patient will ask many questions: Will it work? Will I get sick? How will this affect my mate and/or my family? Should I practice birth control? What kind of contraception should I use? Patients should discuss these questions frankly and thoroughly with their doctors.

American Cancer Society

Discussion Questions

1. Identify the essay's formal definition.
2. What purpose do the headings serve?
3. By what writing method is paragraph 3 developed? Explain your answer.
4. Point out evidence that the piece is addressed to a general audience.

Suggestions for Writing

Write an extended definition, using one of the suggestions listed here or a term approved by your instructor. You might define a word that has special meaning for you. Expand your definition by any combination of the methods discussed in this chapter. Make sure you include a formal definition.

1. Salesmanship	8. The client or customer
2. Worker alienation	9. Routine
3. Radiation	10. Stress
4. The "grease monkey"	11. Water table
5. Evidence	12. Erosion
6. The secretary	13. Viscosity
7. The boss	14. Handgun

15. The police officer
16. Hospitality
17. Nutrition
18. Refrigeration
19. Fashion design
20. Retailing
21. Isometric exercises
22. Central processing unit
23. Drag race
24. Preventive dentistry
25. Restorative dentistry
26. Microcomputer
27. A slang term (*nerd, jerk,* or the like)
28. Courage
29. Auditing
30. Success
31. Leader pricing
32. Vocational education
33. The nurse
34. Pitch
35. Some term from your field of study or occupation
36. Word processing
37. Anesthesia
38. Hospice
39. Electrocardiogram
40. Yuppie (young urban professional)

9
Business Letters

Letters are indispensable to the operation of any business and organization. They are used for countless purposes, but most often to ask questions, provide answers, sell products and services, and register and respond to complaints. Learning to write effective business letters benefits your organization and enhances your usefulness as an employee.

The Language and Tone of Business Letters

Tone is the attitude conveyed by a writer or speaker. Whether or not you intend it, everything you write has a tone—desirable or otherwise. When writing a business letter, strive for a tone that suits your audience and purpose and arouses the desired emotional reaction from your reader. Failure to convey the right tone may cause your message to be rejected, create ill will, or even damage your organization's business. You can achieve the right tone by avoiding wordiness, using the proper degree of formality, and showing courtesy at all times.

AVOIDING WORDINESS

Wordiness results in dull, hard-to-read messages and benefits neither writer nor reader. It can take two forms: business jargon and deadwood.

Business jargon uses inflated and often elaborately polite expressions. *Deadwood* occurs when the writer repeats the same message or uses several words when only one or two would suffice. Following are some examples of wordiness and corrections for them.

Wordy Expression	Correction
at the present time	now
basic fundamentals	fundamentals
cognizant of	know
completely eliminate	eliminate
enclosed please find	we are enclosing
exactly identical	identical
I am in receipt of	I have
in view of the fact that	because
pursuant to your request that	as you requested
will you be kind enough to	please
we wish to acknowledge receipt of	we have, *or* thank you for

As you can see, the corrected versions are more relaxed and natural than the wordy originals.

As noted on pages 68–69, computer programs are available that evaluate letters and other documents and flag wordy expressions and jargon. Frequently, these programs also suggest substitute phrasing. Use of the programs can help you improve your letter's effectiveness.

USING THE PROPER DEGREE OF FORMALITY

The business letters you write for people outside your field will require *informal language*. Much like ordinary, educated conversation, informal language is casual and relaxed, using simple words and sentence structures as well as personal pronouns like *I*, *me*, *your*, and *yours*. At the same time, it avoids slang and overly casual expressions that may cast doubt on your seriousness. The following paragraph uses informal language.

> Customers who have purchased our board brush kit have written us many letters praising its ease of installation and its performance. The kit mounts directly on the chassis of the Zamboni ice resurfacing machine and cleans snow from the boards as the ice is resurfaced. The brush taps right into the hydraulic system of the Zamboni, so there is no need for an additional pump. I have enclosed an instruction sheet so that you can see just how easy the kit is to install and operate.
>
> *Zoren Lupescu*

The business letters you write for people within your field will require *technical language*. Unlike informal language, technical language employs specialized words that the general reader is not likely to understand. Its sentences tend to be long and complex, and its tone is objective and authoritative without being pompous. The following passage uses technical language.

> This new hypertensive agent is a synthetic prostaglandin of PGE1. It is a beta blocker which is selective for the beta receptors of the heart and, by sparing the beta receptors of the lungs, avoids many of the common side effects of this class of substances. Extensive clinical testing revealed that it significantly reduced blood pressure in 95 percent of the test subjects with renal hypertension and 82 percent of those with malignant hypertension.
>
> *Janice Delancy*

SHOWING COURTESY

Courtesy, as important in business letters as in face-to-face conversation, results from adopting a "you" attitude in your letters. The "you" attitude involves viewing matters from your reader's perspective rather than your own. Here are several ways of doing this.

First, never resort to sarcasm and insults, as these create ill-will and may cause your reader to delay taking the desired action. For example, in asking that an overdue order be shipped immediately, resist the urge to say, "I know it's asking a lot of you, but do try to ship my order right away, so I can have it for next week's sale." Instead, consider your reader's feelings and say something like, "Please ship my order right away, so I can have it for next week's sale."

In addition, avoid expressions with resentment-breeding overtones. When you write, "We have your letter *claiming* that the oscilloscopes we sold you were defective," you call the reader's honesty into question. When you write, "*It is our position* that this offer is very attractive," your statement suggests that the reader is quarrelsome and likely to dispute you. In the following example, note how rewriting has created a friendly, courteous tone.

We are sorry to learn that the oscilloscopes you purchased from us were defective.

We think that you will find this offer very attractive.

Cold impersonality is as destructive to courtesy and the "you" attitude as are sarcasm and insults, so take pains to avoid it. The following letter does not.

Dear Mr. Furman:

Reference is made to the March 17, 19--, agreement between your company and ours in which you contracted to provide cafeteria catering services for our employees.

In accordance with paragraph 5(b) of the said agreement, we have elected to discontinue your services. Accordingly, the said agreement is hereby terminated in accordance with its terms without any further obligation or liabilities between the parties.

Sincerely yours,

The writer of this letter handles the cancellation in an abrupt, unfeeling manner that takes no account of the caterer's effort in developing his service. Concern for the reader's feelings demands an expression of regret and an explanation for the action. Although this is more difficult to accomplish when you must present disagreeable information, you can achieve your objective by adopting a positive manner. The following revision shows the improved tone that results from this approach.

> Dear Mr. Furman:
>
> As you will recall, on March 17, 19--, we signed an agreement with you in which you contracted to provide cafeteria catering services for our employees.
>
> At that time, our company had approximately one hundred more employees than now and no plans for decreasing the workforce. However, a recent commitment to automated production has led to the present reduction and made further cutbacks likely in the near future. Because cafeteria sales would not be high enough to justify any further expense on your part, I am sorry to inform you that we must cancel our agreement. As you know, paragraph 5(b) provides for this cancellation.
>
> Thank you for the excellent service you have provided over the past fifteen months. We share your disappointment and wish you every success with your catering services.
>
> Sincerely yours,

If you follow these guidelines, your letters will reflect favorably on your organization and yourself.

Mechanics of Business Letters

FORMATS

There are two common formats for business letters: *modified block* (sometimes called *balanced block*) and *full block*. The primary differences between the two formats are described in the text of the sample letters shown in Figures 9–1 and 9–2.

PARTS

The business letter has six basic parts.

1. Heading
2. Inside address

Figure 9–1.   **Modified-Block Format**

```
                              219 Abbott Road
                  HEADING     East Lansing, MI  48823
                              November 15, 19--


Mr. Wilfred Sims
237 Lincoln Drive
Pittsburgh, PA  15235    INSIDE ADDRESS

Dear Mr. Sims:    SALUTATION

This letter illustrates the modified block format.  In
this format, the heading, the complimentary close, and
the signature begin at the center of the page.  All other
elements, including the first lines of paragraphs, begin          BODY
at the left-hand margin.

This format is popular because it has a balanced appearance
on the page.

      COMPLIMENTARY         Sincerely yours,
      CLOSE

      SIGNATURE             Paul M. Leonelli
                            Paul M. Leonelli

PML/br    STENOGRAPHIC REFERENCE

cc: Mr. L. P. James    CONCURRENT COPY NOTATION
```

MODIFIED BLOCK FORMAT

Figure 9–2. **Full-Block Format**

```
219 Abbott Road
East Lansing, MI  48823      HEADING
November 15, 19-- -



Mr. Wilfred Sims
237 Lincoln Avenue           INSIDE ADDRESS
Pittsburgh, PA  15235

Dear Mr. Sims:     SALUTATION

This letter is typed in a full-block format.  With this
format, every line begins at the left-hand margin.

The full-block format can be typed more quickly than the      BODY
modified block format, but unless balanced by a properly
designed printed letterhead it sometimes looks lopsided
on the page.
                       COMPLIMENTARY
Sincerely yours,       CLOSE

    Paul m. Leonelli         SIGNATURE

Paul M. Leonelli

PML/br     STENOGRAPHIC REFERENCE

cc: Mr. L. P. James      CONCURRENT COPY NOTATION
```

FULL-BLOCK FORMAT

3. Salutation
4. Body
5. Complimentary close
6. Signature

In addition, it may include a subject line, stenographic reference, enclosure notation, concurrent copy notation, and headings for additional pages.

Heading. If you use plain white stationery, the heading consists of your address—street, city, state, and ZIP code—and the date. Use the two-letter U.S. Postal Service abbreviations for states (see pages 181–182), but spell out all other words, including the name of the month. Here is a typical typed heading.

325 South Bond Street
Los Angeles, CA   90020
October 6, 19--

In the modified-block format, the heading begins at the center of the page (see Figure 9–1). In the full-block format, it appears at the left margin (see Figure 9–2).

With rare exceptions, organizations use letterhead stationery—that is, stationery imprinted with the organization's name and address. Letterheads are arranged in many ways and may include decorative type, illustrations, and such abbreviations as *Inc.*, *Co.*, and *Corp.* The only part of the heading that you supply is the date. For modified-block letters, the date begins at the center of the page and for full-block letters at the left margin, two or three lines below the preprinted address.

Inside Address. The inside address gives the name and address of the organization or person receiving the letter. It always begins at the left margin, two lines below the date in long letters and three to eight lines below in shorter ones.

When writing to an individual, give his or her personal title and full name in the first line.

Mr. Harold L. Calloway
Professor Morris Berger
Miss Jane Fontaine
Mrs. Myra R. McPhail
Ms. Noreen Wyman

The job title, if any, should follow the name, either on the same line or one line below it.

Ms. Noreen Wyman, Comptroller
Mr. Harold L. Calloway
Personnel Manager

If you know the job title but not the name of the person you wish to reach, begin the inside address with the title.

Vice-President for Research
Chairperson, Board of Directors

When both name and title are unknown, begin with the organization's name.

Rockland Manufacturing Company

A complete inside address should look like this.

Mr. Mark Thornton
Director of Sales
White-Inland, Inc.
1100 Front Street
Baltimore, MD 21202

Except for the personal title and state name, avoid abbreviations in the inside address unless the organization you are writing uses one in its official title.

Salutation. The salutation, a formal greeting, begins at the left margin, two lines below the inside address. When you write to an individual, it takes the following form.

Dear Mr. Nowicki:
Dear Ms. McCarthy:
Dear Dr. Corelli:

Letters addressed to departments within an organization should use the salutation "Dear Sir/Madam" or the job title itself.

Sales Department
Calmath Chemical Company
239 Dorman Drive
Birmingham, AL 35207

Dear Sir/Madam:

Sales Department
Calmath Chemical Company
239 Dorman Drive
Birmingham, AL 35207

Dear Sales Manager:

Letters addressed to organizations should use the salutation "Gentlemen/Ladies."

Able Tool and Die Corporation
188 South Cedar Lane
Topeka, KS 72163

Gentlemen/Ladies:

Sales Letters use a variety of salutations, such as "Dear Homeowner," "Dear Booklover," and "Dear Friend of the Environment."

Body. The body of the letter contains the message to the reader. It begins two lines below the salutation unless a subject line intervenes (see page 179) and is single-spaced, with an extra space between paragraphs. To enhance its appearance and readability, try to use short beginning and ending paragraphs, and vary the length of the middle paragraphs. Aim for an average sentence length of sixteen to twenty words, but use shorter or longer sentences if needed. Note also that paragraphs are not indented.

Complimentary Close. The complimentary close, a formal good-bye, is placed two lines below the last line of the body. Only the first word is capitalized, and the last is followed by a comma. In the modified-block format, the complimentary close begins at the page's center (see Figure 9–1), and in the full-block format, at the left margin (see Figure 9–2). The most common forms include the following.

> Yours truly,
> Very truly yours,
> Sincerely yours,
> Sincerely,

Other possibilities include "Cordially yours," appropriate when you write close acquaintances, and "Respectfully yours," used to show special esteem or acknowledge much higher rank.

Signature. The typewritten signature appears four lines directly below the complimentary close. When writing on behalf of your company, follow your name with your title or your title and department.

> James W. Terry
> Manager, Finance Department

A woman should include her personal title, in parentheses, along with her typewritten signature to show how she prefers to be addressed in future correspondence.

> (Mrs.) Mary J. Mifume
> (Miss) Nancy K. Parker
> (Ms.) Deborah Kuhn
> (Mrs.) Jack Kasonovich

Write your name, without the personal title, in the space above the typed signature.

If your company specifies that its legal name accompany your signature, type the name in capital letters one line below the complimentary close and four lines above the typewritten signature.

Sincerely yours,
THE MORTON CORPORATION

James W. Terry

James W. Terry
Manager, Finance Department

Subject Line. The subject line tells what the letter is about. It refers to a specific policy number, file number, invoice number, or the like.

Subject: Your invoice LR-237
Subject: Account number 78-375-162

The subject line is positioned between the salutation and the body, with one line space above and below. It may begin at the left margin or be centered on the page.

Stenographic Reference. The stenographic reference is used when someone other than the writer types the letter. It includes two sets of initials—the writer's, in capital letters, and the typist's, in lowercase letters. The two sets may be separated by a colon or slash mark.

DLS:crt
DLS/crt

The reference appears two lines below the last line of the signature and starts at the left margin.

Enclosure Notation. Whenever a brochure, drawing, check, money order, or other document accompanies a letter, type the notation "Enclosure" or "Enc." on the line following the steno-graphic reference. If more than one item accompanies a letter, in-dicate the number.

DLS:crt
Enclosure
DLS/crt
Enc. 2

Documents of special importance are often named.

DLS/crt
Enclosure: Contract

Concurrent Copy Notation. A concurrent copy notation (also known as a courtesy copy notation) is used when two or more copies of a letter are sent. It consists of the lowercase letters "cc" followed by a colon and the name of the person receiving the copy. If more than one person will receive copies, type the additional names directly below the first one.

cc: Dr. N. R. Prince
cc: Mr. N. A. Ames
    Ms. S. L. Hanska

Position the notation on the line following the stenographic or en-closure notation.

Headings for Additional Pages. When a letter has more than one page, type the additional pages on plain stationery with the same margins as on the first page. Provide each additional page with a heading that includes the reader's name, the date, and the page number, and position this heading six spaces from the top of the page. Any of these three heading styles is acceptable.

Ms. Jennifer Arnett   2   July 23, 19--

Ms. Jennifer Arnett, July 23, 19--, page 2

Ms. Jennifer Arnett
July 23, 19--
Page 2

Leave two lines of space below the heading.

PUNCTUATION

Today's business letter omits all end-of-line punctuation in the heading, inside address, typewritten signature, and any special part such as the subject line and enclosure notation. Only when a line ends with an abbreviation is a period used. The sample letters in this chapter illustrate these conventions as do Figures 9–1 and 9–2.

MARGINS

The size of the margins depends on the length of your letter. For a full-page letter (200 to 300 words), use 1-inch side margins and type the first line of the inside address 2.5 inches below the top of the sheet. For a 100- to 200-word letter, use 1.5-inch side margins and a 3-inch top margin. For a very short letter—50 to 100 words—use 2-inch side margins and a 3.5-inch top margin. (The layout of certain letterheads may dictate somewhat different sizes for top margins.) Bottom and top margins should be roughly equal.

PREPARATIONS FOR MAILING

Use the block form for both addresses on the envelope, and single-space between lines. To make sure that the post office's optical scanners can read your envelope, type the recipient's address entirely in capital letters, omit any punctuation, and position the address so that all of it is between 1.5 and 3 inches from the bottom of the envelope. Leave about a 2-inch right-hand margin. The envelope shown in Figure 9–3 illustrates this format.

Use the two-letter postal abbreviations for the names of states and territories.

Alabama	AL	Arizona	AZ
Alaska	AK	Arkansas	AR

Figure 9–3.   **Sample Addressed Envelope for a Business Letter**

```
Mark P. Dwyer
209 Foster Hall
Case Western Reserve University
Cleveland, OH   44106




                        MR   FRANCIS C RHYTE
                        ASSISTANT ADVERTISING MANAGER
                        MINE SAFETY APPLIANCE COMPANY
                        400 PENN CENTER BOULEVARD
                        PITTSBURGH  PA   15235
```

California	CA	Nevada	NV
Colorado	CO	New Hampshire	NH
Connecticut	CT	New Jersey	NJ
Delaware	DE	New Mexico	NM
District of Columbia	DC	New York	NY
Florida	FL	North Carolina	NC
Georgia	GA	North Dakota	ND
Hawaii	HI	Ohio	OH
Idaho	ID	Oklahoma	OK
Illinois	IL	Oregon	OR
Indiana	IN	Pennsylvania	PA
Iowa	IA	Puerto Rico	PR
Kansas	KS	Rhode Island	RI
Kentucky	KY	South Carolina	SC
Louisiana	LA	South Dakota	SD
Maine	ME	Tennessee	TN
Maryland	MD	Texas	TX
Massachusetts	MA	Utah	UT
Michigan	MI	Vermont	VT
Minnesota	MN	Virginia	VA
Mississippi	MS	Washington	WA
Missouri	MO	West Virginia	WV
Montana	MT	Wisconsin	WI
Nebraska	NE	Wyoming	WY

Figure 9–4.   **Folding Procedure for a Business Letter**

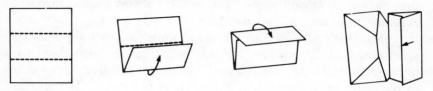

Proofread your letter carefully, sign it, and then fold it neatly into thirds so that it will fit into a business envelope (see Figure 9–4).

Common Types of Business Correspondence

LETTERS OF INQUIRY

A letter of inquiry asks for information. You may, for example, use it to ask for:

1. more detailed data or specifications on a piece of equipment your company might buy.
2. a fuller explanation of a research project described in a magazine article.
3. more details about a safety program or an employee-rating system developed by another organization.
4. statistical data for a term paper.
5. clarification of an inadequate or ambiguous set of directions.

Do not, however, bother your reader by asking for data that you could readily obtain in the library.

There are two basic types of inquiry letters. The first asks for information needed to complete a task or make a decision. The second asks that directions be supplied or clarified.

Type I Inquiry Letter. Begin by identifying yourself, indicating the general subject, and stating that you want information. Be sure to explain how you plan to use it; the recipient will then be more inclined to help you and in a better position to meet your exact needs. If appropriate, mention why you are writing that person or organization. You can then make some favorable comment that may help you obtain what you want.

Next, list the questions you want answered or the points you want clarified. To make the reader's job easier, keep them to a minimum, make them brief, and, whenever possible, word them so they can be answered in a few short sentences. If there are three or more items, arrange them in a numbered list to lessen the chances that one will be overlooked. Finally, indicate that you will welcome any additional information.

Consider possible ways to repay the reader for help provided. If, for example, you want information for use in a survey, offer to supply a copy when it is completed. Sometimes, of course, repayment is not possible. Close the letter with an expression of appreciation, such as "Thank you for any help you can give me" or "Any information you can provide will be appreciated." The following letter meets these requirements.

Indicates general subject and why recipient is receiving letter	I have read with great interest your article in the November 199- issue of *Health* magazine, in which you mention your survey of smoking regulations in Michigan hospitals.
Identifies writer and why information is needed	I am a college student on a trainee assignment and would like to conduct a similar survey of hospitals in our state. Would you please help me by answering the following questions?
Questions: set up as numbered list, brief, worded for ease in answering	1. How were the hospitals contacted—by phone or letter? 2. Were all hospitals in the state contacted or just a representative sample? 3. What did you accomplish by this survey?
Indicates additional help will be appreciated	If you have any additional information or material that might prove helpful, I would welcome it too.

Offers to repay reader
for help and expresses
appreciation

When the survey has been completed, I will be happy to send you a copy of the results. Thank you for any help you can provide.

James T. Brown

Type II Inquiry Letter. Start the type II letter by providing any necessary background information. Next, state the problem, explain the inconvenience it has caused, and then request the directions. Conclude by asking your reader to respond as soon as possible. Maintain a courteous tone throughout your letter; discourtesy will hurt your chances of receiving a prompt reply. Here is an example.

Provides background
information

In early October, I installed one of your Winter-Warm Model CR-1Z wood-coal furnaces in my house.

States problem
and resulting
inconvenience

The furnace worked very well for two months, but then the fan stopped switching on automatically when the temperature in the house drops below the thermostat setting. Now I have to switch the fan on manually, a situation that has caused me considerable inconvenience.

Asks for directions

Since the fan and thermostat are factory-installed, I have no directions for checking them. Therefore, please send me the needed information.

Requests prompt
response

I would appreciate a prompt reply, so that I can put a quick end to this problem.

Bryan Woidan

REPLIES TO LETTERS OF INQUIRY

Replies to letters of inquiry may be favorable or unfavorable. In either case, answer as soon as possible, preferably within one day.

Favorable Replies to Type I Inquiry Letter. Begin by mentioning the original inquiry and noting that you are, or soon will be, supplying the requested information. Occasionally, you might have to refer an inquiry elsewhere for an answer. In this case, name, if possible, the person or department handling it and mention a probable date for the reply.

If your letter provides answers, arrange them to correspond to the order of the original questions, and number them if the originals were numbered. Whenever possible, make your job easier by providing brochures, reports, or other material that contains the desired information. If you cannot supply an answer, say so and tell why. Never bypass a question without comment. If you have other material that might prove useful, send it. Similarly, if you can name someone who might furnish other information, do so. Conclude by offering further help if it is needed and making some pleasant comment. Following is a typical reply.

Mentions original inquiry and notes information is being supplied

Thank you for your December 8 letter requesting information about the survey we conducted to determine smoking regulations in Michigan hospitals. We hope the following answers to your questions will be helpful:

Answers original questions in order requested

1. Hospitals were contacted by letter, addressed personally to the administrator. Each letter included a questionnaire and return envelope. (A sample of each is enclosed.) If we did not receive a reply within ten days, we mailed a follow-up letter or contacted the hospital personally.
2. All hospitals in the state were contacted in order to obtain a complete analysis.
3. Hospitals became more aware of the hazards of permitting smoking around people who were already ill; consequently, many changed their regulations to permit smoking only in specified areas.

Indicates additional material is being supplied

Under separate cover we are sending you a complete copy of our survey results and also samples of our smoking literature.

Makes pleasant ending comment and offers to supply further information	We are pleased that you are planning a similar survey in your state and will be happy to receive a copy of your results. If we can assist you further, please let us know.

James T. Brown

Favorable Replies to Type II Inquiry Letter.   Start by apologizing for any difficulty the customer has experienced; then provide the directions. Arrange them in a numbered list so the separate steps stand out clearly and are in proper order, and present them in the form of commands. Note any steps that must be performed simultaneously, explain the purpose of any step that might seem unnecessary, and provide a warning if a step might be carried out improperly.

End by expressing the belief that the information will solve the reader's problem and by offering to provide more help if it is needed. If you wish, repeat your apology. The letter that follows reflects these guidelines.

Apologizes for difficulties customer has experienced	We are sorry to learn that the fan on the Winter-Warm furnace you purchased from us is not operating properly. If you follow the procedure below, you should soon have it functioning normally again.

Provides directions for correcting problem, in form of commands and in proper order	1. Remove the cover of the thermostat by taking out the corner screws with a Phillips screwdriver. 2. With a regular screwdriver, turn the black "adjustment" screw clockwise one full turn. 3. If the fan starts blowing air, the thermostat is adjusted. Repeat step 2 if the fan does not start blowing. If the fan does not start after three full turns of the screw, the thermostat needs replacing. In that case, call us and we will send a service person to do the job free of charge.

Express belief information will correct problem, offers further help, and repeats apology

This information should enable you to correct your problem without difficulty. If you do have difficulties, however, call us collect at (313) 555-2792 between 9:00 a.m. and 5:00 p.m. Again, we are sorry for the inconvenience you have experienced.

Bryan Woidan

Unfavorable Replies. Writing a good refusal letter is not easy. Unless you exercise special tact, you are likely to offend your reader and jeopardize any further business dealings. Whatever the reason for your refusal, try to be courteous and helpful throughout your letter.

Begin with a friendly comment; then state your refusal and the reason for it. Be specific. Perhaps the reader wants information that is not yet available. Or perhaps the information was obtained under a contract with another company and cannot be released to third parties. In the latter case, you could suggest that the reader write the other company, and then provide an address.

If you can, soften your refusal by supplying articles, bulletins, or reports that might prove useful or by directing the reader to another source. Consider the possibilities carefully; the goodwill you generate will amply repay your efforts.

End courteously by wishing the reader success in his or her venture and offering help in other matters. Here is an example of a refusal.

Opens courteously, states refusal, and notes reason for it

Thank you for your letter requesting information about our new comprehensive safety program. Although we would like to answer your questions, we are unable to do so. Because our program is relatively new, we have not yet compiled any statistical data on its effects.

Suggests other source of information

Although we cannot help you, the Grigsby Tractor Company may be able to provide comparable data since their program is very similar to ours and has been in operation for

several years. In fact, we modeled our program after Grigsby's because of their success.
Address your letter to

> Mr. John Aldo
> Grigsby Tractor Company
> 149 Maplewood Street
> Line, NJ 08043

Wishes the recipient
success and offers help
on other matters

Mr. Aldo is the coordinator of the Grigsby
program. We hope that any information he
might provide will help you to establish a
successful program in your organization.
Please write whenever you need assistance on
other matters. We are always ready to help
whenever we can.

Monica LaBree

Exercise

1. Assume that you are an environmental health student who is interested in rodent control. You have read an advertisement for glue
   traps and write for more information about them. Specifically, you
   ask whether (1) the glue will spill out of an overturned trap, (2) rodents can be easily removed to allow for trap reuse, and (3) dust or
   water will lessen the effectiveness of the trap. Send your letter to the
   research and development department of the manufacturer.

2. Answer the preceding inquiry letter. Indicate that if a trap is in-
   verted, glue will slowly run out, so traps should not be placed where
   glue can damage machinery or clothing. Recommend against reuse
   because of the hazards of removing rodents. Note that moderate
   amounts of dust and water will not affect the trap's performance and
   that a small roof offers protection against excessive atmospheric contamination. Finally, warn against placing the traps in areas fre-
   quented by pets, as the glue is hard to remove from fur.

3. Some instructors assign letters of inquiry and replies to two-person
   teams whose members write back and forth and criticize each other's
   efforts. If your instructor does this, you and your partner should first
   decide who will write, and who respond to, the initial letter. If you
   are the writer, prepare a list of possible topics, show them to your
   partner, choose one together, write the letter, and give it to your
   partner to criticize. If you are the recipient, prepare a written criti-

cism of the letter, send a response, and then meet with your partner to review each other's criticisms and letters.

Next, switch roles and repeat the above procedure. If the first reply was favorable, make the second one unfavorable, and vice versa.

Finally, give the two sets of letters and the accompanying criticisms to your instructor for evaluation and grading.

EXAMPLES OF LETTERS OF INQUIRY AND REPLIES

Elmhurst Bakery

11 Cicero Street
Elmhurst, IL 60126

February 10, 19--

Plant Manager
Kellogg Bakeries
129 Blanck Street
Hazelwood, MO 63131

Dear Plant Manager:

Two weeks ago, while attending the American Bakers' convention, I
met Mr. Orville Wales, your plant superintendent, who mentioned
the participative management program you are using at your
company.

As plant manager for Elmhurst Bakery, I am now looking into the
possibility of introducing participative management into our plant.
You can help me by providing me with information about your
program. I would primarily like to know

1. What part does the character of the work force play
    in the success of such a plan?

2. How much resistance do employees show toward set-up
    changes?

3. How willing are employees to help in departments other
    than their own?

4. Is your program working as well as you had hoped? If
    not, in what way has it proved disappointing?

Thank you for any help you can give me.

Sincerely,

David L. Cobb

David L. Cobb
Plant Superintendent

DC/ma

Kellogg Bakeries
129 Blanck Street • Hazelwood, MO 63131

February 18, 19--

Mr. David L. Cobb
Plant Superintendent
Elmhurst Bakery
11 Cicero Street
Elmhurst, IL 60126

Dear Mr. Cobb:

We are gratified to learn of your interest in our participative
management program and happy to provide the following answers to
your questions:

   1. The character of our work force has had much to do with
       the success of our program. Hazelwood is a solid work-
       ethic community, a fact that has had an important bearing
       on worker reaction.

   2. On the whole, employees do not show any appreciable
       resistance to set-up changes. Being directly involved in
       management, they know in advance about any changes and
       the reasons behind them.

   3. Similarly, employees are willing to help out in depart-
       ments other than their own because they can see how such
       a contribution helps the entire plant.

   4. Yes, this program has worked every bit as well as we had
       hoped. The whole work climate is much healthier and more
       dynamic--so much so that production has increased 15
       percent.

The person chiefly responsible for setting up our program is
Mr. Robert Melin of Melin Management, Inc., 1819 Jones Street SE,
Grand Rapids, Michigan 49504. If you write him, I am sure he
will be able to give you detailed information about the participative management concept.

I hope that, if you adopt this type of program, it will work as
well for you as it has for us.

Sincerely yours,

Charles Taylor

Charles Taylor
Plant Manager

CT/sr

Discussion Questions

1. What formats do these letters follow? How can you tell?
2. Explain how these letters conform to the requirements for inquiry
   letters and favorable responses.
3. Explain these notations in the two letters:
   DC/ma
   CT/sr
4. Why does David Cobb's letter begin with the salutation "Dear Plant
   Manager?"

410 Main Street
Boise, ID 83424
November 26, 19--

Aquarium Filters, Inc.
162 South Main Street
Alhambra, MI 48702

Gentlemen/Ladies:

In October, I ordered your Model R-200 Aquari-Rite under-gravel
filter for my home aquarium.

About two weeks ago, the filter stopped bubbling and since that
time has not worked properly. To prevent the water from
becoming dirty and the fish from dying, I have had to change
the water every few days.

Because the literature you supplied with the filter does not
tell how to correct this problem, please supply me with
directions for doing so.

I would appreciate a reply as quickly as possible, for the
problem has resulted in serious inconvenience.

Sincerely yours,

John Beebe

~~~~~~~~~~~~~~~~Aquarium Filters, Inc.~~~~~~~~~~~~~~~~
162 SOUTH MAIN STREET
ALHAMBRA, MICHIGAN 48702

December 1, 19--

Mr. John Beebe
410 Main Street
Boise, ID 83424

Dear Mr. Beebe:

We are sorry to hear that the Aquari-Rite under-gravel filter
you purchased from us is not bubbling. Please don't be alarmed.
Occasionally bacterial growth will plug the air hose leading to
the filter. Here are several simple steps to clear the clog
without removing the filter from your aquarium.

   1. Separate the air hose from the air pump.

   2. Suck on the hose until the water in the tank has risen
       halfway up the hose. You may or may not see the clog
       at this point.

   3. Now blow forcefully into the air hose until you see
       bubbles coming from the filter. Repeat steps two and
       three if you can't see any.

   4. If this procedure does not work, the small stem on the
       filter is probably clogged, and you can open it by
       running a wire through it.

I hope this will solve your difficulty. If you have any further
problems, please call us collect at (717) 635-1424 between
8 A.M. and 5 P.M. Again, we are sorry for the inconvenience you
have suffered.

                    Yours truly,

                    Thomas Waun

                    Thomas Waun
                    Customer Relations Department

TW:net

Discussion Questions

1. Explain how these letters conform to the requirements for inquiry
   letters requesting directions and the replies to such letters.
2. Why does John Beebe use the salutation "Gentlemen/Ladies" in his
   letter?
3. Why do you think Thomas Waun ends as well as begins his letter
   with an apology?

239 Denton Drive
Waterford, WI 53474
October 18, 19--

Ms. Della McCarthy
Propagation Manager
Princeton Nurseries, Inc.
Box 501
Princeton, NJ 20113

Dear Ms. McCarthy:

I am enrolled in the ornamental horticulture program at Brett
Junior College, and for one of my courses I must prepare a report
on plant propagation methods.

While reading the July 19-- issue of Nursery Management, I noted
in the "Research Briefs" section that you have developed a new
water-immersion system of propagation. Can you help me by
providing me with information about it for my report? I am
especially interested in obtaining answers to these questions:

  1. How do the misting nozzles differ from those used
      with other misting systems?

  2. Can any water source be used, and if not how must the
      water be treated?

  3. How often is the foliage misted and what misting
      pattern is used?

  4. What rooting hormones proved most effective?

  5. Must the greenhouse be heated or is an unheated
      house satisfactory?

I would greatly appreciate your assistance and will be happy to
provide you with a copy of my report as soon as it is completed.

                         Yours truly,

                         Dennis L. Scanlon

                         Dennis L. Scanlon

_____**PRINCETON NURSERIES, INC.**_____
BOX 501 • PRINCETON, NJ 20113 • 609-924-1789

October 24, 19--

Mr. Dennis L. Scanlon
239 Denton Drive
Waterford, WI 53474

Dear Mr. Scanlon:

Thank you for your interest in our new propagation system.
Much as we would like to supply the information you wish, we
cannot do so. Just two weeks ago, our company signed a
contract with Norton Greenhouse Company, which plans to
further develop and then market the water-immersion system.
The lawyers involved have instructed both companies not to
discuss the system until a patent application has been filed.

To help you with your project, however, I am sending you two
reports that you might find useful. The first is by Dr. Robert
Blakely, the head of our research department; it deals with
root grafting compatibilities. The other is by Ms. Irma
Hardesty and describes our winter cutting operations.

Good luck with your paper, and please don't hesitate to write
again if you have questions about either report.

Sincerely yours,
PRINCETON NURSERIES, INC.

Della McCarthy

(Mrs.) Della McCarthy
Propagation Manager

DM/ro
Encl. 2

Discussion Questions

1. Explain why the notation "PRINCETON NURSERIES, INC." appears beneath the complimentary close of the Della McCarthy letter.
2. Why does the notation "Mrs." appear in parentheses before McCarthy's typed signature?
3. Show how the McCarthy letter conforms to the requirements for unfavorable responses.
4. Explain the "Encl. 2" notation in the McCarthy letter.

SALES LETTERS

A sales letter offers a product or service to selected individuals or organizations. If you work for a small company or are self-employed, writing sales letters may be part of your duties.

A successful sales letter must address the right audience persuasively. Mailing lists can be purchased from companies that group people according to their likely buying habits. Or you can develop your own lists from the names of your customers, the membership rosters of organizations, news items, and the like. For example, if you operate a photography studio, you might compile a list of yearbook advisers at nearby high schools or note the wedding announcements in your local paper.

A good sales letter does four things.

1. attracts attention
2. sparks interest in the product
3. convinces the reader that the product is the best available
4. motivates action

Before starting to write, ask yourself what features of your product or service will most likely appeal to your reader. Some possibilities include convenience, durability, economy, performance, appearance, safety, healthfulness, or status. Whatever you decide, make your message plausible and accurate. Wildly exaggerated claims arouse skepticism and could result in lawsuits.

Attracting Attention. Because sales letters flood the mail, many recipients pay little attention to them. Unless you catch your reader's attention right away, your efforts will be wasted.

You can use several techniques to gain attention. *The intriguing question*, one of the most common, prompts the reader to continue in order to find the answer. Here is an example.

Is there a thief in your car's engine?
Start of letter advertising an air filter

A second technique, the "*If . . . then . . .*" opening, also works well—provided the "if" part applies to the reader.

If you own or expect to own a home, securities, saving bonds, or other assets with your wife or someone else, you should know the drawbacks of joint ownership.

Start of letter by the Research Institute of America, Inc.,
advertising its weekly bulletin Recommendations

Beginning with a *quotation* is a third popular option. If you use it, be sure the quotation relates clearly to the subject of your letter.

There's an old adage that says, "Where there's smoke, there's fire." What better reason for buying our First Alert smoke detector?

Start of a letter by a home products
supplier to local homeowners

Yet another effective way to start is by *offering the reader a gift or some product or service at a savings.*

We at Michigan Bankard are pleased to present at no cost for the next six moths—that's correct—ABSOLUTELY FREE—a vital credit card protection service from the Hot-Line Credit Card Bureau of America.

Start of letter to Visa/MasterCard cardholders

Now you can own the latest edition of one of the finest dictionaries in print—and at the same time save $40. This giant reference work, over 2,300 pages long and more than 4 inches thick, was originally published at $59.95. But Barnes & Noble—the world's largest bookstore—is offering it to you for the incredibly low price of only $19.95. That's less than ⅓ the original publisher's price.

Start of a letter to Barnes & Noble customers

Salutations can also gain the reader's attention, and sales letters use a great variety of them. A letter to a prospective bookclub member might begin "Dear book lover," while one offering seat covers might begin "Dear new car lover." For more informality, the salutation often ends with a comma rather than a colon.

Whatever technique you select, keep your opening short. A lengthy beginning is uninviting and decreases your chances for a sale.

Sparking Interest. To interest the reader in purchasing your product or service, you can describe it, note its benefits, or both. The presentation may appeal deliberately to the reader's emotions or senses, or it may rely entirely on facts. The following example combines description and taste appeal.

> There are a variety of ways to enjoy Goodbee pecans . . . fresh, whole, and in the shell . . . Fancy mammoth whole halves . . . Pecan halves, slightly salted and roasted in pure, natural peanut oil . . . The divinity bar, rich and creamy candy smothered in fresh pecans . . .
>
> *Goodbee Pecan Plantations*

The following excerpt focuses on reader benefits and uses a factual approach.

> LIFE PLAN 55 PLUS is an uncomplicated whole life insurance policy that requires no medical exam or health questionnaire of any kind. If you're age 55 to 87 you cannot be turned down during this Guaranteed Acceptance Period . . . and your policy cannot be cancelled for any reason as long as you continue to pay your premiums.
>
> Furthermore, your premiums will never increase, and your benefits will never decrease. And cash values continue building after the first or second year, depending upon your age when you become insured.
>
> *Colonial Penn Insurance Company*

The same appeal can combine product features and benefits as well as blend facts and emotion.

Convincing. To convince readers that your product or service is worth purchasing, you may present facts, offer guarantees, or provide testimonials. The following example uses facts.

> Webster's Unabridged Dictionary has been a standard reference for more than 40 years. *The New Unabridged Twentieth Century Dictionary* continues that fine tradition and is one of the most complete and up-to-date dictionaries available today. Just look at what it contains:

- clear and accurate definitions for 320,000 words and phrases used in American English, including new additions to the language from physics, chemistry, biology, and other specialized fields;
- more than 3,000 black-and-white drawings;
- 32 beautiful pages of full-color illustrations;
- a complete collection of maps of the world;
- thumb-indexing for easy reference.

Barnes & Noble Bookstores, Inc.

Guarantees frequently help sell a product, assuring readers that they have nothing to lose by ordering.

Mother Nature blessed our small area of Georgia with ideal growing conditions for pecans. And because this is so, we can boldly and flatly guarantee all of our pecan products. If they are in any way unsatisfactory, you have our inviolate promise of either your money being refunded or a replacement order. Your option.

Goodbee Pecan Plantation

Testimonials—statements vouching for the merits of a product or service—can be persuasive provided they are accurate and credible. Large companies often use testimonials by movie stars, athletes, and other celebrities. However, the best testimonials are those offered by qualified individuals—for example, people who have tested or used a product.

"I really enjoy using *Yes*. The lightweight plastic bottle is easy to carry, and I love the springtime-fresh scent of my clean clothes!" says a letter we received just last month from Wilkes-Barre, Pennsylvania.

Texize Chemicals Company

Motivating Action. The conclusion of your letter asks the reader to take some action: purchase your product or service, request samples or more information, complete a questionnaire, or the like. To make responding easy, you can enclose an order form, allow customers to place orders through collect calls, offer to charge orders to credit cards, delay billings for a specified time, offer to provide a demonstration in the reader's home or workplace, and so forth. Include a postage-paid addressed envelope for responses by mail. If you want your readers to visit your place of business, supply directions for getting there. Here are several effective conclusions.

> To get your copy of *Webster's Unabridged Twentieth Century Dictionary*, simply fill in the enclosed order form and return it in the postage-paid envelope we've provided. If you are not absolutely convinced it's the finest dictionary you have ever used, you may return it for a full and prompt refund. So why not order a copy for your home or office today?
> *Barnes & Noble Bookstores, Inc.*

> For your convenience, we have enclosed an addressed, postage-paid card. Just indicate which evening would be most convenient for our representative to visit your home and give you our free landscaping analysis and cost estimate. And please accept the enclosed packet of geranium seeds with our compliments.
> *Local landscaping service*

> Visit our local office supply store and see for yourself how the Apple computer can help you to run your home more efficiently. Our trained, professional staff will be happy to answer all your questions and show you our fully equipped service center. With our special payment schedule, we can help you sink your teeth into an Apple.
> *Local office supply company*

This sales letter follows the typical pattern.

Opening attracts attention by combining intriguing question and free gift offer

May I send you two free issues of *The Country People?*

What's the catch?

There isn't any.

I've agreed to make this no-strings-attached offer because it's proven to be one of the best ways to get a certain kind of individual to try *The Country People.*

Sparks interest with factual information on contents of magazine

This kind of individual knows the satisfaction of self-sufficiency. In this magazine there's valuable how-to information on everything from solar energy and wind power to growing your own foods. And because nature is so close to the life you choose to lead, you'll find articles on wildlife, conservation, and outdoor activities for every season. The magazine also features hints on gardening and—to tempt your taste buds—recipes for delicious country cooking.

In short, *The Country People* is the most informative, no-nonsense country magazine on the market.

To take advantage of this opportunity, just return the enclosed card in the post-paid envelope. Send no money! I'll see to it that a 25-week trial subscription is started for you with two sample issues free.

Convinces by guaranteeing to cancel subscription if magazine proves unsatisfactory

If you're not completely sold on *The Country People*, write "cancel" on your subscription bill and pay nothing. You may keep the sample issues with our compliments.

If you decide to continue your subscription, just send us $19.95 and receive 23 additional issues.

Motivates action; order form accompanies letter to facilitate responding

As you can see, you have nothing to lose and a great deal to gain by taking me up on this special offer. So be sure to mail the enclosed order form right away.

Susan J. DeLaney

Exercise

Bring several examples of sales letters to class for a discussion of how they attract attention, spark interest, convince the reader of the product's or service's worth, and motivate action.

EXAMPLE OF A SALES LETTER

DENBY OFFICE SUPPLY COMPANY

129 SOUTH MICHIGAN AVENUE
GARY, INDIANA 46401

October 18, 19--

Dear Gary Office Manager,

Would you like to double the output of your stenographers and typists? Have your official letters and documents filed electronically, replacing bulky filing cabinets with small disk storage boxes? An MTR 8000 word processor can do these things for you, and it's available right here in Gary at the Denby Office Supply Company.

The MTR 8000 offers a totally different, totally superior approach to typing. Instead of reaching for typing paper and inserting it the way you would in a typewriter, you begin typing immediately. What you type appears on an easy-to-read screen that actually looks like a sheet of paper: full-size, with black characters on a white background. (The black-on-white screen is a major feature of the MTR 8000. Some competitive word processors have only a partial-page display on a green-on-green, computer-like background.) Because nothing is on paper yet, you can type at full rough-draft speed without worrying about typos and other errors. Mistakes are corrected easily right on the MTR screen. Words or paragraphs can be changed, added, or deleted, while the entire text is adjusted electronically. Only when the document is letter-perfect do you transfer it from the screen to paper. Just touch a button and the MTR 8000 printer produces a crisp original at the amazing speed of up to 540 words a minute.

<u>WHAT OTHER FEATURES MAKE THE MTR 8000 REMARKABLE?</u>

Everything you type on the MTR 8000 can be captured on small magnetic memory disks. Each disk holds up to one hundred business letters. Individual documents can be recalled to the screen in seconds. So you can update documents any time--as easily as you made corrections on the originals. With MTR's electronic filing system, you can replace <u>rows</u> of bulky filing cabinets with small disk storage boxes.

A new feature, found only on the MTR 8000 and other advanced word processors, is called "software programming." Preprogrammed disks allow you to prepare payrolls, keep ledgers, and handle bookkeeping and more. It's so simple that no special computer language or knowledge is necessary.

(continued)

- 2 -

EXECUTIVES AND SECRETARIES PRAISE THE MTR 8000

Although a comparative newcomer to the word-processing scene, the MTR 8000 has already won the warm acceptance of executives in hundreds of business offices. Here's what James Madigan of Adams Industries in Chicago writes: "I'm impressed. We got our MTR's just six months ago. Since then, they've almost doubled the output of our office workers and in so doing more than paid for themselves."

Secretaries are also strong advocates of the MTR 8000. They like it because it is easy to use, eliminates the drudgery of retyping to make simple revisions, and produces cleaner, crisper copy than any typewriter can.

Why not let us show you and your office staff just what an MTR 8000 can do for you? Just call 823-8100 and we'll be happy to arrange for a demonstration in your own office at any time that is convenient to you. Or if you prefer, you can stop by our store any weekday between 9:30 a.m. and 5:30 p.m. We're located just one block south of the new Mid-Gary Shopping Mall.

We look forward to meeting with you either at your place of business or ours and showing you why so many business people are turning to MTR 8000 word processor.

Sincerely yours,

Patricia Van Dyke

Patricia Van Dyke
Manager, Marketing Group

PVD/ol

Discussion Questions

1. What type of opening does this letter use?
2. Which paragraphs attempt to spark the reader's interest? Do they focus primarily on describing the product or on noting its benefits? What type of appeal does the letter make?
3. Which paragraphs attempt to convince readers of the product's worth? How does the writer accomplish this?
4. What techniques are used to motivate action?

CLAIM LETTERS

Writing claim letters is an unpleasant but necessary task in any organization and sometimes for private individuals as well. Claims arise for many reasons—orders may be improperly filled, packed, or shipped; merchandise may be damaged or substandard; or disputes may arise over terms of payment or pricing. The claim letter points out the problem situation and asks that it be corrected.

Courtesy may require special effort when you prepare a claim letter. Faced with a costly, time-consuming mistake, you may well feel anger and resentment; but avoid showing these feelings. Remember your aim—to obtain a satisfactory settlement. A tactful letter improves your chances of success and keeps the reader's goodwill.

Begin by telling exactly what happened and when, citing colors, sizes, model number, finish, or whatever else the reader must know to investigate and make an adjustment. If you have suffered inconvenience, mentioning it may help generate a sympathetic response, as may appealing to the organization's reputation for fairness and commitment to its customers.

Next, name the desired adjustment, backing your position with whatever supporting arguments are likely to sway the reader. Possible adjustments may include replacement of all or part of the merchandise, a partial or total refund, a discount, or new terms of payment. Perhaps you may also want to set a date for the settlement. To help speed action, you may enclose copies of orders, canceled checks, or other supporting documents. If so, make sure your letter has an enclosure notation. If appropriate, offer to return incorrect or faulty merchandise when the claim is settled.

End your letter courteously, perhaps by hoping for a quick settlement, offering to supply more information if it is needed, or commenting pleasantly on any past business dealings. Here is a typical claim letter.

Presents details of purchase	On March 20, I ordered one Campbell Model RN-530 HC-CO emission analyzer from your company, charging it to my account, number 365-18-003-6265. This item, usually priced

at $295.00, was listed at $265.00 in your latest sale catalog.

Presents details of
problem

Today, I received my monthly statement, but
instead of being charged the sale price I was
billed for the full amount.

States adjustment
desired

Please correct this billing error and send me a
new statement at your earliest convenience.
As soon as it comes, I will send you a check in
full payment.

If you are writing to a large company and do not know the
name of the department that handles claims, address your letter
to "Customer Adjustments Department" or "Customer Relations
Department." If the organization is relatively small, address it to
the "Sales Manager."

REPLIES TO CLAIM LETTERS

Replies to claim letters, like those to inquiry letters, may be
favorable or unfavorable. In either case, answer within one day, if
possible, to demonstrate that the problem concerns you. Maintain
a pleasant tone and avoid terms like *complaint* and *claim*, which
suggest that the reader is being a nuisance or that the request is
unjustified.

Favorable Replies. Begin by apologizing for the problem;
then tell what you are doing to correct it. Next, briefly discuss its
cause, if appropriate. Perhaps the problem occurred because the
company was switching to a computerized order-filling system.
Or perhaps a temporary malfunction in the assembly line resulted
in a faulty product. Whatever the cause, explaining it will help
reassure the reader that the problem will not reoccur. To maintain goodwill, end on a positive note. You might mention how
highly you value your business relationship, offer to deal with any
future problems, repeat your apology, or comment pleasantly on
something the reader has said. The following letter meets these
requirements.

Apologizes for problem and notes it is being corrected

Thank you for calling our attention to the error in our bill for the emission analyzer you ordered on March 20. We regret the mistake and are taking steps to correct it. You should receive the corrected bill in about ten days.

Explains reason for problem and assures there will be no future mishaps

Our sale brought an unexpectedly large influx of orders. As a result, our employees became rushed, and the one who entered your bill into the computer apparently failed to give you the discount. To prevent similar occurrences during future sales, we will supplement our staff with trained temporary help.

Offers to provide help with future problems

If any future problems occur, please do not hesitate to let us know.

James Davies

Unfavorable Replies. Gracefully refusing a claim presents a greater challenge than perhaps any other writing task. Your reader expects good news, but will receive just the opposite. You must therefore draft your letter carefully to retain the reader's goodwill.

Try to strike a harmonious note at the outset. For example, you may thank the person for writing, express regret over the problem, or agree with some statement in the original letter. Be careful, however, to avoid any impression that you will grant the adjustment.

Next, explain exactly why you must refuse the claim. For example, an investigation may have found that supposedly faulty merchandise was improperly used or maintained. In such cases, note the findings and tell how to prevent the trouble from recurring. To avoid suggestions of blame, which will only antagonize the reader, avoid expressions like *faulty care*, *misused*, and *improperly maintained*. Unwarranted claims for discounts, special credit terms, or refunds can be countered by pointing out that granting the claim would involve extra expense and be unfair to other customers.

Conclude as you began—pleasantly and, if possible, helpfully. Perhaps you can grant a special concession or provide some special service, thus softening the blow. Offers of future help are also effective. If you follow these suggestions, your letter may disappoint the reader, but it will also go a long way toward eliminating resentment.

The following example responds to a letter from a garage owner who had been forced to repeat repairs on several auto bodies when the filler failed. The garage owner wants the filler manufacturer to bear the cost of the repairs.

Begins pleasantly
without implying
claim will be granted

We agree that our P.Z.11 epoxy auto body filler should last much longer than a polyester body filler. For that reason we took immediate steps to determine why your problem occurred.

Rejects claim and
explains refusal

As soon as we received your sample of failed epoxy filler, I inspected it visually but could find nothing wrong, so I sent it to our New Jersey laboratories to be checked. There, our technicians found that an excessive amount of catalyst had been added when it was used. The ratio of catalyst to filler is very important. If excess catalyst is used, the filler is weakened, a condition leading to blistering and loss of adhesion. For this reason, we cannot reimburse you for the failure that you experienced.

Provides information
to prevent recurrence
of problem and grants
special concession

To help you avoid further difficulties of this sort, we are enclosing a booklet that lists the recommended catalyst-filler ratio for every filler we manufacture. And because we want you to continue using our products, we are also enclosing a certificate that will entitle you to a 30 percent discount on your next order with us.

Offers to answer
questions about
products

If you have any questions about any of our products, please feel free to call us collect at (906) 466–2207 between 8 a.m. and 5 p.m.

David Holmes

This writer has made a convincing case for the refusal, one that any fair-minded reader would find difficult to reject.

Exercise

1. Write a letter to the customer adjustments department of the Garcia-Mitchell Corporation, 111 Front Street, Bozeman, MT 88998, and note that you recently ordered a Model 408 open-faced spinning reel from them. After you had used the reel for just two hours, its gears started slipping when line was retrieved. Upon inspecting the reel, you found that the main gear had four broken teeth. Indicate that you are returning the defective reel with your letter and ask for a replacement.

2. Answer the preceding letter and refuse the claim. Point out that an inspection of the reel showed that the problem was caused by the use of too-heavy line. Refer to the owner's manual to support your position. Provide the address of an authorized service person who can replace the gear. End by expressing the hope that the reader will continue to buy Garcia-Mitchell products.

3. Your instructor may assign claim letters and replies to two-person teams whose members write back and forth and criticize each other's efforts. If so, you and your partner should first decide who will write and who respond to the initial letter. If you are the writer, prepare a list of possible topics, show them to your partner, choose one together, write the letter, and give it to your partner to criticize. If you are the recipient, prepare a written criticism of the letter, send a response, and then meet with your partner to review each other's criticisms and letters. Next, switch roles and repeat the above procedures. If the first reply was favorable, make the second one unfavorable and vice versa. Finally, give the two sets of letters and accompanying criticisms to your instructor for evaluation and grading.

EXAMPLES OF CLAIM LETTERS AND REPLIES

1816 Dupont Road
Mayton, IL   61327
October 11, 19--

The Clothes Horse
805 Main Street
Jamesville, OH   45335

Gentlemen/Ladies:

On September 5, 19--, while visiting relatives in Jamesville,
I purchased a beige-and-blue horizontally striped Toledo
sweater from your store.

After wearing it several times, I laundered it, but upon
removing it from the drier, I found that it had shrunk badly.
Although I tried to stretch it back to its original size, I was
unsuccessful. Because I can no longer wear the sweater, I am
requesting that you refund the $49.95 I paid for it. When I
receive the refund, I will return the sweater to you collect.

I hope to hear from you soon, as I am anxious to settle this
matter to our mutual satisfaction.

Sincerely yours,

Daniel Farmer

Daniel Farmer

THE CLOTHES HORSE
805 MAIN STREET
JAMESVILLE, OH 45335

October 15, 19---

Mr. Daniel Farmer
1816 Dupont Road
Mayton, IL 61327

Dear Mr. Farmer:

I want to thank you for shopping at The Clothes Horse and
buying a Toledo sweater. We appreciate your patronage.

In your letter, you ask for a refund because your sweater
shrank in the drier after you had laundered it. If you will
examine the care instructions on the label inside the collar,
you will see that they specify dry cleaning only. Therefore,
we are unable to grant the refund.

However, since The Clothes Horse does value your patronage,
we are enclosing a coupon that will entitle you to a five-
dollar discount on another Toledo sweater. Just mail it to
us along with a check for the remainder of the purchase price.

I hope that this solution meets with your approval and that
you will visit us again the next time you are in Jamesville.
I look forward to doing further business with you.

Sincerely yours,

Helen L. Hart

Helen L. Hart
Manager

HLH/nt

Discussion Questions

1. What information has Daniel Farmer provided to help in evaluating his claim?
2. In what ways does Farmer achieve a courteous tone in his letter?
3. Explain how the reply by Helen Hart conforms to the requirements for letters refusing claims.

**Johnston
Sales
and
Service** | 2359 South Street · Los Angeles, CA 90046 · (213) 439-6519

February 3, 19--

Customer Adjustments Department
Diesel Recon
145 Wayne Road
Austin, TX 78731

Dear Sir/Madam:

On January 24, we ordered twenty-four reconditioned barrels and
plungers (part number AA-40065) for PTD injectors. Today, the
order arrived, and we immediately used twelve of the units to
rebuild two sets of injectors for one of our customers.
Following our normal procedure, our technician installed the
reconditioned barrels and plungers and air-checked the injectors
on the ST34465 injector leakage tester. The manufacturer's
specifications call for a maximum leakage of 8 cc, but three of
the twelve failed at 10.0 cc, 10.5 cc, and 13.2 cc. We replaced
these with three others and completed the job.

Our schedule calls for us to use the other barrels and plungers
to repair another customer's injectors next Tuesday, February 10.
However, unless we get replacements for the defective items by
then, we cannot do so. To prevent us from having to delay the
job, and thus perhaps lose the customer's goodwill, please rush
three good AA-40065 barrels and plungers as fast as possible.
We are enclosing a copy of the invoice for our order and
returning the defective items under separate cover. We hope for
a speedy delivery of these items.

Sincerely,

David Johnston

David Johnston
Manager

DJ/co
Enclosure

DIESEL RECON
145 WAYNE ROAD• AUSTIN, TX 78731

February 5, 19--

Mr. David Johnston
Johnston Sales and Service
2359 South Street
Los Angeles, CA 90046

Dear Mr. Johnston:

We are very sorry to learn that three of the AR-40065 barrels
and plungers in your recent order proved defective. As soon
as your letter arrived, we checked, packed, and sent replacements to you via Emery Air Freight. They should arrive about
the same time that you receive this letter.

The problem occurred because we have recently started using a
new process of chroming worn plungers and then honing the
enlarged plunger to the exact size of the barrel. Some of the
worn plungers, including your three, were not properly cleaned,
so the chrome plating flaked off. Our workers are now
thoroughly familiar with the cleaning procedure, and I assure
you that the three we are sending you are within specifications.

We at Diesel Recon greatly value your business, and we hope
this mistake will not stop you from ordering from us in the
future.

Sincerely,

Elaine Rogers

(Mrs.) Elaine Rogers
Customer Service Department

ER/nt

Discussion Questions

1. David Johnston has addressed his letter to Diesel Recon's Customer
   Adjustments Department, but the signature on the answering letter
   indicates that Elaine Rogers is in the Customer Service Department.
   Explain the discrepancy.
2. What information has Johnston provided to expedite settlement of
   his claim?
3. Explain how the reply by Elaine Rogers conforms to the requirements for letters granting claims.

Suggestions for Writing

1. Write a letter of inquiry making one of the following requests.

   a. More detailed information concerning the procedures used in a project reported in a magazine or newspaper article
   b. Additional details concerning a safety program, employee-rating program, inspection system, time-study system, or traffic-routing system developed by another organization
   c. Performance data or specifications on a piece of equipment your organization might buy
   d. Clarification of an inadequate or ambiguous set of directions
   e. Detailed information concerning the pricing, credit, and discount policies of a company with which your organization might do business
   f. Information and data for a student research project or term paper
   g. Curriculum (or certification) requirements for a given career or profession

2. Write a reply to your own letter of inquiry, either supplying the information or refusing the request.
3. Write a sales letter offering to supply some product or service. Use whatever techniques are appropriate to attract the reader's attention, spark interest in the product or service, convince the reader of its worth, and motivate action.
4. Write a claim letter calling attention to one of the following and requesting an adjustment.

   a. An order that was improperly or incompletely filled
   b. An order that was delivered late
   c. Merchandise shipped by the wrong carrier or route
   d. Merchandise damaged in transit because of improper packing
   e. Substandard merchandise
   f. Improper billing for a recent order
   g. A request for a grade reappraisal and adjustment
   h. Faulty service or repairs on an automobile or a household appliance

5. Write a reply to your own claim letter, either granting or refusing the adjustment.

10

Memorandums

Memorandums (also called *memoranda* and *memos*) are short letters used within organizations to present data, schedule meetings and announce their results, suggest policy changes, request action, ask for recommendations, give directions, and perform a host of other functions. Many common types of reports—such as proposals, travel reports, progress reports, and investigation reports—may, when brief, be presented in memo form. The members of an organization keep one another informed primarily through memos. Occasionally, they may also pass between two organizations carrying out a joint enterprise.

Most memos deal with matters that require immediate attention. Generally, the topic is quite narrow. For example, you would use memos to announce meetings held as part of a research project but probably not to announce the research results.

The Value of Memos

Memos transmit information horizontally or vertically. With *horizontal memos*, the information flows between persons and departments of similar rank. With *vertical memos*, it travels up or down the organizational chain of command. The design engineer who asks the testing laboratory for tensile-strength data on a new copper-alloy wire is communicating horizontally. The company president who announces a more liberal vacation policy is communicating vertically down the chain of command. The superintendent who informs the president that a new filing system has been adopted for the company offices is communicating vertically up the chain of command.

The value of memos extends far beyond merely transmitting information. They can be used in the following ways:

1. *To maintain a permanent record of the course and outcome of meetings and other oral discussions.* Without such a record, the participants may later forget important details or disagree about what was decided.
2. *To transmit complicated material accurately.* The employee who must carry out a multistep procedure is much less likely to make an error if the instructions are presented by memo rather than orally. Similarly, transmitting detailed data by memo greatly reduces the chances that the receiver will misinterpret it.
3. *To communicate information to large groups of people* (such as the members of a department or the entire workforce of a company). Often, work schedules or the amount of worktime that would be lost rules out a meeting. By sending a memo to each person or posting it on bulletin boards, however, the writer can reach everyone easily and economically.

The Language and Tone of Memos

Memos range from informal to highly formal, depending on their purpose and the rank of the writer and reader. *Informal memos* feature everyday words and uncomplicated sentence structures, use personal pronouns generously, and do not shy away from contactions. As a general rule, horizontal memos and those passing down the chain of command tend toward informality, although especially important situations may dictate more formality. *Formal memos* feature longer, more complicated sentences, decreased use of personal pronouns, and the absence or near-absence of contractions. Memos going up the chain of command show greater formality.

Courtesy plays as important a role in memo writing as in writing business letters. It is achieved in the same ways: by writing from your reader's perspective rather than your own, avoiding insults and sarcasm, and presenting disagreeable information in a postive manner.

Pages 168–172 offer a detailed discussion of language and tone, together with illustrative examples.

Memo Forms

Because memos are so widely used, most large and medium-sized organizations provide printed memo forms for employee use. The most common memo size is 5 by 8½ inches, although other sizes are also used. A memo consists of two main parts, the *heading* and the *body*. Ordinarily, the heading includes lines for the sender's and receiver's names, the date, and the subject. Some memo forms also have lines for the departments of the sender and receiver, the sender's phone number, and the names of persons receiving copies. Also, some forms are imprinted with letterheads and/or the word *Memorandum*. Two examples are shown in Figure 10–1.

Unlike a business letter, a memorandum omits the complimentary close and typed signature. Some writers, however, put their initials after the typed signature in the heading or sign their memos at the end.

When a memo runs to more than one page, the headings for the additional pages are identical to those used for a business letter (see page 180).

Writing the Memo

In the heading, include your job title and that of your reader along with the names in order to provide more precise identification. If copies are being distributed, type the names of the recipients in alphabetical order or by organizational rank, with the highest-ranked person listed first. Make certain that the subject line accurately reflects what you are writing about. Otherwise, it

Figure 10–1.   Two Types of Memo Headings

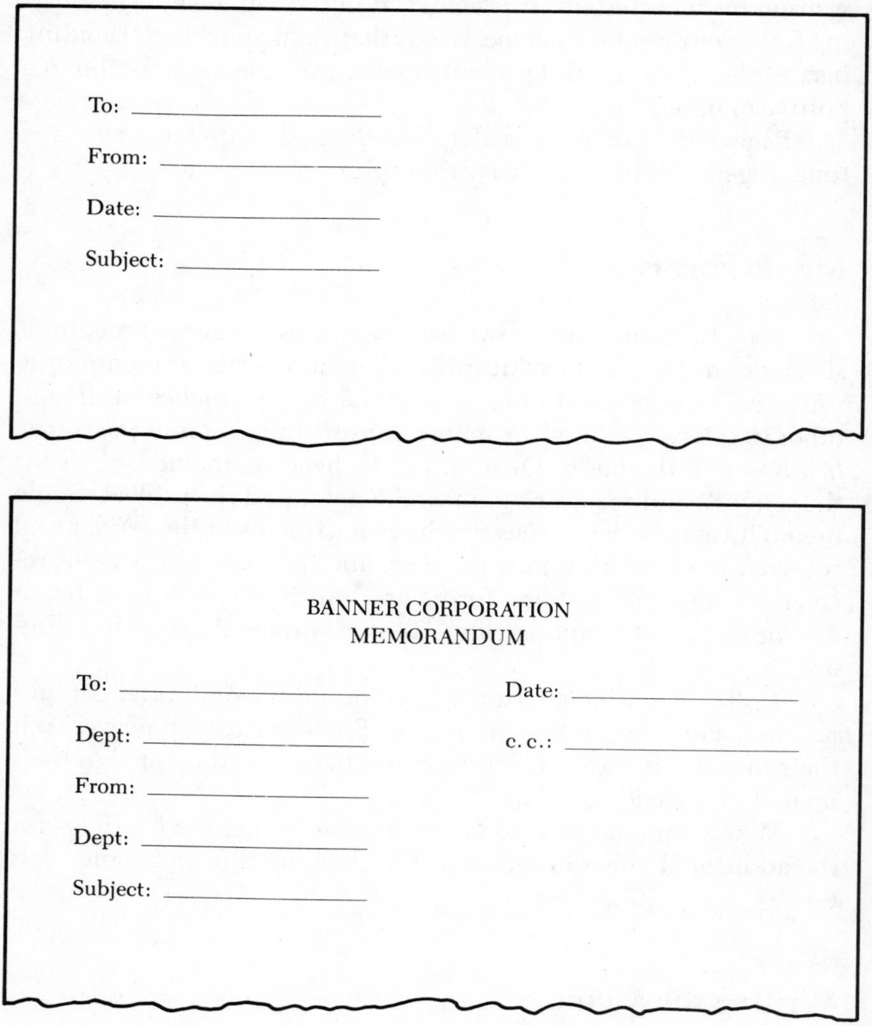

To: _____

From: _____

Date: _____

Subject: _____

BANNER CORPORATION
MEMORANDUM

To: _____   Date: _____

Dept: _____   c. c.: _____

From: _____

Dept: _____

Subject: _____

may mislead your reader temporarily or cause the message to go unread. For example, the subject line "Special Meeting" offers no clue to the nature of the meeting. Will the sender discuss plant safety? High employee absenteeism? Changes in a production schedule? Revising the subject line to "Special Meeting to Discuss

Changes in Production Schedule for Part CR-12" clears up the confusion.

Next, decide whether your memo needs an introduction. Often your reader will know enough about the subject so that the subject line provides the necessary background. If not, draft a brief introduction to prepare the reader for what follows. The content of the introduction will depend on the type and purpose of the memo. If you are announcing a change in some procedure, you might explain why it is necessary. If you are presenting the agenda of a forthcoming meeting, you might mention when, where, and why it will be held, as in the following example.

> Engineering has recently made a number of design changes in the Delta star unit. As a result, we must rework all the CPU boards in stock, retool our production line to modify parts produced in the future, and notify our customers of the design changes and their benefits. To deal with these matters, I am calling a special meeting of all department supervisors for Thursday, July 7. The meeting will be held in the East Conference room beginning at 1:30 p.m. The agenda is as follows.
>
> *Gregory Conti*

The body of the memo details what the reader needs or wants to know. The following list indicates the type of information you should provide in several common kinds of memos.

ANNOUNCEMENT OF AN APPOINTMENT: name of appointee and position; appointee's background and qualifications; duties of job if unfamiliar to reader

TRIP REPORT: name, title, and affiliation of each speaker or discussion leader; subject of discussion; conclusions, evaluations, or recommendations offered; significant exhibits, printed materials, and conversations with others in attendance

REPORT OF SAFETY VIOLATIONS: location and nature of each violation; unless the information is obvious, why it is dangerous and how to correct it

ANNOUNCEMENT OF NEW PRODUCT: properties; features; advantages; different forms

REPORT OF MINOR MISHAP: when, where, and why mishap occurred; results of mishap; steps to prevent recurrence of mishap

SETS OF DIRECTIONS: numbered list of steps, written as commands that include the articles *a*, *an*, and *the*, and presented in the order they are to be performed; mention of simultaneous steps; reasons step is necessary and warning against improper performance whenever reader may question the need for a step or perform it incorrectly.

Finally, decide whether you need a conclusion. Memos can conclude in numerous ways. Among the most common endings are those that offer to provide more information, that make recommendations, and that set starting dates for procedures and policies or deadlines for taking specified actions. Do not provide a conclusion unless one is clearly needed.

Some types of memos, including those already mentioned, are simple and require almost no writing guidelines. Others require detailed instructions. Chapters 11 and 12 discuss proposals, progress reports, and investigation reports, three complex types of writing that often take the form of memos.

Exercise

Write a memo announcing an opening for the position of welding line supervisor. This position is available because of the retirement of the former supervisor, John Walters. Application must be made within two weeks of the date on the memo, and the decision will be based on the attendance records, past performance, and leadership qualities of those applying. The supervisor will be responsible for keeping the welding line operating smoothly and for settling disputes among workers. The salary will be determined by the qualifications of the person chosen and renegotiated after nine months.

Examples of Memorandums

To: Elmira Postiff, Owner, Postiff Surveying Company
From: Jonathan Kobylarz, Supervisor, Crew Chiefs
Date: February 6, 19--

Subject: Attendance at State Convention, American Congress on
          Surveying and Mapping

As you suggested, I spent January 28 at the state convention of
the American Congress on Surveying and Mapping, where I attended
the three sessions that your preview of the program indicated
might provide us with useful information. Here are my comments.

9:00 A.M. - 10:30 A.M. Session

This session featured two speakers, William Ballenger of the
state Department of Licensing and Regulation, and Frank O'Meara,
a state representative, who discussed two legislative proposals
for revamping the licensing and regulation of surveyors and
surveying companies. Following their presentations, several
people in the audience offered comments, sometimes acrimonious,
from the floor. Accompanying this memo are copies of the two
proposed bills. When you have read them, you may perhaps wish
to write our state senator and representative regarding them.

10:30 A.M. - 11:30 A.M. Session

T. R. Tucker, Lands Division, State Department of Natural
Resources, described the survey of state lands that was conducted
during the 1840s. Tucker advised that the field notes from that
survey still exist and he handed out sheets that told how to
obtain them. These notes would serve us in good stead for perhaps half of this year's upcoming projects.

2:00 P.M. - 3:30 P.M. Session

At this meeting, Gary D. Lester, a registered land surveyor who
is with the Gillis County Surveyor's Office, reported on his
county's efforts to remonument all of the section corners in the
county. His report, which was very detailed, covered the cost of
monumenting, the special procedures that were employed, the
number of individuals involved and their titles, and the time
required to complete the project. Copies of Lester's talk will
be available in about one week, and I have asked him to send me
one. As soon as I get it, I will pass it along to you. The
information in it should enable us to remonument the eastern
half of Winnebago County more easily and inexpensively than we
otherwise could.

3:45 P.M. - 5:00 P.M.

Following the Lester talk, I visited the exhibit area and talked
with the representatives of several companies that had exhibits
there. Of all the surveying instruments on display, the Wild

Elmira Postiff   2   February 6, 19--

D13S Distomat interested me the most. This instrument, the most
versatile surveying unit on the market today, can measure
distances of over a mile and, at the push of a button, will also
measure vertical angles. Angles and distances are read from a
digital source. Best of all, perhaps, the Distomat is competitive in price with other measuring units. I have brought back
with me a copy of the owner's manual for the unit and would like
to review it with you. I think you'll agree that we should
seriously consider replacing all of our older surveying units
with the Distomat.

I strongly recommend that you preview the ACSM's convention
program next year and have someone attend any sessions that
appear promising.

                                        Jonathan Kobylarz

Discussion Questions

1. Discuss the adequacy of this memorandum's heading.
2. Show that the writer has done an adequate job of reporting on the convention.

To: Bernard Smith, Radar Maintenance Section Supervisor
From: Douglas Apsey, Safety Engineer
Date: October 1, 19--   *D.a.*

Subject: Safety Violations in Radar Maintenance Section

During my September 28, 19--, safety inspection of your section,
I observed a number of violations that require immediate corrective action.   Noncompliance with safety regulations endangers the
lives of the workers and may result in the destruction of equipment.   Therefore, in order for your section to continue operating,
these violations must be corrected within 30 days.

The most serious violation, and the one requiring the most urgent
attention, is the improper grounding of the AFP-960 radar trans-
mitter test console.   The cable now being used is too light in
gauge and is connected to the cable tray, which does not provide
adequate grounding.   This condition creates a serious electrical
shock hazard for technicians using the console and could result
in serious damage to the console.   This condition can be
corrected by running a 6-gauge copper cable from terminal 8 on
the main power panel of the console to the common ground of the
section's electrical system.   The exact grounding procedure is
described in the <u>AFP-960</u> <u>Radar</u> <u>Transmitter</u> <u>Test</u> <u>Console</u> <u>Instal-
lation</u> <u>and</u> <u>Maintenance</u> <u>Manual</u>, which you can obtain from the
shop's technical data file.

Another serious violation is the lack of rubber safety mats
around all of the test consoles.   Under regulation 6-12-73A, each
piece of electrical equipment must be surrounded for a distance
of three feet by an approved electrical safety mat.   I recommend
the mat manufactured by the Midwest Rubber Company, stock
number 3269-71-9356.

Finally, I noticed a number of personal violations by technicians in your section.   These violations included the wearing of
watches and jewelry around energized equipment, failure to wear
ear plugs in high-noise areas, and failure to consult technical
manuals when equipment was being repaired.   Each of these violations likewise represents a threat to employee well-being or
safety.

As section supervisor, you are responsible for insuring that
your personnel comply with company safety regulations at all
times.   I suggest that you monitor your section more closely and
stress the importance of complying with these regulations.   On
October 30, I will reinspect your section.   Please correct these
violations by then so that I will not have to suspend the
operation of your section.

Discussion Questions

1. Cite several ways in which Douglas Apsey achieves a courteous tone
in this memorandum.
2. What kind of conclusion has Apsey used?

MEMORANDUM

To: All Pruning Crew Foremen
From: Tom Foster, Superintendent
Date: April 30, 19--

Subject: Directions for Assembling New Bullhorse Chain Saws

As you will recall, the Parks and Recreation Department decided last fall to replace our old chain saws with the new Model X-15 Bullhorse chain saws. Yesterday, the new saws arrived, but only one set of assembling instructions was included. To permit you to start assembling the saws right away, I am reproducing the instructions here. If you follow them step-by-step, no problem should arise.

1. Remove the cover from the right-hand side of the saw by loosening the hex bolt with the Allen wrench included with the saw.

2. Place the blade arm with the two slotted holes over the stationary and moveable posts, which are located under the cover.

3. Next, unwrap the chain and slip one end around the clutch, making sure to seat the chain in the groove. The clutch is the small wheel-like part located just behind the stationary and moveable posts.

4. Place the other end of the chain around the entire blade arm, making sure to seat the chain in the groove.

5. When the chain is in place, put the cover back on the saw, making sure that the hex bolt is <u>not</u> tightened. Turn the bolt just far enough to hold the cover in place.

6. Lift the blade arm up and turn the adjusting screw clock-wise with a flat-bladed screwdriver. (The adjusting screw is located on the front of the saw just below the blade arm.) Continue to turn the screw until you can lift the chain easily and can see a one-quarter inch gap between the chain and the blade arm. You must lift the arm while adjusting if you are to achieve the proper tension on the chain.

7. Once the proper tension has been achieved, tighten the saw cover securely with the Allen wrench.

If you have any difficulty in assembling your saw, don't hesitate to get in touch with me right away.

Discussion Questions

1. Why has the writer provided an introduction?
2. Discuss the adequacy of the directions presented in this memo.

MERRILL CORPORATION
MEMORANDUM

To: Nora Johnson, Plant Superintendent

From: Robert Burtch, Safety Engineer

Date: December 21, 19--

Subject: Use of Defective Vehicles

On December 13, 19--, while making a delivery in Westville,
Michigan, one of our drivers passed through the Michigan State
Police Vehicle Inspection Point. The police found that the
brake lights on the truck were defective and issued a citation.
A memorandum reporting the defective lights was then relayed to
you and to John Anderson, head of Vehicle Maintenance. However,
due to the unavailability of parts and our shortage of trucks,
the vehicle was kept in service.

On December 20, 1981, this vehicle was involved in an accident at
the east end of the intersection of Oak and Maple in Westville.
While the vehicle was traveling east on Oak, a car pulled out of
a parking place and into its path. To avoid an accident, our
driver slammed on the brakes and stopped. Because the brake
lights did not work, the driver behind did not react soon enough
and collided with our truck. The damage to the truck was
estimated at $500, and the car was totally wrecked. We are
fortunate indeed that no one was injured.

To prevent similar occurrences, I suggest you issue a directive
informing all drivers that operating a defective company vehicle
is forbidden. If our own maintenance personnel are unable to
repair the vehicles, then we should contract with an outside
automotive repair shop. By taking these steps, we can prevent
accidents of the sort described above.

Discussion Questions

1. Does this memorandum represent a horizontal or vertical flow of information?
2. Two paragraphs are devoted to presenting background information and one short paragraph to presenting the writer's recommendation. Explain why.

Suggestions for Writing

Write a memorandum dealing with one of the following on-the-job situations.

1. Announcement of a meeting to discuss a new research project, advertising program, building project, or similar activity that will soon get under way. Outline several points that the meeting will cover and ask those attending to come prepared to talk about them.

2. Recommendation that employee lunch hours be staggered to prevent congestion in the cafeteria. Point out some of the problems congestion has caused.

3. Summary of the results of a meeting to discuss ways of coping with high employee absenteeism. Ask for employee comments.

4. Report that a procedure is being carried out incorrectly by employees. Point out the error and explain how the procedure should be performed.

5. Announcement of a change in the procedure for testing a particular material or product. Explain the new procedure and tell why the changes were made.

6. Request that the recipient inventory the laboratory stockroom, note any items that are out of stock, and order them. Ask the recipient to report by memo the result of the inventory.

7. Summary of safety violations in some organization or department and suggestions of ways of correcting them.

8. Announcement of a meeting to discuss some production, inspection, or shipping problem that has arisen. Explain why the problem is serious, give several possible solutions, and ask those attending the meeting to come prepared to discuss them.

9. Recommendation that your organization change a policy. List specific changes and tell why you think each is desirable.

10. Summary of several additional duties that an employee will be expected to perform. List the various tasks and explain how each is to be carried out.

11. Announcement that the development of a new device or product will be delayed at least two months. Give three reasons for the delay and indicate how you have tried to compensate for it.

12. Explanation of how to connect a tape deck to a stereo set, collect a potable water sample, turn an angle in surveying, test the resistance of some electronic device, trigger an oscilloscope, package some delicate device, charge a sale with a credit card, make some kind of report, or perform some other task in your field of study.

13. Report of your attendance at a convention, conference, or meeting.
14. Report on the features and performance characteristics of two devices your organization is considering buying. Conclude by recommending the purchase of one of them.
15. List the papers or reports already completed in your technical writing class and those yet to be done. Summarize briefly the contents of the ones to be completed.

11

Proposals

A *proposal* may (1) offer to provide a product or service or (2) suggest an action within an organization.

Proposals of the first sort, called *external proposals*, go to actual or potential customers, usually in response to a request. Depending on your organization's type of business, you may offer to construct an office building, paint a water tower, overhaul a heating system, survey viewers' tastes in television programs, conduct a time-motion study, prepare a service manual, or analyze the work-flow pattern in a factory, to name just a few possibilities.

Internal proposals, the second type, show similar versatility. You may, for instance, suggest that your company buy a new piece of office equipment, liberalize its vacation policy, establish a safety program, reroute traffic within the plant, or change a work procedure.

External and internal proposals use different formats and serve different purposes; therefore, we discuss them separately.

External Proposals

Many companies and government agencies specify elaborate guidelines for the proposals they will consider. However, for the

228

short external proposal of the sort you will probably write, a memo format will serve nicely. It can include all or most of the following sections:

1. Heading
2. Introduction
3. List of required items
4. Cost breakdown
5. Job schedule
6. List of supplementary materials
7. Conclusion
8. Appendix
9. Other parts

HEADING

The heading of an external proposal includes the name and position of both the sender and receiver, the date, and the subject. The subject line should be brief, yet describe the proposal clearly. Here is an example.

To: Jack Roth, Chair, Harper Creek Board of Education

From: Lawrence Quick, for Ceresco Locker Company

Date: January 23, 19--

Subject: Proposal to Install New Locker System in Varsity Locker Rooms

INTRODUCTION

Begin an external proposal by stating what you are proposing and its total cost, if known, as well as any noteworthy features of your product or service. In proposing to supply chairs for an airport lobby, you might emphasize their heavy-duty chrome-plated frames. In other cases, you might point out low installation costs, ease of operation, increased productivity, or high capacity. Note also when the project can be started and completed, as well as any limitations. For example, if you do not intend to finish the interior woodwork of a house you are proposing to build, say so. Unless the reader knows exactly what to expect, hard feelings, and perhaps even a lawsuit, may result. End the introduction with a brief statement designed to create a favorable impression. Examples include mentioning your firm's excellent reputation or your employees' skills.

Here is a complete introduction.

Ceresco Locker Company proposes to install 700 Safe-Lok heavy-duty ventilated lockers in the male and female varsity locker rooms at Harper Creek High School for the total price of $32,650. This locker system features heavy 16-gauge frames, backs, and shelves, and reinforced doors. The lockers are 6 feet tall, 30 inches wide, and 32 inches deep, with heavy-duty chrome plated handles and a maximum security locking device. The price includes assembling and floor-mounting the system with lug bolts. The installation will take our three-person crew four working days to complete, and they can begin work within ten days after you accept our proposal.

The Safe-Lok heavy-duty ventilated locker system has a 10-year warranty, but in actual practice, no system has ever had to be replaced in less than 20 years. Our company has been installing this system for the past 15 years without one customer complaint. I am sure that you will have no complaints either.

LIST OF REQUIRED ITEMS

The list of required items may include materials, equipment, and supplies, often accompanied by brief descriptions. Do not provide too much detail; rather, supply pamphlets of specifications if your reader needs extensive information. If the listing contains numerous items, put it in an appendix and indicate its location in the supplementary materials section. To continue with our example:

Locker shells — Rolled, formed 16-gauge channel frame with continuous strike, 13-gauge expanded metal mesh on sides, 16-gauge on shelves and back members.

Doors — Framed with 11-gauge angles, 13-gauge expanded metal mesh, three heavy-duty welded-on hinges, maximum security 3-point locking device.

Handles	Heavy-duty chrome-plated handles, mounted on 11-gauge handle plate with embossed padlock eye.
Closed bottoms	20-gauge steel fastened by rivets.
Sloping tops	45-degree angle, 11-gauge steel fastened by rivets.
Hooks	Chrome-plated steel; riveted inside lockers.
Lug bolts	Half-inch hardened steel 8-inch bolts.

COST BREAKDOWN

Include every expense that will be incurred, such as the cost of materials, equipment, supplies, labor, transportation, building fees and permits, inspections, and room and board. Overlooking any anticipated cost will cause hard feelings and possibly even legal trouble. If costs are numerous, summarize them in the body of the proposal and provide a detailed breakdown in the appendix.

Here is the cost breakdown section of our example proposal.

700 Locker shells ($21.50 each)	$ 15,050.00
700 Doors ($13.60 each)	9,520.00
700 Handles ($.98 each)	686.00
700 Bottoms and rivets ($3.50 each)	2,450.00
700 Tops and rivets ($4.50 each)	3,150.00
4200 Hooks ($.15 each)	630.00
2800 Lug bolts ($.09 each)	252.00
Labor (96 work-hours at $9.00/hour)	864.00
Delivery charges	48.00
Total cost	$ 32,650.00

JOB SCHEDULE

The job schedule should state exactly when each phase of the work will be carried out. Your customer can then plan around your activities, minimizing disruptions and slowdowns. The schedule for installing the high school lockers might read as follows:

Day 1   Bolt lockers into place and install bottoms—female varsity locker room.

Day 2   Install tops, doors and handles—female varsity locker room.

Day 3   Bolt lockers into place and install bottoms—male varsity locker room.

Day 4   Install tops, doors, and handles—male varsity locker room.

This schedule shows that each locker room will be unavailable to students for two days. If the work will not interfere with the customer's operations, you need not include a job schedule.

LIST OF SUPPLEMENTARY MATERIALS

This section names the materials accompanying the external proposal. These may include blueprints, pamphlets, specification sheets, price lists, and—if lengthy—the listing of required items. You may also want to furnish evidence of your firm's capabilities, such as reports describing similar successful projects or testimonial letters from customers. For the locker-installation proposal, the list of supplementary materials might read as follows:

Accompanying this proposal is a photograph of an assembled locker, a set of specifications, and a copy of the 10-year locker warranty.

Proposals without accompanying materials omit this section.

CONCLUSION

The conclusion for an external proposal should note how long the prices quoted will remain in effect. This information prevents future misunderstandings and—if prices are expected to rise soon—may speed the proposal's acceptance. You might also review your organization's qualifications for carrying out the project or suggest possible modifications. End by expressing your assurances that the work will prove satisfactory, offering to provide more information, and perhaps thanking the reader for considering the proposal. The conclusion to our example proposal is typical.

> The prices in this proposal will remain in effect until March 15, at which time the costs of the locker components will rise by 5 percent. If you need more information or have any questions, please call me at 796–4500. I am confident that the Safe-Lok heavy-duty ventilated locker system will serve your needs for many years to come.

APPENDIX

The appendix contains the items mentioned in the list of supplementary materials.

OTHER PARTS

Occasionally, a proposal to supply equipment may require a section discussing the resulting personnel requirements. With some nonroutine projects, it may be necessary to discuss the methods that will be used or to offer reassurances of feasibility. Personnel requirements, methods, and reassurances of feasibility are discussed on pages 240–241. Generally, such discussions follow the job schedule section.

Exercise

Choose a topic on which you are qualified to write an external proposal. Then, using the brainstorming technique discussed in Chapter 3, prepare a list of the details you will need to develop the proposal's parts.

Examples of External Proposals

Identifies receiver, sender, date, and subject of proposal	To:	Mr. and Mrs. Arthur Scoll
	From:	Harry Dreck, for Sanford Brother Heating, Inc.
	Date:	August 5, 19--
	Subject:	Proposal to Install Luxaire Furnace

Section Heading	*Introduction*
States what is being proposed and cost	Sanford Brothers Heating, Inc., proposes to install a new Luxaire Model B counterflow furnace in your house for the total estimated cost of $1,654.00. This estimate

Sanford Brothers Heating, Inc., proposes to install a new Luxaire Model B counterflow furnace in your house for the total estimated cost of $1,654.00. This estimate includes the furnace, duct work, gas piping, wiring, and one thermostat. The furnace is a compact model that has been designed for easy maintenance and that will provide clean, reliable, and economic heat. The entire installation can be completed in three days, after an agreement has been reached. We have been in business for over thirty years and pride ourselves on our top-quality workmanship. We are confident that you will be pleased with our work.

Section Heading

Introduction

States what is being proposed and cost

Names items included in cost figure

Presents noteworthy features of furnace

Notes how long job will take

Attempts to create favorable impression of contractor

Section heading

List of Required Items

Names and briefly describes required items

Furnace	One Luxaire 110 B.T.U. Natural Gas Furnace, Model B Counterflow
Ductwork	28-gauge sheet metal, 9 runs complete with registers
Chimney assembly	24-gauge double-lined flue with roof flange and weather cap
Thermostat	One Honeywell thermostat Model BK-100
Cold-Air returns	Four 5 × 13-inch in-floor units
Filters	Two 16 × 20 one-inch-thick fiberglass filters
Gas line	32 feet of 3/4-inch Schedule 40 black iron pipe with shut-off valve
Wiring	6 feet of armored wire complete with three-lead plug and box

Section heading

Cost Breakdown

Furnace $ 690.00

Includes all costs
project will incur

Associated items (ductwork,
chimney assembly, thermostat,
cold-air returns, filters,
gas lines, wiring)   475.00

Labor (24 Work-hours at
$17.00/hour)   408.00

Permit and inspections   81.00

Total cost $1,654.00

Section heading

List of Supplementary Materials

Notes items
accompanying
proposal

   These include specifications for the fur- 2
nace, a brochure describing its operation,
and a certificate of warranty covering any
mechanical defects for 10 years.

Section heading

Conclusion

Indicates how long
price will remain in
effect, offers to
answer questions,
thanks recipient for
considering proposal

   The price indicated in this proposal will 3
remain firm until September 15, 19--. If you
have any questions regarding this proposal,
please feel free to call me at 697–4901. Thank
you for the opportunity to be of service to
you.

To: Frank Lamintino, Owner, Club Paradise
By: William U. Sturm, Owner, Sturm & Son Cleaning Ser-
           vice
Date: September 24, 19--
Subject: Proposal to clean carpeting in Club Paradise

Introduction

Sturm & Son Cleaning Service proposes to clean the entire   1
carpeted surface at Club Paradise for the total price of $1,000.00.
This service will not interfere with the club's operation. Cleaning
would begin on a Sunday morning and be completed in seven
hours. The carpets will be totally dry by 9 P.M. on Sunday. We
can do the job any weekend following your acceptance of this
proposal.

Our company utilizes the latest in high-technology carpet   2
cleaning equipment. Our powerful steam-cleaning unit removes
95 percent of the moisture it applies. During the steam-cleaning
process, we hand brush carpet cleaner into the carpet, which not
only removes deep-rooted dirt and stains but also acts as a groom-
ing aid and helps to restore the pile to its original condition. The
final step is to apply a carpet protector that will increase the life
of your carpet by as much as 20 percent.

We have been cleaning carpets in this area for over 20 years   3
and enjoy an outstanding reputation for the quality of our work. I
am certain that our results will please you, too.

Cost Breakdown

20 gallons Z-50 carpet cleaner at $5.50/gal.	$ 110.00
10 gallons carpet protector at $9.50/gal.	95.00
Labor: 35 work hours at $10.00/hour	350.00
Profit	445.00
Total cost	$ 1,000.00

List of Supplementary Materials

Accompanying this proposal are photographs showing car-   4
pets before and after we have cleaned them.

Conclusion

The prices indicated in this proposal are not expected to in-   5
crease until after the first of next year, but after that time may
rise by 5 percent. If you have any questions or require any additional information, please feel free to call me at 492–0127. We
appreciate the opportunity to serve your needs.

Discussion Questions

1. Show how the heading of this proposal meets the requirements given in this chapter.
2. Why has the writer omitted a list of required items?

Internal Proposals

Internal proposals, which address problems within organizations, offer solutions, and note the resulting benefits, can include all or most of these sections.

1. Heading
2. Introduction
3. Statement of the problem
4. Recommendations
5. List of supplementary materials
6. Conclusion
7. Appendix
8. Other parts

For short internal proposals, the statement of the problem and the recommendations can be included in the introduction.

HEADING

Internal proposals have the same four-part heading as external proposals.

To: James Murniak, Owner, Ace Body Shop
From: Michael R. McKay, Service Manager
Date: May 2, 19--
Subject: Proposal to Replace our Present Spray Paint Booth

INTRODUCTION

The introduction should state exactly what is being proposed. Often, the costs will not be known, but when they are, note the total. Here is the introduction section to the preceding proposal.

I propose that our shop purchase one Nova Verta 2000 downdraft spray paint booth. This booth will cost approximately $49,000, which includes installation, Nova Verte's new filtration system, and a 10-year warranty.

STATEMENT OF THE PROBLEM

In this section, specify the problem and its consequences and establish that a solution is needed. Sometimes a discussion of the problem's history can help. To continue with our example proposal:

> In the last year, the quality of our paint jobs has decreased markedly because of the age of our paint booth, which is now 20 years old. Dust and dirt leak between the door and door frame, contaminating the paint as it is applied to the cars and making it necessary to repaint many of them. Furthermore, the energy efficiency of the booth is steadily decreasing because the heat exchanger is wearing out. In the last eight months, our repainting costs have totalled $10,400, and during this same period excess energy costs have topped $3,000. Because our present model booth is no longer made, the parts needed to restore it to full operating efficiency are no longer available.

Often you can support your case by presenting statistics, opinions, or personal experience. To be useful, statistics must be adequate. Do not use the results of a one-day traffic count to argue that a certain corner needs a traffic light. Your employer might reject the results as nontypical. To make a strong case, you would need to continue the counts for several days. Note that the statistics in the preceding example cover eight months.

Opinions may represent the thinking of trained experts or of untrained persons who have firsthand experience with the issue. In proposing that your factory install dust-control equipment, for example, you might cite statements by the plant physician and also by workers who have suffered respiratory problems.

Your own experience can sometimes outweigh any other type of support. Suppose you were once severely injured by a tornado and are now proposing that your plant establish a tornado-warning system. By describing your injury and lengthy hospitalization, you might influence management's decision more than you could in any other way.

RECOMMENDATIONS

In the recommendations section, offer your suggestions for correcting the problem. To bolster the proposal, try to mention one or two advantages that it would provide. Here, too, statistics, opinions, or personal experience may prove useful, as may the experience of other organizations. For example, if you want your company to purchase a certain piece of equipment, you might mention how it benefited some other company. The recommendation section of our example proposal is typical.

> The Nova Verta 2000 downdraft spray booth will eliminate our current painting problems. This spray booth is more advanced than any other on the market. It has the only filtration system that eliminates harmful fumes without the use of paint filters. The system pulls paint overspray from the air and into water ducts, thus greatly reducing maintenance problems and expenses. The average energy cost per car with the Nova Verta system is $3.00, as compared to our present cost of $10.00 per car.
>
> Last spring, Al's Body Shop in Carrollton purchased a Nova Verta booth. Since then, no cars have had to be repainted, and energy costs have dropped 65 percent. I am sure we will enjoy similar results.

LIST OF SUPPLEMENTARY MATERIALS

As in an external proposal, this section lists the materials accompanying the proposal. Page 230 explains what the listing may include, and the following example illustrates such a section.

> Accompanying this proposal is a brochure that includes sections on specifications, operation, maintenance, and safety, together with a photograph and a detailed internal diagram of the unit. In addition, I have included the telephone number of the nearest dealer and a copy of the manufacturer's warranty.

CONCLUSION

The conclusion offers you a final chance to sell your proposal. To do this, you might restate its benefits, note the consequences of adoption or nonadoption, or mention the ease of carrying the project out. You can also offer to meet with the reader, provide more information, or help in whatever way you can if the proposal is adopted. The conclusion to our example proposal has several of these elements.

The Nova Verta 2000 downdraft spray paint booth is exactly what our body shop needs. The booth will pay for itself in approximately three and one-half years while delivering top-quality performance. The manufacturer's 10-year warranty and extensive servicing network make this a no-lose deal. If you have any questions, I will be happy to discuss them with you at your convenience.

APPENDIX

The appendix contains material that supplements the information in the body of the proposal. All materials in the appendix should be mentioned in the list of supplementary materials section of the proposal.

OTHER PARTS

Occasionally, a proposal will require one or more additional sections. When used, they are positioned after the recommendations section.

Discussion of Methods. Discuss the methods of carrying out the project whenever they will be unfamiliar to the reader. Generally, this discussion will be necessary only with special studies or surveys, research projects, or important changes in an organization's operations. Develop each step or test specifically, and provide details on any necessary designs, blueprints, flowcharts, or similar materials.

Assurances of Feasibility. If the reader might doubt the feasibility of the proposal, offer reassurances, such as laboratory findings, information about a similar successful project, or any other convincing data. Except for highly unusual projects, assurances are not needed.

Personnel Requirements. Most internal proposals do not require a list of personnel. When one is needed, however, it should indicate the number of employees who will be involved in the project, their departments, and, if necessary, their names. Management can then evaluate and compensate for shifts in personnel. If new employees will be needed, give their number and qualifications.

The following example notes the personnel needed to operate a proposed telecommunication system.

Two technicians will be required to maintain, program, and operate the system. As noted in the introduction, we will provide the needed training. Two telephone operators will also be needed to operate the system's consoles.

Bernard Schwartz

Cost Breakdown, Job Schedule. Occasionally, an internal proposal must include a cost breakdown, job schedule, or both. If so, follow the guidelines on pages 230–31.

Exercise

Choose a topic on which you are qualified to write an internal proposal. Then, using the brainstorming technique discussed in Chapter 3, prepare a list of the details you will need to develop the proposal's parts.

Examples of Internal Proposals

Identifies receiver, sender, date, and subject of proposal

To: Jack Nesmith, President, Dayton-Hudson Corporation
From: Katherine Nelson, Vice-President for Planning and Development
Date: February 2, 19--
Subject: Proposal to Purchase IBM 38-41EF Computer System

Section Heading

Introduction

States what is being proposed and cost

I propose that our company purchase one IBM 38-41EF computer system, four IBM 38-41EF monitors, four IBM 38-41EF keyboards, one IBM 38-41EF printer, and the associated program software. Four monitors and keyboards will enable all four of our top executives to use the system simultaneously. This equipment will cost approximately $21,500.00, a price which also includes software, installation, and four training sessions.

Section Heading	*Statement of Problem*

Indicates the difficulties stemming from lack of computers

As you know, I have been conducting a study of managerial efficiency within our firm. This study shows that our lack of a sophisticated computer system has seriously handicapped our managers in conducting marketing studies as well as carrying out such day-to-day activities as arranging meetings, preparing copies of reports, and making airplane reservations. Within the last six months, our Marketing Research Department has failed to meet deadlines for completing twelve out of a total of fourteen studies. These delays have ranged from two weeks to over six weeks. As a result, several very important studies that should now be under way have had to be postponed.

Section Heading	*Recommendations*

Repeats recommendation and notes an advantage of computer system

The 38-41EF computer system and its associated equipment will solve our present difficulties. This computer is IBM's newest system. It lets users draw upon information from both corporate and noncorporate data bases. Because of the speed with which it performs calculations, executives can play "what-if" games with figures to see how changes in various pricing or cost components could affect production costs and sales.

Myrna Barnes of Pfizer Pharmaceuticals uses such a computer to analyze pricing, competitive product lines, and promotional allocations. A typical study might look at the potential impact of a 50 percent cut in promotion for a Pfizer product. To develop such a study, the Pfizer executive would search the computer's memory to determine how a competitor that had tried a similar strategy fared in the marketplace. If the executive had to consult market research books, the search would take weeks. With the 38-41EF computer, it is completed in a matter of an hour or so.

Benjamin Heineman, President of Northwest Industries, uses his company's 38-41EF computer to call up information on current or past performances of Northwest subsidiaries, along with comparative industry and economic information from outside data bases. The computer allows him to notice anything out of the ordinary—for example, an unusual pattern in production—and take whatever corrective action is warranted.

Clearly, the 38-41EF computer system is an extremely versatile and useful marketing tool.

List of Supplementary Materials

Accompanying this proposal you will find copies of my study and of the Pfizer and Northwest Industries reports from which I obtained the information cited in the preceding section. In addition, I have included brochures and specification sheets for the components of the 38-41EF system.

Conclusion

The IBM 38-41EF system is just what we need at Dayton-Hudson. With this system,

Margin notes:

Provides an example of a "what if" game and points out its utility

Notes, through an example, a second advantage of the system

Section Heading

Notes items accompanying proposal

Section Heading

Makes final argument for adoption of proposal

Paragraph numbers: 5, 6, 7, 8

our managers will be able to make decisions by combining information developed within the company with outside data bases, including economic and industry statistics. Such data will allow our managers to put together studies—complete with easy-to-understand charts and graphs—of markets, competition, pricing, and forecasts in a few hours, studies that now take months of work.

Offers to discuss proposal   If you have any questions, I will be glad   9 to meet with you at some convenient time.

Submitted to: Wilbur R. Budd, Executive Vice-President
From: Wendell Moore, Personnel Director
Date: May 1, 19--
Subject: Proposal to Create Van Pool for Employees

Introduction

I propose that our company purchase five three-quarter-ton   1 passenger vans in order to form an employees' van pool. The total cost of purchase will be between $55,000 and $56,625. The exact amount will depend on the make of vehicle chosen.

Statement of Problem

As you know, our present parking facilities are woefully in-   2 adequate, and we have no room for expanding them. Many employees must therefore leave their vehicles in commercial parking garages or lots and walk long distances to work. This situation has given rise to considerable employee discontent and has helped create a serious tardiness and absentee problem which has at times led to a disruption of our operations.

Recommendations

As noted above, five vehicles will be needed. The vehicles I   3 propose will have power steering, power brakes, a seating capacity of 10 exclusive of the driver, and the ability to get not less than 27 miles per gallon.

Within the last two years, the West Bend Corporation and 4 the Sun Company have successfully established similar pools. In each case, absenteeism and tardiness have been reduced by nearly two-thirds. Assuming we achieved the same reductions, our annual savings would be about $10,000 per year.

The idea of a van pool has been well received by all the em- 5 ployees with whom I have discussed it, and putting my proposal into effect will undoubtedly improve management-employee relations.

Costs

The estimated cost per vehicle and total cost of all vehicles 6 are given in Supplement A. These costs, less the estimated discount and including taxes, total $55,500 for the least costly vehicle and $56,625 for the most costly. These figures are only estimates, and bidding should lower them.

Supplement B indicates the weekly gasoline expenses for each 7 vehicle, assuming the proposed pickup routes are adopted, while Supplement B-1 shows total weekly gasoline expenses. Since the routes differ in length, the gasoline costs likewise differ. Total gasoline cost for the vehicles is $18.30 per week.

Supplements C and C-1 show the estimated weekly income 8 from the vehicles, after gasoline expenses are deducted. The income after gasoline expenses amounts to $401.70. Supplement C-2 calculates the final yearly income after all expenses have been deducted. This final income comes to $19,688.40.

Method

The county will be divided into five areas, each serviced by a 9 different van. Each area will have a central pickup point with an ample parking lot for employee cars. These lots will be checked hourly by the Sheriff's Patrol, so parked cars will be safe from vandalism. The vehicles will be placed in charge of our regular motor-pool personnel, who will maintain a log book containing a record of miles driven, gasoline and oil costs, and other maintenance expenses. Vehicles will be operated by present personnel from our driver pool. Each driver will spend about three hours per day busing employees.

This proposal not only offers the advantages mentioned ear- 10
lier but will establish our company as a leader in fighting city air
pollution.

List of Supplementary Materials

Accompanying this proposal are detailed cost and income es- 11
timates for this project.

Conclusion

The estimated costs for vehicles apply to this year's models 12
only. Late this summer, when next year's models come out, costs
will undoubtedly rise. I therefore urge quick approval of the proposal. I realize the proposal may generate questions, and I am
ready to provide any additional information you may wish. Call
me anytime at ext. 275 or, if you like, I will be happy to meet
with you in your office whenever you wish.

Appendix

Supplement A: Vehicle Cost Estimate

Vehicle type	Chevrolet	Dodge	Ford
Standard cost, including tax	$11,800	$11,600	$11,900
Less estimated discount	− 550	− 500	− 575
Total estimated cost	$11,250	$11,100	$11,325
Number of vehicles purchased	× 5	× 5	× 5
Estimated total cost (tax & license inc.)	$56,250	$55,500	$56,625

Supplement B: Maintenance and Expense Estimate

Vehicle number	1	2	3	4	5
Miles traveled per day	9	14	17	21	24
Days per week used	× 5	× 5	× 5	× 5	× 5
Total miles per week	45	70	85	105	120
Divided by average mpg	÷ 27	÷ 27	÷ 27	÷ 27	÷ 27
Total gallons per vehicle per week	1.7	2.6	3.2	3.9	4.5
Average price per gallon	$1.15	$1.15	$1.15	$1.15	$1.15
Gasoline cost per week per vehicle	$1.96	$2.99	$3.68	$4.49	$5.18

Supplement B-1: Total Weekly Gasoline Cost

Vehicle 1	$ 1.96
Vehicle 2	2.99
Vehicle 3	3.68
Vehicle 4	4.49
Vehicle 5	5.18
	$18.30

Supplement C: Estimated Income Provision

Vehicle number	1	2	3	4	5
Number of passengers	7	8	9	9	9
Cost per week to passenger ($0.40 per day × 5)	$10.00	$10.00	$10.00	$10.00	$10.00
Gross income per vehicle	$70.00	$80.00	$90.00	$90.00	$90.00
Less gasoline per week	− 1.96	− 2.99	− 3.68	− 4.49	− 5.18
Income per vehicle after gas	$68.04	$77.01	$86.32	$85.51	$84.82

Supplement C-1: Total Net Weekly Income

Vehicle 1	$ 68.04
Vehicle 2	77.01
Vehicle 3	86.32
Vehicle 4	85.51
Vehicle 5	84.82
	$401.70

Supplement C-2: Total Net Yearly Income

Weekly income after gasoline expense	$ 401.70
Times 52 weeks per year	× 52
Total	$20,888.40
Less estimated expenses (oil, antifreeze, maintenance, etc.)	− 1,200.00
Final income after deducting all expenses	$19,688.40

Discussion Questions

1. What kinds of evidence does the writer use to support this proposal? Where is each kind found?
2. This proposal is quite long, yet it is clear and the reader can follow it easily. Show how clarity has been achieved.
3. Why is the conclusion effective?

Suggestions for Writing

1. Write an external proposal offering to do one of the following.

   a. Design an interdisciplinary course, an advanced placement test, or an independent study course for a college or technical institute
   b. Paint a house or some other structure
   c. Study the traffic-flow pattern of a campus or industrial plant and suggest improvements
   d. Redecorate an office or a room in a private residence
   e. Buy a generator, furnace, or some other piece of equipment
   f. Install a sewage or water system for a single-family dwelling
   g. Compare the cost and performance characteristics of two furnaces, drying ovens, refrigeration systems, or other devices or systems
   h. Run comparative tests on two or more adhesives, coatings, fibers, castings, or other materials or products
   i. Provide outside secretarial or stenographic services to some business firm
   j. Design a system to control dust, chemical vapors, noise, or radiation in a laboratory or other facility
   k. Investigate the effects of water pollution on a lake or stream
   l. Conduct a survey to determine public attitudes toward a local political candidate or an existing or proposed ordinance
   m. Develop and carry out a sales campaign for a local department store

2. Write an internal proposal making one of the following requests.

   a. Your company stagger its work hours or change its vacation policy

b.   Your town switch to a different type of traffic light, rezone a particular section of town, or spray for mosquitoes

c.   Your school extend the library hours, change its grading system, or provide expanded parking facilities

d.   Your company improve its lighting, reduce the noise level, install vending machines, provide an employee lounge, or develop a new traffic-flow pattern

e.   Your office reorganize its filing system

f.   Your office adopt job-sharing

g.   Your apartment-house owner install a security system

h.   Your English instructor permit you to conduct research and write a paper on a topic of your choice

i.   Your school reevaluate its policy on student parking, its course offerings in your major field, or its intramural athletic program

j.   Your school provide a post-office mini station, typing service, exercise facility, book exchange, picnic area, or some other facility or service

k.   Your school redesign the traffic patterns on campus to provide safer conditions or better traffic flow

12

Other Professional Reports

Progress reports and investigation reports rank among the most versatile and useful forms of on-the-job writing, being used in almost every field. This chapter explains how to write them.

Progress Reports

Progress reports trace the development of a project or the activities of an individual or organization. The project may be carried out for a customer or within the writer's own organization. Progress reports are written in every field and for projects of all sorts. For example, your employer might ask you to summarize the following:

1. The progress of a laboratory or research project.
2. The progress in the construction of a building, dam, bridge, or highway.
3. The course of an advertising or public-relations campaign.
4. The stages in the remodeling of a building or other facility, or in the installation of new machinery or equipment.
5. The activities of your organization over a six-month or one-year period.

6. The progress of an in-service training program (for management trainees) or of an on-the-job educational program.

Progress reports are valuable for several reasons. By reading them, project directors know when each new phase of a project is expected to start and can make sure equipment and supplies are on hand when needed. Progress reports also allow managers to alter the direction and emphasis of a project. Suppose early reports show that a compound being tested as a soil fumigant and a grain fumigant is ineffective for the first application but better than expected for the second. Knowing this, managers can stop work on the first application and expand it on the second. Furthermore, when a project cannot be completed within budget, progress reports provide advance warning. Managers can then increase the budget or cancel the project and save the unspent money. Similarly, progress reports can prevent last-minute crises caused by project delays. If a supplier's strike has delayed completion of a dormitory beyond its scheduled fall opening date, progress reports would give college officials sufficient time to make other arrangements for housing the students.

Progress reports help the writer as well as the reader. Without them, you may waste time on unimportant aspects of a project or even forget a primary aim, causing delays or the repetition of some work. Each new progress report forces you to reconsider your aims, thus preventing these types of problems.

Depending on the project, progress reports may appear weekly, monthly, quarterly, annually, at some other set interval, or irregularly—such as when major steps in the project are completed. With a few exceptions, such as sales reports and the annual reports issued to company stockholders, progress reports are written for projects with definite completion dates. One- or two-week projects seldom require reports. For complex projects, progress reports may extend to dozens or even hundreds of pages. For simple projects, though, a memorandum format like the one shown here works nicely.

PARTS OF PROGRESS REPORTS

A typical progress report has two parts: a heading and a body. The first report in a series also includes an introduction.

Heading. The *heading* of a progress report is identical to that of any other memorandum except for the final line, which shows the time period covered by the report. Do not give the dates for the entire project. This heading for a restaurant inspection report is typical.

To: Jack Powers, Commissioner, Monroe County Health Department

From: Paul Lewis, Sanitarian, Monroe County Health Department

Subject: Progress Report on Improving Restaurant Inspection Scores in Monroe County

Time Covered by Report: January 1, 19-- through January 1, 19--

Introduction. The *introduction* presents the background and goals of the project, notes its completion date, and points out any special requirements, such as specifications, that must be met. In addition, the introduction should note any special test materials needed as well as any limitations that must be observed. If the project involves only a few people, the introduction customarily includes their names. As changes in personnel occur, future reports note them. Here is the introduction to the restaurant inspection report.

This is the first progress report on our department's program to improve the overall scores of restaurant inspections. A survey showed that Monroe County had the worst restaurant inspection scores of any county in the state. The average at that time was 30 points, but Monroe County's average was 42.

To correct this situation, the present program was put into effect January 1, 19--. The program aims to lower the average inspection score for the county to 30 and to eliminate all scores over 40 by January 1, 19--. It involves doing these things:

1. inspecting restaurants more frequently and enforcing the food code more stringently
2. establishing mandatory management certification programs for restaurant managers
3. establishing a cooperative board of sanitarians, restaurant owners and managers, and restaurant employees to coordinate the program and deal with any problems that arise

Body. Although the practice varies, the *body* of most progress reports includes three sections.

1. *Work completed*—what has been done since the last report; that is, during the time period indicated in the heading of the report.
2. *Present status*—where the project stands as of the second date in the heading.
3. *Work remaining*—what will be done during the next reporting period and those following it.

When there are long intervals between reports, it is useful to summarize the activities of the previous reporting period or the state of the project at that time. Do this in a paragraph at the beginning of the body. A typical example follows.

> During the last reporting period, all remaining drainage structures were installed, the interior concrete floors were poured, and the underground electrical connections were completed. In addition, the housing for catch basin C-B 14 was rebuilt after its accidental destruction by a caterpillar operator, and two defective sections of the water main were replaced.
>
> *Donald R. Burgin*

The complexity of the report determines whether you should include headings to identify each section. Brief reports that discuss present status in one or two sentences can omit headings entirely. Most other reports, though, should include them.

Ordinarily, you need identify only the processes that have been carried out. However, unfamiliar ones may require you to provide some details of the procedure or refer readers to a separate explanation. If problems have occurred or the project has fallen behind schedule, explain what happened and how the problems have been or will be corrected. When the evidence warrants, do not hesitate to recommend changing the direction of a project or even abandoning it. If more materials, equipment, and supplies will be needed, ask for them. Finally, do not hesitate to offer cautious predictions about the outcome of the project or the chances of finishing it on schedule.

Position your information at appropriate places in the body of the report. For example, discuss unfamiliar procedures in the

"Work Completed" section and predictions in the "Work Remaining" section. In some cases, you may need to include tables and graphs. However, use such devices sparingly so they do not interfere with the discussion. Position tables and graphs at the end of the report but discuss them in the body. The body of the restaurant inspection report illustrates many of these points.

Work Completed

This program has now been in effect for one year. During this period, restaurants were inspected every three months rather than semiannually, as in the past. The average inspection score has been reduced 6 points below the 19-- figure. Much of the improvement is due to the increased strictness of the inspectors, who were instructed to suspend the license of any restaurant that scored over 40 points on two successive inspections. Once this fact became known, most restaurant owners quickly complied with the food-service code.

The first mandatory management certification course got under way on June 2, and the first meeting of the cooperative board was held on July 1.

Present Status

The management certification program is off to a good start; over 30 restaurant managers have completed the two-month course. This training has already resulted in the elimination of many food-code violations.

Because of the rapid turnover of restaurant employees, the cooperative board has been without an employee representative for five of the six months it has been in existence. Without the employee voice, the board has become largely a management-health department group. As a result, many employees believe their opinions are not wanted and refuse to work with the board. A public-relations consultant has been called in to work on the problem.

Work Remaining

During 19--, we hope to reduce the average restaurant inspection score by another 3 points. To help achieve this goal, we plan to continue inspecting restaurants on a quarterly basis and to suspend licenses whenever more than 40 points are scored on two successive inspections. By the end of the year, some 90 restaurant managers—about one-half the total in the county—will have completed the management certification program.

ORGANIZATION BY TASKS

Reports on complicated projects involving several simultaneous activities should be *organized by task* rather than by time. Arranged in this way, a report on the construction of a large apartment complex would have such main headings as "Plumbing," "Wiring," and "Heating." Within each major section, however, the discussion should follow a past-present-future pattern.

Exercise

Using the brainstorming technique discussed in Chapter 3 (see pages 36–38), prepare a list of specific details needed to write a progress report on a project you are supposedly carrying out.

EXAMPLES OF PROGRESS REPORTS

Identifies receiver, sender, project, and time covered by report

To: Ronald Beatty, Chairperson, Onaway County Chamber of Commerce

From: Mary M. Schwartz, Leader, Clean-Up Crew

Subject: Progress Report on Onaway Back-to-Nature Cleanup Project

Time Covered by Report: May 15, 19-- through June 15, 19--

Introduction

Provides background information

On May 15, the Onaway Chamber of Commerce announced that it was sponsoring a campaign to clean up the camps and recreational facilities in the Presque Isle area and asked for twenty-five high-school-student volunteers. On May 18, these volunteers met with representatives of the Chamber, chose a   1

Indicates details of project

leader, and received details of the project. The project will include four sites: Camp Norwood, Ocqueac Falls recreational facility, Ocqueac Falls hiking trails, and Tomahawk Campground. The participating students will receive extra credit in high school biology and be paid $4.00 per hour. The project is scheduled to be completed on August 15.

States deadline date

Heading

Work Completed

Discusses past activities; written in past tense

Work has been completed at Camp Norwood. Each campsite was first cleared of debris, raked, and mowed; then the beaches were also cleared and raked and the latrines disinfected and painted. Finally, the posts marking each campsite were repainted as were the signs marking the entrances to the campsite.

2

Heading

Present Status

Discusses present activities; written in present tense

Volunteers are now working at the Ocqueac Falls recreational facility, where operations are proceeding on schedule. All objects that pose a hazard to swimmers are being removed from the swimming area, and the crew is varnishing the picnic tables as well as restoring the fire pits. Completion of this phase of the project will also involve repainting the campsite posts and signs and cleaning up the parking lot.

3

Heading

Work Remaining

Discusses future activities; written in future tense

We will complete work at the Ocqueac Falls recreational facility in about one week; then we will turn our attention to the Oc-

4

queac Falls hiking trails. There, we will remove debris from the trails and the surrounding woods and once again repaint signs.
Approximately ten miles of trails will be covered.

Finally, the back-to-nature cleanup   5
crew will move to Tomahawk Campground,
where it will carry out the same tasks as at
Camp Norwood and in addition will enlarge
the beach area by clearing small trees and
underbrush from about 100 feet of shoreline.

Indicates deadline
date will be met
If we continue to maintain our present   6
schedule, we should finish the project by our
deadline date.

To: Kimberley Gillette, Professor of Engineering
From: Ronald Jones, Student
Subject: Progress Report on Design of Pump No. P10400
Time Covered by Report: January 30, 19-- through
February 28, 19--

On January 30, you supplied Christopher Lichty, Kurt   1
Myers, and me with specifications for a small pump and asked us
to design a pump that would meet them. The pump is to be constructed as an integral unit that is driven by a belt and pulley
powered by a small air-cooled engine. Its height must not exceed
10 inches, and its weight must be less than 10 pounds. It must be
capable of delivering 10 gallons per minute at 550 revolutions per
minute, and its parts must withstand a maximum pressure of 400
pounds per square inch. The pump is to be designed and drawn
by April 30.

On February 1, the group decided in a brainstorming session   2
that a positive displacement pump would be adequate to meet the
required specifications. Cast 1013 aluminum was selected as the
material of construction for most parts because of its low cost and
ability to withstand vibration. Two pistons, each with a diameter
of 1¾ inches and a 1-inch stroke, will provide an even displace-

ment. The cylinder walls be be ⅛ inch thick—a thickness easily capable of withstanding the 400 psi load specified. Rough sketches of the internal assembly are now being drawn.

Two major parts of the pump must still be designed. I will $_3$ design the type and size of valves needed to produce the correct volume of flow, while Myers will determine the size of the shaft and its material. Finally, Lichty will design the other parts required. These determinations will be completed by March 5, and further analysis of the design will be completed within three weeks thereafter. Final assembly and detail drawings will then be started, and they will be finished by the April 30 deadline date if everything goes as planned.

Discussion Questions

1. Why does this report include a discussion of the project's background?
2. In which paragraphs does the writer discuss work completed, present status, and work remaining? What techniques besides paragraphing are used to distinguish between these three segments of the report? Why is the present status not discussed more fully?
3. Why have headings been omitted from this report?

Suggestions for Writing

Write a progress report on one of the following projects.

1. A research, design, or construction project carried out as part of a course
2. The reorganization of the floor plan of some retail business establishment or small shop
3. The construction or remodeling of a store or house
4. The reorganization of a factory assembly line
5. The resurfacing of a section of roadway
6. A sales campaign for a local store or other business
7. A public immunization campaign
8. The remodeling of a laboratory or X-ray facility in a hospital
9. A local fund-raising drive
10. The installation of machinery in a shop

11. The installation of a furnace or air-conditioning system in a commercial building or private house
12. The activities of a professional or student organization
13. The reorganization of a town's traffic-flow pattern
14. A survey being conducted among the citizens of a community
15. Your progress in one of your courses
16. A program to improve the safety of a shop or laboratory
17. The landscaping of an office or a home
18. The installation of a sewage disposal system or electrical wiring system for a trailer park
19. A campaign to recruit new members for a campus organization
20. The renovation of a house or commercial building
21. The expansion of a shop, store, greenhouse, or other facility
22. Your progress in writing a library research report, carrying out a term project, or obtaining a summer internship
23. Your progress in obtaining the degree, license, or other credentials needed to pursue your career

Investigation Reports

An *investigation report* describes and evaluates the results of a test or other inquiry carried out in the laboratory, shop, or field. Unlike a library research paper, which depends largely on published material, the investigation report relies on data developed or gathered by the writer or writer's colleagues.

This type of report helps an instructor gauge how well you have mastered the apparatus, procedures, theory, and calculations involved in the investigative work. It helps you to reinforce what you have learned, and it familiarizes you with this format of on-the-job writing. Investigation reports are used to improve products and procedures, to correct undesirable conditions, and to take other types of appropriate action.

PARTS OF INVESTIGATION REPORTS

An investigation report may include all or most of the following parts.

1. heading   5. results
2. purpose   6. discussion of results
3. theory   7. recommendations
4. procedure   8. appendix

Heading. The *heading* of most investigation reports follows the typical four-part memorandum format shown earlier in the chapter. Here is a heading for a report on a water sample.

To: Jan Winkelman, Director, County Health Department
From: Walter Barrons, Student Intern
Subject: MPN—Presumptive Test, Oxbow Lake
Date: September 1, 19--

Purpose. In stating the *purpose* of the report, identify precisely what has been tested. For example, if you are running tensile strength tests on aluminum and brass wire, give the formal designation for each alloy—aluminum AZ 210 and brass B 12—and tell why the investigation was carried out. Four or five sentences at most should do. Here is the purpose section of the water-sample study.

> The purpose of this study was to determine the most probable number (MPN) of coliform organisms present in a sample of water taken from Clear Lake in Dale Township. The department conducted the study because several cases of dysentery have recently been reported by persons who own cottages on the lake.

Theory. The *theory* is the underlying principle that makes the investigation possible. Generally, procedures in chemistry, physics, and the other sciences rest on some clear principle, whereas nonscientific procedures do not. Any report on a scientific procedure should include a theory, unless the reader already knows it. Science instructors often ask students to include a theory to demonstrate their knowledge of the principle. Here is the theory section from the water-sample report.

> The coliform group of bacteria is capable of fermenting lactose sugar to form gas. The presence of gas in an inoculated tube

indicates that coliform organisms were present in the water sample; the number of tubes showing gas provides a measure of the degree of contamination.

Procedure. The *procedure* section of the report explains how the investigation was carried out. When writing it, do not try to produce a set of directions for readers to follow. Rather, just give enough information to provide readers with a general idea of the procedures involved. A few sentences are generally adequate. The procedure section of the water-sample report follows.

> Five lactose-broth tubes, each containing a smaller inverted tube, were inoculated with 10 ml. of the water sample under sterile conditions. The tubes were then incubated at 35°C for 48 hours and examined for evidence of gas formation.

Results. The *results* are the findings of the investigation. They may consist of the actual measurements, readings, or observations or of figures derived from them by means of a formula, chart, or graph. In the latter case, the section should include everything used to arrive at the results as well as the results themselves. Here is the results section of our example report.

Observations

tube no. 1—gas
tube no. 2—no gas
tube no. 3—gas
tube no. 4—gas
tube no. 5—no gas
The MPN Index was then calculated from the following chart.

Number of Tubes with Gas	MPN Index/100 ml. Sample
none	less than 2.2
1	2.2
2	5.1
3	9.2
4	16.0
5	infinite

Since three tubes showed the presence of gas, the most probable number of coliform organisms was 9.2/100 ml. of the water sample.

Sometimes the results include so many individual measurements that putting them in the body of the report would interfere with the flow of the text. In this case, divide the measurements into several equal groups, average each group, cite the averages in the body of the report, and list the individual measurements in an appendix.

Discussion of Results. In the *discussion of results*, the findings are evaluated and their significance pointed out. Depending on the investigation and its purpose, you might:

1. Compare your findings with some standard and try to account for any difference.
2. Point out how well one or more materials meet the requirements for a particular application.
3. Indicate whether a certain condition exists.
4. Note the need for more work.

The discussion section of our example report indicates that further investigation is needed.

Although the results show an MPN Index of 9.2 coliforms/ 100 ml., this presumptive test indicates only the presence or absence of gas production, and it is possible that the gas produced in the tubes was due to some other type of organism capable of fermenting lactose sugar to form gas. Additional and more precise tests are therefore required before a definite conclusion can be reached.

Be sure to note any gaps or irregularities in your data and any defects in measurement, and to discuss their possible effects on the results.

Recommendations. If the results will decide some future course of action, include a *recommendations* section in the report. Because most student reports do not lead to any future action, they do not usually include recommendations. However, on-the-job reports almost always make some recommendation.

The recommendations will depend, of course, on the investigation. You might, for instance, recommend that your organization do one of the following.

1. Replace one material, process, or device with another.
2. Take a product off the market or start selling a new one.
3. Overhaul a piece of equipment.
4. Expand the investigation by carrying out certain clearly specified additional work.

Here is the recommendations section of our example report.

> Confirmation and completion tests should be carried out on samples of the water to obtain positive proof that the gas produced in this test was generated by coliform organisms.

Cost often determines the recommendation. For instance, if one test material meets the requirements for an application and a second but more expensive test material surpasses the requirements, the less expensive material might well be recommended for use.

The discussion and recommendations are often combined in a single section, especially if both are brief (see the example on page 265).

Appendix. The *appendix* contains material that supplements information given in earlier sections of the report. The appendix may include these types of supplementary material.

Test data too detailed to include in the body of the report
Mathematical calculations used in preparing the report
Brochures, bulletins, letters, and reports
Drawings, graphs, maps, photographs
Field, laboratory, and shop notes
Case histories
Equipment lists
Specifications

When the appendix includes more than one type of material, group and label each type separately. Mention appendix material at appropriate points in the body of the report.

EXAMPLES OF INVESTIGATION REPORTS

Identifies receiver, sender, subject, and date of report

To: Edward Gein, Supervisor, Vernon Tool and Die Company
From: Randall Stroup, Foreman
Subject: Comparison of Borazon and Aluminum Oxide Grinding Wheels
Date: May 5, 19--

Heading

Purpose

Indicates precise purpose of test

Indicates what prompted work

Omits theory: test not dependent on clear underlying principle

The purpose of this test was to compare the wheel life of Borazon grinding wheels and aluminum oxide grinding wheels, which are now used in our shop. The work was prompted by growing dissatisfaction with the present wheels.

1

Heading

Procedure

Provides sufficient information to understand the procedure but not to repeat it

Two different tests were carried out, each involving one wheel of each type. The first test consisted of grinding fifty one-half-inch diameter two-flute end mills. The two wheels were set up on identical Cincinnati cutter grinding machines in accordance with the manufacturer's specifications and the parts ground in the standard manner. The second test was performed on the Deckel Pantograph cutter grinder, using two new wheels. Each wheel was used to grind seventy-five single-point cutters, again following standard procedures. After each test, the two wheels were measured with a mi-

2

crometer to determine the amount of wear, and the percentage of wheel life used was then calculated.

| Tabulates findings of tests | **Results** |

Results

Test No.	Wheel Type	% Wheel Life Used
1	Borazon	10
	Aluminum Oxide	60
2	Borazon	15
	Aluminum Oxide	68

Heading

Discussion and Recommendations

Evaluates results by comparing percent of wheel life used

Test results reveal that the Borazon 3
wheels are greatly superior in performance to the aluminum oxide wheels. The latter showed six times as much wear as the Borazon wheels in the first test and four times as much wear in the second test. Furthermore, the Borazon wheels required much less wheel dressing, a feature that saves operator time and increases production rates. Although

Assesses performance in light of costs

Borazon wheels cost three times as much as their aluminum oxide counterparts, their performance far outweighs the price disadvantage.

Recommends course of action

I therefore recommend that our tool 4
room switch to Borazon grinding wheels.

To: Willard Holden, Service Manager
From: Otis Barnes, Mechanic
Subject: Oil Consumption Test
Date: June 24, 19--

Purpose

This test was conducted to determine whether the 305-cubic-   1
inch V-8 engine in the 1988 Chevrolet Caprice owned by Mrs.
Alice Palovitch was burning enough oil to justify engine repairs
under the terms of its warranty. The owner requested the test because she suspected excessive oil consumption.

Procedure

Before the test was begun, the oil pressure was checked, the   2
PCV Valve System was evaluated, the engine was thoroughly
cleaned and checked for oil leaks, the oil and filters were
changed, and the mileage was noted. During the next 2,000 miles
of driving, the owner brought her car into the service department
whenever it needed oil. The oil was added, and the mileage was
noted. When the 2,000 miles had been driven, the oil consumption rate was calculated.

Results

The results obtained when the above procedure was followed   3
are shown below.

Miles Driven	Quarts of Oil Added
650	1
1,325	1
2,000	1

Discussion of Results

These results show that the engine burned an average of one   4
quart of oil every 667 miles. According to the engine specifications, however, the oil consumption should not exceed one quart
every 800 miles. Consumption is therefore excessive.

Recommendations

It is recommended that the intake manifold gasket, guide   5
valve, and guide valve seals be checked, a wet-dry compression

test be run, and any faulty condition be corrected under warranty.

Discussion Questions

1. Comment on the adequacy of the heading. Support your comments with specific evidence.
2. Note that this report does not include a statement of theory. Why is the omission justified?
3. Why has the writer of this report omitted an appendix?

To: Malcolm O'Reilly, Director of Research and Development
From: Thomas Gauthier, Test Engineer
Subject: Road Testing Radial Highway Tires Model XT-225
Date: April 9, 19--

Purpose

This work was carried out to test the mileage capability of   1
our newly developed Model XT-225 radial highway tire. The
study is the first segment of a field-testing program designed to
determine whether or not our tire is equal or superior in wear-
ability to the corresponding models made by our three competitors. Laboratory testing had previously shown the XT-225 to be
slightly superior in wearability to the others.

Procedure

The National Bus Company was contacted and agreed to   2
participate in the tests. One set of our tires was installed on a bus,
and one set each of Ace T-34, Mercury R-29, and All-Grip M-40
tires was placed on three other buses. Each of these buses operated on the same 350-mile run.

The tires were inflated to the manufacturers' recommended   3
pressures, the depth of the tread measured with a dial indicator,
and the average depth calculated for each of the four models. After 7,000 miles, the depth of tread was again measured, and the

number of miles required to produce each one-thousandth inch of wear was calculated (see Appendix).

Results

Tire	Miles per One-Thousandth Inch of Wear
XT-225	79.9
Ace T-34	80.1
Mercury R-29	78.6
All-Grip M-40	79.5

Discussion and Recommendations

Test results show our XT-225 to be slightly inferior in wear-ability to the Ace T-34 tire but slightly better than the Mercury R-29 and All-Grip M-40.

It is recommended that the remaining phases of the field-testing program and the safety-testing program, outlined in report 23-597RHT, be carried out. Preliminary market research and pricing studies should also be initiated as soon as feasible.

Appendix

Tire Tread Wear Data

Make of Tire	Tire Number	Original Tread Depths, Thousandths Inch	Final Tread Depths, Thousandths Inch	Difference, Thousandths Inch	Average Difference Thousandths Inch
	1	500	416	84	
	2	500	410	90	
	3	500	412	88	
XT-225	4	500	412	88	87.6
	5	500	414	86	
	6	500	415	85	
	7	500	411	89	
	8	500	409	91	

Tire Tread Wear Data (continued)

Make of Tire	Tire Number	Original Tread Depths, Thousandths Inch	Final Tread Depths, Thousandths Inch	Difference, Thousandths Inch	Average Difference Thousandths Inch
Ace T-34	1	501*	413	88	
	2	499	415	84	
	3	500	416	84	
	4	502	414	88	87.4
	5	503	411	92	
	6	500	413	87	
	7	505	420	85	
	8	501	410	91	
Mercury R-29	1	504	415	89	
	2	501	415	86	
	3	504	411	93	
	4	502	411	91	89.0
	5	497	409	88	
	6	496	404	92	
	7	503	416	87	
	8	501	415	86	
All-Grip M-40	1	498	413	85	
	2	498	410	88	
	3	497	407	90	
	4	502	411	91	88.1
	5	503	419	84	
	6	497	406	91	
	7	496	407	89	
	8	503	416	87	

*Variations probably occurred because tires were made in different molds.

Calculation, Miles per One-Thousandth Inch of Wear

XT-225
$$\frac{7000}{87.6} = 79.9$$

Ace T-34
$$\frac{7000}{87.4} = 80.1$$

Mercury R-29
$$\frac{7000}{89.0} = 78.6$$

All-Grip M-40
$$\frac{7000}{88.1} = 79.5$$

Discussion Questions

1. Discuss the adequacy of the procedure section of this report.
2. Why does the report include an appendix?
3. Do the average values presented in the results section accurately reflect the value of the individual measurements from which they were derived? Support your answers with specific evidence.

Suggestions for Writing

Write an investigation report on work carried out to determine one of the following problems or situations.

1. The traffic flow pattern on a campus or in a trailer park
2. The attitude of a town's voters toward a particular candidate or proposal
3. The pricing practices of the merchants in a small town
4. A problem in your campus's physical plant
5. The reaction of students at a college toward a proposed change in some campus regulation
6. The adequacy of the recreational facilities in a town
7. The performance characteristics of one or more personal computers
8. The stability of transistor bias circuits or the effect of a diode in a simple AC circuit
9. The validity of Ohm's Law, the transformer turns equation, or some other equation
10. The concentration of particulate matter in air
11. The specific heat of aluminum, brass, or some other metal
12. The most probable number of organisms in water or a standard plate count on milk
13. The normality of an acid or base, the identity of a chemical compound, or the aspirin content of aspirin tablets
14. The maximum density and optimum water content value for a soil
15. The acreage of a parcel of land
16. The moisture content of aggregate for concrete
17. The nitrate and detergent levels in sewage effluent
18. The cylinder pressures, oil pressure, or dwell angle for an automobile

19. The physical characteristics of two or more adhesives, coatings, fibers, castings, or other materials or products

20. The performance characteristics of two furnaces, drying ovens, refrigeration systems, or other devices or systems

13

Abstracts

An *abstract*—sometimes called a summary, precis, or synopsis—is a condensed version of the main points made in a piece of writing or oral presentation.

The ability to abstract is a necessary skill. When you take lecture notes, underline the important points in a text, or summarize passages for a library research paper, you are performing part of the abstracting procedure. When you combine underlined passages and several weeks' lecture notes into a writeup to prepare for an exam, you complete the process.

In school, an instructor may ask you to summarize the plot of some piece of fiction, the contents of an article, or a textbook chapter. On the job, your supervisor may ask you to summarize the contents of a report, an article, or a chapter in a book or to write the abstract of a long report. And when you attend a talk or meeting, note taking helps you capture the essence of what you hear.

Abstracts are vital to the functioning of any large organization. Without them, executives could not begin to cope with the flood of reports that crosses their desks. During a single week, these reports might number in the dozens, many of them lengthy and all requiring some sort of action. Abstracts reduce an otherwise impossible reading task to manageable proportions. The executive merely reads the abstracts and then routes each report to the appropriate person, perhaps reserving a few to handle personally.

Further, abstracts allow professionals at all levels to keep up with new developments in their fields. Thousands of technical and professional journals are now published in the United States and elsewhere, and each year they print several million articles. To impose order on this enormous mass of information, numerous *abstract journals* are published. These journals subdivide the articles published in fields like chemistry, economics, and education, making it easier for interested readers to locate them. Some of the more important abstract journals are listed here.

Abstracts in Anthropology
Abstracts of English Studies
Abstracts of World Medicine
Biological Abstracts
Chemical Abstracts
Education Abstracts
Employment Relations Abstracts
Engineering Abstracts
Geological Abstracts
Geophysical Abstracts
Highway Research Abstracts

International Aerospace Abstracts
Journal of Economic Abstracts
Library Science Abstracts
Mathematical Reviews
Mineralogical Abstracts
MLA (Modern Language Association) Abstracts
Nuclear Science Abstracts
Psychological Abstracts
Science Abstracts
Social Science Abstracts
Sociological Abstracts

Types of Abstracts

Two types of abstracts are widely used—descriptive and informative.

A *descriptive abstract* names the topic of the original piece of writing and notes the main points that it covers but does not reveal any findings. It is seldom more than ten lines long. An *informative abstract* is a highly condensed version of the original. Besides naming the topic and noting its main parts, it also presents the most important findings of the original, including any decisions, recommendations, and conclusions. Its length may range from 25 percent of the original for short pieces to less than 1 percent for long chapters or books. The following examples illustrate the difference between the two types of abstracts.

Descriptive Abstract

This report analyzes the July operating statement of Granger Autos, Inc., Baltimore, Ohio. It compares net profit and various operating expenses to total sales volume, as well as the salespersons' compensation to the gross profits on vehicle sales. It notes that the parts and service department is operating at a loss and suggests several ways of correcting the situation.

Informative Abstract

Granger Autos, Inc., is a Baltimore, Ohio, dealership employing 22 persons and selling approximately 500 vehicles per year. The July operating statement showed the net profit to be 4.5 percent of the total sales volume. Advertising, rental costs, and fixed and semifixed expenses totaled 0.7, 1.3, and 7.8 percent, respectively, of the total sales volume, while salespersons' compensation totaled 18 percent of the gross profit from all sales of vehicles. The sales department sold 42 vehicles during the survey month, 18 more than necessary to break even, for a gross profit of $37,800. Because of decreasing business, the parts and service department showed a loss of $2,555. The report suggests that the company institute a customer follow-up program to correct the situation, offer more liberal credit to customers, boost its charges for labor, and decrease by one person the parts and services staff.

Joe Mayer

A descriptive abstract indicates whether the original piece of writing contains information that will interest you, and thus it helps you decide whether to read it. Although a descriptive abstract cannot substitute for the original, informative abstracts frequently do stand in for the original. The user consults the original only when it is necessary to review the evidence supporting a finding or recommendation given in the abstract.

Descriptive or informative abstracts often precede chapters in technical books and journal articles and are a standard feature of lengthy company reports. In addition, they often accompany the titles on the table of contents pages of magazines. Because abstracts produced in school and on the job are nearly all informative, this chapter explores that type.

Writing an Abstract

When you abstract, it is important to follow a systematic procedure.

1. Begin by scanning the original, paying particular attention to the title, the headings and subheadings, and the opening and closing paragraphs for clues to the central message. Next, read the material carefully and familiarize yourself with its content and organization. As you read, look for the thesis statement—it often occurs in the first or second paragraph, although sometimes it appears in the conclusion. If the thesis statement is implied, state it in a sentence or two in your own words.

2. Now look for the main points that support the central idea. If you own the original, underline the points; otherwise, copy them as complete sentences in their original order on separate sheets of paper or make a photo copy of the original and mark it. Often the topic sentences of paragraphs state the main points—ideas, opinions, findings, or events. Do not underline or record specific details; similes, metaphors, or other figurative language; illustrative examples; or repetitive statements. If part of an idea occurs in one sentence and the remainder in another, underline the appropriate parts or record them as a single sentence.

3. Using the main parts of the original, prepare a first draft of the abstract. Follow the original order of presentation unless starting with the conclusion makes more sense or a poorly written original makes rearrangement necessary. Use the original wording or a close approximation of it and do not accidentally omit anything important. If your abstract is too long or poorly written in spots, you can correct these faults later on.

4. When you write the final draft of the abstract, condense by substituting words for phrases and clauses and by rewriting long sentences in a shorter form. Do not, however, omit *a*, *an*, or *the* or abbreviate anything that is not abbreviated in

the original. At times, you may need to summarize several separate points in a general statement. Make any changes in phrasing and add any linking devices needed to ensure a smooth flow of thought. If the original has technical terms that your readers may not understand, define them in everyday terms.

5. When your draft is complete, check it against the original to make sure you have not omitted an important point or distorted the emphasis. Polish the draft by correcting the misspellings, word omissions, and errors in grammar and punctuation.

When the abstract is completed, add a title. For abstracts of journal articles and chapters of books, use the following forms.

Abstract of "Sodom and Gomorrah: A Volcanic Disaster," by Joel Block, *Journal of Geological Education*, (May 1975): 74–75.

Abstract of Chapter 3, "Air Contaminants," by R. W. Allen et al., *Industrial Hygiene*, Englewood Cliffs, N.J., Prentice-Hall, 1976.

If the abstract will accompany the original, use only the word *Abstract* for the title.

An Example of Abstracting

Here is an original piece of writing in which the important points are italicized and the marginal notes serve as a guide to abstracting. Following the original passage are rough and final drafts of an abstract prepared for a general audience.

Omit generally known fact

Everyone knows that a human being, 1 like a chicken, comes from an egg. *At a very early stage, the human embryo forms a three-layered tube, the inside layer of which grows into the stomach and lungs, the middle layer into bones, muscles, joints, and blood vessels, and the outside layer into the skin and nervous system.*

Usually these three grow about equally,   2
so that the average human being is a fair mixture of brains, muscles, and inward organs.
In some eggs, however, one layer grows more than the others, and when the angels have finished putting the child together, he may have more gut than brain, or more brain than muscle. When this happens, the individual's activities will often be mostly with the overgrown layer.

We can *thus* say that while the average   3
human being is a mixture, *some people are* mainly "digestion-minded," some "muscle-minded," and some "brain-minded," and correspondingly *digestion-bodied, muscle-bodied, or brain-bodied. The digestion-bodied people look thick; the muscle-bodied people look wide; and the brain-bodied people look long.* This does not mean the taller a man is the brainier he will be. It means that if a man, even a short man, looks long rather than wide or thick, he will often be more concerned about what goes on in his mind than about what he does or what he eats; but the key factor is slenderness and not height. On the other hand, a man who gives the impression of being thick rather than long or wide will usually be more interested in a good steak than in a good idea or a good long walk.

Medical men use Greek words to de-   4
scribe these types of body-build. For the man whose body shape mostly depends on the inside layer of the egg, they use the world **endomorph.** If it depends mostly upon the middle layer, they call him a **mesomorph.** If it depends upon the outside layer, they call him

Margin notes:

Omit figurative language

Omit repetition

Omit secondary points

Omit derivation of names and their connection with body types an **ectomorph**. We can see the same roots in our English words "enter," "medium," and "exit," which might just as easily have been spelled "ender," "mesium," and "ectit."

Since the inside skin of the human egg,   5
or endoderm, forms the inner organs of the belly, the viscera, the endomorph is usually belly-minded; since the middle skin forms the body tissues, or soma, the mesomorph is usually muscle-minded; and since the outside skin forms the brain, or cerebrum, the ectomorph is usually brain-minded. Translating this into Greek, we have the viscerotonic endomorph, the somatotonic mesomorph, and the cerebrotonic ectomorph.

Words are beautiful things to a cerebro-   6
tonic, but a viscerotonic knows you cannot eat a menu no matter what language it is printed in, and a somatotonic knows you cannot increase your chest expansion by reading a dictionary. So it is advisable to leave these words and see what kind of people they actually apply to, remembering again that most individuals are fairly equal mixtures and that what we have to say concerns only the extremes. Up to the present, these types have been thoroughly studied only in the male sex.

Include basic physical description

Viscerotonic endomorph. *If a man is*   7
definitely *a thick type* rather than a broad or long type, *he is likely to be round and soft, with a big chest but a bigger belly.* He would rather eat than breathe comfortably. *He is likely to have a wide face, short, thick neck, big thighs and upper arms, and small hands and feet. He has overdeveloped breasts* and

Omit simile

looks as though he were blown up a little like a balloon. *His skin is soft and smooth, and when he gets bald,* as he does usually quite early, *he loses the hair in the middle of his head first.*

Omit specific example of type except for behavioral information that applies to all thick types

The short, jolly, thickset, red-faced politician with a cigar in his mouth, who always looks as though he were about to have a stroke, is the best example of this type. The reason he often makes a good politician is that *he likes people, banquets, baths, and sleep; he is easygoing, soothing, and his feelings are easy to understand.*   8

Omit secondary point

His abdomen is big because he has lots of intestines. He likes to take in things. He likes to take in food, and affection and approval as well. Going to a banquet with people who like him is his idea of a fine time. It is important for a psychiatrist to understand the natures of such men when they come to him for advice.   9

Include basic physical description

Somatotonic mesomorph *If a man is* definitely *a broad type* rather than a thick or long type, *he is likely to be rugged and have lots of muscle. He is apt to have big forearms and legs, and his chest and belly are well formed and firm, with the chest bigger than the belly.* He would rather breathe than eat. *He has a bony head, big shoulders, and a square jaw. His skin is thick, coarse, and elastic, and tans easily. If he gets bald, it usually starts on the front of the head.*   10

Omit specific examples of type

Dick Tracy, Li'l Abner, and other men of action belong to this type. Such people make good lifeguards and construction workers. They like to put out energy. They have lots of muscles and they like to use them. They go in for adventure, exercise, fighting, and getting the upper hand. *They are bold and unrestrained, and love to master the people and things around them.* If the psychiatrist knows the things which give such people satisfac-   11

Include behavior information

Omit secondary point

Include basic physical description

Omit simile

Include basic behavioral information

Omit secondary point

Omit repeated behavioral information

tion, he is able to understand why they may be unhappy in certain situations.

Cerebrotonic ectomorph. *The man who is definitely a long type is likely to have thin bones and muscles. His shoulders are apt to sag and he has a flat belly with a dropped stomach, and long, weak legs. His neck and fingers are long, and his face* is shaped like a long egg. *His skin is thin, dry, and pale, and he rarely gets bald.* He looks like an absent-minded professor and often is one. 12

Though *such people* are jumpy, they like to keep their energy and don't fancy moving around much. They *would rather sit quietly by themselves* and keep out of difficulties. *Trouble upsets them, and they run away from it.* Their friends don't understand them very well. They move jerkily and feel jerkily. The psychiatrist who understands how easily they become anxious is often able to help them get along better in the sociable and aggressive world of endomorphs and mesomorphs. 13

In the special cases where people definitely belong to one type or another, then one can tell a good deal about their personalities from their appearance. When the human mind is engaged in one of its struggles with itself or with the world outside, the individual's way of handling the struggle will be partly determined by his type. If he is a viscerotonic he will often want to go to a party where he can eat and drink and be in good company at a time when he might be better off attending to business; the somatotonic will want to go out and do something about it, master the situation, even if what he does is foolish and not properly figured out; while the cerebrotonic will go off by himself and think it over, when perhaps he would be bet- 14

ter off doing something about it or seeking
good company to try to forget it.

Since these personality characteristics   15
depend on the growth of the layers of the little egg from which the person developed,
they are very difficult to change. Neverthe-
Include thesis   less, *it is important for the individual to
know about these types, so that he can have
at least an inkling of what to expect from
those around him,* and can make allowances
for the different kinds of human nature, *and
so that he can become aware of and learn to
control his own natural tendencies,* which
may sometimes guide him into making the
same mistakes over and over again in handling his difficulties.

> *Eric Berne, "Can People Be Judged
> by Their Appearance?"*

Here is a rough draft made from the italicized portions of the
original article by Berne.

Abstract: First Draft

At a very early stage, the human embryo forms a three-
layered tube, the inside layer of which grows into the stomach
and lungs, the middle layer into bones, muscles, joints, and
blood vessels, and the outside layer into the skin and nervous system. Usually these three grow about equally. In some eggs, however, one grows more than the others, and thus some people are
digestion-bodied, muscle-bodied, or brain-bodied. The
digestion-bodied people look thick, the muscle-bodied people
look wide, and the brain-bodied people look long. If a man is a
thick type, he is likely to be round and soft, with a big chest but
a bigger belly. He is likely to have a wide face, short, thick neck,
big thighs and upper arms and small hands and feet. He has
overdeveloped breasts. His skin is soft and smooth, and when he
gets bald, he loses the hair in the middle of his head first. He
likes people, banquets, baths, and sleep; he is easygoing, soothing, and his feelings are easy to understand. If a man is a broad
type, he is likely to be rugged and have lots of muscle. He is apt

to have big forearms and legs, and his chest and belly are well formed and firm, with the chest bigger than the belly. He has a bony head, big shoulders, and a square jaw. His skin is thick, coarse, and elastic, and tans easily. If he gets bald, it usually starts on the front of the head. He is bold and unrestrained and loves to master the people and things around him. The man who is definitely a long type is likely to have thin bones and muscles. His shoulders are apt to sag, and he has a flat belly with a dropped stomach and long, weak legs. His neck and fingers are long, as is his face. His skin is thin, dry, and pale, and he rarely gets bald. Such people would rather sit quietly by themselves. Trouble upsets them, and they run away from it. It is important to know about these types, so that one can have an inkling of what to expect from those about him and so that he can become aware of and learn to control his own natural tendencies.

This first draft includes all the main points of the original article, but it makes no attempt to condense or tighten the write-up or to ensure a smooth flow of prose. These shortcomings are corrected in the final draft that follows.

Abstract: Final Draft

The human embryo very early forms a three-layered tube. The inside layer grows into the stomach and lungs, the middle layer into bones, muscles, joints, and blood vessels, and the outer layer into the skin and nervous system. Sometimes one layer grows more than the others, and thus some people are digestion-bodied, some muscle-bodied, and some brain-bodied. A digestion-bodied man has round, soft physical features, soft, smooth skin, and a belly that is larger than his chest. He is easygoing, soothing, and likes people. A muscle-bodied man has rugged, prominent physical features, thick, coarse, elastic skin, and a chest that is bigger than his belly. He likes to master the people and things around him. A brain-bodied man has thin, weak-looking physical features, thin, dry, pale skin, and a flat belly with a dropped stomach. He like quiet and solitude, and avoids trouble. Knowing about these types helps a person to anticipate the behavior of others as well as to recognize and control his own natural tendencies.

This final version is about 60 percent shorter than the first draft. Brevity has been gained by shortening sentences, summarizing individual points in general statements, and omitting some relatively unimportant points. For example, the final sentence of the first draft reads:

> It is important to know about these types, so that one can have an inkling of what to expect from those about him and so that he can become aware of and learn to control his own natural tendencies.

The same sentence in the final draft reads:

> Knowing about these types helps a person to anticipate the behavior of others as well as to recognize and control his own natural tendencies.

Thirty-nine words have become twenty-four. Also, most comments about specific physical characteristics have been replaced with general remarks that capture the essence of the more detailed statements. The following two passages, the first from the rough draft and the second from the final draft, illustrate this generalizing.

> If a man is a thick type, he is likely to be round and soft, with a big chest but a bigger belly. He is likely to have a wide face, short, thick neck, big thighs and upper arms, and small hands and feet. He has overdeveloped breasts. His skin is soft and smooth, and when he gets bald, he loses the hair in the middle of his head first.

> A digestion-bodied man has round, soft physical features, soft, smooth skin, and a belly that is larger than his chest.

Baldness patterns have not been mentioned because of their relative unimportance.

Suggestions for Writing

1. Read the following article carefully, noting its central point and main ideas. Then follow the guidelines in this chapter to prepare an informative abstract.

Several times a year, a tailor shows up at investment man- 1
ager John Crockett's office at Beacon Group in Boston. The tailor who works for Tom James Co., shows Crockett swatches of
fabric and takes his measurements, then returns for fittings and
comes back in two weeks with a finished garment. The suits cost
$400 to $600 each.

Crockett could find less expensive suits at a store, but then 2
he'd "have to leave the office and kill an hour going to and from
some other place," he says.

Convenience. It's one reason the luxury of going nowhere 3
has returned.

Delivery of products and services was nearly wiped out 4
when gasoline prices rocketed in the early 1970s. Gone were the
milkman and the housecalling TV repairman. Only florists and
a few other businesses held out. But now shops-on-wheels are
spreading again—to gourmet dining, videotape movies and oil
changes for your car.

A new generation of busy business people and lazy couch 5
potatoes is demanding delivery—and is willing to pay for it.
And marketers are learning to use the service to stand out from
the pack down at the shopping mall.

Some companies have made delivery their reason for being. 6
That shouldn't be any surprise to a nation that has nearly four
times more Domino's pizza drivers (85,000) than physicists and
astronomers combined (22,000). Detroit-based Domino's has no
dining tables in any of its 4,600 pizza delivery outlets, and its
quick, reliable delivery (it promises you'll get your pizza in 30
minutes) by mostly young men driving their own cars is a bench-
mark for the industry.

In services, Decorating Den is among those leading the way. 7
In the past four years, the network of 700 franchises that brings
wallpaper and decorating services to homes has seen its customer list quadruple to 35,000 this year.

Delivery is spreading so rapidly that there's even a direc- 8
tory, *L.A. Delivers*, in Los Angeles that lists more than 100
stores, restaurants and services that bring their goods to your
home. A complex map shows who will deliver what to where,
and you can get anything from dry ice to health food from
Yolanda's, which lists Linda Ronstadt and Bill Murray as clients.
A smattering of what's happening elsewhere:

Food: In one Atlanta neighborhood, Kroger Co. now deliv- 9
ers groceries. Many small, neighborhood grocers do that, but

Kroger is a chain of 1,321 supermarkets in 32 states. Through Prodigy—a joint venture of Sears, Roebuck and Co. and IBM Corp. that allows consumers to shop, bank and read news through personal computers—customers can call up a list of more than 3,500 items. Then they can place an order for a flat delivery charge of $8. Most orders arrive the same day. For now, the system is experimental, designed to test the waters for what Kroger calls "The Electronic Grocery Store."

You can often get a gourmet meal delivered in a major city. But Sundborn Ltd., a unit of Chipwich Inc. (of ice cream sandwich fame), is taking that a step further, delivering to just about anywhere. Say you live in central Kansas, you're planning a big date and you'd like to serve veal chops with prosciutto, fontina and sage. You pick up Sundborn's catalog and phone in your order. Delivery comes within 24 hours; you reheat the meal in your microwave. The veal is $13.75 an order, $2.75 for delivery.   10

Other goods: In Chicago, you can have an evening's entertainment—a video and an Italian dinner—delivered from one of Chicago's four Video Plus stores. The video rental chain has gone into the delivery business with a restaurant. Price: Whatever the meal costs plus $2.50 for the video rental and $1 for delivery. From 25 to 50 customers a week use the service.   11

In Charlotte, N.C., you can get a book without going to the bookstore. By October, Fort Lauderdale, Fla.-based Books by Wire plans to offer its service nationally. In the test phase in Charlotte, the company says some customers even pay the $5 delivery charge for a single $4.95 paperback. After ordering from a catalog, delivery (by United Parcel Service) takes two to three days.   12

Sak's Fifth Avenue is seeing its delivery business grow. The company has informally delivered goods for years—in 1980 it started its Executive Service in one store. But now it's in 34 of Sak's 44 stores. For a one-time fee of $50, you can register your sizes at one of the stores. If you spill soup on your tie during lunch, they'll deliver a new one before you meet a client for drinks.   13

"I think today you really need to be serviced," says Executive Service director Susan Olden. "We're all running in 20 directions to accomplish our workload."   14

Services: In Irvine, Calif., you can get your cleaning picked up at the office. Rainbowman Dry Cleaners picks up your shirts, launders them and delivers them back to you for $1.40 each. A   15 sign of the company's success: Before delivery began last November, Rainbowman's sales were $1,900 a month. Today, sales are more than $20,000 a month.

If you must go shopping, you can even get some services delivered at the mall. For example, while you're strolling, Mobi-Care, a franchise based in Gettysburg, Pa., will do a 17-point maintenance check on your car for less than $25. The company's 23 vans in 23 cities come to malls, office buildings or any parking spot.   16

What's behind all this? "People do prefer to stay at home," says Cheryl Russell, editor in chief of *American Demographics* magazine. Baby boomers are often two-career couples shuffling kids from day care to piano lessons, and they'd often rather not have to run out for bread or to check a new drapery pattern. Companies find that such customers are willing to pay a premium—from 12.5% to 100% in some cases—for goods to come to them.   17

But delivery is still an emerging factor in business and experts aren't sure how big it will get. One key test will be the fast-food industry. The potential is huge: A study by Campbell Soup Co. and the Food Marketing Institute found we already spend $62.4 billion on take-home meals. So the wheels are turning at giant corporations to see if we'd rather have those meals delivered.   18

General Mills Inc. is experimenting with home delivery through The Order Inn, which makes complete meals that customers re-heat. Lasagna costs $5.25 and prime rib goes for $10.95. After eight months of tests in Minneapolis, General Mills has decided to double—to 90,000—the number of homes it serves.   19

On the other hand, Popeye's Famous Fried Chicken, a New Orleans–based chain of 701 fast-food stores—tested delivery and found that customers didn't use it.   20

Othes are finding the same thing. Safeway Stores Inc. spokesman John Shepherd says one problem for grocers is that people are picky about produce. He says customers want "to go into the store and pick from among the apples, check for bruises, squeeze the oranges."   21

Some retailers say home delivery doesn't make sense for them. "As a store, our main object is to get people into the store to shop," says Sue Sorensen, a spokesperson for Dayton Hudson Corp. in Minneapolis. That way, while you're looking for one thing, you may buy a few other things, too.   22

A big hurdle: delivering is expensive. To keep costs down, today's deliverers use computerized inventory systems and they keep office or store space and staff to a minimum. They make appointments—saying they'll be there at 4 p.m. rather than just "next Tuesday"—so they don't make any unnecessary calls.

2. Abstract a journal article on a topic that interests you. Follow the guidelines presented in this chapter.

3. Compare a published abstract of an article with the original publication, noting the abstracting techniques it uses.

14

The Library Research Paper

Writing a library research paper involves gathering information about a topic from books, magazines, newspapers, government documents, and other library sources, and then presenting that material in a formal report that documents the sources. Preparing such a paper familiarizes you with library resources and services, promotes careful reading and note-taking, and provides experience in assimilating and evaluating printed material—valuable skills that can be applied in any field, both in school and on the job.

The procedure for writing a research paper involves (1) choosing a topic, (2) using the library to assemble sources and information related to the topic, (3) developing and organizing that information, and (4) writing and revising the paper.

Choosing Your Topic

Instructors differ in assigning topics for library research papers. Some assign a specific topic, others specify a general subject area for students to limit, and yet others allow students free choice of topic. If you are asked to select from a general subject area, you still have some control over your topic. Let your interests guide your choice. If you are an avid astronomer and are asked to write on some aspect of America's space program, "The Significance of Voyager II" would be more appropriate than "The Politics of NASA Appropriations for Cape Canaveral Maintenance."

TOPICS TO AVOID

If you are asked to choose a topic, avoid overly broad ones. For example, "The Effects of Chemical Food Additives" or "Recent Medical Advances" could not be covered adequately in a book, much less a paper, but could be sufficiently limited to "The Effects of Sodium Nitrite As a Meat Preservative" or "Eye Surgery with Laser Beams." The materials in your library, the assigned length of your paper, the time you have to complete it, and your purpose and audience will all help you determine how much to limit your topic.

Other topics to avoid include those that can be explained fully in a single source and those based entirely on personal opinion. For example, process explanations and descriptions of geographical locations do not require you to evaluate and coordinate material from several sources. Although many books and articles related to these topics may be available, they will all report the same basic information. Furthermore, topics based on personal opinion or experience are unsuitable because they cannot be supported by library research. However, you can use personal insights, judgments, and conclusions to support or contradict research material.

THE FOCUSING PROCESS

If your instructor has asked you to choose a topic, you will need to do some *focusing*. A good topic sometimes comes to mind suddenly and spontaneously. An instructor's lecture, for instance, might spark a desire to investigate an intriguing business trend or a medical milestone, a technological development or a scientific discovery. A discussion with a friend might whet your curiosity about the economics of solar heating, or a television documentary on Charles Darwin might interest you in the current controversy between creationists and evolutionists. Reflecting on your own interests, experiences, observations, and reading can also lead to a suitable topic. So can suggestions from classmates, friends, and family members. Instructors in other fields can point you toward topics in their academic disciplines. If your major is business and your assignment in English composition is a research paper on some recent development in business or technology, your business instructor might suggest such topics as teleconferencing or computerized record-keeping.

At times, though, neither reflection nor discussions with others will lead to a suitable topic. In this case, turn to one or more of the prewriting strategies discussed in Chapter 3—brainstorming, free writing, and asking a series of basic questions—to help you narrow a broad topic or expand your thoughts on a limited one.

Once you have chosen what seems to be a workable topic, do some background reading in standard reference works to orient yourself to it, to make sure it is sufficiently limited, and even perhaps to determine how you might approach it in the paper. The material to consult depends, of course, on your topic. For example, sources related to the topic of robots in industry would include *McGraw-Hill Encyclopedia of Science and Technology, Van Nostrand's Scientific Encyclopedia*, and articles in general encyclopedias like *Encyclopedia Americana* and *Encyclopedia Britannica*. If you are in doubt about which background sources to consult, ask the reference librarian to suggest some appropriate reference works.

Exercise

Narrow two of the following subjects to topics suitable for a research paper of 2,000–2,500 words.

1. The early impact of a scientific discovery
2. An expedition to a remote part of the world
3. An important educational development
4. An aspect of space exploration
5. A new medical or surgical tool
6. A new development in business
7. A new electronic device
8. An economic event with far-reaching consequences

Using Your Library to Assemble Sources

Several reference tools are available to help you locate appropriate source material for your paper. The most useful are encyclopedias, the card catalog, and periodical indexes. The research procedures discussed in this section yield a set of cards that contain bibliographical information taken from the sources consulted in the library. These cards become your *working bibliography*— the list of sources you will draw from when writing your research paper.

ENCYCLOPEDIAS

Encyclopedias are collections of articles on an array of general subjects or subjects within restricted fields, such as education or physics. Encyclopedias are a useful starting point for research because their articles can provide an overview of the field into which your topic fits. Suppose you are investigating the impact of commercial television on its first audiences during the early 1950s. General encyclopedia articles about television would supply you with concise background information. Further, the bibliographies that often follow encyclopedia articles might provide additional references for your research. On the other hand, for some technical aspect of television such as the development of the color picture tube, you would consult one or more general encyclopedias as well as specialized encyclopedias like *Harper's Encyclopedia of Science* and *McGraw-Hill Encyclopedia of Science and Technology*. The following list includes many of the best-known general and specialized encyclopedias.

General Encyclopedia

Collier's Encyclopedia	*Encyclopedia Americana*
Encyclopaedia Britannica	*New Columbia Encyclopedia*

Specialized Encyclopedias

Encyclopedia of Accounting Systems	*Encyclopedia of Higher Education*

Encyclopedia of Advertising

Encyclopedia of Banking and Finance

Encyclopedia of Biological Science

Encyclopedia of Chemical Technology

Encyclopedia of Chemistry

Encyclopedia of Computer Science

Encyclopedia of Ecology

Encyclopedia of Education

Encyclopedia of Educational Research

Encyclopedia of Environmental Science

Encyclopedia of Human Behavior: Psychology, Psychiatry, and Mental Health

Encyclopedia of Management

Encyclopedia of Occupational Health and Safety

Encyclopedia of Physics

Encyclopedia of Social Work

International Encyclopedia of the Social Sciences

McGraw-Hill Encyclopedia of Science and Technology

Universal Encyclopedia of Mathematics

Van Nostrand's Scientific Encyclopedia

Most libraries shelve encyclopedias alphabetically and keep them in the reference room.

As you read about your topic, note any points that you might work into your paper and any promising references in article bibliographies. For each article that appears promising, jot down the following information on a 3 × 5-inch index card for easy reference.

Title of article

Author(s) of article (This information is not always available. Sometimes an author is identified only by initials at the end of an article. In such cases, check the list of contributors at the front of the first volume for the full name.)

Name of encyclopedia

Year of publication

A typical bibliography card for an encyclopedia reference is shown in Figure 14–1.

THE CARD CATALOG

Conventional Card Catalogs. The conventional *card catalog*—a file of 3 × 5-inch cards—alphabetically indexes all

Figure 14–1.   Sample Bibliography Card for an Encyclopedia
Reference

Sorenson, Garth. "Personnel Work."
Encyclopedia of Educational Research.
1982 ed.

the books in the library. In some libraries, the catalog also lists
magazines, newspapers, government documents, records, and
tape recordings. In others, these materials are listed separately.
The librarian can tell you what your catalog includes.

The card catalog has three types of cards—author, title, and
subject—for each nonfiction book in the library and two types—
author and title—for each book of fiction. The three types of
cards may be filed together, separately, or in some other way such
as author and title cards together and subject cards elsewhere. A
set of catalog cards—author, title, and subject—is shown in Figure 14–2. Except for the top line of each card, they are all identical. In addition to providing the call number for the book, the
cards offer other valuable information. The publication date may
indicate whether a book will serve your needs (for example, an
aeronautics book dated 1943 will not have information on jet engines). The cards also indicate whether the book includes an index, which can help you locate useful information. At the bottom
of the cards is a list of the subjects under which the book is cataloged, which can lead you to books you might otherwise overlook.
If you are writing about some aspect of computers, for example,
you would check the subject card for _computers_ as a matter of
course. However, if you also examined the subject headings at the

Figure 14–2.   **Sample Catalog Cards for One Book**

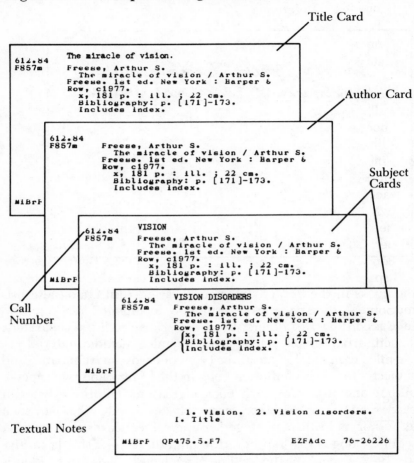

bottom of the card, you would find the categories *artificial intel-ligence* and *calculating machines*.

For every promising source you find in the card catalog, copy down the following information on a 3 × 5-inch index card.

Call number
Author(s)
Title
Editor(s) and translator(s), as well as author(s) of any supplementary material

Total number of volumes (if there is more than one) and the
   number of the specific volume that you want to consult
City of publication
Name of publisher
Date of publication

A typical bibliography card for a book is shown in Figure 14–3.
The call number indicates where the library shelves the book.
Each book is assigned a call number that is imprinted on its spine.
Most libraries store books in *stacks*, which may be open for
browsing or closed. If the stacks in your library are closed, give
the librarian a list of the call numbers and ask to see the books. If
the stacks are open, find the general area where each book is located. Most libraries post charts to guide you. If yours does not,
ask the librarian. Once you are in the right area, check the call
numbers posted on the end of each row of stacks to find which
row contains the book you want; then follow the figures on the
book spines until you locate it. Also look at other books in the
same general vicinity; you may find other useful titles that you
overlooked in the card catalog.

Examine each promising book by skimming its preface, introduction, table of contents, and other front matter material to
determine its scope, approach, and relevance to your topic. Also

Figure 14–3.   **Sample Bibliography Card for a Book**

HD
30.5
.W 73
1979

Wren, Daniel. *The Evolution of
Management Thought*. New York:
Wiley, 1979.

check the book's index for discussions related to your topic; then skim this material. Finally, check any bibliographies following chapters for other promising references. If this examination shows that the book does not contain helpful information, throw the bibliography card away and replace the book in the stacks.

Computerized Card Catalogs. Many libraries have converted to a computerized system of cataloging, which stores the information in the card catalog on magnetic tape or compact discs. Those libraries still using the conventional card catalog will undoubtedly install a computerized one in the near future. Some computerized card catalogs list only the holdings of the library where they are located; others include the holdings of nearby libraries as well. Some computerized catalogs can even tell you if a book is checked out and when it is due back. Other features of the system can include a map of the library that shows you where a particular book can be found and abstracts of journal articles. Needless to say, computerization has revolutionized library research, making it easier for libraries to update their holdings and for students to obtain working bibliographies in only minutes.

A typical library computer terminal consists of a viewing screen and keyboard, along with directions telling you how to type requests for information. For example, to learn what is available about and by Linus Pauling, you would type his last name or a shortened version such as Pau. Once you have this list, you can then call up detailed information on any book it includes by typing one or more significant words of the title. Similarly, typing in a subject heading like *diet therapy* provides a list of related subject headings—*nutrition, food composition*, and *nursing*, in this case. You can then explore subject headings by calling up a list of the books cataloged under each one. If you wish to know whether the library has a certain book, typing in the title will give you the answer. Another option allows you to retrieve lists of titles that begin with or contain a certain word or words.

PERIODICAL INDEXES

Periodical indexes catalog articles published in magazines, journals and newspapers. The entries are generally listed by subject and author, and sometimes also by title. These indexes are issued biweekly or monthly, then combined in volumes that cover six months or a year. Because they appear so frequently, periodical indexes provide access to recent information that might not appear in books for several years—if at all.

Reader's Guide to Periodical Literature (1900–date) indexes subjects that have been discussed in popular magazines. It lists nonfiction articles by subject and author and creative works by author and title. The first pages of the Readers' Guide identify the abbreviations for the 150 or so magazines that are indexed. The following example illustrates the arrangement of a typical entry. Note the "see also" cross-references that point to related subject headings.

MINES and mineral resources
  see also
  Ore deposits
  Quarries and quarrying
Mineral crisis. M. Sheils and J. Buck-
 ley. il Newsweek 96:98 N 10 '80
More than just oil in short supply
 here. il U.S. News 89:38 N 24 '80
Resource wars. M. T. Klare, Harpers
 262:20 + Ja '81

Entries in the Readers' Guide list article titles, authors, whether an article is illustrated (il), periodical titles, volume numbers (before the colon), page numbers (after the colon), month, day, and year.

Several new periodical indexes are available only on microfilm or similar microforms. *Microfilms* are filmstrips on which printed material is photographically reduced page by page. They are read through an enlarging viewer that your librarian can explain how to use. Do not be intimidated by microfilms and other microforms: they are easy to use and, for some material, the only available way to locate sources.

Among microfilmed indexes, *The Magazine Index* is particularly useful. Indexing some four hundred popular publications by subject, author, and title, each monthly issue covers the past five years and includes material that may be no more than two weeks old. The coded entries are read on a screen attached to a television-like device that allows both fast, motorized film movement for skipping through the index and slow, manual movement for browsing. Accompanying this device are coded reels of microfilm containing the indexed articles, together with a reader/printer that allows you to read the articles and to obtain photocopies. The librarian can show you how to use these machines. In addition, *The Magazine Index* publishes a list of recent articles on twenty to thirty current topics.

The *National Newspaper Index* covers five national papers—the *Christian Science Monitor*, the *Los Angeles Times*, the *New York Times*, the *Wall Street Journal*, and the *Washington Post*. Each monthly microfilm issue includes three years of references and is read on a viewer identical to that of *The Magazine Index*.

Two newspaper indexes—the *New York Times Index* and *NewsBank*—are issued in printed form and refer readers to photographically reduced materials. The first one (1913–date) lists news articles, book reviews, commentaries, and features that have appeared in the *New York Times*. The index's preface explains how to read entries that relate to the final "Late City Edition" of the paper—the one that is on microfilm in most libraries. *NewsBank* indexes stories of local, state, and regional interest from over 120 newspapers in every state. It is issued monthly as a looseleaf notebook, and the articles indexed are reproduced on microfiche—small cards with a series of reproduced pages that can be read only on microfiche viewers.

Specialized periodical indexes such as the following are also available.

Accountants' Index, 1921–date (indexed by subject)

Agricultural Index, 1916–1964 (indexed by subject; titled *Biological and Agricultural Index* from 1964 on)

Applied Science and Technology Index, 1958–date (indexed by subject)

Biological and Agricultural Index, 1964–date (indexed by subject)

Business Index, 1979–date (indexed by subject, author, corporation, and persons mentioned in articles; microfilmed)

Business Periodicals Index, 1958–date (indexed by subject)

Consumer's Index, 1974–date (indexed by subject and product)

Criminal Justice Periodicals Literature, 1975–date (indexed by subject and author)

Cumulative Index to Nursing and Allied Health Literature, 1977–date (indexed by subject and author)

Cumulative Index to Nursing Literature, 1956–1976. (indexed by subject and author; titled *Cumulative Index to Nursing and Allied Health Literature* from 1977 on)

Education Index, 1929–date (indexed by subject and author)

Engineering Index, 1884–date (indexed by subject and author)

Environment Index, 1971–date (indexed by subject and author)

Index to Dental Literature, 1963–date (indexed by subject and author)

Index to Legal Periodicals, 1909–date (indexed by subject and title)

Industrial Arts Index, 1913–1958 (indexed by subject; divided, 1958, into *Business Periodical Index and Applied Science and Technology Index*)

Legal Resources Index, 1979–date (indexed by subject, author, statute, and case; microfilmed)

Public Affairs Information Service Bulletin, 1915–date

Quarterly Cumulative Index Medicus, 1927–date (indexed by subject and author)

Technical Book Review Index, 1935–date (indexed by subject, author, and title)

Vision Index, 1975–date (indexed by subject and author)

Wall Street Journal Index, 1958–date (indexed by company and subject)

Although your topic will determine which indexes you should consult, it is usually good to begin with the *Readers' Guide* and *The Magazine Index* and then move on to the specialized indexes. For each promising article you find, copy the following items on a 3 × 5-inch index card.

Author(s), if identified

Title of article

Name of periodical

Volume or issue number (for professional and scholarly journals only)

Date of periodical

Pages on which article appears

Figure 14–4. **Sample Bibliography Card for an Article**

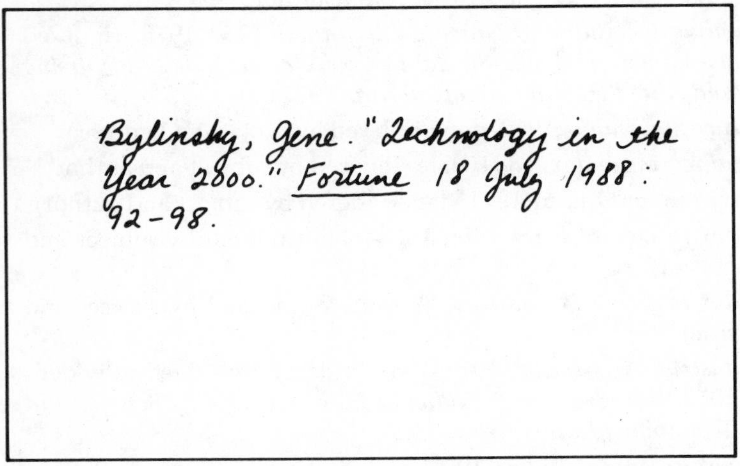
Bylinsky, Gene. "Technology in the Year 2000." Fortune 18 July 1988: 92–98.

Figure 14–4 shows a typical bibliography card for an article.

Look up each article referenced in *The Magazine Index* by using the coded microfilms and the reader/printer. Check the topic sentences of the paragraphs to determine the article's essential points, or scan the abstract or summary if there is one. Keep your bibliography cards for articles that appear promising. Take the remaining cards to whatever catalog your library uses to index its periodicals; then determine which periodicals your library holds and where they can be found. Recent issues are often kept in a special place, such as a periodical room. Back issues of magazines may be bound into volumes and shelved with books, or they may be kept on microfilm. Most newspapers are also on microfilm.

DATA BASES

Most libraries have access to *data bases*, computerized indexes that provide much more extensive listings of articles than your library's holdings. Because data-base listings are updated weekly or monthly, they can provide unparalleled access to the most recently published material on a topic. Increasingly, data bases not only index articles but also can provide complete copies of them. If your topic calls for current information and your library makes use of a data base, ask your librarian how to use it to search for relevant articles and to obtain copies of articles not in your library.

Because the companies that provide services charge libraries a subscription or an access fee, you will probably be charged for any material you obtain. However, the cost is often minimal, as many college libraries underwrite part of the expense to ease the financial burden on students.

ALMANACS, HANDBOOKS, AND DICTIONARIES

Almanacs, handbooks, and dictionaries are often the most efficient sources for clarifying a concept or verifying a fact.

Almanacs. General *almanacs* contain up-to-date facts on a broad array of topics. If you are writing about federal budget deficits, a current general almanac, unlike an encyclopedia, could supply a table showing the deficits for past fiscal years. Especially useful are *World Almanac and Book of Facts, Information Please Almanac,* and *Reader's Digest Almanac.*

Handbooks. More specialized than almanacs, *handbooks* supply background information in addition to facts. They also describe practices, processes, and methods in particular occupations. Here is a list of some noteworthy handbooks.

Handbook for Community Professionals
Handbook for Environmental Planning
Handbook for Managers
Handbook for Nurses
Handbook for the Technical and Science Secretary
Handbook of Air Conditioning, Heating, and Ventilating
Handbook of Chemistry and Physics
Handbook of Community Health
Handbook of Environmental Control
Handbook of Highway Engineering
Handbook of Industrial Engineering and Management
Handbook of Industrial Noise Control
Handbook of Industrial Research Management

Handbook of Industrial Waste Disposal
Handbook of Occupational Safety and Health
Handbook of Pharmacology
Handbook on Contemporary Education
Handbook on Urban Planning

Dictionaries. There are two types of *dictionaries*. The more familiar type defines words and shows their pronunciation, development, and use. The second type, like handbooks, provides concise information on specialized subjects. Whatever your topic, always use the first type to find the meanings of new words encountered in your research and to check spellings and usage in your final draft. Following are lists of useful standard dictionaries—unabridged and abridged—and specialized dictionaries.

Unabridged Dictionaries

Funk and Wagnall's New Standard Dictionary
Random House Dictionary of the English Language
Webster's Third New International Dictionary

Abridged or Desk-Type Dictionaries

The American Heritage Dictionary of the English Language
Funk and Wagnall's Standard College Dictionary
Webster's Ninth New Collegiate Dictionary
Webster's New World Dictionary of the American Language

Specialized Dictionaries

Chambers' Technical Dictionary
Comprehensive Dictionary of Psychological and Psychoanalytical Terms
Dictionary of Business and Science
Dictionary of Criminal Justice
Dictionary of Economics and Business
Dictionary of Education

Dictionary of Genetics
Dictionary of Geology
Dictionary of Law
Dictionary of Personnel Management and Labor Relations
Dictionary of Psychology
Dictionary of Scientific and Technical Terms
Dictionary of Sociology
Dictionary of Sociology and Related Sciences
Dictionary of Visual Science
Dictionary of Water and Waste Engineering

After searching for useful books and magazines, you may find that you need to modify the scope or emphasis of your topic. Your most diligent efforts sometimes yield insufficient information, forcing you to expand your topic and your working bibliography. Or, you may be so swamped with sources that you must narrow your topic and trim your working bibliography. Any significant change should be approved by your instructor. Unfortunately, no firm rule governs how many sources you need to produce a good research paper. At this point, however, you can probably judge what your needs will be.

Exercise

1. Select three of the following topics and find one book about each in the card catalog. List each book's call number, author, title, publisher, and date of publication. Because subject headings may vary, investigate related headings, if necessary, to find a book.

   a. Aging
   b. Alcoholism
   c. Crocodiles
   d. Death
   e. Ecology
   f. Epidemics

   g. Fertility
   h. Fiber optics
   i. Holography
   j. International trade
   k. Quasars
   i. Stock exchange

2. Select three of the following topics and find one periodical article about each. Use at least two periodical indexes. For each article, list the name of the author (if given), the title of the article, the name of the periodical, its date, volume and page numbers, and the name of the index.

a. Alien labor
b. Calculators
c. Diesel engines
d. Free enterprise
e. Microwaves
f. Nuclear fusion

g. Protectionism
n. Quantum theory
i. Relaxation therapy
j. Stereoisomerism
k. Unemployment
l. X-ray astronomy

Developing and Organizing Your Information

With your topic and sources in hand, you can now gather specific information and consider how to develop and organize it for your research paper.

TAKING YOUR NOTES

Before starting to take notes, think about your ultimate goal. Your review of the sources may have already suggested a tentative plan for your paper. If, for example, your topic is teleconferencing, your initial reading might suggest these main subdivisions.

1. Kinds of teleconferencing
2. Advantages of teleconferencing
3. Applications of teleconferencing

Until you have finished taking notes, you cannot create a comprehensive outline. But determining your general direction now will help focus your investigation.

Note-taking involves reading your sources carefully and recording any useful information they contain. Because you will write your paper directly from these notes, you must pay careful attention to certain note-taking strategies.

First, copy each note on a separate 4 × 6-inch (or larger) index card to avoid confusion with your smaller-sized bibliography cards. Record only one note on a card even when you take several notes from a single page: you may use them at different points in your paper. Do not copy notes into a notebook; the sheets cannot be easily rearranged in the proper order.

Copy the source for each note at the bottom of the note card so you can give proper credit when you write the paper. In most cases, the author's last name and the page number or numbers are sufficient. Occasionally, though, you may need to add initials to distinguish between two authors with the same last name, and sometimes you may need partial titles to distinguish between different works by the same author. *Do not forget to include the page number or numbers for each note.* If you do, you will have to look them up later when you document. Key each note card to a division in the tentative outline by penciling the proper heading at the top of the card. If you are unsure where the note will go, indicate its general subject.

A note may be a summary, a paraphrase, or a direct quotation.

Summary. A *summary* condenses the original material primarily in your own words. It may include brief quotations, provided they are enclosed with quotation marks. Usually ranging in length from 10 to 33 percent of the original, a properly written summary states concisely the core idea of the original. It presents points in their original order without distorting their emphasis or meaning, and it omits specific examples and supporting details. Summaries allow you to produce a much shorter paper than you otherwise could. Figure 14–5 shows a summary note card produced from this original passage:

> The burning of 180 grams of sugar in cellular respiration yields about 700,000 calories, as compared with the approximately 20,000 calories produced by fermentation of the same quantity of sugar. This process of combustion extracts all the energy that can possibly be derived from the molecules which it consumes. With this process at its disposal, the cell can meet its energy requirements with a minimum expenditure of substance. It is a further advantage that the products of respiration—water and carbon dioxide—are innocuous and easily disposed of in any environment.
>
> It is difficult to overestimate the degree to which the invention of cellular respiration released the forces of living organisms. No organism that relies wholly upon fermentation has ever amounted to much. Even after the advent of photosynthesis, organisms could have led only a marginal existence. They could indeed produce their own organic materials, but only in quantities sufficient to survive. Fermentation is so profligate a way of life that photosynthesis could do little more than keep up with it. Respiration used the material of organisms with such

Figure 14–5.   **Sample Summary Note Card**

> *Impact of cellular respiration*
> *Cellular respiration produces 35 times more energy from a given amount of sugar than does fermentation. Fermentation provided a precarious existence for living organisms. The advent of cellular respiration provided a surplus of energy and made organic evolution possible.*
>
>   *Wald, p. 53*

enormously greater efficiency as for the first time to leave something over. Coupled with fermentation, photosynthesis made organisms self-sustaining; coupled with respiration, it provided a surplus. To use an economic analogy, photosynthesis brought organisms to the subsistence level; respiration provided them with capital. It is mainly this capital that they invested in the great enterprise of organic evolution.

> *George Wald, "The Origin of Life,"* Scientific American,
> *191 (Aug. 1954):53.*

Paraphrase. A *paraphrase* restates original material in your own words but, unlike a summary, does not shorten it substantially. Paraphrasing makes technical and specialized material more understandable than the original. Suppose a source says that "toxicological testing of dioxin revealed that low dosage levels can cause chloracne reponses, hyperplasia, and teratogenic effects." This statement would puzzle or antagonize a general audience. In contrast, a paraphrase stating that "low levels of dioxin can cause skin eruptions, abnormal increases in body tissue cells, and malformed fetuses" would be easily understood.

Exercise

1. Submit summaries of two pieces of information that you plan to use in writing your library research paper, along with photocopies of the

originals; *or* select a two- or three-paragraph passage from an article on some current topic and prepare a summary of it.
2. Select a short technical passage from one of your textbooks and paraphrase it for a reader unfamiliar with that field.

Quotation. A *quotation* is a word-for-word copy of original material. Because a research paper should demonstrate your mastery of your sources, do not rely extensively on quotations. In addition, reproducing the words of others gives you no practice in expressing yourself.

Generally, use quotations only when the original is especially clear and forceful or when you need the support of an authority. The following quoted passage would be nowhere near as effective if presented in any other way.

> Man is himself, like the universe he inhabits, like the demoniacal stirrings of the ooze from which he sprang, a tale of desolation. He walks in his mind from birth to death the long resounding shores of endless disillusionment. Finally, the commitment to life departs or turns to bitterness. But out of such desolation emerges the awful freedom to choose beyond the narrowly circumscribed circle that delimits the rational being.
> *Loren Eisley*, The Unexpected Universe

Special rules and conventions govern the use of quotations. If, for clarity, you need to alter the original by adding some explanation or substituting a proper name for a personal pronoun, enclose the addition in *brackets*.

> Our admiration for this splendid man [Johannes Kepler] is accompanied by another feeling of admiration and reverence, the object of which is not man but the mysterious harmony of nature into which we are born.
> *Albert Einstein*, Ideas and Opinions

Reproduce any grammatical and spelling errors exactly as they appear in the original. To indicate that the original author, not you, made the mistake, insert within brackets the Latin word *sic* (meaning "thus") immediately after the error.

> As Walsh notes, "The threat to our envionment [sic] comes from many directions."

If you want to exclude an unneeded part of a quotation, indicate the omission by using *ellipsis marks*—three spaced periods. Indicate omissions within sentences in the following way.

> Gamow concludes his discussion of the problem by saying, "We can not demonstrate this proof, since it is fairly complicated . . . but the reader can find it in various books on topology and spend a pleasant evening (and perhaps a sleepless night) in contemplating it."
>
> *George Gamow*, One, Two, Three . . . Infinity

When an omission comes at the end of a sentence and the quoted part can stand as a complete sentence, use an unspaced period followed by three spaced periods.

> As one analyst noted; "Williamson's campaign focused primarily on the issue of hazardous chemical wastes because he hoped to capitalize on the fears of voters in his district. . . . Nevertheless, he was unsuccessful in his attempts to unseat the incumbent."

When you omit material from a quotation, be careful not to change or distort the original meaning; doing so is unethical and can get you into trouble if your instructor discovers your tampering. The following example shows such distortion.

Original passage	VitaHelth vitamin products are advertised as being superior to other brands, but laboratory tests have shown them not to be significantly better than competitive vitamin supplements.
Quotation distorting meaning	"VitaHelth vitamin products are . . . significantly better than competitive vitamin supplements."

At times you may wish to summarize or paraphrase the original but retain a few words or phrases that indicate a precise shade of meaning or add vividness. In such cases, use quotation marks but omit ellipsis marks.

Because of the "passionate advocacy" of its supporters, the push to halt the use of strip mining gained considerable support across the state.

When you copy a quotation onto a note card, put quotation marks at the beginning and end so that you will not mistake it for a paraphrase or summary when you write the paper.

As you read and take notes, don't expect to find useful material on every page. Sometimes a page will yield several notes; other times you will read several pages and find nothing. If you are uncertain about the value of any information, make a note. Too many notes are always better than too few.

Use of a Word Processor. If you have access to a word processor, you can copy your summaries, paraphrases, and quotations, along with the bibliographic references for them, into the unit for later expansion and reorganization. If your system has a bibliographic function, you can enter your references separately as you go along and then print out the bibliography at the end of the project.

PREPARING YOUR OUTLINE

When your notes are completed, you are ready to prepare a *formal outline*. This blueprint indicates the divisions and subdivisions of your paper, showing how you will arrange your ideas and what details will support them. Chapter 3 covers the two types of formal outline—topic and sentence—and the system of numerals, letters, and numbers used to designate the divisions and subdivisions. The sample library research paper at the end of this chapter includes a topic outline.

Develop your outline by sorting your note cards into stacks according to the subject headings you have penciled at the tops. Change or combine these headings where necessary. Next, review each stack carefully to determine further divisions and subdivisions, and use these divisions to write your formal outline. Phrase items of equal rank in similar or parallel fashion to help clarify the relationships among items.

When your outline is completed, key your note cards to it. Write at the top of each card the letters and numbers—such as II.

A. or III. B. 2.—for the appropriate outline category. Now arrange the cards into stacks according to the major headings: one stack for I, one stack for II, and so on. Next, arrange each stack internally, grouping together all cards with the same number and letter codes. Finally, start with the first card in category I and number all of the cards consecutively. Then, if they fall off the table or slide out of place, you can easily put them back in proper order. A few note cards may be left over when you finish keying. Some may go unused. Some you might work into your paper later on as you write or revise it.

PREPARING YOUR THESIS STATEMENT

As noted in Chapter 3, a *thesis statement* presents the central idea of a paper. Perhaps a thesis statement occurred to you as you took notes or prepared your outline. If not, prepare one now. Evaluate your purpose, audience, method of organization, and attitude toward your topic; then construct a thesis statement that reflects these considerations.

Here is a possible thesis statement for a teleconferencing paper.

> This technology, which now includes three kinds of teleconferencing, offers important advantages over conventional meetings and is enjoying growing popularity.

This statement indicates that the paper will first discuss the different types of teleconferencing, then its advantages, and finally its uses.

Writing and Revising Your Paper

You already know how to write a paper that is entirely your own. For a research paper, however, you must work other people's material into your own writing. Many students mistakenly believe that a research paper consists merely of a series of quotations, paraphrases, and summaries. Although you do use the material of others, *you* select and organize it, *you* develop insights about it, and *you* draw the conclusions.

In addition, you must know how to document your sources, handle quotations properly, avoid plagiarism, and prepare bibliographic references. These matters, as well as information about proper format, are discussed in this section.

WRITING YOUR DRAFT

Generally, the thesis statement appears in the introduction, but sometimes—such as when you analyze a problem and offer a solution—you may choose to reserve it for the conclusion. In the latter case, state the problem clearly at the outset.

Write your draft paper section by section, linking the material from your note cards with your own comments and assessments. Smooth writing is not necessary at this point; just get the information down on paper. You can work out the kinks and work in the transitions later. Allow this version to sit for a day or two before you polish and revise it.

DOCUMENTING SOURCES IN YOUR PAPER

The sources for borrowed material—whether summarized, paraphrased, or quoted—must be identified in the paper. The system of parenthetical citation recommended by the Modern Language Association (MLA) is illustrated in the following examples. Note that the documentation is the same for books, periodicals, encyclopedias, and government publications. Examine each example carefully, including the punctuation. (For additional examples consult the *MLA Handbook for Writers of Research Papers*, 3rd ed.).

Author's Name Not Used in Text. Whenever you introduce a summary or paraphrase without noting the author, the parenthetical citation includes the last name(s) of the author(s), *unless* there are more than three authors, and the page numbers in the source.

> In the two decades that have elapsed since their introduction, synthetic pesticides have been so thoroughly distributed throughout the animate and inanimate world that they occur almost everywhere (Carson 15).

Four major factors contributing to the increasing interest in solar energy include the rising cost of fossil fuels, the rising consumption of energy, the rapid advancement of solar energy technology, and the growing willingness of consumers to consider
utilizing solar energy (Stobaugh and Yergin 211).

For sources with more than three authors, use *et al.* to designate
all but the first-named one.

The most effective solar heating system utilizes water for space
heating. Corrugated metal roofing is painted black and installed
on the roof of the dwelling. A perforated metal pipe is positioned
along the upper edge of the roofing so that water runs down the
corrugations. Because the black metal absorbs the sun's heat, the
water running down it becomes hot. This hot water is collected
in a gutter at the low edge of the metal roofing and sent to a res-
ervoir (Thompson et al. 13).

If your sources include authors with the same last name, include
their initials to distinguish them.

In 1950, thirty-two billion passengers rode commuter trains
each year. By 1970, automobile ownership was so deeply in-
grained in the American way of life that the number of commuter train passengers dropped to less than eight billion (M. L.
Davis 79). . . . By the late 1960s, most cities utilized at least one
third of their downtown areas for parking, and newly constructed roadways had consumed another 20 percent of inner-
city property (R. O. Davis 30–31).

When the author is a corporation, government agency, or private
organization, use all or part of its name in the citation.

NIOSH has estimated that 1.5 million workers are exposed annually to inorganic arsenic, which is primarily produced
through the smelting of ores, particularly copper (U.S. Public
Health Service 24).

Author's Name Used in Text. If you introduce a paraphrase,
summary, or quotation by using the author's name, include only
the page number in the parenthetical citation. Position the cita-

tion just after the author's name or at the end of the borrowed material.

> According to Metz (229), the organizing and bargaining powers that labor gained via the Wagner Act would prevent a considerable number of strikes and thus prove a boon to interstate commerce, rather than a detriment.

> According to Metz, the organizing and bargaining powers that labor gained via the Wagner Act would prevent a considerable number of strikes and thus prove a boon to interstate commerce rather than a detriment (229).

When you cite more than one work by a single author, the citation consists of a shortened title and the page number. Underline titles of books and set off titles of articles with quotation marks.

> Dr. Kenneth H. Cooper points out that the nicotine in a cigarette overstimulates the production of hormones, which eventually cause scarring of the heart muscle (*The Aerobics Way* 31).

> Cooper further notes that heavy cigarette smokers are three times as likely to suffer heart attacks as nonsmokers or even moderate smokers (*Aerobics* 183).

Unsigned Sources. When no author is given for a source, the parenthetical citation includes all or part of the title and the appropriate page number. If you use a partial title, indicate the omission with ellipsis marks.

> Not everyone is satisfied that the legally established tolerances for pesticides are safe. Skeptics point out that food may carry pesticides in unpredictable combinations that can injure us even though each pesticide is present at a safe level ("Better Pesticide Detection . . . " 26–27).

Quotations. For short quotations that are run into the text, position the citation after the closing quotation marks and follow it with a period.

> Dr. Richard Seiden, of the University of California's School of Public Health, suggests that lack of confidence contributes to

the high suicide rate of college students: "As opportunities for education and employment increase, there's more opportunity for things to go wrong" (74).

With longer block quotations, position the citation as shown here.

> Dr. Leon R. Kass, of the National Academy of Sciences, suggests that cloning poses a threat to the family:
>
>> The family is rapidly becoming the only institution in an increasingly impersonal world where each person is loved not for what he does or makes but simply because he is. The family is also the institution where most of us, both as children and as parents, acquire a sense of continuity with the past and a sense of commitment to the future. . . . It would be a just irony if programs of cloning or laboratory-controlled reproduction to improve the genetic constitutions of future generations were to undermine the very institution which teaches us concern for the future. (56)

Notice that the citation follows the final period, and that a double space separates the two. If the length of the last line does not allow positioning, place the citation one space below the last line.

> . . . institution which teaches us concern for the future.
>   (56)

If the author's name is not mentioned in the text, the citation includes the name and the page number.

> Other observers, of whom the following may be taken as typical, have reached similar conclusions.
>
>> No matter how crowded the area in which we humans live, each of us maintains a zone or territory around us—an inviolate area we try to keep for our own. How we defend this area and how we react to an invasion of it, as well as how we encroach into other territories, can all be observed and charted and in many cases used constructively. (Fast 136)

HANDLING QUOTATIONS

As the preceding examples indicate, the way to handle direct quotations depends on the length of the quoted material. Quotations that are less than five lines long are set off by quotation marks and run into the text of the paper. With longer quotes, omit quotation marks and indent the material ten spaces from the left-hand margin. If more than one paragraph is quoted, indent the first line of each an additional three spaces. If only one paragraph is quoted, no further indentation is necessary. Type longer quotes double-spaced and leave no extra space above and below the block quotation.

Occasionally, you may need to indicate a quotation within the material you are quoting. Use single quotation marks for a quotation within a quotation as shown here:

> The report further stated that "All great writing styles have their wellsprings in the personality of the writer. As Buffon said, 'The style is the man'" (211).

However, use the regular double quotation marks ("   ") when a quotation appears within a long quotation presented in block format.

Whenever you use someone else's words, provide some context for the quoted passage. This informs the reader of what to expect and makes for smoother writing. When you first cite a work, for example, you might give its author's full name and expertise, along with the source of the quote.

> Writing in *Vogue* magazine, Terry Weeks told of her experience in returning to college at middle age: "Forms and procedures which young students handled with ease were frighteningly complex to me. I had moments of stark panic and fear of failure" (42).

Or, you may elect to give the author's full name and expertise, but note the occasion that prompted the quote rather than where it appeared.

> At a meeting of the Iron and Steel Institute, David M. Roderick, chairman of the United States Steel Corporation, told his fellow

executives, "It's important that Washington realize just how bad the recession is" (35).

Yet another option allows you to note the author's full name and expertise only.

> Dr. Conway Hunter, Jr., of Atlanta's Peachford Hospital, said, "Withdrawal from Valium is more prolonged and often more difficult than that from heroin" (43).

When the author of the quotation is unidentified, introduce it by noting the name of the publication from which it is taken.

> As economic conditions worsened, *Iron Age* magazine noted that "a jolt of good news anywhere . . . might just strengthen the resistance and end the recession" ("The Wait for News . . . " 35).

Once you have cited an author's full name, use only the last name in subsequent citations.

> In assessing the reasons for his company's difficulties, Roderick stated, "Our company was too steel-sensitive. We were subject to the most violent movements in the economic cycle" (36).

AVOIDING PLAGIARISM

Plagiarism is the intentional or unintentional use of another person's words or ideas without acknowledging the source. It is a serious offense because it robs the original writer of recognition. Some instructors, suspecting plagiarism, will ask to review students' notes and rough drafts. Students who plagiarize risk failure in the course and even suspension from school.

Any information obtained through your reading and used in your paper—whether as a quotation, paraphrase, or summary—requires documentation, unless it is a well-known fact available from many sources (such as the date World War II ended in Europe or the size of the 1989 budget deficit). If you are unsure about the need to document a source, do so anyway to avoid the risk of plagiarism.

The following passages illustrate the improper and proper use of source materials.

Original passage   The whole process of spraying seems caught up in an endless spiral. Since DDT was released for civilian use, a process of escalation has been going on in which ever more toxic materials must be found. This has happened because insects, in a triumphant vindication of Darwin's principle of the survival of the fittest, have evolved super races immune to the particular insecticide used; hence, a deadlier one has always to be developed— and then a deadlier one than that. . . . Thus the chemical war is never won, and all life is caught in its violent crossfire.

Rachel Carson, Silent Spring
(Boston: Houghton, 1971:8)

Deliberate plagiarism   The whole process of spraying seems caught up in an endless spiral. Since DDT was released for civilian use, a process has been going on in which ever more toxic materials must be found. This has happened because insects have evolved super races immune to the particular insecticide used; hence, a deadlier one has always to be developed. Thus, the chemical war is never won, and all life is caught in its violent crossfire.

This is deliberate plagiarism. The student's failure to mention Carson's name and to set the passage off with quotes leads readers to think that the writing represents the student's original thoughts.

Partial plagiarism   Rachel Carson notes, in *Silent Spring*, that <u>spraying seems caught up in an endless spiral. Since DDT</u> became available <u>for civilian use, ever more toxic materials</u> have had to be developed. <u>This has happened because insects have</u> become <u>immune to the particular insecticide used;</u> hence, it becomes necessary to find <u>a deadlier one. Thus the chemical war is never won.</u> (8)

Although this passage credits Carson for the ideas expressed, the student has plagiarized by copying the underlined parts of the passage word-for-word from the original without enclosing them in quotation marks. As a result, the reader will assume that the words are the student's rather than Carson's.

Proper use of original material

In *Silent Spring*, Rachel Carson notes the futility of spraying. She points out that, starting with DDT, insects have developed an immunity to each new insecticide produced, forcing scientists to develop a more lethal replacement (8).

Here the student has avoided plagiarism by identifying the author and using original phrasing.

PREPARING THE LIST OF WORKS CITED

The *list of works cited*, prepared from your bibliography cards, provides all pertinent information for each source you used in writing your paper. The listing begins on a new page, headed "Works Cited," and follows the last page of the paper. (See the sample list on pages 339–40.)

Each entry in Works Cited is listed alphabetically according to the author's last name or, if no author is given, the first significant word in the title. For a work with more than one author, alphabetize according to the name that appears first. Begin the first line of each entry at the left margin; indent subsequent lines in each reference five spaces. Double-space all lines and within and between entries. The formats used for different types of entries are shown in the examples that follow, which are based on the *MLA Handbook for Writers of Research Papers*, Third Edition (1988). If you need more information, consult the *MLA Handbook*.

Format for Books. The basic MLA-style format for a book includes the following information, which you should already have on your bibliography cards.

The name of the author, last name first
The title of the book, underlined

The place of publication
The publisher
The date of publication

Other facts of publication are added as necessary. Carefully examine the following sample entries, paying particular attention to the punctuation used and the arrangement of the information.

A book with one author:

Himmelfarb, Gertrude. <u>The Idea of Poverty.</u> New York: Knopf, 1984.

A book with two or three authors (the second and third authors' names are not reversed because they are not used in alphabetizing the list):

Bolt, A. B., and M. E. Wardle. <u>Communicating with a Computer.</u>
      Cambridge, Eng.: Cambridge UP, 1970.

A book with more than three authors uses the first author's name followed by "et al."—a Latin abbreviation meaning "and others":

Alder, Roger William, et al. <u>Mechanisms in Organic Chemistry.</u> New
      York: Wiley, 1971.

A book with corporate authorship and no author identified by name treats the corporation as authors:

United Nations, Public Administration Division. <u>Local Government
      Training.</u> New York: United Nations, 1968.

An edition other than the first:

Turabian, Kate L. <u>A Manual for Writers of Term Papers, Theses, and
      Dissertations.</u> 4th ed. Chicago: U of Chicago P, 1973.

A book with an editor rather than an author:

Deetz, James, ed. <u>Man's Imprint from the Past: Readings in the
      Methods of Archaeology.</u> Boston: Little, 1971.

A book with both an author and an editor:

Chiera, Edward. They Wrote on Clay. Ed. George C. Cameron. Chicago:
    U of Chicago P, 1938.

A translation:

Piaget, Jean. The Child and Reality. Trans. Arnold Rosin. New York:
    Penguin, 1976.

An essay or chapter in a collection of works by one author:

Eisley, Loren. "The Judgement of the Birds." The Immense Journey.
    New York: Random, 1956. 174-75.

An essay or chapter in a collection containing several authors' contributions compiled by an editor:

Seltzer, Richard. "The Art of Surgery." The Sense of the 70s. Ed.
    Paul J. Dolan and Edward Quinn. New York: Oxford UP, 1978.
    375-80.

Format for Periodicals. The basic MLA-style format for a periodical article includes the information you should already have on your bibliography cards.

    The name of the author, last name first
    The title of the article, within quotation marks
    The name of the periodical, underlined
    The volume number of the periodical
    The year of publication, within parentheses
    The pages on which the article appears

If the periodical is published weekly, monthly, or seasonally and each issue is paged separately, specify the full date of publication. For popular magazines and newspapers, omit the volume number and parentheses.

An article in a technical or scholarly journal consecutively paged throughout the year:

Holden, Gerald L. "Nation's Income and Maintenance Policies."
     American Behavioral Scientist 15 (1972): 673-95.

An article in a journal that pages each issue separately:

Block, Joel W. "Sodom and Gomorrah: A Volcanic Disaster." Journal
     of Geological Education 23.5 (1976): 74-77.
"Business' New Communication Tool." Dun's Review 117.2 (1981):
     80-81.

An article in a popular magazine:

Schwartz, Tony. "Second Thoughts on Having It All." New York 15
     July 1985: 32-41.

A signed article in a daily newspaper (if sections are paginated separately, the section is also identified: the city is underlined if it is part of the newspaper's title):

Walker-Lynn, Joyce. "The Marine Corps Now Is Building Women, Too."
     Chicago Tribune 30 Oct. 1977: I5.

When no city is specified in the newspaper's title, note the city and state in brackets following the title, unless the paper has national circulation:

Atkins, Ralph, "U.S. To Export More Grain to Russia." Daily Press
     [Burton, CO] 8 April 1977: A9.

An unsigned article in a daily newspaper:

"Lawmakers Unite on Mileage Rules." Detroit Free Press 21 Oct.
     1975: B3.

Format for Encyclopedia Articles. The basic MLA-style format for an encyclopedia article includes the information you should already have on your bibliography cards.

The author's name, last name first
The title of the article, within quotation marks
The name of the encyclopedia, underlined
The year of publication

```
Davis, Harold S.  "Team Teaching."  The Encyclopedia of Education.
    1974 ed.
```

If the article is unsigned, the reference begins with the title of the article.

```
"Hydrography."  The American People's Encyclopedia.  1969 ed.
```

REVISING YOUR PAPER

To revise your library research paper, follow the general guidelines given on pages 51–54. In addition, ask yourself these questions:

Is my material clearly organized? Do my outline and paper reflect the relative importance of the points I discuss?

Have I gathered information from a variety of sources and integrated it with my own observations?

Is each quotation properly introduced? Does it follow the proper format? Have I avoided overuse of quotations?

Are paraphrases and summaries stated in my own words?

Does each paraphrase, summary, and quotation have a parenthetical citation?

Does each source in my list of works cited follow proper format?

PREPARING YOUR FINAL COPY

Type your final draft on 8½ × 11-inch white paper, leaving one-inch margins on all four sides except at the top of the first page. Double-space the text, including indented block quotations and the list of works cited.

Number each page except the first in the upper right-hand corner, and precede each number with your last name. In the upper right-hand corner on the first page, type your name, the course number, and the date. Two lines below this, center the title, and then double-space twice before typing your first paragraph. If your instructor requires a title page instead of this heading, include the title of the paper, typed in upper- and lowercase letters and centered about two inches below the top of the sheet; your name, centered in the middle; and the course designation, instructor's name, and date, centered about two inches from the bottom. In this case, repeat the title on the first page, centering it about two inches from the top.

Sample Library Research Paper

The sample library research paper that follows includes a title page and a topic outline. The student writer uses MLA-style documentation, including parenthetical citations and a list of works cited, to acknowledge her sources. The marginal notes that accompany the paper point out some of the conventions of research papers discussed in this chapter.

Teleconferencing: Meetings for an Electronic Age

Carol Nash

English III, Section 1010

Mr. Abbott

November 3, 19--

Nash i

Topic Outline

I. Introduction: Establishes historical context,
   defines teleconferencing, and presents thesis
   statement: ''This technology, which now includes
   three kinds of teleconferencing, offers its users
   important advantages over conventional meetings
   and is enjoying expanding popularity''
II. The development of teleconferencing
    A. Period before mid-1960s
    B. Mid-1960s and after
       1. The first innovation
       2. Later innovations
III. Kinds of teleconferencing
    A. Audio teleconferencing
       1. Features
          a. Familiarity of equipment
          b. Speed and versatility
       2. Kinds and capabilities of equipment
          a. Telecopier
          b. Tablet/screen audiograph
          c. Micrographics projection unit
    B. Video teleconferencing

1. Kinds of systems available
   a. Full-motion system
   b. Compression-video system
   c. Freeze-frame system
2. Capabilities of different systems
   a. Full-motion system
   b. Freeze-frame system
   c. Compression-video system

C. Computer teleconferencing
   1. Length of conferences
   2. Alterations of input
   3. Characteristics of input

IV. Advantages of teleconferencing
   A. Reduced travel costs
      1. Possible decreases in face-to-face meetings
      2. Savings even with modest decreases in face-to-face meetings
   B. Improved marketing operations
      1. Operations involving customers
      2. Operations involving salespeople

V. Limitations of teleconferencing
   A. For reducing face-to-face meetings
      1. Audio teleconferences
      2. Video teleconferences

B. For reducing need to travel

VI. Acceptance of teleconferencing

  A. By industry

    1. Full-motion systems

    2. Freeze-frame systems

    3. Hotel teleconferencing services

  B. By other organizations

    1. By the government

    2. By colleges

    3. By professional organizations

VII. Conclusion: Importance, possible future uses

Title: centered on
page, typed in
upper- and
lowercase letters,
not underlined

Teleconferencing: Meetings for an Electronic Age

     Since the dawn of commercial enterprise,
communication has played an important role in its
operations. For centuries, letters and reports
provided the only means of long-distance
communication, and as a result weeks or even months
were often required to make decisions and complete
transactions. The invention of the telephone in 1876
ushered in the era of telecommunications, allowing two
individuals to communicate over long distances in a
matter of minutes. As time passed and business grew
ever larger, more and more decision making came to be
invested in meetings involving participants from
several widely scattered company locations. Often,
however, time and distance made such meetings
expensive and difficult to arrange. To avoid these
drawbacks, businesses--along with other
organizations--are making increasing use of
teleconferencing. Just what is teleconferencing
anyhow? Christine H. Olgren and Lorne A. Parker,

authors of <u>Teleconferencing Technology and
Applications</u>, define it as follows:

> . . . two-way electronic communications
> between two groups, or three or more
> individuals, who are in separate locations.
> In order to interconnect people,
> teleconferencing systems use
> telecommunication channels that range from
> regular telephone lines to satellite links.
> The only requirement is that the medium be
> interactive, giving people at each location
> the opportunity to actively participate in
> the meeting.(1)

<u>This technology, which now includes three kinds of
teleconferencing, offers important advantages
over conventional meetings and is enjoying expanding
popularity</u>.

Teleconferencing got its start in the 1930s but
for years was tied to the nation's basic telephone
network. Then, beginning in the mid-1960s, a series of
technical innovations ended this period of stagnation.
The first of these, developed by Robert F. White,
consisted of a unit comprising a color TV projector, an
11x14-foot TV screen, and a powerful sound system, and

Context for
quotation: name
and expertise of
authors

Extended block
quotation, indented
ten spaces without
quotation marks,
double-spaced

Thesis statement

Parenthetical citation: author's name provided because not mentioned elsewhere

Parenthetical citation: source with corporate authorship

was designed specifically for conferences (Johnson 5). Other developments included satellite transmitters and receivers, new and vastly more sophisticated telephone terminal equipment, and most significant of all, the modern digital computer (U.S. Congress 6-7). Today there are three major kinds of teleconferencing: audio, video, and computer conferencing.

Audio conferencing links conferees together by means of telephones and a core connector that allows a large number of people to participate. This system has the advantage that the telephone is a familiar device which is comfortable for most people to use. Conferences can be arranged in a short time without a great deal of planning and at relatively low cost. Current audio teleconferencing systems can accommodate conferences involving participants in up to 200 separate locations (Olgren and Parker 7-8). Audio teleconferencing allows two or more organizations to hold joint meetings, called meet-in conferences, if they wish. Participants use a common telephone number and have the services of a stand-by operator in case trouble arises or a late caller wishes to join the conference. Loudspeaking telephones and multiple tabletop or around-the-neck microphones make speaking and listening easy (Gold 30, 36).

With audio conferencing, there is often a need to
transfer written material as well as graphs, diagrams,
and tables. To accomplish this, several types of
audiographic equipment are available. One such device,
the telecopier, can transmit a document to any
designated location in 1 to 6 minutes. Another, the
tablet/screen audiograph, is ideally suited for
handling illustrative material. The device consists
essentially of a tablet, stylus, and video monitor. As
graphs and diagrams are recorded on the tablet in one
location, they are transmitted to the video monitors of
the participants in other locations, who can then use
their own tablets and styli to make modifications.
Finally, there is available a micrographics projection
unit that provides its users with access to the images
on a microfiche. Before the conference, each
participant is provided with a copy of the microfiche.
To call up an image on the device's screen, the
participant uses a Touch-Tone telephone pad (Gold 31-
32). This equipment makes it possible for participants
in audio conferences to utilize the same kinds of
information as participants in face-to-face meetings.

Video conferencing allows participants to see as
well as hear one another and, unlike audio conferencing, can be used to transmit images of three-dimen-

Independent
insight: no citation
necessary

sional objects. Three types of video systems are available. The first of these, the full-motion color system, utilizes broad-band channels and provides images indistinguishable from those received on home-viewing sets. Compression video, a relatively new technique, compresses the picture and sends it over a narrower channel, thus reducing transmission costs. Because the technique is still new, the picture may at times be blurred. The final system, freeze-frame video, transmits a series of still, rather than moving, images. This system, the cheapest of the three, can make use of ordinary telephone lines (Olgren and Parker 10).

Because of the differences in the images they produce, these systems possess very different capabilities. Full-motion systems, which yield the most realistic images, are well suited for simulating face-to-face meetings. Freeze-frame systems find application for transmitting images of three-dimensional objects, graphs, and individuals. Although compression video remains in the developmental stage, AT&T and International Business Machines are readying a system that will probably be used to transmit charts, graphs, and the faces of speakers (Schaffer 13).

Computer teleconferencing, unlike the other two kinds, does not involve the transmission of voices or images. Instead, the conferees communicate by typing their messages into terminals that are linked to a central computer (Edwards 50). This kind of teleconferencing frees participants from the constraints of time. Participants enter their inputs into the computer at whatever times are most convenient for them; and a conference may last for hours, days, weeks, or even months, during which period participants may augment their original contributions or modify their original positions (Olgren and Parker 11). In addition, computer conferencing allows anonymous messages to be transmitted and, because participants never see one another, is especially conducive to emotion-free communication (Edwards 50).

Perhaps the chief attraction of teleconferencing is the savings in travel costs that it provides. With teleconferencing, face-to-face meetings to resolve conflicts, share information, present reports, or conduct negotiations can be reduced by as much as 62 percent (Olgren and Parker 26). Savings can be significant even when reductions are more modest. Atlantic Richfield, for example, estimates that it will reduce travel costs by 20 percent and save $4 to $10 million per year when the teleconferencing system it is now installing goes into operation. According to Paul Snyder, the company's vice-president for communications services, the biggest problem will probably be getting the managers and supervisors to adjust to the new system. ''Communication . . . has to be handled by people who understand how others act and react. We don't want to produce cultural shock. We want to achieve cultural change without shock'' (''Business' New . . . Tool'' 81).

Besides reducing travel costs, teleconferencing can be used to improve marketing operations and thereby enhance company profits. Through teleconferencing, companies can reach new or specialized markets, furnish potential customers with product information, and put experts directly in touch with clients who require special assistance. Teleconferencing also allows companies to offer low-cost training seminars to users of their products and to provide quick trouble-shooting if difficulties develop. Finally, teleconferencing can be used to inform salespeople of new products and altered marketing strategies as well as to provide better communication between the sales

Short quotation provided with context, run into text, and enclosed with quotation marks. Ellipsis shows omission from quotation

Parenthetical citation: source with no author given

force and the home office (Olgren and Parker 28-29).
Because of these advantages, teleconferencing should
become increasingly attractive as an alternative to
face-to-face meetings.

Independent insight: no citation necessary

These benefits do not mean, however, that
teleconferencing lacks limitations or is suited for
every organization. To begin with, laboratory
investigations have revealed that although audio
conferencing is as effective as face-to-face meetings,
video conferencing causes participants to feel awkward
and therefore to function less effectively. The
researchers concluded that 40 percent of all face-to-
face meetings could be replaced by audio conferences
but only 10 percent by video conferences. A full 50
percent of all meetings, they said, would require
participants to meet face-to-face (Elton 258). Nor is
there any guarantee that teleconferencing will reduce
the time and money spent traveling to meetings. In
fact, by generating new ideas, it may actually increase
the need to travel and thus increase travel costs
(Siverd 123).

On balance, however, the benefits of teleconferencing far outweigh its limitations. As a
result, it has become widely used by industry,

government agencies, and educational institutions.
Industry has been particularly receptive to video
teleconferencing. In 1981, for example, Aetna Life and
Casualty, Inc., began using full-motion teleconferencing as part of its management training program and for
sales meetings. That same year, Westinghouse took the
first steps toward establishing a satellite-linked
connection between its home office in Pittsburgh and a
facility in Baltimore. Both Westinghouse and Sperry
Univac are using freeze-frame systems to allow
engineers and other technical personnel in widely
separated locations to discuss blueprints and drawings
(''Business' New . . . Tool'' 81). In 1982, Johnson and
Johnson held a video press conference involving some
600 reporters in 30 cities in order to introduce its new
tamper-resistant packaging for Tylenol. By the start
of 1984, over 1,000 of the country's 8,000 large
commercial hotels were providing satellite-linked
teleconferencing for their guests. In doing so, they
followed the trail blazed by Holiday Inns, which
introduced the service at the start of the decade
(Morris 1-2).

Computer teleconferencing has found its widest
use in nonindustrial applications. For over a decade

and a half, the Federal Preparedness Administration
has used computer teleconferencing to disseminate
information concerning national disasters and
shortages of commodities. For over 10 years, the
University of Michigan has used this same technology to
offer courses in a variety of fields. At the University
of Colorado students are being offered a course that
explores the effects of automated office technology on
business executives. Scientists and technicians find
computer teleconferencing an especially valuable
device for conducting professional conferencing and
seminars. A conference sponsored jointly by the
Institute for the Future and the Lily Endowment will
serve nicely as a case in point. This conference,
conducted to develop a data base for secondary
education, involved participants in this country and
England and spanned several months. Without computer
teleconferencing, the whole project would have been
financially impossible (Olgren and Parker 290-92).

    Within the last 20 years or so, technical
innovations have revolutionized teleconferencing and
created a whole new spectrum of options for communication between groups of individuals in different
locations. As time passes, we can expect the revolution

Independent
insight: no citation
necessary

to continue, lowering teleconferencing costs still
more and ushering in a wider range of applications.
Some day, perhaps, politicians may use teleconferencing to raise campaign funds, union leaders to keep
in touch with the rank and file at locals, and
international organizations to avoid in-person
gatherings and the heavy travel costs they incur.
Conceivably, even the United Nations might someday
conduct sessions via teleconferencing. But whatever is
in the offing, one thing is certain: teleconferencing
will continue to play an expanding role both in
industry and elsewhere.

Nash   12

Works Cited

''Business' New Communications Tool.'' <u>Dun's Review</u>   Journal article with
    117.2 (1981): 80-81.   no author given

Edwards, Morris. ''Stay-at-Home Conferences: More   Journal article with
    Than Just an Energy-Saver.'' <u>Infosystems</u> 28.8   volume and issue
    (1981): 48-54.   numbers

Elton, Martin C. J. <u>The Practice of Teleconferencing</u>
    <u>in the U.S.: Trends and Policies</u>. Dedham, MA:
    Artech House, 1981.

Gold, Elliot M. ''Teleconferencing: Communications
    Bridge Between Geographically Dispersed Sites.''
    <u>Telephony</u> 203 (26 July 1982): 30-32, 36.

Johnson, James W. ''Some Observations on Tele-   Book with editor
    conferencing.'' <u>The Teleconferencing Hand-</u>   and contributions by
    <u>book</u>. Ed. Ellen A. Lazer. White Plains, NY: several authors
    Knowledge Industry Publications, 1983. 1-12.

Morris, Betsy. ''Hotels Start Luring Video
    Conferences.'' <u>Wall Street Journal</u> 25 Feb. 1983:   Newspaper article
    1-2.

Olgren, Christine H., and Lorne A. Parker. <u>Telecon-</u>   Book with two
    <u>ferencing Technology and Applications</u>. Dedham,   authors
    MA: Artech House, 1983.

Schaffer, Edward A. ''Video Conferences Are Seen
        Becoming More Popular in '84.'' Wall Street
        Journal 3 Aug. 1984: 13.

Siverd, Bonnie. ''The Economics of Teleconferenc-
        ing.'' The Teleconferencing Handbook. Ed. Ellen
        A. Lazer. White Plains, NY: Knowledge Industry
        Publications, 1983. 103-23.

U.S. Congress. Adverse Report Together with
        Additional and Supplemental Views,
        Telecommunications Act of 1980. 96th Congress,
        2nd Session, Report 96-1252, Part 2.

Document with
government
authorship

15
Oral Presentations

While in college you may be asked to give oral presentations even if you never take a speech course. Your English composition instructor may ask you to speak about your background, some campus issue, or the reasons you chose to attend your college. In a technical writing course you may be required to recast the content of a technical report orally, so that students in other fields can understand it. In a major-field course that requires a lengthy term paper, you may be asked to explain why you chose your topic, how you gathered material for it, what problems you encountered, and how you solved them. Assignments like these familiarize you with speaking before an audience and, through the comments of your instructor and classmates, provide insights into improving your delivery.

On the job, oral presentations may be part of your duties. At a meeting, your supervisor might ask you to speak extemporaneously about some item on the agenda. This assignment can include considerable give-and-take: a listener may interrupt you with a question, or you might inquire whether anything needs further explanation. Because such talks are impromptu, they involve no advance preparation.

In contrast, *formal oral presentations*, the type we discuss in this chapter, require considerable advance planning and preparation. These presentations can address a great variety of situations and topics in both school and the workplace. For example, your supervisor may ask you to explain a new departmental policy, describe a new test procedure, show how to operate a device, report on the progress of a research project or sales campaign, or discuss the possible impact of some regulatory legislation. Some of these talks may occur after working hours. An environmental group may want to know about your company's efforts in preventing air and water pollution, or the local merchants' association may ask to hear about the economic impact of your company's expansion or retrenchment plans. Situations like these require speaking skills that result in interesting and effective presentations.

Speeches may be informative, persuasive, or a combination of the two. *Informative speeches* explain or teach, whereas *persuasive speeches* aim to change listeners' attitudes or to arouse them to action. These four steps are involved in preparing and delivering an effective formal speech of any type:

1. Understanding your audience
2. Determining your purpose
3. Developing your presentation
4. Making your presentation

Understanding Your Audience

Understanding your audience is as important when you talk as when you write. Unless you are aware of your listeners' interests and expectations, you cannot communicate effectively, and you may even irritate or antagonize your audience. When you speak to members of your own department, you should already know them quite well. However, for less familiar audiences, you must answer key questions: "Are they technical, professional, or unskilled workers?" "What is their general level of education?" "How much do they know about my topic?" Explaining a new procedure to employees from another department often requires that you define some technical terms. And, for an audience with no technical background, you should probably omit most technical terms.

Determine which aspects of your topic are most likely to interest your audience. Suppose, as a school nutritionist, you want to persuade your listeners that the federal school-lunch program should be expanded to include more children. Speaking to a group of farmers, you might focus on the added income they would receive; to health-care officials, on the expected improvements in the children's health; and to school officials, on improved classroom performance. Tailoring your message to your audience greatly improves its chances of acceptance.

Also consider the probable size of your audience. With small groups, there is often plenty of time for questions and answers after the talk. With larger ones, though, a question-and-answer period may not be practical.

To obtain information about the audience for an off-the-job talk, question the person who asked you to speak. If possible, talk also with some people who will be listening to you. Successful audience analysis and successful speaking go hand-in-hand, so pay careful attention to this phase of your presentation.

Determining Your Purpose

To determine the purpose of your oral presentation, decide first what you want your audience to know, believe, or do. On the job, the situation often determines your purpose. Suppose several changes have been made in your department's safety regulations, and your superintendent asks you to explain them at the next safety meeting. No doubt you would present the changes as positive steps.

Off-the-job talks require considerable thought. Suppose you are a police captain in a town where the local college has just established a degree in criminal justice. A prominent business group, knowing that you helped set up the program, asks you to talk about it at their monthly luncheon meeting. They are considering a possible scholarship fund, and you want to persuade them that the program deserves their support. First, you must decide which aspects of the program are most likely to interest your audience. Because they probably do not care about the actual details of establishing the criminal justice program, you might decide to focus on its benefits to the community. These might include graduate police officers trained in all major aspects of law enforcement and in coping with many kinds of emergencies. The interests of your audience and your own attitude toward the topic should determine your purpose.

Developing Your Presentation

Developing an oral presentation consists of (1) making an outline, (2) supporting it with details, (3) writing a thesis statement, (4) preparing an introduction and conclusion, and (5) choosing the mode of delivery.

PREPARING YOUR OUTLINE

The outline for a speech, like that for a paper, serves as a road map of your ideas and helps ensure that your listeners will be able to follow those ideas easily. Depending on the length of the talk, you may use a topic or a sentence outline (see pages 44–46) or a less formal written plan. Here is a topic outline for the police captain's talk.

    I. Introduction
   II. Training in law enforcement
      A. Police administration
      B. Laboratory techniques
      C. Evidence collection
      D. Defense tactics
      E. Combating juvenile delinquency
  III. Training for emergencies
      A. First aid
      B. Emergency childbirth
      C. Fire fighting
      D. Handling natural disasters
  IV. Conclusion

Speeches can follow any of the patterns used to develop pieces of writing. If you explain how to perform a test, each major division of your outline should represent a stage in the procedure. When tracing the development of an advertising campaign, you might adopt a time-sequence approach. To discuss changes in a set of safety regulations, a comparison-contrast format might work best. When describing a new office building or other facility, you might use a spatial pattern, listing each different area in turn. The preceding outline reverses the order-of-climax pattern: it first covers primary police training and then moves on to auxiliary training.

PROVIDING SUPPORTING DETAILS

Much of your oral presentation will be based on your own knowledge and observations. Sometimes, though, you may need to draw on written materials or to ask other people for help. If you report on a research project, you might have to reread the proposal that helped create it or check the progress reports tracing its history. Similarly, in preparing the talk about the criminal justice program, you might consult college brochures on it or ask a fellow officer to clarify a point for you.

On occasion, you may need to support your talk with library information. If so, the procedure is the same as for a research paper (see Chapter 14). Record enough bibliographical information so that you can mention the sources and add authority to your presentation.

WRITING YOUR THESIS STATEMENT

If you have not already prepared a thesis statement, do so now. Here is a possible thesis statement for the speech on the criminal justice program.

> The new criminal justice program at Carter College will benefit this community and others by turning out police officers who are versed in all major aspects of law enforcement and who know how to cope with several kinds of personal and community emergencies.

Note that this thesis statement reflects the arrangement of the outline shown earlier.

PREPARING YOUR INTRODUCTION AND CONCLUSION

Generally you will encounter less trouble with your introduction and conclusion if you prepare them at this point rather than earlier.

The Introduction. A good introduction catches the listeners' attention and sets the stage for what is to come. To accomplish these goals, you might begin with an attention-getting statement, a quotation, a true or fictionalized story, an interesting question, or any other device that fits the situation. If you are talking about a new and highly promising product your company has developed, you might start by saying, "Today, I'm going to tell you about a product that has more money-making potential than anything we have marketed so far." If you are talking about recent advances in coping with childhood leukemia, you might mention an afflicted child who was cured by a new type of chemical therapy. Whatever approach you use, your introduction must prepare listeners for the ideas you will convey in the body of the speech.

The Conclusion. In contrast, the conclusion wraps up your ideas and creates the sense that you have fulfilled your purpose. Any of the techniques used for ending a paper can also end a speech. The criminal justice speech might conclude with a brief restatement of its main points. To end your talk on childhood leukemia, you might predict that a time will come when this affliction will no longer menace our children. Other effective ways to conclude a speech include offering an evaluation, quoting a recognized authority, or challenging listeners to take some action.

CHOOSING YOUR MODE OF DELIVERY

You can use one of three approaches to deliver a speech:

1. Memorize the speech and repeat it word-for-word.
2. Write it out and read it from manuscript.
3. Talk from a set of note cards.

A speech given from memory poses several problems. First, unless you are trained in acting, your delivery is likely to be stilted and flat. Also, if you temporarily forget a sentence or two, you may accidentally repeat or skip part of your message when you start talking again. Reading from a manuscript eliminates the danger of forgetting but increases the chance of a dull, mechanical performance. As you read, you may also neglect to maintain eye contact with your audience and thereby reduce the effectiveness of your presentation. Some situations, however, do require use of a manuscript, such as when the speech includes direct quotations or statistics that must be presented accurately. Also, when you have a strict time limit, a manuscript helps ensure that you complete the speech on schedule.

Unless circumstances dictate otherwise, your best approach is to talk from note cards. Note cards lessen your chances of giving a mechanical performance, of losing contact with your audience, or of accidentally skipping important points. When making notes, copy each item in your outline onto a 4×6-inch index card. Then expand the notes with cards that contain additional material. Since notes are only guideposts to keep you on track, use short phrases or clauses rather than complete sentences, which take too long to read. Also, avoid making too many cards—so many that you must spend most of your time shuffling through them. By leaving most of your message unwritten, you can make your speech more spontaneous, natural, and interesting.

Making Your Presentation

To give an effective oral presentation, you need to consider what you wear, counter any nervousness you might feel, begin properly, and use your voice, body, hands, and eyes effectively. In addition, you must use any visual aids properly and know how to handle questions after your talk.

CHOOSING APPROPRIATE CLOTHING

Before you utter a word, your audience will undoubtedly begin to judge you on the basis of your overall appearance. It is important, then, to dress appropriately. If you speak to a group of co-workers, wear on-the-job clothing. For an audience of supervisors, dress more formally than usual. Occasionally, it is appropri-

ate to wear on-the-job clothing for talks to outside groups. A police officer who talks about crime prevention to a group of
townspeople might appear in uniform to lend authority to the
speech.

COPING WITH NERVOUSNESS

Despite adequate planning and preparation, nervousness affects many speakers as speech time approaches. Thinking ratio-
nally about your sweating, trembling, and other reactions often
lessens their intensity. It also helps to sit in a relaxed position and
take deep breaths. To ease tense throat muscles, drop your chin
slightly and move your head inconspicuously from side to side.
Review one final time your opening remarks and message. Once
you start speaking, any remaining tension will probably diminish
or disappear entirely. As you gain experience in giving talks, nervousness should not be a problem.

BEGINNING YOUR TALK

When your time comes to speak, rise slowly, take your position at the speaker's stand, place your note cards in front of you,
and briefly scan your audience. Experienced speakers often begin
with a few preliminary remarks before starting their actual presentations. If you choose this strategy, thank the person who introduced you, note that you appreciate the opportunity to speak,
and, if appropriate, comment on the importance of the occasion.
Remember that you and your audience need some time to adjust
to each other, so if time permits, a moment or two of   pleasantries
helps establish the needed contact.

USING YOUR VOICE

As you talk, listen to yourself and correct any harshness,
squeakiness, or other voice faults. Without shouting, modulate
your voice so everyone can hear you. Be careful to speak clearly
and smoothly. A series of "dontcha's," "goin's," and other slurred
words, punctuated with "er's," "uh's," "you know's," and "I
mean's," makes you appear careless and lessens the acceptance of
your remarks.

To show enthusiasm and help keep your audience alert, vary the speed of your delivery. You might speak more rapidly to convey excitement or more slowly to emphasize an important point. Rehearsals are invaluable for detecting and overcoming voice problems. The evening before your presentation, rehearse it while a knowledgeable friend listens, or make a tape recording. Then have your friend criticize your performance or play the tape back and evaluate it yourself. Repeat the procedure until you are satisfied with the effectiveness of your voice.

USING BODY MOVEMENTS AND HAND GESTURES

Body movements and hand gestures are important in effective oral communication. Start your talk by standing comfortably without slouching or swaying back and forth. It is not necessary, however, to remain rooted to one spot during the presentation. To dramatize an important point, you can lean forward or move from behind the lectern and take a few steps toward your audience. To show disbelief, you can step back slightly. And, if you use visual aids, you will undoubtedly have to move about to manipulate them.

Hand gestures are useful providing you keep them natural. You can raise your index finger to call attention to a point or make a jabbing motion for added emphasis. You can turn your palms down to reject information or ideas, turn them up to signal acceptance, or extend them toward the audience to show caution or to deliver a warning. You can clench your fists to show anger or strong resolve, or place your hands on your hips to show skepticism. Never use your hands to play with pencils or chalk, straighten your tie, smooth your hair, or otherwise fidget. These actions betray nervousness and distract your listeners from your message.

MAINTAINING EYE CONTACT WITH YOUR AUDIENCE

To create a bond with your audience, look directly at them, not down at the floor or toward some remote spot beyond them. If the audience is small, look directly at one person for a few seconds, then shift your attention to someone nearby. Try to make eye contact with all of your listeners before you finish the talk. If the audience is large, mentally divide the room into sections and proceed as with smaller audiences, shifting each time to someone in a different part of the room. Maintaining eye contact allows you to gauge the response of your audience and to correct any undesirable developments. Thus, when you notice people straining forward as if unable to hear, you can raise your voice. If people seem puzzled, you can slow down and provide more details.

USING VISUAL AIDS

Visual aids can add clarity, precision, and variety to an oral presentation. As you plan your speech, take time to consider where they might be used effectively. Four visual aids—chalkboards, posters, flip charts, and overhead projectors—are especially useful for oral presentations.

Chalkboards. A chalkboard works well when you need to present an occasional figure, formula, short list, or brief outline. You can also use it to present more extensive information, providing you put the information on the board in advance rather than interrupt your talk to write it. If you use a portable chalkboard, keep prewritten material covered until it is time to show it; otherwise, it may distract your listeners.

Posters and Flip Charts. A poster is a card, usually 2 × 3 feet or larger, made of pasteboard or some similar material. A flip chart is a set of similarly large sheets that are hinged together at the top. Both are suitable for presenting a series of tables, graphs, drawings, and other written matter.

Posters and flip charts are prepared in advance, usually with colored felt-tip markers. Posters are arranged in a suitable sequence, placed on a viewing stand at appropriate points during the talk, and then removed. A flip chart is fastened to an easel and each page is flipped over and out of view as the speaker finishes discussing its content and purpose. Posters are somewhat more awkward to handle than flip charts, but they can be arranged in any order—an important advantage if the speaker must give different versions of the same talk.

Overhead Projectors. An overhead projector throws an enlarged image from a transparency onto a wall or screen. The material to be shown is first placed on opaque sheets, usually about the size of business stationery, which are then run through a transparency maker. An overhead projector allows the use of overlays and masking. An overlay is a transparency that is placed over another one to add more information to what is being shown. For example, a speaker may superimpose a sales curve for the current year over the curve for the previous year. Masking consists of covering up part of a transparency and then removing the cover when it is time to reveal the hidden information. During the presentation, the speaker can use a grease pencil to mark the transparencies. Afterward, these markings can be removed for the next presentation.

Make sure that your visuals are not overcrowded or too complicated and that all your listeners can see them clearly. Otherwise, they may confuse and irritate, rather than help, your audience. To ensure readability, use sixteen-point or larger sized type.

Never just show a visual; go over it to make sure your audience has grasped the material; then put it away so it will not be a distraction. When you have finished showing your transparencies, turn off the projector. If you use handouts, wait until after the talk to distribute them. Otherwise, some people may read them instead of listening to you.

ANSWERING QUESTIONS AFTER YOUR TALK

Question-and-answer periods allow listeners to learn more about points they do not understand and to raise other points. Make sure your audience understands each question before you answer it. If the question is ambiguous, you might say, "If I haven't misunderstood you, you would like to know . . ." If the questioner was hard to hear, you might repeat the question. Answer each question straightforwardly, taking as long as time allows or the question merits. If you do not know an answer, say so rather than trying to bluff. If a questioner is hostile or sarcastic, never respond in kind. Instead, reply courteously and move on to the next question. A civil reply can help win acceptance for your ideas.

Most question-and-answer periods have some definite time limit. When the time has about expired, tell your listeners that you can take just one or two more questions. If the number of people wish to continue, do so at your option, providing the room is still available. Be sure to thank your audience for listening to you.

Suggestions for Speaking

Complete one of the following assignments or another approved by your instructor. Determine your audience and purpose, prepare a thesis statement and an outline, provide suitable supporting details, develop an introduction and a conclusion, and prepare a set of note cards for your speech.

1. Prepare a three- to five-minute talk for the graduating class of your high school, telling the seniors what to expect in college.

2. Convert one of the papers or reports you have written for this course into a three- to five-minute oral presentation that includes the use of at least one visual aid.

3. Prepare a three- to five-minute talk on the opportunities in your career field. Obtain pertinent background materials by checking your placement office, consulting one or more periodical indexes in your college library, and asking the librarian for pertinent government documents and other materials.

4. Prepare a three- to five-minute talk on some controversial issue in your community. You might discuss a local bond issue, traffic congestion, industrial pollution, mosquito control, or a rezoning proposal. Check back issues of the local newspaper for news stories, editorials, and letters on the issue.

5. Prepare a three- to five-minute talk on an article you have read or a report you have written for another course, and follow the talk with a question-and-answer session.

6. Prepare a three- to five-minute oral presentation in which you demonstrate how to operate one of the devices listed on pages 136–37 of Chapter 7 or some other device you are familiar with.

16

Tables, Graphs, and Drawings

Tables, graphs, and drawings often accompany on-the-job reports and support oral presentations. These visual aids allow writers and speakers to do the following:

Add variety and interest to the presentations;
focus attention on important parts of reports and speeches;
reduce the length of explanations; and
present, in an easily understandable form, information that otherwise would be difficult to convey.

This chapter explains how to prepare and use tables, graphs, and drawings for written and oral presentations.

Tables

A *table* groups related facts or figures in rows and columns for easy reference. Certain information is better shown in tables than in other kinds of visual aids. Tables are useful for showing slight differences in values. For example, the difference between

589 and 596 would be made more clear in a table than in bars of different length, which would exaggerate the difference or make it too slight to detect. Tables can also present large quantities of information without confusing the reader. Suppose, for instance, you wish to compare widely varying monthly production figures for some item over an eight-year period. You could do this easily in a table that lists the monthly figures in eight columns, one for each year. However, presenting this same information in written form would make understanding the comparisons quite difficult.

When you prepare a table, follow these seven guidelines.

1. Give the table a brief but accurate title. If you use more than one table, number them consecutively. Use either of the two styles that follow.

Style 1

Table 1
Physical Properties of Tungsten

Style 2

Table 1. Physical Properties of Tungsten

2. Provide each column with an appropriate heading. If several columns contain related kinds of information, center a single major heading over them; then provide each column with an appropriate subheading. Use capital and lowercase letters for major headings and subheadings unless numerals are needed. An example follows.

Monthly Hirings in Electronics Industry			
Month	1986	1987	1988	1989

3. Align columns of whole numbers on the right-hand digit and columns of decimals on the decimal point.

25	3.5
3,284	0.81
8	14.051

4. Document any table or statistical data taken from another source. If the table or data appeared in an article, book, or company publication, you must obtain permission to reproduce it and give whatever credit line the source specifies. If the table or data come from a government publication, no permission to use it is necessary but credit should be given. In this case, follow the documentation formats explained on pages 311–314.

5. Position any explanatory footnotes at the bottom of the table. Precede each footnote with a raised lowercase letter (for example, a, b, c) and place the same raised character after the item to which each footnote refers.

6. Whenever a lengthy table must run vertically on the page, position it so that its title is to the left when the page is in the horizontal reading postion. If a table must occupy more than one page, write *continued* or *cont.* immediately below the first page. Repeat the title and column headings at the top of the second page, with *continued* or *cont.* following the title.

7. Refer to tables at the most appropriate points in the text and position them as nearby as possible, preferably on the same page if space allows.

Table 1 shows the sizes of anchors to use with different-length boats.

Table 1. Hi-Tensile Anchor Selection Guide

Anchor Size	Horizontal Holding Power in lbs[a]		Recommended Boat Length (feet)	Recommended Rope Size (Open Laid Nylon Only)
	Soft Mud	Hard Sand		
5-H	400	2,700	17–24	$5/16$
12-H	900	6,000	25–38	$3/8$
20-H	1,250	8,750	39–44	$7/16$
35-H	1,600	11,000	45–54	$1/2$
60-H	2,400	17,000	55–70	$5/8$
90-H	2,900	20,000	71–90	$3/4$
150-H	3,100	21,000	over 90	$7/8$
190-H	3,500	23,000	over 90	1

[a]Refers to the pulling force on the anchor, not the weight of the boat.
Source: Reprinted by permission of Danforth Division, the Eastern Company.

Graphs

A *graph* is a pictorial presentation of numerical data. Three types of graphs—line, bar, and circle—are most common. A line graph has a vertical axis, a horizontal axis, and one or more lines that show the relationship between two or more sets of value. A bar graph has the same two axes but uses vertical or horizontal bars instead of lines. A circle graph looks like a pie that has been sliced into several pieces.

Often, data are easier to grasp and understand when presented in graphs rather than in tables. Presenting the monthly fluctuations of a store's sales in a line graph would make the magnitude of changes and the spotting of any trends much easier to grasp. On the other hand, the exact monthly sales figures would require a table. Because tables and graphs complement each other so well, they are often used together.

Document graphs exactly as you would tables, refer to each one at the appropriate spot in the text, and position it as close as possible to the text discussion, preferably on the same page. When you use more than one graph, identify them as "Figure 1," "Figure 2," and so on. Titles may appear above or below the graphs and follow the figure number.

LINE GRAPHS

A *line graph* shows the relationship between one or more sets of items—one measured by a horizontal scale and the other by a vertical scale. The horizontal scale, which usually appears at the bottom of the graph, measures time or some other regular-type progression. The vertical scale measures something that fluctuates or changes in the horizontal scale. Suppose you want to graph a hospital's monthly admissions for a one-year period. You would plot the twelve months of the year on the horizontal scale and a series of numbers representing admissions on the vertical scale. A line graph such as this could be expanded to compare the monthly admissions of several hospitals.

Line graphs do not always measure time. For example, such a graph could be used to chart the freezing points of a series of antifreeze-water mixtures or to plot the changes in an automobile's fuel consumption over a range of speeds.

Follow these guidelines to prepare a line graph.

1. Draw a vertical axis and a horizontal axis that intersect (they look L-shaped, as in Figure 16–1).

Figure 16–1.   **Line Graph Drawn to Proper Scale**

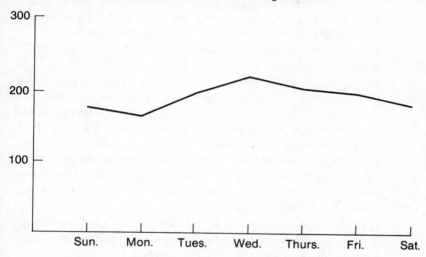

Choosing a scale of 150-250 would cause the differences to appear much greater than they actually are.

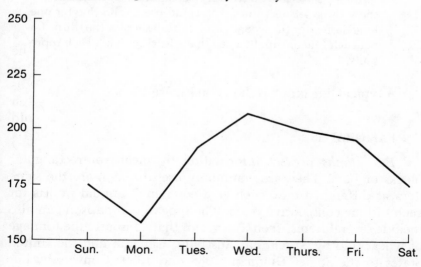

2. Divide each axis into a series of labeled segments. For the horizontal axis, work from left to right; for the vertical axis, work from bottom to top. In labeling the vertical axis, choose a range of numbers that does not distort the fluctuations you want to show. If you wanted to graph the number of daily visitors to a park during a certain week and the numbers ranged from 150 to 210, a vertical scale of 0–300 would accurately reflect the magnitude of the differences. (See Figure 16–1.) On the other hand, choosing a vertical scale of 100–250 would make the differences seem greater than they actually are, and a scale of 0–1,000 would make them nearly impossible to distinguish.

3. Pinpoint the fluctuating values by placing a series of points at the proper heights above the segment markers along the horizontal axis. If you are graphing, at five-minute intervals, the temperature of a solution over a one-hour period and the temperature after five minutes is 550°F, you would place a point directly above the five-minute marker on the horizontal scale and at the height corresponding to 550°F on the vertical scale. Plot the other temperatures the same way and connect the points with a line.

4. If the vertical axis requires a short identifying label, position it at the top of the axis. Position longer labels vertically along the axis, reading upward. (See Figure 16–2.)

5. If the graph has two or more sets of fluctuating values, use a different style line to identify each value. For example, to show three sets of values, you could use a solid line for one, long dashes for the second, and short dashes for the third. Label each line or supply a key that identifies what each represents.

A typical line graph is shown in Figure 16–2.

BAR GRAPHS

Bar graphs present information by means of rectangular blocks or bars. They are commonly used to compare the same item at different times, such as a company's annual profits for each of four consecutive years. The type of comparison can also include several items, such as a graph that compares the tonnage of wheat sold by Argentina, Australia, Canada, and the United States to the Soviet Union in 1988 and 1989. Conversely, bar

Figure 16–2.   **Specific Gravity of Aqueous Ammonia**

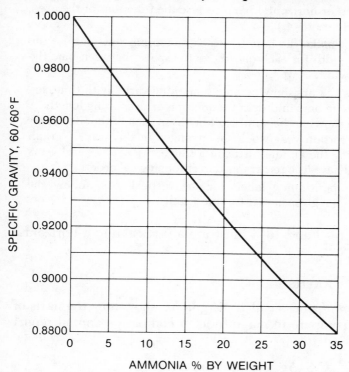

Source: Reprinted by permission of The Dow Chemical Company. Data from W. C. Ferguson, *Lange's Handbook of Chemistry*, 7th ed. New York: McGraw-Hill, 1949.

graphs offer a way of comparing different items at the same time, such as last year's welfare budgets for the fifty states.

Not all bar graphs, however, involve time comparisons. You might use one, for instance, to show the levels of illumination in different areas of a factory or the percentages of different soil types in a county.

Ordinarily, the direction in which the bars are drawn does not matter, but there are exceptions. For example, it would be more appropriate to use vertical bars to compare heights and horizontal bars to compare mileages.

Follow these guidelines to prepare bar graphs.

1. Draw a horizontal axis and a vertical axis that intersect. For vertical bars, plot the scale of measurement on the vertical

axis and label each bar on the horizontal axis. (See Figure 16–3.) For horizontal bars, reverse the functions of the axes. (See Figure 16–4.)

2. Do not make the bars too thick or too narrow, and use the same width for each one. Keep the spaces between bars the same width as well.

3. Unless you are showing how something varies with time, arrange the bars in order of increasing or decreasing length. A graph showing the number of births in each of the fifty states for a certain year would be arranged in this way. A graph showing the annual births in a single city over several years would have its bars arranged in chronological order.

4. When positioning labels for the vertical axis, follow the guidelines given earlier for line graphs.

Figures 16–3 and 16–4 illustrate a vertical and a horizontal bar graph.

CIRCLE GRAPHS

Circle graphs, also called *pie graphs*, show how the parts of some whole compare in magnitude. A company's annual report

Figure 16–3.   **U.S. Agricultural Exports**

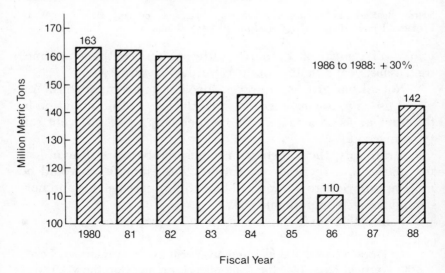

Source: Reprinted from *1988 Agricultural Chartbook*, Washington, D.C., 1988.

Figure 16–4.   **Size of Michigan Income Tax Personal Exemption**

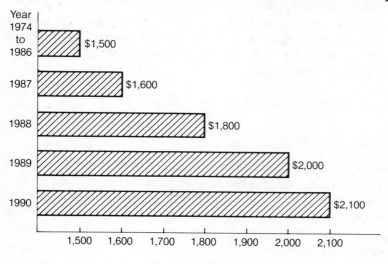

Amount of Exemption

Source: Reprinted from *1987 Michigan Income Tax Return.*

might include a circle graph that compares that year's outlay for wages and salaries, payments to stockholders, debt retirement, and the like. A time-motion study might include a circle graph that compares the time a worker spends performing different tasks during a shift.

To make a circle graph, follow these guidelines.

1. Using a compass, draw a circle with a suitable diameter. Ordinarily, four inches is sufficient. Since a circle is 360° in circumference, each 3.6° segment equals 1 percent of whatever you are graphing.

2. If the parts being graphed are not given as percentages, calculate them; then check to be sure they add up to 100 percent.

3. Draw a vertical line from the center of the circle to the 12-o'clock position. Using a protractor and proceeding clockwise, measure off the longest segment. Continue around the circle, measuring off the smaller segments.

4. If what you are graphing has several very small parts, try to group them into a single segment to reduce clutter. Label this segment "Other" or "Miscellaneous," and if a breakdown is

needed, provide a key to what the segment includes. This segment should follow all the others.

5. Provide each segment with a label and include any other pertinent information, such as percentages or hours. If necessary, position this information outside the circle and draw a line from it to the segment.

Figure 16–5 shows a typical circle graph.

COMPUTERIZED GRAPH-MAKING

Several computer programs are available that greatly facilitate the preparation of graphs. *Spreadsheets* are electronic worksheets that allow you to enter and tabulate data. For example, if you work for a store, you might enter its daily or weekly gross sales and its various expenses and then enter a formula that tabulates net sales automatically. The information can be presented as figures or in graphical form. Some programs even offer a choice of line, bar, or circle graphs.

Many of the more sophisticated computer programs allow users to create a graph, alter its size, and position it optimally in a

Figure 16–5.   Sources of CO^2 from Burning Fossil Fuels

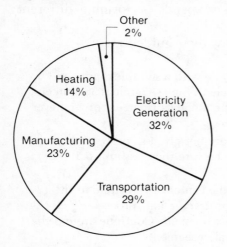

Source: Reprinted from Anthony Ramirez, "A Warming World: What It Will Mean," *Fortune,* July 4, 1988, 102–110.

report. Thus, a graph could be reduced from, say, 8½ × 11 inches to 2 × 3 inches, then placed next to the text it illustrates.

Drawings

A *drawing* is a representation of an object, a scene, or the like. Drawings are particularly useful because they allow you to omit the unimportant elements of what you are drawing and thereby to emphasize its important details.

Drawings can provide interior as well as exterior views of an object by means of cutaways an exploded views. A *cutaway drawing* omits part of the casing of an object, allowing the viewer to see the internal parts and their arrangement. An *exploded-view drawing* shows the device disassembled, with the parts arranged in the same relative positions they occupy when assembled. Figure 16–6 shows a cutaway drawing and Figure 16–7 an exploded-view drawing.

Follow these guidelines for preparing drawings.

1. If the object has several parts, be sure to draw them in the proper proportions.
2. Label each part with its name, positioned either on or next to the part. (See Figure 16–6.) If the object has so many parts that they cannot be labeled in this way, number each one and identify it in an accompanying key. Use connecting lines as necessary. (See Figure 16–7.)
3. Position the figure title and number, if any, either above or below the drawing. Document, position, and mention drawings in accordance with the guidelines for tables given earlier in the chapter.

Various computer programs, usually designated *CAD* (computer-assisted drawing), are available to draw complex, three-dimensional, and overlaid figures that can be printed on a dot-matrix printer. Users of these programs can modify parts of a drawing rather than redoing it entirely and can magnify parts for greater clarity. The magnified portions can be entered into the unit and used as separate illustrations.

Figure 16–6.   **Floguard Check Valve**

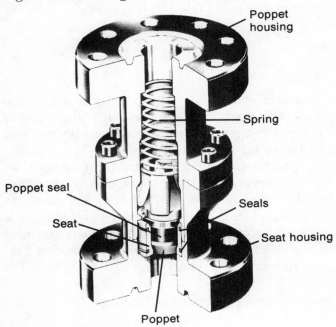

Source: Reproduced by permission of Flocon Products, Inc.

Suggestions for Making Tables, Graphs, and Drawings

1. Make a table that compares the monthly housing starts in the city of Midville for 1988 and 1989. Use the following data.

   1988: January (155), February (140), March (165), April (178), May (186), June (205), July (215), August (220), September (190), October (165), November (150), December (130).

   1989: January (120), February (108), March (133), April (145), May (130), June (163), July (160), August (150), September (143), October (130), November (116), December (110).

2. Make a line graph that gives a month-by-month comparison of the housing starts in the city of Midville during 1988 and 1989. Use the data from the preceding item, and chart each year with its own line.

3. The summer production record for a certain company is as follows: June—575 lathes, 850 shapers, 600 drill presses; July—690 lathes, 950 shapers, and 800 drill presses; August—450 lathes, 700 shapers,

Figure 16–7.   **Belt-Guard Assembly for Econo-o-mitre Saw**

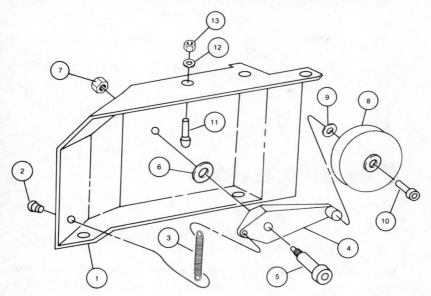

Part #	Part Name
1	Belt Guard R&L Hand
2	Idler Spring Anchor
3	Idler Spring
4	Idler Arm
5	Idler Axle
6	Idler Spacer
7	Idler Axle Lock Nut
8	Idler Pulley
9	Idler Pulley Spacer
10	Idler Pulley Axle
11	Idler Damper
12	Idler Damper Washer
13	Idler Damper Lock Nut

Source: Reproduced by courtesy of LeTarte Company, Smith Creek, Michigan.

and 675 drill presses. Prepare a bar graph comparing the production of these items for each of the three months.

4. Prepare a circle graph showing the percentage of different appliances sold by the kitchenwares department of a store during a one-month period. The items and percentages are as follows: refrigerators, 43 percent; stoves, 31.5 percent; dishwashers, 13 percent; blenders, 6 percent; coffeemakers, 3.5 percent; toasters, 1.8 percent; electric can openers, 1.2 percent.

6. Prepare a cutaway or an exploded-view drawing of some relatively simple object or device used in your field of study.

7. Prepare a table, graph, or illustration that is appropriate for a proposal, investigation report, or some other type of report that you have written.

17

Finding a Job

Successful job hunting requires a well-organized campaign that begins with a search for openings in your field. Unfortunately, many potential candidates overlook important sources of information about the jobs they seek, and others are not considered because they do a poor job of presenting themselves. This chapter is designed to help you avoid such pitfalls in your search for a job. It tells how to locate job openings; how to write effective application letters, resumes, and postinterview letters; and how to prepare for and handle job interviews.

Locating Job Openings

Most job openings are located through campus placement offices, word-of-mouth information, or newspaper and periodical advertisements. Sometimes, job openings are discovered by writing directly to the companies in your field or through a professional employment service that can refer you to prospective employers.

CAMPUS PLACEMENT OFFICES

Perhaps the best place to start looking for job openings is your campus placement office. Find out where it is located; then, early in your final year of school, visit it and ask what services it performs. Explain your job interests, and find out how recruiter visits are announced as well as how to sign up for interviews. Complete the placement registration form and provide certificates of commendation, instructor evaluations, letters of recommendation, and similar materials so the office can create your placement file. This material will be reviewed by company representatives before they speak to you or be sent to prospective employers, after you contact them. If you have not already done so, check to see whether your college has internship or cooperative education employment arrangements with organizations. Often, these are excellent stepping stones to permanent positions. Also, if your college publishes a placement newsletter, ask to be added to its mailing list. If your college sponsors an annual job fair, attend it. Before leaving the placement office, review the *College Placement Annual*, which lists the job requirements and locations of several hundred industrial, business, and government employers, whom you may contact directly.

WORD-OF-MOUTH INFORMATION

Word-of-mouth information may come from your instructors, friends, or acquaintances. Start by listing all the people who might possibly help you, and then phone or visit each one to inquire about suitable job openings. Be sure to explain the type of position you are seeking and to ask whether you can use the person's name when you apply.

ADVERTISEMENTS

Advertisements of job openings appear in the classified sections of newspapers and trade publications—that is, periodicals devoted to particular occupations or professions. Read every advertisement carefully, noting the qualifications required for the job and any information concerning the size and location of the organization, job duties, job benefits, and salary.

DIRECT INQUIRIES

Like the *College Placement Annual*, corporate directories can provide names of organizations to contact. Standard corporate directories include *Dun and Bradstreet's Million Dollar Directory, Standard and Poor's Index, Moody's Industrials*, and *Thomas Register of American Manufacturers*. For names of smaller companies not included in these publications, consult the manufacturing directories issued for different states and large cities. Go to your college or city library and ask a librarian where they are shelved. Before using any directory, study the front pages to learn how it is organized.

The yellow-page section of the telephone directory is another good source of company names. Many libraries have statewide collections of telephone books as well as books for all major U.S. cities. If the library does not have one you want, check the local office of your telephone company.

REFERRAL SERVICES

Many professional organizations operate employee referral services. If you belong to the student chapter of one that does, ask it to supply your name to prospective employers.

Writing the Application Letter

If a campus interview is your first contact with an organization, no letter of application is required. In all other situations, you will need to write one.

Your application letters may be among the most important writing you ever do. Like many job seekers, you probably have a good idea of the sort of company you wish to work for as well as geographical preferences. Perhaps you prefer a large organization on the East Coast or a medium-sized company in the South or Southwest. A well-written application letter greatly increases your chances of getting what you want.

Unfortunately, few job seekers know how closely most companies examine the application letters they receive and how ruthlessly they discard those that fail to measure up. Some companies, for instance, automatically reject any letter that is not on business-sized stationery or does not follow one of the standard business letter formats, and no organization will accept a handwritten letter. Even a single misspelled word or insufficient information about the applicant can send the letter to the "reject" file. Obviously, you must prepare your letter with great care to compete successfully with other applicants.

Before you start writing your application letter, analyze the job you are applying for and your qualifications for it. Make a list, itemizing the job qualifications in one column and your own qualifications in another. Although the two columns should be similar, they need not be identical. If you lack one qualification partially or even completely, you may have another that compensates for it. Here is how a typical list might look.

Qualifications Specified	My Qualifications
Associate's degree in drafting	Associate's degree in drafting
One year's work experience in drafting	Nine months' work experience in drafting
	Two elective courses in technical illustration

Assuming you have the proper qualifications for the job, you are ready to start writing your letter. But how can you make the desired impression? To begin, address your letter to a specific person, if possible. Make every effort to learn the name of the personnel manager or supervisor who hires for the position. The job advertisement may provide it, you may find it out through word of mouth, or you can call the company and ask. Do not write to "Personnel Manager" unless securing his or her name is impossible.

Since your aim is to sell yourself, consider your application letter as a specialized kind of sales letter. A successful sales letter does the following things:

Catches the reader's attention.

Creates a desire for the product or service by establishing its superiority.

Causes the reader to act.

ATTRACTING ATTENTION

Beyond naming the position you want and telling how you heard of the vacancy, the opening paragraph should spark the reader's interest in you. Begin by stating a service you can provide or naming one of your outstanding qualifications. Three common attention-getters are the summary, name, and challenging question openings.

A *summary opening* presents the required information as a direct statement.

> I feel my college training in biology and art qualifies me for the position of scientific illustrator that you advertised in the July 20 *Detroit Free Press*.

> Because of my training in chemistry and two summers of laboratory work experience, I believe I can fill any opening you may have for a chemical laboratory technician.

As the second example shows, you can use the summary opening to inquire about possible openings as well as to answer advertisements.

If you use this opening, be sure to include all necessary information. If you merely say, "I wish to be considered for the position of laboratory technician in your firm," you have not mentioned a qualification or a service you can provide. As a result, you are less likely to succeed.

Above all, never let the employer think that you are not a serious job hunter. If you begin by saying, "I happened to be reading the *Boston Globe* and saw that you are looking for a computer programmer," you will destroy your chances with the very first sentence.

The *name opening* identifies the person who told you about the job. This opening can be especially effective because it suggests a recommendation by that person.

> Ms. Loretta Naegele, head of your firm's drafting department, has told me that you plan to hire two more drafters next month. I believe that my B+ record at Newton Technical Institute and two years of summer employment as a drafter's assistant will enable me to meet your requirements for this position.

Note that a summary of the writer's qualifications immediately follows the opening sentence.

The *challenging question opening* asks a question and is used most often by persons inquiring about possible job openings. However, it is also effective for answering advertisements of positions.

> Can your company use someone with two years' experience in designing specialized heating and air-conditioning systems for office buildings?

> Would the engineer's assistant you advertised for in today's *Washington Post* be more valuable to your company if he also had worked three years as a maintenance technician in the army?

Avoid this kind of opening unless you have a special qualification that the employer is likely to find useful. Mentioning a farfetched special qualification will hurt, not help, your job chances.

ESTABLISHING SUPERIORITY

To establish superiority, expand on the qualities you mention in your opening and present others that suit you for the position. Start by discussing your course of study and your grades (if outstanding); then turn to your work experience and extracurricular activities.

In discussing your employment, do not mention the names of the organizations, the dates of employment, or your specific duties. Instead, reserve this information for your resume. Do, however, try to relate your experiences to the job you want. If you want a salesperson's position and have worked as a cashier in a supermarket, indicate that this earlier job taught you how to deal with the public. If the opening is for an office manager and you have worked as a bell captain at a summer resort, note that your previous work provided experience in supervising others. Even if you have never had directly related work experience, try to think of some aspect of a past job—even a part-time or summer job— that you can relate to the position you want.

If you have paid part or all of your educational expenses or held one or more elective offices, say so. The first suggests ambition; the second, the ability to lead—both highly desirable qualities. Mentioning membership in student chapters of professional organizations shows that your interest in your profession is not just monetary. Rather than mentioning every job or office you have held, try to single out those that are most likely to interest the prospective employer, and take up any others in the resume.

If you wish, you may conclude the section by noting that a resume accompanies the letter. The following excerpt from a job application letter establishes superiority. The writer is applying for the position of welding engineer.

> In May 19--, I shall complete a two-year program in welding technology. This program provides a thorough grounding in blueprint reading, template layout, metallurgy, physics, and welding. I have a 3.3 average in my major field.
>
> To help defray the costs of my education, I have worked for two summers in a small metal fabricating shop. This job has given me practical experience with a number of welding processes.
>
> Since entering college, I have been a member of the American Welding Society and during my first term received an educational grant from the Western Michigan Chapter of that organization. I am a tactful, disciplined, hard-working individual who has the ability to set high goals and to achieve them.
>
> William R. Madden

SUGGESTING ACTION

The closing section of your application letter should try to secure an interview. If the hiring organization is nearby, request an interview directly, as in the following example.

> May I come in for an interview at some mutually convenient time? You can reach me at the above address or by phone at (616) 796-3962.

When the organization is far away, the expenses of an interview will be high, and there is no tactful way to request one directly. Instead, ask if a representative will be in your area soon and offer to meet with him or her at that time. Similarly, if you plan to visit the city in which the company is located, suggest an interview then. These approaches often result in interviews.

Applicants for positions in journalism and the graphic arts should also offer to let employers see samples of their work.

> Should you wish to review my portfolio, please call or write, and I shall send copies of my drawings.

THINGS TO AVOID

You can increase your chances of being hired if you avoid the following pitfalls in your application letter.

1. Your writing should not be long-winded. People who must read dozens of application letters naturally prefer brevity, so keep your letter to a single page. However, include all the information needed to sell yourself as a desirable candidate.

2. Never mention how badly you need work. Companies are not charitable institutions, and your appeal will arouse little more than, perhaps, sympathy. If you are unemployed, merely note that you can begin work immediately.

3. Avoid mentioning how eager you are to work for that organization. Such comments, unless carefully phrased, tend to sound insincere and create an unfavorable impression. The employer, after all, wants to know how you can benefit the company, not how it can benefit you.

4. If you do not have on-the-job experience, do not say so, as it may suggest a lack of self-confidence. Stress instead how your training has prepared you for the position.

5. Avoid the question of salary until the job interview. If you are answering an advertisement that asks you to state a salary, suggest deferring the matter until the interview. You might write as follows:

> May I suggest that the matter of salary be deferred until we have discussed the position? Once I know more about the duties, I will be better able to talk about an amount.

Remember, your goal is to sell your services. Your best approach, then, is to ask yourself, "What can I do for this company?"—and then tell your reader as clearly and succinctly as you can.

POLISHING YOUR LETTER

After you write your letter, proofread and polish it with care. The application letter you send must not have a single misspelled word, correction, or incorrect sentence. After all, the employer will use the letter to judge your conscientiousness and attention to detail.

When typing your letter, follow either the modified-block or the full-block format (see pages 172–75). If you know the format the company prefers, use it. Otherwise, follow the modified block, the more common of the two. Some examples of application letters follow.

Examples of Job Application Letters

20900 Moxon Drive
Mt. Clemens, MI 48043
March 16, 19--

Ms. Mary Ann Buday
Personnel Director
Allan Dee-Fraser Senior Citizens'
  Residential Center
33300 Utica Road
Fraser, MI 48026

Dear Ms. Buday:

Uses name opening, identifies position desired, and mentions two qualifications.

Mrs. Diane Schebil, director of your activities department, has informed me that you intend to hire an assistant administrator soon. I feel that my training in health services management and experience in the field of allied health qualify me for this position. Please regard this letter as my formal application.

Provides facts concerning graduation, major program, and area of concentration

On May 21, 19--, I shall receive a Bachelor of Science degree in health services management from Ferris State University. This program offers a thorough background in health science, personnel and financial management, and plant operations, as well as training in leadership techniques. My area of concentration is health care for the aged.

Discusses employment experience; omits specifics of positions but relates experience to job being sought

As an intern, I worked in the administration department of a public health clinic. I have also worked as a hospital ward clerk for one summer and served as a counselor for a summer recreation program. This experience has taught me to apply business practices to the operation of health care facilities and prepared me to hold a supervisory position.

Notes membership in professional and civic organization

While in college, I have been a member of the Ferris Health Services Management Association. I belong to the Clinton Township chapter of the Goodfellows Association. The enclosed resume will provide a fuller picture of my background and experience.

Asks for interview and provides phone number

May I have a personal interview with you to discuss my qualifications in more detail? You can reach me by calling (313) 468-4861 or writing to the above address.

Sincerely,

Susan M. Santine

Susan M. Santine

Enc.

62E West Campus Apartments
Grolier College
Medina, ND 58467
February 14, 19--

Mr. Jonas Dupree
General Manager
Cherry Hill Country Club
100 Hillside Drive
Jordan, AR 72548

Dear Mr. Dupree:

I believe that my formal college training, together with nearly
one summer of management experience, has provided me with the
skills needed to fill the position of assistant maintenance
manager that you advertised in the December issue of Weed and
Turf Magazine.

My graduation this coming May will mark the completion of a two-
year program in ornamental horticulture technology that includes
courses in plant, grass, and vehicle maintenance, use of pesti-
cides and herbicides, and management practices. I have earned
an A average in my major field.

To help pay for college, I have worked for two summers at a
local golf course and one summer in a small nursery. When the
owner of the nursery was hospitalized for ten weeks, I assumed
its complete management for that period. Besides providing
maintenance and supervisory experience, these jobs have given me
the opportunity to meet and deal with the public.

I have played varsity golf for both Grolier College and my high
school. To keep abreast of developments in golf course
management, I have become a student member of the Golf Course
Superintendent's Association of America.

If my qualifications interest you, I would welcome the opportunity to meet with you and discuss them in greater detail. I will
be visiting your area for ten days starting March 11 and can
come in for an interview any time during that period. Please
call me at (701) 349-2500, extension 62, or write to the above
address.

Sincerely yours,

James N. Skellinger

James N. Skellinger

Enc.

Discussion Questions

1. Which type of opening does this letter illustrate?
2. Generally, a job applicant would not cite athletic accomplishments
    in an application letter. Why does this writer mention playing var-
    sity golf in high school and college?
3. Why does the writer suggest that he be interviewed when he visits
    the employer's area rather than asking for an interview at the em-
    ployer's convenience?

216 Burnam Hall
Byron Technical Institute
Dublin, NC 28332
March 14, 19--

Mr. Reginald Washington
Manager
Ames Heating and Cooling Company
1500 Monroe Street
Durham, NC 27701

Dear Mr. Washington:

Does your company have an opening for a serviceman whose background combines academic training with extensive practical
experience? If the answer is yes, I would like to be considered
for the position.

In June, I will receive an Associate in Applied Science degree
in heating, air conditioning, and refrigeration. My chief
interest is in air conditioning.

Before starting my program at Byron Technical Institute, I
worked for two years as a service assistant of a small air
conditioning and refrigeration company. This job has given me a
solid foundation in troubleshooting air conditioning units.
While in school, I have worked part-time as a desk clerk at a
local motel, thus learning to deal with many types of people.

Would it be possible to arrange for an interview? I am
available any weekday except Thursday.

Sincerely,

Kenneth Hollingbeck

Kenneth Hollingbeck

Enclosure

Discussion Questions

1. Which type of opening does this letter illustrate?
2. What does the writer accomplish by mentioning that he is chiefly interested in air conditioning and by naming his major field?
3. Why doesn't the writer name the company he worked for and the
   specific duties he performed there?
4. What is the significance of the "Enclosure" notation in this letter and
   the "Enc." notations in the two preceding letters?

257 Maple Street
Big Rapids, MI 49307
March 30, 19--

Ms. Nancy J. Newman
Personnel Director
Great Lakes Surveying, Inc.
27657 Wide Track Drive
Pontiac, MI 48402

Dear Ms. Newman:

Mr. Donald Lange, of your firm's public relations department, has told me you have several summer openings for surveyor's assistants. I believe my schooling at Ferris State University has provided me with the qualifications to fill one of these positions.

I am a junior in the surveying program at Ferris and expect to receive my Bachelor of Science degree in May, 19--. My overall academic average is 3.5 on a 4.0 scale, and I have a 3.75 in my major field.

I have worked two summers as a carpenter's helper and one summer as a member of a farm crew, jobs that provided practical experience in teamwork and cooperation. I am capable, responsible, and quick to learn, and I believe I will prove an effective member of your surveying crew.

If you require further information concerning my background and qualifications, the Ferris Placement Office can supply you with copies of my placement registration form and instructor evaluations. I would be happy to come in for an interview. Just call me at (616) 796-0713. I look forward to hearing from you.

                    Sincerely yours,

                    Kermit Hulman

                    Kermit Hulman

Discussion Questions

1. Why does the writer note that his previous summer employment gave him experience in teamwork and cooperation?
2. Why does the writer mention that further information is available from the campus placement office?

Preparing the Resume

A job application letter is accompanied by a *resume*, sometimes called a *personal data sheet* or *vita*. The resume summarizes, in one or two pages, the qualifications mentioned in the application letter and presents other information useful to the employer. It also allows you to keep your letter brief so that it functions effectively as a sales tool.

Group the information in the resume under five headings: "Employment Objective," "Education," "Employment Experience," "Personal and Professional Interests," and "References." Include references only when answering an advertisement that asks for them.

Although there is no single correct format for a resume, the format you choose should make it attractive, well organized, and easy to read. The following rules are helpful.

1. Underline and/or capitalize the headings so they stand out on the page.
2. To condense information, use phrases and clauses rather than complete sentences.
3. List your most recent education and employment experience first and work backward so the employer can readily find what is most recent.
4. Avoid cramming too much material onto a page. Ample white space is important.
5. Do not reproduce a resume by mimeographing or xerography. Instead, reproduce the original on a high-quality photocopy machine or have copies printed. Use high-quality paper.

RESUME HEADING

The heading includes your name, address (including zip code), and telephone number. Generally, it is centered at the top of the page, although other arrangements are possible (see the sample resumes on pages 384–89). You may type your name in upper- and lowercase letters or use just capitals. Do not include the date of preparation, as it will make your resume obsolete more quickly.

EMPLOYMENT OBJECTIVE

The employment objective section states your immediate work goal and, if appropriate, the direction you hope your career will take. Here are two examples.

To learn the duties of a librarian and later qualify for the position of head reference librarian.

To begin work as a management trainee or assistant buyer and eventually become a marketing specialist or head buyer.

Your employment objective should convey the impression that you are ambitious, have confidence in your ability, and know your possible avenues for advancement. Do not, however, imply that you see the job as a stepping stone to a better one elsewhere or to establishing your own business.

EDUCATION

In the education section, include information about your post-high school education and any vocational or skill-center programs you have completed. Begin by giving the date of graduation, the degree or certificate you received, your major field of study, and the name and location of the institution. If you have earned a 3.0 grade point average or better, especially in your major field, call it to the employer's attention. Also mention any other academic honors you have received.

Since major field courses are somewhat standard, do not mention them unless the program is so new that an employer would not know its content. Do include minors and elective courses that relate to the job you are seeking. For example, if you majored in diesel and heavy equipment service but are applying for a job with an automobile dealership, list any courses you have taken in automobile repair. Extracurricular activities also create a desirable image, so mention the significant ones you have participated in. Membership in one or more campus clubs, social and professional organizations, or similar groups suggests that you are an outgoing person with numerous interests. Holding office in an organization shows a capacity for leadership. Employers look for these and other positive qualities in job applicants.

If you are a recent high-school graduate, provide your date of graduation, the name and location of the school, and your major field of study. Otherwise, do not mention your high school experience.

Following is the education section of one student's resume.

May 1990, Associate in Applied Science degree, building construction, Ferris State University, Big Rapids, MI 49307.

Academic Honors:

3.5 G.P.A. (4.0 scale) in major field
3.2 G.P.A. overall

Extracurricular Activities:

Captain intramural baseball team one year
Member Pi Kappa Alpha, a social fraternity
Member Associated Building Construction Technologists, a campus professional organization; treasurer senior year

June 1988, graduated from Cannon High School, South Park, PA 15102, industrial arts program.

EMPLOYMENT EXPERIENCE

In the employment experience section of your resume, include the full-time jobs and part-time or temporary jobs you have held. List them in reverse chronological order, most recent first, and separate them clearly on the page. Begin by telling when you held the job, and then give your job title, if any, and the name and address of the organization. Briefly specify your duties if they are pertinent to those of the job you are seeking. Otherwise, just provide the job title. For example, if you apply for a position as a highway technologist, do not discuss the duties you performed as a gas-station attendant or supermarket checkout clerk.

Mention any bonuses, raises, or promotions you received as well as any supervisory experience you gained. All of these reflect superior job performance and make you a more attractive candidate.

Here is the employment experience section of one student's resume.

November 1987 to September 1989	Sanitarian Assistant, Chester County Health Department, West Chester, PA 16529. Inspected restaurants and mobile home parks; conducted mosquito surveys; collected water samples. Starting salary, $860/month; final salary, $990/month.

Discuss military service at the appropriate chronological section. Give the dates, branch of service and your specialty, and places you served. Discuss your duties if they relate to those of the job you are seeking. Since military promotions, like those in civilian life, indicate satisfactory performance, note your rank on discharge. If you supervised others, mention this as well.

December 1986 to November 1989	Electronics repairperson, United States Air Force, Washington, D.C., and Wiesbaden, Germany. Supervised a five-person crew. Honorably discharged as sergeant (E-5).

PERSONAL AND PROFESSIONAL INTERESTS

In this section list any memberships in technical and professional societies, participation in civic activities and organizations, special training (such as lifesaving), and hobbies. This information shows you have a commitment to your profession, a concern for your community, a liking for others, and a variety of interests—all qualities that employers find attractive.

Member National Association of Printers and Lithographers.
Enjoy music, backpacking, swimming, bowling.

REFERENCES

If you answer an advertisement that asks for references, include a list of them along with your letter and resume. Otherwise, simply indicate, under the "References" heading, that you will furnish references on request. Common courtesy requires that you obtain permission before using a person's name as a reference. A good letter of reference is hard to write. Anyone unexpectedly asked to supply one might either refuse or do a slipshod job. Seeking permission also enables you to make sure that the reference will speak well of you. Three or four references should suffice. A smaller number might cause the employer to question your ability or character; more might not provide significant additional information.

For each reference, list the name, title, and address, including the zip code. If you know the phone number, supply it, including the area code. The employer can then call and ask any desired questions.

References can be former employers, instructors, co-workers in responsible positions, or prominent people in your community who know you. Never list relatives or neighbors. Some employers may specify the types of references to include. If so, include only those types.

A typical set of references follows.

Mr. Robert Carlson
Instructor, Drafting Department
Ferris State University
Big Rapids, MI 49307
Phone: (616) 592-5553

Mr. James Stryker
Owner, Stryker's Lakeside Marina
5891 South M–30
Edenville, MI 48620
Phone: (616) 689-4555

Mr. Donald Rynearson
Instructor, Drafting Department
Ferris State University
Big Rapids, MI 49307
Phone: (616) 592-5050

Ms. Sally Momsma
Manager, Poloczech Café
397 Elgin Street
Brandle, MI 48729
Phone: (517) 392-2263

Examples of Resumes

Susan Marie Santine
20900 Moxon Drive
Mt. Clemens, MI 48043
Telephone: (313) 468-4861

EMPLOYMENT OBJECTIVE

Includes short-term and long-term objectives

To become a member of the staff of a private institution or community agency in the health-care field and eventually assume managerial responsibilities.

Gives facts of graduation, academic honors, electives, extracurricular activities

EDUCATION

May 1990, Bachelor of Science degree, health services management, Ferris State University, Big Rapids, MI 49307.

Academic Honors:

   3.6/4.0 G.P.A., health services and science courses.

Electives Related to Major:

   Problems of Aging
   Biomedical Ethics
   Communicable Disease Control

Extracurricular Activities:

   Member of Zeta Tau Alpha, a social sorority.

June 1982. Graduated from Chippewa Valley High School, Mt. Clemens, MI 48043, college preparatory program.

Lists internship, full-time jobs, part-time job in reverse chronological order, and specific duties when related to job being sought

EMPLOYMENT EXPERIENCE

December 1989	Manager trainee (internship program)
	Muskegon Health Center
to	Muskegon, MI 49444
	Assisted with accounting, purchasing,
February 1990	personnel, and maintenance.

Summer of 1989	Ward clerk, Mt. Clemens General Hospital, Mt. Clemens, MI 48043 Answered phone, updated patients' charts and records, handled secretarial duties.
Summer of 1988	Counselor, Clinton Township Parks and Recreation Department, Mt. Clemens, MI 48043 Conducted recreation programs at area playgrounds and parks.
September 1985 to July 1987	Part-time theater cashier, Parkway Theater, Mt. Clemens, MI 48043

PERSONAL AND PROFESSIONAL INTERESTS

Notes membership in professional and civic organizations, lists hobbies

Treasurer, Ferris Health Services Management Association. Member, Clinton Township Goodfellows Association. Enjoy swimming, doll collecting, racketball, softball, and reading.

REFERENCES

Offers to provide references

Will be furnished on request.

James N. Skellinger
62E West Campus Apartments
Grolier College
Medina, ND 58467
Telephone: (701) 349-2500 Ext. 62

Employment Objective

To learn the maintenance and management practices of the golf
course that employs me and eventually become maintenance manager
or head greens superintendent.

Education

May 1990, Associate in Applied Science degree, ornamental
horticulture technology, Grolier College, Medina, ND 58467.

Academic Honors:

   3.8/4.0 G.P.A., ornamental horticulture technology;
   3.2 G.P.A. overall

Extracurricular Activities:

   Varsity golf team two years
   Treasurer senior class
   Yearbook editor junior year

June 1988, Graduated from Dwight D. Eisenhower High School, Rider,
ND 58779, college preparatory program.

Employment Experience

Summer of 1988   Greenhouse worker, Marshall Nursery,
                        Medina, ND 58467
                        Planted and propagated flowers and shrubs,
                        waited on customers, managed business while
                        owner was hospitalized. Received bonus at
                        end of summer.

Summers of 1986   Maintenance worker, Riverview Golf Course,
and 1987   Medina, ND 58467
                        Mowing, watering, fertilizing, spraying
                        weeds, maintaining bunkers.

Personal and Professional Interests

Golfing, swimming, bicycling, coin collecting, photography.

References

Will be furnished on request.

Discussion Questions

1. Why does the writer mention his experience as class treasurer and yearbook editor?
2. What do the writer's personal and professional interests suggest?

```
                        Kenneth Hollingbeck
                        216 Burnam Hall
                      Byron Technical Institute
                        Dublin, NC  28332
                Telephone:  (919) 866-3196, ext. 216
```

EMPLOYMENT OBJECTIVE

   To work as a commercial air conditioning service mechanic, gain more
   experience in troubleshooting, and later hold a service manager's
   position.

EDUCATION

   June 1989, Associate in Applied Science degree, heating, air
   conditioning, and refrigeration, Byron Technical Institute, Dublin,
   NC 28332.

   June 1982, certificate, refrigeration and air conditioning, Dublin Area
   Skills Center.

EMPLOYMENT EXPERIENCE

August 1985   Part-time desk clerk, Manor House Motel, Dublin, NC 28332.
  to Present

July 1982 to   Service assistant, Dixie Air Conditioning and
  August 1985   Refrigeration Company, Effand, NC 27243.
                   Troubleshooting commercial and industrial air conditioning
                   units; some experience installing home and commercial
                   heating units. Starting wage, $5.00/hour; final wage,
                   $6.50/hour.

PERSONAL AND PROFESSIONAL INTERESTS

Bowling, fishing, operating a ham radio. Member of ASHRAE.

References

Will be furnished on request.

Discussion Questions

1. Why does the writer note the wage increase he received as a service
   assistant?
2. What does the writer accomplish by mentioning that he has earned a
   certificate in refrigeration and air conditioning at a skills center?
3. Hollingbeck does not mention his duties as a desk clerk but does specify his duties as a service assistant. Why?

The Interview

Before being hired, you will have a job interview. Sometimes a company recruiter visiting your campus will conduct the interviews, but it usually takes place at the company's personnel offices after the employer reviews your application letter and resume. An interview can last from twenty minutes to several hours and may involve several persons, all of whom you must impress favorably. Obviously, you must plan and execute your interview with great care.

ADVANCE PREPARATION

Before the interview, try to learn as much as you can about the organization. This information enables you to show a real interest in the organization and to discuss your possible role more intelligently.

For a large company, visit the library and read about it in the corporate directories (such as *Dun and Bradstreet's, Moody's Industrials*). These publications tell you the company's credit rating, sales volume, and products, as well as the locations of its plants, the names of its chief officers, and other important facts. For smaller companies, consult the manufacturing directories issued for states and large cities.

A company's annual reports can also provide important information. They give financial statements, discuss building programs and other projects, describe new and promising products, and outline company plans for the future. Many college libraries subscribe to a service that provides on microfiche the annual reports of some eleven thousand companies whose stocks are traded on the major exchanges. An accompanying booklet lists the companies alphabetically and provides a code number that directs you to the proper microfiche. Libraries that do not subscribe to this service often maintain files of annual reports, as do placement offices. If an annual report is not available at your college, write company headquarters or visit a brokerage firm to obtain it.

For government agencies and many private institutions (such as hospitals), consult the pamphlets they issue that describe their facilities and services. If your school placement office does not have these pamphlets, obtain them directly from the organization.

If you are interviewing for a position with a very small organization, such as a locally owned garage, printing shop, or construction company, try speaking with an employee before the interview.

DRESS AND MANNERS

Interviewers weigh a job applicant's dress and manners with care, so you should try to make the best impression possible.

Generally, you should dress formally and conservatively, even if the job you are seeking will not require formal dress. For men, this requires wearing a suit or a sport coat and slacks, together with dress shoes, a dress shirt, and a tie. For women, it means wearing an office dress or a skirt, jacket, and blouse. Also, pay attention to the condition of your clothing. If they are soiled, ripped, or sloppy, the employer may assume that your work habits are also sloppy. Personal cleanliness is viewed in the same light. If well groomed, you will make a better impression.

When the interview is held at school or on-campus, clothing rules are generally more relaxed, and you can then wear shop or laboratory clothing. Do not, however, wear blue jeans, cut-offs, or T-shirts. Start the day with fresh clothing so you will be as neat as possible for the interview.

The employer will also observe your manners during the interview. Once you are called into the interviewer's office, wait for him or her to shake hands and begin the conversation. Remain standing until you are offered a seat, and then sit up straight and maintain good eye contact. You will make a poor impression if you slouch, sprawl, or fuss with items on the desk. Never chew gum or smoke during an interview. Try to appear relaxed and confident. When the interview is over, thank the interviewer. Good manners always leave a favorable impression.

ANSWERING QUESTIONS

Different interviewers adopt different approaches. Some do almost all the talking, while noting how closely and intelligently you listen. Others say almost nothing, forcing you to make your case virtually unaided. Generally, though, the interviewer obtains information by asking questions. Advance preparation will improve your responses. A day or so before the interview, list the questions that you might be asked. Here are some possibilities.

Tell me something about yourself and your family background.

Why did you choose your field of work?

What qualifications do you think will ensure your success?

What special courses have helped prepare you for this job?

What previous jobs have you held and how will the experience help you in this job?

What do you know about opportunities in your field?

What percentage of your college expenses did you earn? How?

What do you know about our company?

Why do you wish to work for us?

What interests you about our product(s) or service(s)?

Do you work best as part of a team or by yourself?

How do you respond to supervision?

Give me an example of a time when you provided leadership.

What are your strengths? Weaknesses?

Do you like to travel?

Are you willing to go where the company sends you?

What future role would you like to play in our organization?

Once you have exhausted the possible questions, begin to outline your answer to each one. Familiarize yourself with the answers and then, if a tape recorder is available, record them so that you can hear yourself as the interviewer will. You may, for example, find you are speaking too quickly or too softly. If you can, ask a friend to act as interviewer and criticize your performance. Even if the interviewer's questions are phrased differently from your own, your efforts will be worthwhile; both sets of questions will undoubtedly cover the same general information.

How you respond to the interviewer's questions will determine in large part whether you will be hired. First, always wait until the interviewer has finished a question before answering. Take a moment or two to organize your thoughts before you start speaking. Say only what is necessary; then stop. At the same time, avoid one-word "yes" or "no" answers, which do not allow the interviewer to learn much about you. Do not hesitate to admit that you cannot answer a question: an honest "I don't know" is far better than a hasty and perhaps incorrect response.

Interviewers occasionally ask "catch" questions just to see how you handle them. If this happens, try to phrase your answer so it will neither offend the speaker nor contradict your own views. If the interviewer says, "The president is certainly catching lots of criticism these days, isn't he?" you might respond, "Yes, but I suppose, any president has to expect quite a bit of that." Such an answer would offend neither a supporter nor a critic of the president, nor would it compromise your own position.

ASKING QUESTIONS

An interview should be as informative to you as it is to the interviewer, helping you determine whether the job, the company, and the community are right for you. Therefore, you should ask questions about matters that have not been covered by the interviewer. Some of these questions might include the following:

> What opportunities for advancement are open to me?
> Might I expect to be transferred periodically or would I work permanently in this location?
> Will my hours be regular or variable?
> What fringe benefits does your organization offer?
> What will be the size of my work unit?
> How do you evaluate employees' job performance?
> What opportunities for furthering my education are available in the area?
> What recreational and cultural activities does the area offer?

You should leave the interview with your key questions answered so that you can make an intelligent job choice. However, avoid asking so many questions that the interviewer does not have time to evaluate you.

DISCUSSING SALARY

At some point, the issue of salary will arise. Although salary is important to you, it is best to let the interviewer mention it first. Otherwise, you may appear to be most interested in the money. Sometimes, however, interviewers deliberately avoid the subject to see how you will handle it. In this case, wait until the interview is clearly drawing to a close and then ask, directly and without embarrassment, "What salary are you offering for this position?" An interview is a business transaction, and there should be candor on both sides.

Occasionally, an interviewer will ask what salary you expect. Unless you know the salary range for your position, this can create an embarrassing situation. In addition, it can lead the interviewer to make a lower offer than you would otherwise receive. Thus, you should investigate the salary range for the job before the interview. Ask your instructors, consult literature in your school's placement office, and check the classified ads in newspapers and professional publications for salary information. Many states have annual occupational guides that list national and state salary levels for all occupations in the state. Ask your library staff whether this guide is available.

Most companies have an established salary range for each job, so unless your qualifications are exceptional, do not try to bargain for more money. This attempt may keep you from getting the job.

KEEPING A RECORD OF THE INTERVIEW

You will probably not receive a job offer at the time of an interview. Instead, the organization will review your qualifications, along with those of other applicants, and then reach a decision. In the meantime, what you have learned can improve your performance in other interviews.

To help you remember each interview, keep a detailed record of it in a notebook. Record the information as soon after the interview as you can, while it is still fresh in your mind. Include the names of the interviewers, a description of the job, a summary of the job qualifications, and the salary range. If you are called for a second interview, the information will be especially helpful. Note, too, any questions that gave you trouble or any mistakes that you made so that you can correct these weaknesses for future interviews.

Post-Interview Letters

There are four common types of post-interview letters: letter of thanks, job acceptance letter, job refusal letter, and follow-up letter.

LETTER OF THANKS

A day or so after the interview, send the interviewer a brief *letter of thanks*. Use the opportunity to say once again that you want the job and why you think you can handle it. A sample letter of thanks follows.

7022 Bailey Road
Howard City, MI 49329
March 19, 19--

Mr. Jerry Elenball
Head, Manufacturing Engineering
Herman Miller, Inc.
Zeeland, MI 49464

Dear Mr. Elenball:

Thank you for a very pleasant interview for the position
of assistant furniture designer.

My academic training in design engineering, along with my
internship in the design department of Harris Furniture
Company, has provided me with the qualifications we
discussed. I am convinced I can handle the job
successfully.

I hope you decide to hire me, and I look forward to hearing
from you.

Sincerely,

Irma Inman

Many job candidates neglect to write letters of thanks. Your note, therefore, will stamp you as especially thoughtful and increase your chances of being hired. If the interviewer has spoken to many other applicants, it also helps ensure that you will be remembered.

JOB ACCEPTANCE LETTER

A *job acceptance letter* is used to accept a written job offer or to confirm the verbal acceptance of a job offered over the phone. Show courtesy—even enthusiasm—but don't go overboard in expressing your thanks.

> Thank you very much for offering me the position of marketing assistant with your firm. I am happy to accept and I am sure that I will be able to justify your confidence in me. As you requested, I will report for work on Monday, July 10. In the meantime, if you need to get in touch with me, I will be at my present address until July 7.
>
> I look forward to working for you.

This letter, though brief, does much more than merely accept the job. It thanks the company for the offer, assures good future performance, confirms the starting date, tells where to reach the new employee until then, and ends by expressing pleasure. In short, its tone is pleasant, and it says everything necessary.

JOB REFUSAL LETTER

The *job refusal letter* is harder to write than the other types of post-interview letters. Remember that the organization you are turning down has spent considerable time, effort, and money in corresponding with you, conducting your interview, and reviewing your qualifications. It also may have counted heavily on your services. Great tact and courtesy are therefore necessary. One good approach is to telephone the interviewer, explain your decision and briefly why you made it, and then follow with a letter reiterating the decision.

Begin a job refusal letter with a courteous remark about the organization, job, or interview. Follow this with a polite refusal and your reasons for choosing another job. End with another pleasant comment.

> I enjoyed meeting you and discussing the duties of your commercial artist position, and I was gratified to receive your job offer last Wednesday. I have given the offer serious thought but have decided to accept a position with another publisher. As you know from our conversation, I wish to concentrate on scientific illustration. The job I have chosen will allow me to spend full time doing so.
>
> I appreciate the consideration you have shown me.

This letter is both pleasant and thoughtful. Although it may disappoint the reader, it should leave no trace of bitterness or resentment.

FOLLOW-UP LETTER

In most cases, you will be hired or rejected within a month of your interview. If you are rejected, it may be because you lack one or more of the job qualifications. With medium-sized and large companies, however, a more suitable opening may perhaps occur a few months later. If you are still unemployed after several months, you might send *follow-up letters* to the companies that interviewed you. For example:

> On August 15, I was interviewed by Union Carbide Chemicals for the job of chemical laboratory technician. Although I was not hired because I lacked courses in organic analysis, I remember both you and your organization very favorably and hope you will consider me for any current opening that fits my qualifications.

A follow-up letter can lead to a review of your credentials and, possibly, to a job offer. Otherwise, your credentials may not be reconsidered. If you are turned down for a job because another candidate has more experience, the company may have several similar postions for which an opening may occur soon. In this case, you could send a follow-up letter like this one:

Early last summer you interviewed me for a sales position with
General Foods. Although I was not hired, you indicated during
the interview that I was qualified for the position. General
Foods remains in my mind one of the top companies to work for.
Should another opening occur in you sales force, I would appre-
ciate your reconsidering my application.

Suggestions for Writing

1. Write an application letter for a specific job that you have seen advertised or that someone has told you about. Use one of the three
   openings discussed in this chapter.
2. Write a letter applying for a specific position with a company that
   may or may not have a vacancy.
3. Prepare a resume to accompany your application letter. Include references.
4. Write the following post-interview letters.
   a. thank someone for interviewing you
   b. accept a job offer
   c. refuse a job offer
   d. express interest in working for a company that has rejected you
      previously.

HANDBOOK

Grammar, Usage, Punctuation, and Mechanics

The Handbook is designed to help you with the questions and problems that arise when you write papers. You can also use it as needed to review the fundamentals of English usage.

The Handbook has three main sections. The first, "Sentence Elements," discusses subjects, predicates, complements, appositives, parts of speech, phrases, and clauses. The second section, "Avoiding Common Errors of Usage," is intended to help you avoid common writing errors. The final section, "Punctuation and Mechanics," tells when and how to use the different types of punctuation marks.

Sentence Elements

Subject and Predicate

SUBJECT

The subject of a sentence tells·who or what the sentence is about. A *simple subject* consists of one or more words that name one or more persons, places, things, actions, qualities, or ideas. A *complete subject* includes the simple subject plus certain other words that describe it. Here are some simple and complete subjects.

Simple Subjects	Complete Subjects
man	the tall man
trees	the slender, leafy trees
complaint	your complaint
baby	the baby
Mr. Davis	old Mr. Davis
bits	rotary drill bits

PREDICATE

The predicate tells something about the subject and completes the idea expressed by the sentence. A simple predicate consists of one or more words, called *verbs*, that show action or existence—what someone or something is, was, or will be. A complete predicate includes the simple predicate plus any other words needed to expand and modify its meaning.

Simple Predicates	Complete Predicates
laughed	laughed loudly
are swaying	are swaying in the wind
will be discussed	will be discussed next Wednesday
is	is in its crib
was	was the neighborhood grouch
must be sharpened	must be sharpened periodically

Combinations like *are swaying* and *will be discussed* are called *verb phrases*—two or more verbs that function as a single unit.

Notice that none of the subjects and predicates convey complete ideas by themselves. However, combining appropriate subjects and predicates gives us complete sentences and therefore complete thoughts.

The tall man laughed loudly.
The slender, leafy trees are swaying in the wind.
Your complaint will be discussed next Wednesday.
The baby is in its crib.
Old Mr. Davis was the neighborhood grouch.
Rotary drill bits must be sharpened periodically.

Recognizing Subjects and Predicates. Here are two of the preceding sentences, this time with their simple subjects underlined once and their simple predicates or verbs underlined twice.

The tall <u>man</u> <u>laughed</u> loudly.
The slender, leafy <u>trees</u> <u>are</u> <u>swaying</u> in the wind.

In each of these sentences, the main idea is expressed by the simple subject and verb—a fact that holds true for every other sentence as well.

Picking out these key parts is not difficult. Simply locate the verb part of the sentence, and then ask yourself who or what controls the verb. Consider the following sentence.

Elmer gave the old beggar a dollar.

The answer to the question "What or who gave?" is clearly *Elmer*, rather than the *beggar*. Thus, *Elmer* is the subject of the sentence.

When identifying subjects and verbs, you should keep a few pointers in mind. First, as already noted, the verb part of a sentence may be a verb phrase. In the following examples, the subjects are underlined once and the verbs twice.

By tomorrow, I will have finished my report.

Sometimes one or more words may interrupt the verb phrase or come between the subject and the verb.

Joyce had completely forgotten her appointment with the dentist. (A word interrupts the verb phrase.)
Marvin has certainly not shown any talent as a writer. (Two words interrupt the verb phrase.)
Do you believe that story? (A word interrupts the verb phrase.)

Note that in the last example the interrupting word is the subject of the sentence. This verb-subject-verb pattern occurs in many sentences that ask questions.

Some sentences have compound subjects (two or more simple subjects), compound verbs (two or more individual verbs), or both.

The house and garage burned to the ground. (compound subject)
He jogs and swims for exercise. (compound verb)
The knight and the squire mounted their horses and rode off. (compound subject and compound verb)

In most sentences, the subject comes ahead of the verb. Sometimes, though, the verb comes first and may be preceded by one or more other words.

> Across the river <u>stands</u> a lone pine <u>tree</u>.
> Here <u>is</u> my house.
> There <u>goes</u> <u>Jack</u>.
> When <u>is</u> your <u>theme</u> due?

If a sentence begins with *here* or *there* or a question begins with *when, where, how,* or *why,* the subject is likely to follow the verb.

In sentences expressing a command or a request, the subject, which is always "you," may be unstated but understood.

> (<u>you</u>) <u>Come</u> here right away!
> (<u>you</u>) <u>Hand</u> me that wrench, please.

Exercise

Place a slash mark (/) between the complete subject and the complete predicate of each sentence; then underline the simple subject once and the verb or verb phrase twice. Some sentences may have more than one subject and one verb. If the subject interrupts the verb phrase, set the subject off with a pair of slash marks. If the subject is unstated, put a slash mark at the beginning of the sentence.

> My <u>boss</u>/<u>is</u> <u>planning</u> the agenda for the safety meeting.
> What <u>will</u>/<u>you</u>/<u>do</u> after graduation?
> /<u>Return</u> the wrench to the tool crib. (The subject *you* is under-
>   stood.)

1. The new helper will finish the job soon.
2. The crew of carpenters worked all day.
3. As an apprentice, Janice will be learning the plumbing trade.
4. Miranda and her family drove to Chicago and visited the Museum of Science and Industry.
5. What did you hear about the accident?
6. I do not understand the directions for this procedure.

7. Where are the minutes of last month's meeting?
8. There are several empty shelves in the stockroom.
9. One man and two women were hired.
10. Behind the barn sat a rusty tractor.

COMPLEMENTS

A sentence may include one or more complements—words or word groups that are part of the predicate and help complete the meaning of the sentence. There are four kinds of complements: *direct objects*, *indirect objects*, *subject complements*, and *object complements*.

Direct Object. A direct object names the person, place, or thing that receives, or results from, the action of a verb.

> The store clerks chose *John* to represent them. (The direct object *John* receives the action of the verb *chose*.)
>
> The Boy Scouts built a *fire*. (The direct object *fire* is the result of the action of the verb *built*.)

Indirect Object. An indirect object identifies someone or something that receives whatever is named by the direct object. It always precedes the direct object.

> Ramona Chavez sold *me* her calculator. (The indirect object *me* identifies who received the calculator. *Calculator* is the direct object.)
>
> They built the *dog* a kennel. (The indirect object *dog* identifies what received the kennel. *Kennel* is the direct object.)

An indirect object can be converted into a prepositional phrase that begins with *to* or *for* and follows the direct object.

> Ramona Chavez sold her calculator *to me*.
>
> They built a kennel *for the dog*.

Subject Complement. A subject complement follows a verb that shows existence—what something is, was, or will be. It renames or describes the subject.

Lucille is an *architect*. (The complement *architect* renames the subject *Lucille*.)

Lucille is *efficient*. (The complement *efficient* describes the subject *Lucille*.)

Object Complement. An object complement follows a direct object and renames or describes it.

The class elected Mary *president*. (The object complement *president* renames the direct object *Mary*.)

They painted the lounge *green*. (The object complement *green* describes the direct object *lounge*.)

Exercise

For each of the following sentences, identify the italicized item as a direct object (DO), an indirect object (IO), a subject complement (SC), or an object complement (OC).

I consider that suggestion *foolish*. (OC)

1. Mona and Rose were very *angry* over their low test scores.
2. I understand the *problem* and how to solve it.
3. They have offered *William* the promotion at least three times.
4. David has been *supervisor* of the stock room for two months.
5. The police checked the *airplane* for a bomb.
6. Everyone in the class thought the instructor *incompetent*.
7. I will be *ready* soon.
8. The local machine shop has donated a *lathe* to the school.
9. I'll certainly give *him* a piece of my mind.
10. Because of the rain, the road was almost *impassable*.

Parts of Speech

Traditional English grammar classifies words into eight parts of speech, based on their function in sentences. These parts are *nouns*, *pronouns*, *verbs*, *adjectives*, *adverbs*, *prepositions*, *conjunctions*, and *interjections*.

NOUNS

Nouns name persons, places, things, qualities, ideas, events, or occurrences. In the following examples, the nouns are italicized.

> *Angelo* drove to *Colorado* in his *car*. (The first noun names a person, the second a place, and the third a thing.)
> He has never shown *compassion* for anyone. (The noun names a quality.)
> *Socialism* has never appealed to me. (The noun names an idea.)
> The *party* was enjoyable. (The noun names an event.)
> Her *departure* was abrupt. (The noun names an occurrence.)

Proper Nouns. When nouns name particular persons, places, institutions, or events, their first letters are always capitalized (*John, Sacramento, American Stock Exchange, World War II*). These nouns are known as *proper nouns*.

Common Nouns. These nouns name general classes that include many individual items (*dog, business, house*). Think of common nouns as names for things, usually concrete and tangible, that can be counted (*one dog, two businesses, three houses*). Common nouns usually add *s* or *es* to indicate a quantity greater than one; that is, their plurals usually end in *s*.

Mass and Abstract Nouns. Nouns also name things that are not ordinarily counted and therefore do not often have plural forms. *Mass nouns* name formless things (*salt, petroleum*) and *abstract nouns* name intangible objects and ideas (*courage, liberalism*).

Collective Nouns. Still other nouns, called *collective nouns*, are singular in form but stand for a group of individual units (*herd, grove*). Collective nouns also have plural forms, which indicate more than one such group (*herds, groups*).

Exercise

List the nouns in the following sentences.

The new senator from North Dakota was met by a delegation that protested his conservatism. (senator, North Dakota, delegation, conservatism)

1. The cowboys rounded up the herd for shipment to Chicago.
2. Sylvia Broom was born in Newark, Ohio.
3. Thoughtlessness has led to many industrial accidents.
4. The Acme Corporation rates aggressiveness above all other qualities in its salespeople.
5. Two members of the committee presented a report on the cost of the project.
6. Scientists believe that the surface of the planet Uranus is cold and barren.
7. In our town, the Knitwell Textile Company is the chief industry.
8. Raymond filled his tank with twenty gallons of gasoline.
9. Professor La Fontaine spent his sabbatical leave in France.
10. Sandra is conducting a survey for the Danbury Merchants' Association.

PRONOUNS

A pronoun is a word that takes the place of a noun in a sentence. There are eight types of pronouns: *personal, interrogative, relative, demonstrative, reflexive, intensive, indefinite,* and *reciprocal.*

Personal Pronouns. Personal pronouns are pronouns that refer to one or more clearly identified persons, places, or things.

Subjective	Objective	Possessive
I	me	my, mine
you	you	your, yours
he	him	his
she	her	her, hers
it	it	its
we	us	our, ours
you	you	your, yours
they	them	their, theirs

The personal pronoun forms listed under "Subjective" are used as the subjects of sentences or clauses; the forms listed under "Objective" are used as direct or indirect objects; and the forms listed under "Possessive" are used to show possession. *My, your, her, our,* and *their* always precede a noun.

> *I* repaired the lawnmower. (pronoun as subject)
> William called *him.* (pronoun as direct object)
> William threw *him* the ball. (pronoun as indirect object)
> The camera is *hers.* (possessive pronoun as subject complement)

Interrogative Pronouns. Interrogative pronouns begin sentences or clauses that ask questions.

who	what
whom	which
whose	

> *What* is wrong with the dishwasher?
> *Which* of these wrenches fits the bolt?

Relative Pronouns. A relative pronoun starts a noun clause (see pages 429–30) or an adjective clause (see pages 430–31). Note that, with the exception of *that,* the relative pronouns in the first column can also serve as interrogative pronouns.

who	(whoever)
whose	(whosever)
whom	(whomever)
what	(whatever)
which	(whichever)
that	

> The field *that* I plan to major in is heating, air conditioning, and refrigeration.
> Harvey Wilson, *whose* printing shop burned last month, is rebuilding in a new location.

Demonstrative Pronouns. A demonstrative pronoun points out or identifies something. There are four demonstrative pronouns.

this	these
that	those

That is the lathe to use.
I like *those*.

This and *these* point out things that are recent or nearby; *that* and *those* point out things that are farther away in time or space.

This is a better calculator than that is.

Reflexive and Intensive Pronouns. A reflexive pronoun turns the action of a verb back upon the doer of the action. An intensive pronoun is used to give emphasis to a noun or a pronoun. Reflexive and intensive pronouns always end with -*self* or -*selves*.

myself	oneself
yourself	ourselves
himself	yourselves
herself	themselves
itself	

The machinist cut *himself* on the metal shaving. (reflexive pronoun)
The manager *herself* answered the customer's complaint. (intensive pronoun)

Do not use a reflexive pronoun as a substitute for a personal pronoun.

John and *myself* will repair the radiator. (incorrect)
John and *I* will repair the radiator. (correct)

The following nonstandard forms should not be used in your writing: *hisself, theirself,* and *theirselves.*

Indefinite Pronouns. This group includes the many pronouns that do not refer to specifically named persons, places, or things. The following are among the common indefinite pronouns.

all	everyone	none
another	everything	no one
any	few	nothing
anybody	many	one
anyone	most	some
anything	much	somebody
each	neither	someone
either	nobody	something
everybody		

Neither of the students writes well.

I saw *nobody* in the chemistry laboratory.

Reciprocal Pronouns. A reciprocal pronoun indicates an exchange of action between two or more parties. There are two reciprocal pronouns: *each other* and *one another. Each other* is used when there are two parties involved in the action; *one another* is used when there are three or more.

Larry and I always help *each other* with chemistry problems. (two persons)

The shop employees congratulated *one another* upon winning the company's safety award. (more than two persons)

In informal speech, *each other* and *one another* are often used interchangeably. However, this practice should be avoided in formal writing.

Exercise

List the pronouns in the following sentences.

They had convinced themselves that neither would be promoted. (they, themselves, neither)

1. He can afford to pay for it himself.
2. Help yourself to whatever you wish to eat.
3. Now, that is the right way to do it.
4. They themselves are to blame for the problem.
5. What is the matter with my micrometer?
6. To whom am I speaking?
7. If we help one another, everyone will find the task easy.
8. Of the two themes, yours is written better than hers.
9. These are problems we can solve by ourselves.
10. Anybody who wishes additional overtime can have it.

VERBS

A verb is a word that indicates action or existence and helps express the main idea of a sentence. Verbs may be classified as *action verbs*, *linking verbs*, and *helping verbs*.

Action Verbs. As its name suggests, an action verb expresses an action or occurrence. Action verbs may be classified as transitive or intransitive. A transitive verb requires a direct object, which receives the action of the verb and completes its meaning.

The mechanic *installed* the carburetor.

In this example, *carburetor* is the direct object and completes the meaning of the action indicated by *installed*.

An intransitive verb, on the other hand, does not need an object to complete its meaning.

Ellen *resigned*.
Water *flows* downhill.

Many verbs can be either transitive or intransitive depending on the sentences in which they are used.

Jerry *stood* the tripod in the corner. (transitive verb)
Jerry *stood* in the doorway. (intransitive verb)

Linking Verbs. A linking verb expresses a condition or state of being rather than an action. Some linking verbs connect the subject of a sentence or clause to a noun or pronoun that identifies or renames the subject. Others connect the subject to an adjective, a word that describes the subject. (For a discussion of adjectives, see pages 418–19.)

> Ms. Kincaid *is* the chief biologist. (The subject, *Ms. Kincaid*, is linked to the noun, *biologist*, which identifies or renames the subject.)
>
> His speech *was* excellent. (The subject, *speech*, is linked to *excellent*, which describes the subject.)

The most common linking verbs are forms of the verb *be* (*is, are, am, was, were, been*). Some other verbs that may be used as linking verbs are *seem, become, appear, remain, feel, look, smell, sound,* and *taste.* When used as linking verbs, words in the second group in effect function as forms of the verb *be.* Thus, in the sentence "The water felt cold," *felt* has the same meaning as *was.* When, however, the words in the second group stand for physical actions, they function as action verbs. For example, in the sentence "The swimmer felt the water," *felt* is an action verb.

Helping Verbs. A helping verb accompanies an action verb or a linking verb, allowing it to express shades of meaning, such as the time when an action takes place. Combining one or more helping verbs with an action verb or linking verb results in a verb phrase. The following list includes some of the most common helping verbs.

has	been	had (to)
have	do	shall
had	does	will
am	did	going (to)
is	used (to)	
are	may	would
was	might	should
were	must	ought (to)
be	have (to)	can
being	has (to)	could

The following sentences illustrate the use of helping verbs.

> The mechanic *will install* the carburetor in the automobile. (helping verb *will* with action verb *install*)
>
> Betty *will have worked* for the O'Hara Electronic Corporation two years this June. (helping verbs *will have* with action verb *worked*)
>
> He *does seem* less competent than the others. (helping verb *does* with linking verb *seem*)
>
> Tuesday *may be* the day when Belinda receives a raise. (helping verb *may* with linking verb *be*)

Several helping verbs can function as verbs by themselves. This dual function is illustrated in the following two sentences.

> I *have* requested a raise. (*have* as a helping verb)
>
> I *have* two jobs. (*have* as a verb by itself)

Principal Parts and Forms. All verbs have three principal parts—the *present*, the *past*, and the *past participle*—from which their tenses are built. Though not a principal part, a fourth necessary part is the *present participle*.

Individual verbs may have as few as three forms or as many as eight forms. Most verbs, however, have four forms, as illustrated below.

	Present	Past	Past Participle	Present Participle
I	*talk*	*talked*	talked	*talking*
you	talk	talked	talked	talking
he, she, it	*talks*	talked	talked	talking
we, you, they	talk	talked	talked	talking

In the table, the four forms are *talk*, *talks*, *talked*, and *talking*. All regular verbs, those which take -*d*, -*ed*, or -*t* endings, have four forms, as do some irregular verbs, those which undergo internal changes. *Swing* is one such irregular verb; its four forms are *swing*, *swings*, *swung*, and *swinging*.

A second group of irregular verbs has five forms.

	Present	Past	Past Participle	Present Participle
I	*write*	*wrote*	*written*	*writing*
you	write	wrote	written	writing
he, she, it	*writes*	wrote	written	writing
we, you, they	write	wrote	written	writing

Here, the five forms are *write, writes, wrote, written,* and *writing.*

A very few irregular verbs—*set, hit,* and *hurt,* for example—have only three forms.

	Present	Past	Past Participle	Present Participle
I	*hit*	hit	hit	*hitting*
you	hit	hit	hit	hitting
he, she, it	*hits*	hit	hit	hitting
we, you, they	hit	hit	hit	hitting

Hit, hits, and *hitting* are the three forms of this verb.

One irregular verb, *be,* has eight forms: *be, am, are, is, was, were, been, being.*

Tense. Verbs show the time of the action or state of being they represent through tense. There are six basic tenses—*present, past, future, present perfect, past perfect,* and *future perfect*—and six corresponding progressive tenses. The different tenses are formed by using the principal parts of the verb, either alone or in combination with helping verbs.

Present Tense

The present tense is used to show present state of being and to state facts that are permanently true; to show general or habitual action; and sometimes, with appropriate adverbs, to denote future action. It is formed by using the present principal part without a helping verb.

Helen *looks* beautiful in her new gown. (present state of being)

Brazil *is* in South America. (permanent truth)

John *lives* on the eighteenth floor. (general action)
I *brush* my teeth each morning. (habitual action)
Monday, I *begin* my new job. (future action)

Past Tense

The past tense indicates that a state of being or an action took place at a particular time in the past. It is formed by using the past principal part without a helping verb.

Robert *felt* unhappy with his performance on the test. (past state of being)
Maria *completed* the computer program yesterday. (past action)

Future Tense

The future tense indicates that a state of being or an action will occur in the future. It is formed by using the present principal part, along with the helping verb *shall* or *will*.

I *will feel* better after a good night's sleep. (future state of being)
We *shall overcome* this problem. (future action)

Present Perfect Tense

The present perfect tense is used when a state of being or an action that began in the past, or its effects, continues until the present time. It is formed by using the past participle with the helping verb *has* or *have*.

The players *have been* irritable since they lost the homecoming game. (State of being continues until present.)
Norman *has worked* as a chemical laboratory technician for five years. (Action continues until present.)
William *has repaired* the snow blower. (Effect of action continues until present.)

Past Perfect Tense

The past perfect tense shows a past state of being or action that was completed prior to another past state of being or action. It is properly used only when two past times are expressed and is formed by using the past participle with the helping verb *had*.

> He *had been* sick for a number of years before he died. (Italicized state of being occurred first.)
>
> Michele bought a new typewriter. She *had wanted* one for several months. (Italicized action occurred first.)

Future Perfect Tense

The future perfect tense indicates that a state of being or an action will be completed at a particular time in the future. It is formed by using the past participle with the helping verbs *shall have* or *will have*.

> The laboratory director *shall have been* with the company ten years next July. (Future state of being will be completed.)
>
> I *will have completed* all the requirements for my degree by next June. (Future action will be completed.)

Progressive Tenses

The six progressive tenses use the present participle with the verb *to be* and denote action going on over a period of time.

> I am talking (present progressive tense)
> I shall be talking (future progressive tense)
> I was talking (past progressive tense)
> I have been talking (present perfect progressive tense)
> I had been talking (past perfect progressive tense)
> I shall have been talking (future perfect progressive tense)

Voice. Transitive verbs have two voices: *active* and *passive*. A verb is in the active voice when the subject performs the action specified by the verb.

Teresa *identified* the organic compound. (The subject performs the action.)

A verb is in the passive voice when the subject does not perform the action but is acted upon. The noun or pronoun that identifies the performer of the action either appears in a prepositional phrase or is not mentioned at all.

The organic compound *was identified* by Teresa. (The prepositional phrase *by Teresa* identifies the performer.)

The organic compound *was identified* as ethyl alcohol. (The performer is not identified.)

Technical and scientific writing commonly employs the passive voice for explanations of processes, where objectivity is desirable. Other kinds of writing should, however, avoid the passive voice except where the action rather than the actor is important. For further discussion of the passive voice, see pages 450–52.

Exercise

List the verbs in the following sentences and identify the tense and voice of each.

Has the chisel been returned to the tool crib? (has . . . been returned; present perfect tense, passive voice)

1. Perry is changing the tire.
2. Can you begin the new job right away?
3. I will supervise every stage of the project.
4. I shall have finished the preparations for the speech by late afternoon.
5. Henry worked diligently on his mathematics assignment.
6. Edmond has worked for the same boss for ten years.
7. We believe that our company's products are without equal.
8. Two months after he enlisted, Neville had earned the rank of corporal.
9. I should have considered other approaches to this problem.
10. In a few days, you will feel better about this decision.

ADJECTIVES

An adjective *modifies* a noun or pronoun by describing or limiting it or in some way making its meaning more exact. Sometimes the adjective is positioned next to the word it modifies. At other times, one or more words may come between the two of them.

> Mary is *beautiful*.
> *Grouchy* men irritate me.
> The *yellow* car belongs to Bob.
> *Three* people have applied so far.

You will notice from the last example that numbers, when used to limit nouns, are adjectives. The words *a*, *an*, and *the*, known as articles, are also considered adjectives. Unlike most adjectives, an article *must* precede the noun it modifies.

> *The* girl brought *an* apple and *a* sandwich to *the* picnic.

Often, two or more adjectives modify the same word.

> *The tall, leafy* tree has *gray* bark.

Several categories of pronouns can function as adjectives.

> *Whose* micrometer is on the floor? (interrogative adjective)
> The repairman *whose* truck was stolen called the police. (relative adjective)
> *This* shop has the best safety record. (demonstrative adjective)
> *Some* chemists have special training in bacteriology. (indefinite adjective)
> She focused *her* microscope on the rod-shaped organisms. (possessive adjective)

Some adjectives, called proper adjectives, are derived from proper nouns.

> That building is a fine example of *Victorian* architecture.
> An *Italian* restaurant is opening across the street.

Exercise

List the adjectives in the following sentences.

A tall, thin man wearing a red ski mask robbed the local bank yesterday. (a, tall, thin, a, red, ski, the, local)

1. Our company gives its employees three weeks of vacation each year.
2. A clean, tidy house will sell faster than a dirty one.
3. Because of the good pay, thirty people applied for the job.
4. The dishonest salesperson cheated me by selling me a defective car.
5. We shared an orange and a banana at lunch.
6. Few people live without some stress.
7. Arnold was delighted when he won the lottery after buying many tickets.
8. Before he could finish his question, the angry chairperson silenced him.
9. Five actors auditioned for the lead in the new musical.
10. The doors were locked when the first speaker began her report.

ADVERBS

An adverb is a word that modifies a verb, an adjective, another adverb, or a whole sentence. Adverbs generally modify verbs and answer the questions "how?" "when?" "where?" "how often?" and "to what extent?"

The painter worked *rapidly*. (The adverb *rapidly* modifies the verb *worked* and answers the question "how?")

The supplies arrived *yesterday*. (The adverb *yesterday* modifies the verb *arrived* and answers the question "when?")

Fred drove *home* after leaving the expressway. (The adverb *home* modifies the verb *drove* and answers the question "where?")

I *sometimes* watch TV in the evening. (The adverb *sometimes* modifies the verb *watch* and answers the question "how often?")

Adverbs that modify adjectives, other adverbs, and whole sentences are also common.

The draftsman's work was *extremely* precise. (The adverb *extremely* modifies the adjective *precise* and answers the question "how?")

The project is proceeding *very* slowly. (The adverb *very* modifies the adverb *slowly* and answers the question "to what extent?")

Perhaps I will be promoted this year. (The adverb *perhaps* modifies the whole sentence but does not answer any specific question.)

Most adverbs are formed by adding *-ly* to adjectives.

The sea is *calm*. (Calm is an adjective modifying *sea*.)

She spoke *calmly* to the dog. (*Calmly* is an adverb modifying *spoke*.)

However, a considerable number of adverbs—including some of the most common ones—do not end in *-ly*. Here is a representative listing.

almost	often	there
here	quite	too
never	soon	well
now	then	

I *never* imagined economics would be so difficult.

We expect our order to arrive *quite soon*.

In addition, certain words—some ending in *-ly* and some not—can function as either adjectives or adverbs.

better	hard	only
close	late	right
cowardly	little	straight
early	much	well
far	near	wrong
fast		

There must be a *better* way to do this. (*Better* is an adjective modifying *way*.)

You'll work *better* after you've rested awhile. (*Better* is an adverb modifying *work*.)

Exercise

List the adverbs in the following sentences.

Soon you will become completely familiar with this procedure. (soon, completely)

1. We went skiing yesterday, and I can barely walk today.
2. Please divide the tasks equally and finish them quickly.
3. If this speech lasts much longer, I'll fall asleep.
4. Actually, we have all made too many mistakes in this project.
5. Each day the old man moved more slowly.
6. I never thought I would be promoted so soon.
7. Alton worked fast to finish his assignment before the late movie began.
8. He tried hard to solve the problem, but it proved too hard for him.
9. Our supply of sheet steel is almost exhausted, but we expect a new shipment tomorrow.
10. The boss told us to move close to the stage and pay close attention to the demonstration.

PREPOSITIONS

A preposition links its object, which consists of a noun or noun substitute, to some other word in the sentence and shows a relation between the two. This relation is often one of location, time, possession, means, or reason or purpose.

The drillpress *in* the corner needs overhauling. (The preposition *in* links its object, *corner*, to *drillpress* and shows location.)

We will wait *until* Tuesday. (The preposition *until* links its object, *Tuesday*, to *wait* and shows time.)

The laws *of* nature sometimes contradict civil regulations. (The preposition *of* links its object, *nature*, to *laws* and shows possession.)

Sally went *by* automobile. (The preposition *by* links its object, *automobile* to *went* and shows means.)

Wilfred bicycles *for* pleasure. (The preposition *for* links its object, *pleasure*, to *bicycles* and shows reason or purpose.)

Here is a list of common prepositions, some of which consist of two or more words.

above	by reason of	of
after	contrary to	on
against	during	onto
along with	except	out of
among	for	over
at	from	since
because of	in	through
before	instead of	to
below	into	toward
beside	like	under
between	near	with
by	next to	without

Occasionally, and particularly in questions, a preposition may be separated from its object.

What are you looking *for*? (The object of the preposition *for* is *what*.)

Whom are you selling your car *to*? (The object of the preposition *to* is *whom*.)

Prepositions, their objects, and words associated with these objects form *prepositional phrases* that may serve as adjectives or adverbs. Prepositional phrases are discussed on page 426.

Exercise

List the prepositions in the following sentences and identify the object of each.

The noise from the apartment above us made sleeping difficult.
   (from [apartment], above [us])

1. The sign on the door said that the office was closed until noon.

2. Jethro covered the dingy walls of the room with brightly colored wallpaper.
3. The house next to ours has been for sale for six months.
4. What are you writing with?
5. After a short nap, I felt ready for an evening of bowling.
6. We have had three days of rain in the last five days.
7. Because of the flu epidemic, several factories in this town have stopped operations for the week.
8. After a term of biology, Sally decided to major in bacteriology.
9. The memorandum from the superintendent said that the productivity of the department had increased by 20 percent in the past year.
10. Over half of our employees have been with the company for a decade or more.

CONJUNCTIONS

Conjunctions join. They are used to connect the parts of sentences or to connect whole sentences. One group of conjunctions connect items of equal rank—words, word groups, and simple sentences. These conjunctions can occur singly (*and, but, or, nor, for, yet, so*) or in pairs (*either—or, neither—nor, both—and, not only—but also*). The single conjunctions are called *coordinating conjunctions*; the paired conjunctions are called *correlative conjunctions*.

Tom *and* his brother are opening a gas station. (The coordinating conjunction connects two nouns.)

Should I call you at home *or* at your office? (The coordinating conjunction connects two prepositional phrases.)

Bill applied to medical school, *but* he was not accepted. (The coordinating conjunction connects sentences.)

Henry *not only* works full time *but also* takes classes at night. (The correlative conjunctions connect two verbs.)

You can study auto mechanics *either* at Ferris State College *or* at Delta College. (The correlative conjunctions connect two prepositional phrases.)

A second group of conjunctions (for example, *because, as if, even though, since, so that, while, whereas,* and *wherever*) are used to show unequal rank between groups of words that contain both subjects and predicates (see clauses, pages 429–33). These conjunctions, called *subordinating conjunctions*, introduce *subordinate* or *dependent clauses*—ideas that are expressed with a subject and a predicate but that cannot stand alone as sentences. Because of the conjunction, these clauses are subordinate to or dependent on a group of words that can stand alone as a complete sentence—a *main clause*.

> The class was canceled *because* the instructor was ill. (The subordinating conjunction connects the subordinate clause *because the instructor was ill* to the main clause.)
>
> Lend me your typewriter *so that* I can finish this report. (The subordinating conjunction connects the subordinate clause *so that I can finish this report* to the main clause.)

The *conjunctive adverb* has characteristics of both conjunctions and adverbs. Like conjunctions, conjunctive adverbs serve as linking devices between clauses of equal rank. Like adverbs, they modify sentences and sentence elements, showing such things as similarity, contrast, result or effect, addition, emphasis or clarity, time, and example. Here are the most commonly used conjunctive adverbs, grouped according to the things they show.

Similarity	consequently	in other words
likewise	hence	indeed
similarly	therefore	that is
	thus	
Contrast		**Time**
however	**Addition**	afterwards
nevertheless	also	later
nonetheless	furthermore	meanwhile
on the contrary	in addition	subsequently
on the other hand	in the first place	then
otherwise	moreover	
		Example
Result or Effect	**Emphasis or**	for example
accordingly	**Clarity**	for instance
as a result	in fact	to illustrate

> The job will require you to travel a great deal; *however*, the salary is excellent.

Andrea misread the instructions for carrying out the experiment; *as a result*, she had to repeat it.

INTERJECTIONS

An interjection is a word that expresses strong feeling or surprise. It has no grammatical relation to the rest of the sentence. An interjection is followed by either an exclamation point or a comma.

Hey! That's my coat you're taking. (strong interjection)
Oh, is it time to leave already? (mild interjection)

Exercise

List and identify the conjunctions (C), conjunctive adverbs (CA), and interjections (I) in the following sentences.

The water looked inviting; therefore, Jan and Marie decided to take a swim. (therefore, CA: and, C)

1. We employ both men and women as machinists.
2. Molly didn't like the instructor even though she earned an *A* in the class.
3. Kimberley did not feel especially energetic; nevertheless, she walked to work rather than taking the bus.
4. Because we all work in the same building, let's form a car pool and save on driving expenses.
5. Gary refused to attend the seminar, so we went without him.
6. Wow! Did you see that shooting star or were you looking the other way?
7. This experiment requires a one-liter Erlenmeyer flask and two small beakers.
8. Renée not only has a full-time job but also does her own housework.
9. Neither her boss nor her fellow employees know why Elaine has asked for a transfer.
10. Audrey has always been interested in navigation; consequently, she eagerly accepted the invitation to see the airport control tower.
11. Hey, will you wait for me while I finish this assignment?
12. Jim breezes through our math problems; however, I have to puzzle over them for hours.

Phrases

A phrase is a group of words that lacks a subject and a predicate and that serves as a single part of speech. There are five types of phrases: *verb phrases, prepositional phrases, participial phrases, gerund phrases*, and *infinitive phrases*. The last three are built around participles, gerunds and infinitives, which are known as verbals. Verb phrases have already been discussed on pages 400–401; this section deals with the four other types of phrases.

PREPOSITIONAL PHRASES

A prepositional phrase is made up of a preposition, one or more objects of that preposition, and any words associated with the object. Prepositional phrases can function as adjectives or adverbs.

> The student *at the microscope* is examining a fly's wing. (prepositional phrase as adjective)
>
> I ran *into the laboratory*. (prepositional phrase as adverb)

PARTICIPIAL PHRASES

A participial phrase is made up of a participle plus associated words. Participles are verb forms (see pages 411–14) that, when used in participial phrases, function as adjectives and therefore modify nouns or noun substitutes. A present participle ends in -*ing* and indicates an action being carried out by the noun or noun substitute it modifies. A past participle usually ends in -*ed*, although there are many verbs with irregular past participles (see page 443). It indicates that the noun or noun substitute it modifies has been acted upon or has carried out an action.

> The typesetter *operating the linotype* is my sister. (present participial phrase)
>
> Mr. Wilson, *disturbed by the noise*, called the police. (past participial phrase)
>
> The typewriters, *worn beyond repair*, are being replaced. (past participial phrase)
>
> *Finished with the operation*, the surgeon removed her gloves. (past participial phrase)

A perfect participial phrase consists of *having* or *having been* plus a past participle and any associated words. It denotes that an action has been carried out by or upon the noun or noun substitute it modifies.

> *Having warned the student to stop talking*, the instructor resumed his lecture. (perfect participial phrase)
>
> *Having been warned to stop talking*, the student fell silent. (perfect participial phrase)

Participial phrases may be restrictive or nonrestrictive. A restrictive participial phrase distinguishes the person or thing modified from others in the same class. A nonrestrictive participial phrase provides more information about someone or something that has previously been identified. The difference between restrictive and nonrestrictive elements is discussed fully on pages 492–93.

GERUND PHRASES

A gerund phrase is made up of a gerund plus associated words. Like present participles, gerunds are verb forms that end in *-ing*, but they serve as nouns rather than as adjectives. Like ordinary nouns, gerund phrases can function as subjects, direct objects, indirect objects, subject complements, appositives (see page 463), and objects of prepositions.

> *Running the X-ray spectrograph* requires specialized chemical training. (gerund phrase as subject)
>
> John enjoys *swimming in the ocean*. (gerund phrase as direct object)
>
> Felice gave *writing the report* her full attention. (gerund phrase as indirect object)
>
> Henrietta's hobby is *collecting stamps*. (gerund phrase as subject complement)
>
> My summer project, *painting my house*, is taking longer than I expected. (gerund phrase as appositive)
>
> He devoted every spare moment to *overhauling the car*. (gerund phrase as object of preposition)

INFINITIVE PHRASES

An infinitive phrase consists of the present principal part of a verb preceded by *to* (*to run, to see, to laugh*)—the infinitive—plus its objects and modifiers. Infinitive phrases can function as adjectives, adverbs, or nouns.

> The student had a project *to complete by Friday.* (infinitive phrase as adjective)
>
> Lenore worked *to earn money for college.* (infinitive phrase as adverb)
>
> Her goal was *to major in environmental health.* (infinitive phrase as noun)

When used as nouns, infinitive phrases can serve as subjects, direct objects, subject complements, and objects of prepositions.

A gerund can often be substituted for an infinitive and vice versa.

> *To identify the chemical compound* took two hours. (infinitive phrase as subject)
>
> *Identifying the chemical compound* took two hours. (gerund phrase as subject)

At times, the *to* in an infinitive may be omitted following verbs such as *make, dare,* and *let.*

> He made the engine (*to*) *run again.* (*To* is omitted but understood.)
>
> She didn't dare (*to*) *challenge the instructor's statement.* (In this sentence, *to* can be kept or omitted.)

Exercise

Identify the italicized words in the following sentences as prepositional, participial, gerund, or infinitive phrases, and indicate whether each is used as a noun, an adjective, or an adverb.

> My purpose in taking this trip is *to conduct a job interview.* (infinitive, noun)

1. *Flying a crop-dusting plane* is an exciting job.
2. Helen's goal was *to major in ornamental horticulture*.
3. The rain *predicted for tomorrow* will prevent us from completing our surveying assignment.
4. The bus *to the Deere Agricultural Museum* will leave in five minutes.
5. Anyone *needing a ride tomorrow* should call 784-4183.
6. *Having worked a double shift*, Jim wanted only to rest.
7. His hobby is *restoring old cars*.
8. Madge studied interior decorating *through an extension course*.
9. Acme Auto Sales has built an enviable reputation by *treating its customers fairly*.
10. Jeremy studied every minute *to make the dean's list*.
11. *Swollen by the spring floods*, Sulter's Creek rushed angrily past us.
12. The boss has given me two reports *to abstract this afternoon*.

Clauses

A clause is a group of related words that includes both a subject and a predicate. There are two types of clauses—independent and dependent (subordinate). An independent clause expresses a complete thought and can stand alone as a simple sentence. A dependent clause does not express a complete thought and therefore cannot stand alone as a sentence. It can function within a sentence as a noun, adjective, or adverb.

NOUN CLAUSES

A noun clause is a dependent clause that functions as a noun. Thus it may serve in any of the ways that other noun substitutes serve.

What I am working toward is a degree in avionics. (noun clause as subject of sentence)

I'll award first prize to *whoever has the highest average in my course*. (noun clause as object of preposition)

His greatest hope was *that he would graduate with high honors*. (noun clause as subject complement)

Noun clauses normally begin with one of the following words.

who	what	when
whom	whoever	why
whose	whomever	where
that	whatever	how
which	whichever	whether

The words in the first two columns are relative pronouns; the words in the third column are subordinating conjunctions. The relative pronoun *that* at the beginning of a dependent clause is sometimes left out when the clause is used as a direct object.

> Marybelle hoped (*that*) *she would graduate with honors*. (*That* is omitted but understood.)

ADJECTIVE CLAUSES

An adjective clause is a dependent clause that functions as an adjective, modifying a noun or a pronoun.

> Mr. Martin, *who now works as a mechanic*, used to sell insurance. (Adjective clause modifies noun.)
> Our company is looking for someone *who has a background in data processing*. (Adjective clause modifies pronoun.)

Adjective clauses usually begin with one of the following words.

who	when
whom	where
whose	why
that	after
which	before

The words in the first column are relative pronouns; the words in the second column are subordinating conjunctions. Sometimes, a relative pronoun at the beginning of an adjective clause can be omitted.

The woman (*whom*) *he hired as a bacteriologist* has her master's degree. (The relative pronoun *whom* is omitted but understood.)

The parts (*that*) *we ordered six weeks ago* have not arrived. (The relative pronoun *that* is omitted but understood.)

Sometimes, too, a preposition comes ahead of the relative pronoun.

The gauge *with which Norman measured the pressure* was faulty. (The preposition *with* is used before the relative pronoun *which*.)

Some adjective clauses are restrictive; that is, they distinguish the person or thing that they modify from others in the same class. Other adjective clauses are nonrestrictive, providing information about someone or something that has already been clearly identified. Restrictive clauses are not set off by commas, but nonrestrictive clauses are. Pages 492–93 provide a detailed discussion of restrictive and nonrestrictive elements.

ADVERB CLAUSES

An adverb clause is a dependent clause that functions as an adverb; thus it may modify a verb, an adjective, another adverb, or an entire clause (or sentence).

You may go *whenever you wish*. (Adverb clause modifies verb.)

The shop looked cleaner *than I had ever seen it before*. (Adverb clause modifies adjective.)

She worked rapidly *so that she could leave early*. (Adverb clause modifies adverb.)

Unless everyone cooperates, we have little chance of success. (Adverb clause modifies entire main clause.)

Some words that commonly introduce adverb clauses are listed here, according to the questions that the clauses answer. The words that signal adverb clauses are always subordinating conjunctions.

When?	**Why?**
while	because
when	since
whenever	as
as	so that
as soon as	now that
before	in order that
after	
since	**Under What Conditions?**
until	if
	once
Where?	unless
where	though
wherever	although
	provided that
How?	
as if	**To What Extent?**
as though	than

Occasionally, an adverb clause will omit one or more words that are not needed for an understanding of its meaning. Such a construction is called an *elliptical clause*.

> *While (he was) watching TV*, Richard stuffed himself with potato chips. (*He was* can be omitted but understood.)

Unlike noun and adjective clauses, adverb clauses can often be moved about in their sentences.

> Richard stuffed himself with potato chips *while (he was) watching TV*.

Exercise

Identify the italicized words in the following sentences as noun, adjective, or adverb clauses.

> I'm switching to Dr. Jekyll *because I don't like Dr. Fell*. (adverb clause)

1. *Whether Melvin passes the course* depends upon his score on the final.
2. Harriet Thomas, *who has just been promoted to vice-president,* started work in this company as a secretary.
3. I wish *I could persuade my boss to raise my salary.*
4. Nick fractured his thumb *while fixing the dented fender.*
5. Give me one reason *why you think that the experiment won't work.*
6. I'll hire anyone *Dr. Stone recommends.*
7. George spoke loudly *because he wanted everyone in the room to hear him.*
8. The candidate *for whom I'm working* is well qualified for the office.
9. Have you heard *why the company failed?*
10. Tell me *where the instruction manuals are filed.*

Avoiding Common Errors of Usage

Avoiding Sentence Fragments

A sentence fragment is a part of a sentence that is capitalized and punctuated as if it were a complete sentence. To be a sentence, a word group must (1) have a subject and a verb and (2) express a complete thought. Following are two examples of fragments.

> If *you* decide to go. (The fragment has a subject and verb but does not make sense by itself; *if* makes the clause dependent.)
>
> An accident in the shop. (The fragment lacks a verb.)

Types of Fragments. Word groups mistakenly written as fragments include phrases, dependent clauses, verbs with their associated words, the second half of compound predicates, and nouns or noun substitutes with their associated words. The following examples illustrate these kinds of fragments. In each case, the fragment is italicized.

> *Having been warned about the washed-out road.* We took another route. (participial phrase)

434

I went to class. *Although I was not prepared.* (adverb clause)

John washed the windows. *And cleaned out the basement.* (second half of compound predicate)

The old gentleman sitting on the park bench. (noun with modifying phrase)

Was once the president of our largest bank. (verb with complement and modifying phrase)

Eliminating Fragments. Getting rid of a sentence fragment in your writing is not difficult. Often, a fragment belongs either to the sentence that precedes it or the one that follows it. In such cases, simply combine the fragment with the appropriate sentence. Sometimes you can convert a fragment into a sentence by adding or changing a word or phrase. Observe how the example fragments presented in the preceding section have been corrected.

Having been warned about the washed-out road, we took another route. (The fragment has been joined to the following sentence.)

I went to class *although I was not prepared*. (The fragment has been joined to the preceding sentence.)

John washed the windows *and cleaned out the basement*. (The fragment has been joined to the preceding sentence.)

John washed the windows. *He also cleaned out the basement.* (The fragment has been changed into a complete sentence.)

The old gentleman sitting on the park bench was once the president of our largest bank. (The fragments have been joined together.)

When combining a fragment and a sentence, put a comma between them if the first element is a long phrase or long adverb clause or if there is a distinct pause between the two elements. Note the use of a comma in the first sentence above.

Appropriate Uses for Fragments. Fragments are commonly used in everyday conversation as well as in writing that reproduces it. They also occur in the works of professional writers, who use them to create special moods or effects. In general, though, fragments should be avoided except in dialogue or for special emphasis.

Exercise

Ten main clauses paired with fragments are presented below. In each case, identify the sentence and the fragment, then eliminate the fragment.

> Stanley has made plans. To retire in August. (sentence, fragment)
> Stanley has made plans to retire in August.

1. In just about a minute. I'm going to lose patience with this task.
2. Harrigan discussed the procedure for checking the tolerances on the part. While the apprentices listened.
3. Because I couldn't find my car keys. I had to take the bus.
4. While in Chicago, I visited the Sears Tower. The tallest building in the world.
5. Living in an apartment house is pleasant. Unless one requires a great deal of privacy.
6. Gail and Olive have gone to Armour Technical Institute. To take a summer course in special education.
7. Dennis bought a pound of peanuts. And ate them in one evening.
8. Frustrated by a boss he could never please. Clayton quit the company.
9. If I leave for Cleveland in the next hour. I'll arrive at the auditorium for the opening of the midwestern electronics suppliers' convention.
10. Gasping and red-faced. The worker stumbled from the smoke-filled building.

Avoiding Run-on Sentences and Comma Splices

A run-on sentence occurs when one complete sentence is run into another without the proper end punctuation and initial capital letter to separate them. A comma splice occurs when there is only a comma between two complete sentences.

> The millwrights voted to strike the electricians decided to stay on the job. (run-on sentence)
> The millwrights voted to strike, the electricians decided to stay on the job. (comma splice)

These two types of errors can be corrected in several ways. First, the sentences may be separated by using a period and capital.

> The millwrights voted to strike. The electricians decided to stay on the job.

Second, the sentences may be separated by using a semicolon.

> The millwrights voted to strike; the electricians decided to stay on the job.

Third, the sentences may be separated with a comma plus a coordinating conjunction.

> The millwrights voted to strike, *but* the electricians decided to stay on the job.

Fourth, one of the sentences may be changed into a subordinate clause introduced by a subordinating conjunction.

> *Although* the millwrights voted to strike, the electricians decided to stay on the job.

Finally, the sentences can be separated by means of a semicolon and a conjunctive adverb.

> The millwrights voted to strike; *however*, the electricians decided to stay on the job.

Unless the conjunctive adverb is *then*, follow it with a comma.

The method of correction to use will depend upon the particular sentence pairs. When the two ideas are not closely related, using a period and capital letter—or a semicolon—is often preferable, unless a choppy effect results. For more closely related ideas, use the method of correction that best shows the relationship between them. If, for example, one idea is subordinate to the other, then the sentence expressing it can be converted to a subordinate clause introduced by a subordinating conjunction. In some cases, several or all of the methods may be used interchangeably.

Exercise

Indicate whether each of the following sentences is a run-on sentence or contains a comma splice; then correct the error.

> Teach me a few magic tricks, I want to surprise my friends. (comma splice) Teach me a few magic tricks, for I want to surprise my friends.

1. Ramón lost his part-time job he couldn't continue in school.
2. Joe is a college senior, his sister runs a beauty shop.
3. I believe that chemistry is an overcrowded profession many experts agree with me.
4. Wesley worked all night that's why he's sleeping now.
5. Harvey worked in Ecuador for five years, consequently, he is very fluent in Spanish.
6. Our employee incentive plan is simplicity itself, make one mistake and you're fired!
7. The card catalog is an important library research tool every student should know how to use it.
8. Gideon wanted to become a doctor Hector chose engineering as his profession.
9. He didn't work hard his boss didn't promote him.
10. Industrial accidents are a serious problem, both management and labor must look for ways to reduce the number of injuries that occur each year.

Making Subjects and Verbs Agree

A verb should agree in number with its subject. If the subject is singular, the verb should be singular. If the subject is plural, the verb should be plural.

Ordinarily, making subjects and verbs agree causes no problems. However, the following special situations can lead to difficulties.

Subject and Verb Separated by a Word Group. Sometimes the subject is separated from the verb by a word group that includes a noun. When you write this sort of sentence, be sure that the verb agrees in number with the subject of the sentence, not a noun in the word group.

Our supply of nails *was* inadequate. (The verb agrees with the singular subject *supply*.)

Several courses required for my major *are* not being offered this term. (The verb agrees with the plural subject *courses*.)

Phrases beginning with words such as *along with*, *as well as*, *in addition to*, *like*, and *with* that follow the subject do not affect the number of the verb. The verb agrees with the subject of the sentence.

Mr. Jones, along with his son and daughter, *operates* a repair shop. (The verb agrees with the singular subject *Mr. Jones*.)

The walls, as well as the ceiling, *were* freshly painted. (The verb agrees with the plural subject *walls*.)

Two Singular Subjects. Singular subjects joined by *and* usually require a plural verb.

The drafting board and T-square *were* initialed by the owner.

Grading papers and preparing lectures *take* up most of my evening.

Few of us would use *was* in the first of these two examples. However, when the subjects are word groups like *grading papers* and *preparing lectures*, singular verbs are often mistakenly used.

Occasionally, two subjects joined by *and* refer to a single person, place, or thing. In such cases, use a singular verb.

The captain and owner *was* on the ship. (The words *captain* and *owner* stand for the same person.)

When two singular subjects joined by *and* are preceded by *each* or *every*, use a singular rather than a plural verb.

Every cup and saucer *was* badly chipped. (*Every* makes a singular verb necessary.)

Each watercolor and etching *has* been signed by the artist.
(*Each* makes a singular verb necessary.)

Singular subjects joined by *or, either/or,* or *neither/nor* require a singular verb.

A doctor or a nurse *is* always on hand.
Neither his house nor his yard *was* in very good shape.
Either Dr. Miles or Ms. Reynolds *is* the speaker for tonight.

One Singular and One Plural Subject. When one singular and one plural subject are joined by *or, either/or,* or *neither/nor,* the verb agrees in number with the subject that is closer to it.

Neither the secretaries nor the office manager *was* there. (The verb agrees with the singular subject, *manager,* which is closer to the verb.)
Neither the office manager nor the secretaries *were* there. (The verb agrees with the plural subject, *secretaries,* which is closer to the verb.)

Pronouns as Subjects. When the following indefinite pronouns are used as subjects, they take singular verbs.

each	anyone	someone
each one	anybody	somebody
either	anything	something
either one	everyone	no one
neither	everybody	nobody
neither one	everything	nothing

Somebody *has* stolen the car.
Neither *was* told about the meeting.

Collective Nouns as Subjects. Collective nouns are nouns that are singular in form but stand for a group or collection of individuals or things. In most instances, collective nouns are regarded as single units and therefore require singular verbs.

The class *is* in the library. (*Class* is considered a unit.)
The convoy *was* headed for the harbor. (*Convoy* is considered a
  unit.)

Occasionally, though, a collective noun is regarded as a group of
individuals acting separately or disharmoniously. In such cases,
the collective noun takes a plural verb.

The Thurston family are hard workers. (*Family* is considered a
  group of individuals acting separately.)

Sentences in Which the Verb Precedes the Subject. Sentences in which the verb precedes the subject may begin with a
phrase or such words as *here, there, how, what,* and *where.* In
each case, the verb must agree in number with the subject that
follows it.

Where *is* my book? (The verb agrees with the singular subject
  book.)
Where *are* my books? (The verb agrees with the plural subject
  books.)
There *are* several ways of checking the acidity of a solution. (The
  verb agrees with the plural subject *ways.*)
There *is* no battery in that flashlight. (The verb agrees with the
  singular subject *battery.*)

Sentences with a Linking Verb and Subject Complement. A
linking verb agrees with its subject, not with the subject complement that follows it.

My favorite fruit *is* bananas. (The verb agrees with the singular
  subject *fruit.*)
Bananas *are* my favorite fruit. (The verb agrees with the plural
  subject *bananas.*)

Exercise

In each of the following sentences, choose the correct verb form from
the pair in parentheses.

The Wilberts, along with their cousin, (sells, sell) real estate. (sell)

1. Either Kevin or Harley (is, are) sure to win this race.
2. All of the tools (needs, need) replacing.
3. The student committee, together with two faculty members, (is, are) drafting a final report.
4. Either the dog or the cats (has, have) been digging in the flower bed.
5. There (is, are) a quick solution to this problem.
6. A completely different set of results (has, have) been obtained this time.
7. Each sword and pistol in my collection (has, have) been owned by a famous person.
8. Neither Penelope nor her brothers (plans, plan) to join the photography club.
9. Where (is, are) the books we got from the library?
10. Each of our employees (owns, own) stock in the company.
11. My favorite breakfast (is, are) ham, eggs, and toast.
12. The team (has, have) all signed contracts for next season.

Choosing the Right Verb Form

Using a verb that does not agree in number with its subject is not the only kind of error involving verb forms. Several other types of verb errors occur so frequently that they merit special attention. These errors include using the wrong *principal part*, confusing *lie* with *lay* and *sit* with *set*, omitting the final -*d* from certain verbs, and using *nonstandard verb forms*.

Using Wrong Principal Parts. As noted on page 413, all verbs have three principal parts—the *present*, the *past*, and the *past participle*. The present principal part may occur without a helping verb or with *shall* or *will*. The past principal part always occurs without a helping verb, while the past participle occurs with one or more helping verbs (*has, have, had, shall have, will have*).

Most verbs have the same past and past participle forms (for example, I *walked*, I have *walked*; she *heard*, she has *heard*).

However, a sizable number have different past and past participle forms, and many usage problems result from confusing these forms (for example, I have *went* for I have *gone*). Following are forty common verbs that are especially likely to cause this sort of difficulty.

Present	Past	Past Participle
arise	arose	arisen
bear	bore	borne
become	became	become
begin	began	begun
bite	bit	bitten
blow	blew	blown
break	broke	broken
choose	chose	chosen
come	came	come
do	did	done
draw	drew	drawn
drink	drank	drunk
drive	drove	driven
eat	ate	eaten
fall	fell	fallen
fly	flew	flown
forget	forgot	forgotten (or forgot)
freeze	froze	frozen
give	gave	given
go	went	gone
grow	grew	grown
know	knew	known
ride	rode	ridden
ring	rang	rung
rise	rose	risen
run	ran	run
see	saw	seen
shake	shook	shaken
sing	sang	sung
sink	sank	sunk

Present	Past	Past Participle
speak	spoke	spoken
spring	sprang	sprung
steal	stole	stolen
swear	swore	sworn
swim	swam	swum
take	took	taken
tear	tore	torn
throw	threw	thrown
wear	wore	worn
write	wrote	written

Memorizing the principal parts of any verb that gives you trouble will help prevent this kind of error. Until you have the parts down pat, check this list or consult a good desk (not pocket) dictionary whenever you cannot decide which form is right.

Confusing "Lie" and "Lay" and "Sit" and "Set." The use of *lay* for *lie* is very common in informal spoken English. ("I'm going to lay down.") Nonetheless, this usage is incorrect. When you write or speak in formal situations, you must distinguish carefully between these verbs.

To lie means "to be or to remain in a horizontal position." Because we cannot "remain" things, this verb never takes a direct object. The following sentences illustrate the three principal parts of *lie*.

I *lie* down for a nap each afternoon. (present)

I *lay* down for a nap yesterday afternoon. (past)

I have *lain* down for a nap every afternoon this week. (past participle)

To lay means "to place." Because we do "place" things, this verb always takes a direct object.

Those two men *lay* bricks for a living. (present)

Those two men *laid* over twelve hundred bricks yesterday. (past)

Those two men have *laid* an average of twelve hundred bricks every day this month. (past participle)

Notice that the past principal part of *lie* and the present principal part of *lay* are identical—a fact that helps explain the confusion between the two verbs.

Sit and *set* do not cause as much trouble as *lie* and *lay*. Nevertheless, they too are often confused, as shown by such errors as "Come in and set awhile" and "I sat the dish on the sideboard."

To sit means "to rest on one's haunches" as in a chair. Like *lie*, it does not take a direct object.

> Sometimes I *sit* on the floor when I watch TV. (present)
> We *sat* on the floor when we ate at that Japanese restaurant. (past)
> I have *sat* through some pretty terrible movies in my time. (past participle)

To set means "to place in position." It almost always takes a direct object. Notice that the verb's three principal parts are identical.

> I *set* my briefcase on the desk when I come home at night. (present)
> I *set* my briefcase on the desk when I came home last evening. (past)
> I have *set* the package on the desk. (past participle)

When used with the subject *sun*, set does not take a direct object.

> The sun *set* behind the hills.

Similarly, when *set* has the meaning "to become hard or firm" or "to begin or get started," it does not take a direct object.

> The cement has *set*.
> The crew *set* to work.
> The gelatin salad *set*.

Whenever you have trouble choosing between *lie* and *lay* or *sit* and *set*, check to see whether the sentence has a direct object. If there is none, use the proper form of *lie* or *sit* except in those special cases that call for *set*. If there is a direct object, use the proper form of *lay* or *set*.

Omitting Endings from Certain Verbs. Omitting endings involves dropping the *-d* or *-ed* from verbs that have the same past and past participle principal parts. The most common errors include the use of *ask* for *asked*, *prejudice* for *prejudiced*, *suppose* for *supposed*, and *use* for *used*. The following sentences illustrate these incorrect usages:

> I *ask* my roommate yesterday to lend me his tweed jacket.
> The governor's reputation as an alcoholic *has prejudice* his chances for reelection.
> Lucinda mistakenly *suppose* that she would receive an invitation to the party.
> Henry *use* to work for General Motors.

Here are the correct verb forms for these sentences.

> I *asked* my roommate yesterday to lend me his tweed jacket.
> The governor's reputation as an alcoholic *has prejudiced* his chances for reelection.
> Lucinda mistakenly *supposed* that she would receive an invitation to the party.
> Henry *used* to work for General Motors.

Use of Nonstandard Verb Forms. Some usages are considered nonstandard and should be avoided whenever you speak or write. Common errors include the use of *busted* for *broke*, *broken*, and *burst*; *drownded* for *drowned*; *swang* for *swung*; and *throwed* for *threw* and *thrown*. Here are four examples of these errors.

> The balloon *busted* when Sam tried to blow it up.
> My typewriter is *busted*.
> When ten years old, I nearly *drownded*.
> The children *swang* all afternoon in the park.

The correct verb forms are as follows:

> The balloon *burst* when Sam tried to blow it up.
> My typewriter is *broken*.

When ten years old, I nearly *drowned*.

The children *swung* all afternoon in the park.

Exercise

In each of the following sentences, choose the right verb form from the pair in parentheses.

It was so cold that the car battery had (froze, frozen). (frozen)

1. The price of gasoline has (rose, risen) every year since the Arab oil embargo.
2. Because of the subzero weather, our water pipes have frozen and (burst, busted).
3. The secretary has (went, gone) to lunch.
4. After mowing the lawn, I (lay, laid) down for an hour.
5. In the morning, (sit, set) the trash out by the curb.
6. A man (come, came) into the gas station and asked for directions to the research center.
7. Manfred (suppose, supposed) that he would be promoted.
8. He said he had (lain, laid) very still in his hiding place while the killers looked for him.
9. You have (set, sat) around long enough; get up and go to work.
10. For his summer job, Rupert (lay, laid) pipe for a building contractor.
11. They (lay, laid) the hero to rest last Friday.
12. The foundations of the electrical generation building (sank, sunk) three inches last year.

Avoiding Errors in Showing Time

Errors in showing time include unwarranted shifts in time and failure to make clear the order in which two past events occurred.

Unwarranted Shifts in Tense. When describing a series of events or a past situation, student writers sometimes make unwarranted and confusing shifts from past tense to present and vice versa. Such shifts are especially likely in summaries of the plots of plays, movies, and stories. The following paragraph contains two unwarranted shifts in tense.

> When Framton Nuttel first *arrives* at Mrs. Sappleton's home, he *is greeted* by her niece, Vera, who *announces* that she *will entertain* him until her aunt *comes* downstairs. Vera, a compulsive storyteller, *proceeded* [shift from present to past tense] to tell Framton a beautifully tragic but completely false tale about the death of her aunt's husband and two brothers. She *said* that three years before, the three *had gone* hunting and *perished* in a bog, and that their bodies *were* never *recovered*. Framton *believes* [shift from past back to present tense] her.

To prevent such shifts, you must pay close attention to the time frame of the events or situation you are describing and shift time only when the narrative time changes. Here is a corrected version of the preceding paragraph, in the present tense.

> When Framton Nuttel first *arrives* at Mrs. Sappleton's home, he *is greeted* by her niece, Vera, who *announces* that she *will entertain* him until her aunt *comes* downstairs. Vera, a compulsive storyteller, *proceeds* to tell Framton a beautifully tragic but completely false tale about the death of her aunt's husband and two brothers. She *says* that three years before, the three *went* hunting and *perished* in a bog, and that their bodies *were* never *recovered*. Framton *believes* her.

The future *will entertain* in the first sentence is correct because the entertainment must follow the announcement. The next-to-last sentence retains the past tense because it deals with an event that supposedly occurred before Framton's visit to Mrs. Sappleton.

Sequence of Past Tenses.   Often you will need to indicate that one past action or condition ended before or after another past action or condition occurred. To do so, use the past tense of one verb and the past perfect tense (*had* plus the past participle) of the other verb, as in the following sentence.

> Bob *bought* a new lamp because he *had broken* the old one.

Failure to do so can cause you to misstate the time relationship of the events, as in the following sentence.

> The team *scored* two touchdowns when the first quarter *ended*.

This sentence indicates that the team scored two touchdowns at the moment the first quarter ended. Such a situation is impossible. When misstatements of this sort occur in your writing, you must decide which verb needs to be changed in order to correct the situation. Usually, it will be the verb for the earlier event.

> The team *had scored* two touchdowns when the first quarter ended. (The verb for the earlier action has been changed.)

If two past events occurred at the same time or nearly the same time, then use the past tense for both verbs.

> When the bell *rang*, the students *rushed* out the door.

Exercise

Indicate whether each of the following sentences is correct (C), contains an unwarranted shift in time (S), or shows past times improperly (I); then correct the faulty sentences.

> When I made the coffee, I sat down and drank a cup. (I) When I had made the coffee, I sat down and drank a cup.

1. General Gung Ho decorated his walls with weapons he captured during his last campaign.
2. I have been working as a landscape architect this summer, and I found the work very interesting.
3. Because I heard so much about Houston, I was delighted when the company transferred me there.
4. Have you received the bonus the company will give its employees?
5. Once the instructor had worked the problem, I saw my mistake.
6. The assembly line starts operating at 7 A.M. and usually ran until 6 P.M.
7. After Tammie has carefully read the instructions for assembling the swing, she got her tools and set to work.

8. Marilyn worked for Ames Products six months when she got her first promotion.
9. After he rested awhile, he began studying again.
10. Students who wish to save money on books will find lower prices at the off-campus bookstore.

Avoiding Overuse of the Passive Voice

Transitive verbs have two *voices: active* and *passive*. A verb is in the *active voice* when the subject of the sentence performs the action named by the verb. A verb is in the *passive voice* when the subject receives the action. The noun or pronoun that tells who performed the action may appear in a prepositional phrase or remain unmentioned.

Joan *planned* the sales meeting. (active voice)

The sales meeting *was planned* by Joan. (passive voice; prepositional phrase *by Joan* identifies performer)

The sales meeting *was held* last week. (passive voice; performer not identified)

Drawbacks of the Passive Voice. The passive voice gives writing a flat, impersonal tone and almost always requires more words than the active voice. Consider the following paragraph, written largely in the passive voice.

Graft becomes possible when gifts are given to police officers or favors are done for them by persons who expect preferential treatment in return. Gifts of many kinds may be received by officers. Often free meals are given to officers by the owners of restaurants on their beats. During the Christmas season, officers may be given liquor, food, or theater tickets by merchants. If favored treatment is not received by the donors, no great harm is done. But when traffic offenses, safety code violations, and the like are overlooked by the officers, corruption results. When such corruption is exposed by the newspapers, faith is lost in the law and law enforcement agencies.

Note the livelier tone of the following revised version, which is written largely in the active voice.

Graft becomes possible when police officers accept gifts or favors from persons who expect preferential treatment in return. Officers may receive gifts of many kinds. Often restaurant owners provide free meals for officers on local patrol. During the Christmas season, merchants make gifts of liquor, food, or theater tickets. If donors do not receive favored treatment, no great harm is done. But when officers overlook traffic offenses, safety code violations, and the like, corruption results. When the newspapers expose such corruption, citizens lose faith in the law and law enforcement agencies.

This version has twenty-three fewer words than the earlier version, and is livelier as well.

Situations in which the Passive Voice Is Preferable. Because of its livelier, more emphatic tone, the active voice is usually the more effective. Nonetheless, there are certain situations in which the passive voice is better. Occasionally, for instance, it may be desirable to conceal someone's identity. Consider this memorandum from a supervisor to a group of employees who have consistently taken overly long coffee breaks.

At the monthly supervisors' meeting, a suggestion was adopted that coffee breaks be suspended permanently unless employees immediately limit them to ten minutes. Please observe the ten-minute limit from now on so that such action will not be necessary.

To prevent hostile comments and harassment, the supervisor deliberately uses the passive voice to conceal the name of the person who made the suggestion.

Technical and scientific writing commonly makes use of the passive voice to explain how processes are or were carried out. In such descriptions the action, not the actor, is important, and an objective, impersonal tone is desirable.

To obtain a water sample for dissolved oxygen analysis, a B.O.D. bottle is completely filled and then capped so no air is trapped inside. Next, 2 ml of manganese sulfate solution is added, well below the surface of the sample, and this is followed by 2 ml of alkali-iodide-oxide agent. The bottle is then stoppered carefully, so as to exclude air bubbles, and the contents are mixed by inverting the bottle at least 15 times.

There are times when the passive voice is preferable in everyday writing.

The garbage is collected once a week—on Monday.
The aircraft carrier was commissioned last August.

In these sentences, just as in the scientific example above, what was done, rather than who did it, is the important thing. Omitting the name of the doer gives the action the necessary emphasis.

Except in such special situations, however, you should try to use the active voice.

Exercise

Indicate whether each of the following sentences is in the active voice (A) or the passive voice (P); then convert each passive-voice sentence to the active.

The drill press has been repaired by the millwright. The millwright has repaired the drill press.

1. The switch is attached to the wall with four screws.
2. By 7 P.M., I will have finished my term paper.
3. Additional fire extinguishers have been purchased for the building.
4. The high rate of employee absenteeism was discussed by the supervisors.
5. For twenty years, I have admired your work in genetics.
6. She has not learned how to be assertive.
7. Witnesses said the getaway car had been driven by Chester Stark.
8. We have scraped all the old putty from the window frame.
9. Wendy's parents gave her a new calculator for her birthday.
10. Our new sales office will be opened in just two weeks.
11. Your suggestion has been adopted by the committee.
12. Copper is being replaced by aluminum as an electrical conductor for high temperature service.

Making Pronouns and Antecedents Agree

The noun or noun substitute that a pronoun refers to is called its antecedent. Like verbs with their subjects, pronouns should agree in number with their antecedents. If the antecedent is singular, the pronoun should be singular. If the antecedent is plural, the pronoun should be plural. The following pointers will help in the special situations that are most likely to cause problems.

Indefinite Pronouns as Antecedents. Indefinite pronouns are pronouns that do not refer to specific persons or things. When the following indefinite pronouns are used as antecedents, the pronouns that follow them should be singular.

each	anyone	someone
each one	anybody	somebody
either	anything	something
either one	everyone	no one
neither	everybody	nobody
neither one	everything	nothing

Neither of the actors has learned *his* lines.

Recently, the use of *his or her* has become common when the sex of the antecedent is unknown.

Each of the performers received tickets for *his* or *her* parents.

Do not, however, use the *his or her* construction so often that your writing becomes awkward and distracting to your reader. Sometimes you can rewrite the sentence in the plural and avoid awkwardness.

All of the performers received tickets for *their* parents.

Occasionally, a ridiculous result occurs when a singular pronoun refers to an indefinite pronoun that is obviously plural in meaning.

Everybody complained that the test was too hard, but I didn't agree with *him*.

Everyone was talking, so I told *him* to quiet down.

In such cases, recast the sentence to eliminate the problem.

Everybody complained that the test was too hard, but I didn't think so.

Everyone was talking, so I asked for silence.

In informal writing and speaking, there is an increasing tendency to use plural pronouns with indefinite pronoun antecedents.

Someone has left *their* muddy footprints on the floor.

However, because many people object to this practice, you should avoid it in your own writing and speaking.

Two Singular Antecedents. Two or more antecedents joined by *and* usually require a plural pronoun.

His car and boat were left in *their* usual places.

Harold, Norman, and Lucinda finished *their* joint presentation ten minutes early.

When two subjects joined by *and* refer to the same person, however, a singular pronoun is needed.

The captain and owner walked up the gangplank and onto *his* ship. (The words *captain* and *owner* stand for the same person.)

When the antecedents are preceded by *each* or *every*, the pronoun should be singular.

Every family and business must do *its* part to conserve energy. (*Every* makes a singular pronoun necessary.)

Each college and university sent *its* budget request to the legislature. (*Each* makes a singular pronoun necessary.)

Singular antecedents joined by *or*, *either/or*, or *neither/nor* require singular pronouns.

> Has either John or Bill finished *his* report?
> Neither Margaret nor Jane has completed *her* preparations for the trip.

Applying this rule will sometimes result in an awkward or ridiculous sentence. In such cases, recast the sentence to avoid the problem.

> Neither Sharon nor Robert has written *his* or *her* thank-you note. (The sentence is awkward.)
> Sharon and Roger have not written thank-you notes. (The sentence has been recast.)
> Neither Sharon nor Robert has written a thank-you note. (The sentence has been recast.)

Singular and Plural Antecedents. If one singular and one plural antecedent are joined by *or*, *either/or*, or *neither/nor*, the pronoun agrees in number with the closer antecedent.

> Either Jim Forbes or the *Mastersons* will lend us *their* car. (The pronoun *their* agrees with the plural antecedent *Mastersons*.)
> Either the Masters or *Jim Forbes* will lend us *his* car. (The pronoun *his* agrees with the singular antecedent *Jim Forbes*.)

Sometimes you must write the antecedents in one particular order to express the desired meaning.

> Neither the superintendent nor the *workers* recognized their peril. (The pronoun *their* agrees with the plural antecedent *workers*.)
> Neither the workers nor the superintendent recognized *his* peril. (The pronoun *his* agrees with the singular antecedent *superintendent*.)

Notice that the meaning is different in these sentences. In the first, the peril is to everyone. In the second the peril is to the superintendent only.

Collective Nouns as Antecedents. Collective nouns (see page 406) are singular in form but stand for a group of individuals or things. If a collective noun is regarded as a single unit, the pronoun that refers to it should be singular. If the noun is regarded as a group of individuals acting separately, then the pronoun should be plural.

> The group presented *its* resolution. (The group is acting as a unit.)
>
> Yesterday the team signed *their* contracts for the coming season. (The team is acting as a group of individuals.)

Exercise

In each of the following sentences, choose the right form of the pronoun.

> The graduating class was unanimous in (its, their) choice of Ralph Nader for commencement speaker. (its)

1. If anyone objects to this proposal, now is the time for (him or her, them) to speak up.
2. Each foreman and superintendent agreed that (he, they) would contribute to the Red Cross drive.
3. Anyone wanting a successful college career must devote much of (his, their) time to studying.
4. The board will announce (its, their) decision next week.
5. When asked to make statements, Doris and Zula insisted on (her, their) right to remain silent.
6. I'm told that neither Betty Myers nor the Engels filed (her, their) income tax on time.
7. No one should force (his or her, their) interests on other members of the family.
8. To cope with the tornadoes, each town and city set up (its, their) special warning system.
9. We watched the crowd leaving the theater and heading toward (its, their) homes.
10. Either the Borom brothers or Ronald Drag will show (his, their) travel slides at the meeting.

Avoiding Faulty Pronoun Reference

A pronoun reference is faulty if the pronoun refers to more than one antecedent, to a hidden antecedent, or to no antecedent at all.

More Than One Antecedent. The following sentences are unclear because they include more than one possible antecedent.

Take the radio out of the car and sell *it*. (It is unclear whether the radio or the car should be sold.)

The supervisors told the sheet-metal workers that *they* would receive a bonus. (It is unclear whether supervisors or workers will receive a bonus.)

Sometimes writers will produce a sentence like the following one.

If the fans don't buy all the pennants, pack *them* away until next season. (In this case, *pennants* is clearly the antecedent, but the presence of *fans* makes the sentence ridiculous.)

You can correct both of these kinds of faults by substituting a noun for the pronoun or by rephrasing the sentence.

Take the radio out of the car, and then sell the car. (A noun has been substituted for the pronoun.)

The supervisors told the sheet-metal workers to expect a bonus. (The sentence has been rephrased to show that the workers will get the bonus.)

The supervisors told the sheet-metal workers that they were expecting a bonus. (The sentence has been rephrased to show that the supervisors will get the bonus.)

Pack away any unsold pennants, and save them for next season. (The sentence has been rephrased so that it is no longer ridiculous.)

Hidden Antecedent. An antecedent is hidden if it serves as an adjective rather than as a noun. Here are two sentences with hidden antecedents.

When I removed the table's finish, *it* proved to be oak. (It should refer to *table*, which in this sentence appears as the adjective *table's*.)

The popcorn bowl was empty, but we were tired of eating *it* anyhow. (It should refer to *popcorn*, which in this sentence is an adjective.)

To correct this error, substitute a noun for the pronoun, or switch the positions of the adjective and the pronoun and then make whatever changes are required by correct English.

When I removed its finish, the table proved to be oak. (The adjective and the pronoun have been switched and their forms have been changed accordingly.)

The popcorn bowl was empty, but we were tired of eating popcorn anyhow. (The noun has been substituted for the pronoun.)

No Antecedent. A no-antecedent sentence has no noun to which the pronoun can refer. Sentences of this sort are common in informal speech, but you should avoid them in formal writing or speaking. The following sentences show this error.

The shop is humming with activity because *they* are working hard.

It says in this article on leukemia that many cases are now being cured.

To correct such a sentence, substitute an appropriate noun for the pronoun, or reword it to avoid the problem.

The shop is humming with activity because the *employees* are working hard. (A noun has been substituted for the pronoun.)

This article on leukemia says that many cases are now being cured. (The sentence has been reworded to avoid the problem.)

Vague Antecedent. Another common feature of informal sentences is the use of *this, that,* and *which* to refer to a whole clause or sentence.

The boss insisted that his employees write weekly progress reports, *which* irritated them very much.

However, sentences of this sort, like no-antecedent sentences, are undesirable in formal writing and speaking. To make a correction, replace the vague antecedent with something specific or recast the sentence.

The boss insisted that his employees write weekly progress reports, *a task that* irritated them very much. (The vague antecedent *which* has been replaced with *a task that*.)

The boss's insistence that his employees write weekly progress reports irritated them very much. (The sentence has been recast.)

Exercise

Indicate whether each of the following sentences is correct (C) or contains a faulty pronoun reference (F), and correct the faulty sentences.

Millie asked Suzanne how she liked her new hat. (F) Millie, sporting a new hat, asked Suzanne how she liked it.

1. Move the car out of the garage and paint it.
2. Caught cheating on the examination, Pam tried to lie her way out of it.
3. Jack's father felt proud when he receive a promotion to manager.
4. As the wolf approached the sheep paddock, they moved to its far side.
5. The lecture was interesting, but they weren't paying attention.
6. When Malcolm walked into the employees' lounge, they burst out laughing.
7. Because my parents like oysters, I served them as an appetizer.
8. When Charles poked the snake's cage, it hissed.
9. They say that the sales force will receive a bonus this year.
10. Albert told Sue that she was tired and needed to rest.
11. The locker room was very noisy because the players were celebrating their victory.
12. The receptionists told the typists that they should be making more money.

Avoiding Unwarranted Shifts in Person

Pronouns can be in the first person, second person, or third person. First-person pronouns (for example, *I, me, mine, we, us, ourselves*) identify people who are speaking or writing about themselves. Second-person pronouns (*you, your, yours, yourself, yourselves*) identify people who are being addressed directly. Third-person pronouns (for example, *he, she, it, his, hers, its, they, theirs, himself*, and any indefinite pronoun) identify people or things that are being spoken or written about.

Student writers often shift needlessly from one person to another, as in these examples.

> If an employee works hard, *he* has many opportunities for advancement, and eventually *you* might become a department supervisor. (The shift is from third to second person.)
>
> An understanding roommate is one *you* can tell *your* personal problems to. This kind of roommate knows when *I* want to be alone and respects *my* wishes. (The shift is from second to first person.)
>
> After working as a cashier for six months, *I* welcomed a promotion to bookkeeper with *her* own office. (The shift is from first to third person.)

You can avoid such errors by paying careful attention to the pronouns you use in each sentence and by making sure that no shifts occur as you go from one sentence to the next. Notice the improved smoothness and clarity of the corrected examples.

> If an employee works hard, *he* has many opportunities for advancement, and eventually *he* might become a department supervisor. (The sentence uses the third person only.)
>
> An understanding roommate is one *you* can tell *your* personal problems to. This type of roommate knows when *you* want to be alone and respects *your* wishes. (The sentences use the second person only.)
>
> After working as a cashier for six months, *I* welcomed a promotion to bookkeeper with *my* own office. (The sentence uses the first person only.)

Not all shifts in person are unwarranted. Consider, for example, the following correct sentences.

I would like *you* to take this sales report to Ms. Carter's office. *She* asked to borrow it.

Here the speaker identifies himself or herself (*I*) while speaking directly to a listener (*you*) about someone else (*she*). In such cases, shifts are necessary in order to get the message across.

Exercise

Indicate whether each of the following sentences is correct (C) or contains an unwarranted shift in person (S), and correct the faulty sentences.

I believe you should buy a set of snow tires for your car this winter. (C)

1. Would you ask John whether he will lend me his biology book for the afternoon?
2. Participants in the meeting should come prepared to discuss the items on the agenda and to bring up any other matters you consider important.
3. When I ask Rochelle to help me with my homework, sometimes she turns you down.
4. Our house was situated in a grove of trees, and you couldn't see the highway from our front window.
5. Once we are committed to a course of action, it is often difficult for people to change their views.
6. When we weren't on duty, employees could use any recreational facilities at the resort.
7. Anyone wishing to attend the department luncheon should sign your name on this sheet.
8. The company must realize that its greatest asset is our employees.
9. We think our boss is wonderful; he is always ready to help you with problems that arise on the job.
10. Unless you have a good grounding in grammar, no one can hope to succeed as a technical writer.

Using the Right Pronoun Case

The term *case* refers to the changes in form that a noun or a pronoun undergoes to show its function in a sentence. There are three cases in English: the *subjective (nominative)*, the *objective*, and the *possessive*. The subjective case is used for subjects and subject complements. The objective case is used for direct objects, indirect objects, and objects of prepositions. The possessive case shows ownership or possession.

Nouns and most indefinite pronouns (*anyone, someone, no one, everyone*, and the like) undergo changes in form for the possessive case only.

> *John* knows *Douglas. Douglas* knows *John.* (The forms are identical in both the subjective and objective cases.)
>
> *John's* college program is very difficult. (The *'s* is added to *John* to show possession.)
>
> *Anyone's* guess is as good as mine. (The *'s* is added to *anyone* to show possession.)

However, several of the most common pronouns have different forms for each case.

Subjective	Objective	Possessive
I	me	my, mine
you	you	your, yours
he	him	his
she	her	her, hers
we	us	our, ours
they	them	their, theirs
who	whom	whose

"We" and "Us" Preceding Nouns. Nouns that serve as subjects take the pronoun *we.* Those that serve as objects take the pronoun *us.*

> *We* managers set a good example for the employees. (The pronoun *we* precedes the subject of the sentence, *managers.*)

The guide took *us* visitors through the nuclear installation. (The pronoun *us* precedes the object of the sentence, *visitors*.)

If you have difficulty choosing the right pronouns, mentally omit the noun and read the sentence to yourself, first with one pronoun and then with the other. The incorrect pronoun will sound wrong, and the correct one will sound right.

Father gave (we, us) girls two large chocolate hearts for Valentine's Day.

Omitting *girls* reveals at once that *us* is the correct choice.

Compound Subjects, Compound Objects, and Appositives. Pronouns in the compound subjects of sentences and of dependent clauses should be in the subjective case. Those in compound objects should be in the objective case.

Sam and *I* plan to work in public health. (The pronoun *I* is part of the compound subject.)

The school awarded Marcia and *her* certificates of academic excellence. (The pronoun *her* is part of the compound indirect object.)

Between John and *me*, we finished the job in one hour. (The pronoun *me* is part of the compound object of the preposition.)

An appositive is a noun or noun substitute—and any associated words—that follows another noun or noun substitute and tells something about it. When the appositive accompanies the subject of the sentence, it should be in the subjective case. When it accompanies an object, it should be in the objective case.

The superintendent selected two people, Loretta and *me*, to receive merit increases. (The noun *people* is the direct object; the appositive *Loretta and me* is in the objective case.)

Two people, Loretta and *I*, received merit increases. (The noun *people* is the subject; the appositive *Loretta and I* is in the subjective case.)

Again the technique of mental omission can help you to pick the right pronouns.

Pronouns in Dependent Clauses. A pronoun that serves as the subject of a dependent clause must be in the subjective case. A pronoun that serves as an object must be in the objective case.

> The recruiter will see all students *who* request a job interview. (The pronoun *who* is the subject of the dependent clause.)
>
> Sheila is the student *whom* we voted most likely to succeed. (The pronoun *whom* is the direct object of the dependent clause.)

Once again there is a simple trick to help you decide whether *who* or *whom* is correct. First, mentally isolate the dependent clause. Second, block out the pronoun in question, and then insert *he* and *him* at the appropriate spot in the remaining part of the clause. If *he* sounds better, *who* is the correct case form. If *him* sounds better, *whom* is correct. Now let's apply this trick to the following sentence, in which the clause has been italicized.

> The man *who(m) I met last night* is a well-known art critic.
> I met (he, him) last night.

Clearly, *him* is correct, and therefore *whom* is the proper form.

Pronoun as Subject Complement. In formal writing and speaking, the subject complements should always be in the subjective case.

> It is *I*.
> It is *he* who is most responsible for this company's success.

However, this rule is often ignored in conversation and informal writing.

> It's *me*.
> That's *him* working in the garden.

Comparisons Using "Than" or "As . . . As." Sentences that make comparisons and include the expressions *than* or *as . . . as* often omit a direct statement about the second item of comparison. When the second naming word is a pronoun, you may have trouble choosing the proper one.

She is taller than (they, them).
Our accounting instructor will grade you as fairly as (I, me).

If such a problem arises, expand the sentence by mentally supplying the omitted material. Next read the sentence with one pronoun and then the other, and see which sounds right.

She is taller than (they, them) are.
Our accounting instructor will grade you as fairly as she will (I, me).

Applying this test to our two examples shows that *they* is the right choice for the first sentence and *me* is the right choice for the second one.

Pronouns Preceding Gerunds. A pronoun that precedes a gerund should be in the possessive case.

I don't understand *his* failing the course.
I dislike *her* constant bickering.

Use of the possessive case shows that it is the *failing* that you don't understand and the *bickering* that you dislike, rather than the person who failed and the person who bickers. *Failing* and *bickering* are gerunds, or verbal nouns, and are the direct objects of *understand* and *dislike*. We can say that the emphasis is on the actions rather than on the actors.

Now consider the following sentence.

William caught *them* sneaking out of the house.

Here, use of the objective case shows that William caught the persons doing the sneaking, not the sneaking itself. *Sneaking* is a participle modifying the direct object *them*. The emphasis is on the actors rather than on their actions.

Whenever you have trouble deciding between the objective and the possessive cases, check to see whether the emphasis is on the action or on the actor. When the emphasis is on the action, the word ending in *-ing* will be a gerund and will require a possessive pronoun; when the emphasis is on the actor, the word ending in *-ing* will be a participle modifying the object—a pronoun in the objective case.

Exercise

In each of the following sentences, choose the right form of the pronoun.

Joseph and (they, them) are officers in the employees' credit union. (they)

1. Although all three of us worked equally hard, our boss praised Sam more than (we, us).
2. There are several reasons for (me, my) leaving school temporarily.
3. The high cost of gasoline is causing (we, us) commuters a great deal of concern.
4. Mary is the sort of person (who, whom) excels at whatever she does.
5. (We, Us) laboratory workers should form a union.
6. The recruiter said that (we, us) fellows would like working for U.S. Steel.
7. Do you think I'll be able to finish this test as quickly as (they, them)?
8. I regret to announce that Mr. Martinez with (who, whom) most of you are well acquainted, has decided to retire this summer.
9. High interest rates have forced our neighbors and (we, us) to postpone buying new homes.
10. (Who, Whom) do you wish to see?

Avoiding Errors with Adjectives and Adverbs

As noted before, adjectives modify nouns and noun substitutes, whereas adverbs modify verbs, adjectives, and other adverbs. Ordinarily, adjectives and adverbs cause little trouble when we speak and write. Three kinds of errors do crop up with some frequency, however: misusing adjectives for adverbs, misusing adverbs for adjectives in subject complements, and using the wrong forms to make comparisons.

Misusing Adjectives for Adverbs. Although almost any adjective can mistakenly be used for the corresponding adverb, the following word pairs are most likely to cause problems. In each pair, the adjective comes first.

awful—awfully	good—well
bad—badly	real—really
considerable—considerably	sure—surely

The following faulty sentences illustrate the sorts of errors that can occur.

> His explanation for the mistake seems *awful* weak to me. (The adjective *awful* is used mistakenly to modify the adjective *weak*.)
> We came *real* close to having a bad accident. (The adjective *real* is used mistakenly to modify the adverb *close*.)

In each of the cases, the adverb is needed. Here are the sentences rewritten in correct form.

> His explanation for the mistake seems *awfully* weak to me.
> We came *really* close to having a bad accident. (In this case, *very* might be used in place of *really*.)

Whenever you do not know whether an adjective or adverb is needed, check the word being modified. If the word is a noun or pronoun, use an adjective. If it is a verb, adjective, or adverb, use an adverb.

Misusing Adverbs for Adjectives in Subject Complements. An adjective used as a subject complement follows a linking verb and describes the subject of the sentence. Linking verbs fall into two groups. The first group includes the different forms of the verb *be*, *(is, are, am, was, were, be, been)*. The second group includes such words as *seem, remain, feel, look, smell, sound,* and *taste*—words that can also function as action verbs.

When used as linking verbs, words in the second group, in effect, function as forms of the verb *be*. They must, therefore, be followed by an adjective rather than an adverb.

> Wanda felt *uncertain* about changing her job.
> My boss looked *angry*.

When the linking verbs in the second group stand for physical actions, they function as action verbs and must be followed by adverbs.

> Wanda felt *uncertainly* in the grass for her lost ring.
> My boss looked *angrily* at me.

The verb *feel* presents complications. First, it can be transitive or intransitive; second, it may be used properly with either *good* or *well*, as in the following sentences.

> I feel *good* about giving ten dollars to the Red Cross.
> I feel *well* today; I was sick yesterday.

The first of these sentences indicates that the speaker is morally and spiritually satisfied. The second sentence means, "I am in good health"; *well* here is an adjective meaning *healthy* rather than the adverb corresponding to the adjective *good*. *Feel* is also commonly used with *badly*, rather than *bad* in these sentences.

> I am feeling *badly* today.
> Sheila feels *badly* about her parents' divorce.

Although such usage is acceptable in informal speech, it is incorrect in formal speaking and writing. Use *bad* instead.

Using the Wrong Forms to Make Comparisons. Adjectives and adverbs change form to show comparison. When one thing is compared with another, short adjectives usually add *-er*; longer adjectives and most adverbs add *more* (for example, *high, higher; defective, more defective; slowly, more slowly*). When something is compared with two or more other things, *-est* is added to short adjectives, and *most* is used with longer adjectives as well as with adverbs (*highest, most defective, most slowly*). A few adjectives and adverbs—for example, the following—have irregular forms.

Adjectives	**Adverbs**
good—better—best	well—better—best
bad—worse—worst	badly—worse—worst
much—more—most	much—more—most

In making comparisons, a person may mistakenly use a double form, as illustrated by these two faulty sentences.

My lamb chops seems *more tenderer* than yours.
That is the *most stupidest* idea he's ever had!

Here are the sentences written correctly.

My lamb chop seems *more tender* than yours.
That is the *stupidest* idea he's ever had!

A second problem involves using the form for three or more things when only two things are being compared.

Eva is the *smartest* of the two girls.

Although such usage sometimes occurs in informal writing, it is incorrect. Use *-est* and *most* only when you actually compare something with two or more other things, as in this sentence.

Wendell is the *richest* of the three brothers.

Exercise

In each of the following sentences, choose the proper word from the pair in parentheses.

You have done an (awful, awfully) good job restoring this painting. (awfully)

1. If I do (good, well) on this assignment, I'll get a good grade for the
   course.
2. As the body becomes (healthier, more healthier), the emotions improve.
3. The bouquet of flowers smelled very (fragrant, fragrantly).
4. I feel (good, well) about my performance in the seminar.
5. We are (real, really) pleased to have you working for us.
6. Fred groped (awkward, awkwardly) along the wall until he found
   the light switch.
7. Killer McGurk clearly proved the (better, best) fighter in that bout.
8. Don't feel (bad, badly) about failing to get that order.
9. This skit is (more clever, more cleverer) than the one we saw last
   week.
10. His voice sounded (harsh, harshly) because of his cold.

Avoiding Misplaced Modifiers

A misplaced modifier is a word, phrase, or clause that is improperly separated from the word it modifies. Because of the separation, sentences with this fault often sound awkward, ridiculous, or confusing. Furthermore, they can be downright illogical.

Misplaced modifiers can be corrected by shifting the modifier to a more sensible place in the sentence, generally next to the
word modified. Occasionally, small changes in phrasing are also
necessary.

Misplaced Adjectives and Adverbs. Misplaced adjectives almost always distort the meaning the writer intends to convey.
Consider, for example, this incorrect sentence.

I ate a *cold* dish of cereal for breakfast today.

The sentence suggests that the *dish*, not the *cereal*, was cold. Positioning the adjective next to the noun it modifies clears up the difficulty.

I ate a dish of *cold* cereal for breakfast today.

Although an adjective must be positioned as closely as possible to the word it modifies, an adverb can often be shifted around in a sentence without causing a change in meaning.

Nervously, he glanced upward at the shaky scaffolding.
He glanced *nervously* upward at the shaky scaffolding.
He glanced upward *nervously* at the shaky scaffolding.

Such flexibility is not always possible, though, as the following sentences show.

Just John was picked to emcee the first half of the program. (No one else was picked.)
John was *just* picked to emcee the first half of the program. (John was recently picked.)
John was picked to emcee *just* the first half of the program. (John will not emcee the second half of the program.)

Each of these sentences says something logical but quite different, and its correctness or incorrectness depends upon what the writer had in mind.

Often, misplacing an adverb not only alters the intended meaning but also yields one that is highly unlikely.

I *only* brought ten dollars with me.
John has *almost* eaten the whole pie.

Like adjectives, adverbs should be precisely positioned in any writing you do. Proper positioning yields sentences that accurately reflect the meaning you intend.

I brought *only* ten dollars with me.
John has eaten *almost* the whole pie.

Misplaced Phrases and Clauses. Like single words, phrases and clauses can be misplaced. The following sentences illustrate this kind of fault.

The dealer sold the Mercedes to the banker *with leather seats.* (The banker appears to have leather seats.)

There is a fence behind the house *made of barbed wire.* (The house appears to be made of barbed wire.)

Here are corrected versions of the preceding sentences.

The dealer sold the Mercedes *with leather seats* to the banker.

Behind the house, there is a fence *made of barbed wire.*

There is a *barbed wire* fence behind the house. (Note the change of wording in this corrected version.)

In attempting to make a correction, do not reposition the modifier so as to create a second erroneous or ridiculous meaning.

I found a photograph in the attic that Father had given to Mother. (Father appears to have given Mother the attic.)

I found a photograph that Father had given to Mother in the attic. (The photograph appears to have been given to Mother in the attic.)

In the attic, I found a photograph that Father had given to Mother. (This version is correct.)

Squinting Modifiers. A squinting modifier is positioned so that the reader cannot tell whether it is intended to modify the part of the sentence that precedes it or the part that follows it.

The teacher said *on Monday* she would return our tests.

As this sentence is written, we cannot tell whether the teacher made the statement on Monday or intends to return the tests on Monday.

This kind of error can be corrected by repositioning the modifier so that the sentence has just one meaning.

On Monday, the teacher said she would return our tests.

The teacher said she would return our tests *on Monday.*

Exercise

Indicate whether each of the following sentences is correct (C) or contains a misplaced modifier (MM), and correct the faulty sentences.

Dr. Mitty only needed ten minutes to remove the brain tumor. (MM) Dr. Mitty needed only ten minutes to remove the brain tumor.

1. I have made nearly fifty dollars this week.
2. My boss told me after the meeting to stop by his office.
3. Shelley read an interesting article in the *New York Times* about cerebral palsy.
4. The instructor told the students that they would only have to write three papers that term.
5. The man who had entered noisily tripped over the carpet.
6. Clayton uses a pen with a gold cap to write his reports.
7. A stranger came to the house where we lived asking directions.
8. The job took scarcely an hour to complete.
9. I've only watched that TV show three times.
10. The president made some vigorous comments about inflation during the news conference.

Avoiding Dangling Modifiers

A dangling modifier is a phrase or clause that is not clearly and logically related to the word or words it modifies. In most cases, the modifier appears at the beginning of the sentence, although it can also come at the end. Sometimes the error occurs because the sentence fails to specify anything to which the modifier can logically refer. At other times, the modifier is positioned next to the wrong noun or noun substitute.

Looking toward the horizon, a funnel-shaped cloud was stirring up the dust.
Tossing the candy wrapper on the sidewalk, a police officer ticketed me for littering.

The first sentence is faulty because the looker is not identified in any way. As the sentence is written, the funnel-shaped cloud seems to be looking toward the horizon. In the second sentence, the modifier is incorrectly positioned next to *police officer*, and thus the police officer appears to have tossed the wrapper away— and then ticketed the writer for doing so! As these examples show, dangling modifiers result in inaccurate and sometimes ludicrous statements. Here are other examples of dangling constructions.

> *Walking to the movies*, a cloudburst drenched me. (The *cloudburst* appears to be walking to the movies.)
>
> A string broke *while playing the cello*. (The *string* appears to have been playing the cello.)
>
> *Fatigued by the long walk*, the lemonade was refreshing. (The *lemonade* appears to have been fatigued by the long walk.)
>
> *When nine years old*, my mother enrolled in medical school. (*Mother* appears to have enrolled when she was nine years old.)

Dangling modifiers may be corrected in two ways. First, the modifier may be left as it is and the main part of the sentence rewritten so that it begins with the term actually modified. Second, the dangling part of the sentence can be expanded into a complete dependent clause with both a subject and a verb. With certain sentences, either method will work equally well. With others, only one of the two methods will be feasible. Here are corrected versions of the preceding sentences.

> Walking to the movies, *I was drenched by a cloudburst.* (The main part of the sentence has been rewritten.)
>
> *While I was walking to the movies*, a cloudburst drenched me. (The modifier has been expanded.)
>
> A string broke *while Lana was playing the cello*. (The modifier has been expanded.)
>
> *Because I was fatigued by the long walk*, the lemonade was refreshing. (The modifier has been expanded.)
>
> *Fatigued by the long walk*, I found the lemonade refreshing. (The main part of the sentence has been rewritten.)
>
> *When I was nine years old*, my mother enrolled in medical school. (The modifier has been expanded into a dependent clause with an expressed subject.)

Exercise

Indicate whether each of the following sentences is correct (C) or contains a dangling modifier (DM), and correct the faulty sentences.

Rewritten for the third time, the essay received a much higher grade. (C)

1. From under a rock, a snake appeared suddenly.
2. At the age of ten, my parents took me to Disney World.
3. When born, we know a baby can't care for itself.
4. Standing on the corner, I watched the fire engines race by.
5. Rubber fins are necessary when skin diving.
6. In order to repair this engine, a special wrench is needed.
7. The mercury in the thermometer must be shaken down before taking the patient's temperature.
8. By inserting a nail in a baked potato, the time required to bake it can be reduced.
9. Because of inexperience, Priscilla lost the job.
10. As a secretary, certain responsibilities were delegated to me.

Avoiding Nonparallelism

Nonparallelism results when different grammatical forms are used to express two or more equivalent ideas. This error can occur with elements in pairs or in series as well as with elements following correlative conjunctions.

Elements in Pairs or in Series. Elements in pairs or in series may include words, phrases, and clauses. The following faulty sentences illustrate some of the many possible nonparallel combinations.

We called the meeting *to present* our new vacation policy, *to discuss* last week's accident, and *for reporting* on the status of our XR-1 project. (The phrases are different in form.)

James's outfit was *wrinkled, mismatched,* and *he needed to wash it.* (The adjectives do not parallel the main clause.)

The instructor complimented the student *for taking part in classroom discussions* and *because she had written a superb library research paper.* (The phrase does not parallel the subordinate clause.)

Note the improvement in smoothness and clarity when the sentences are revised so that the ideas in them are expressed in parallel structure.

> We called the meeting *to present* our new vacation policy, *to discuss* last week's accident, and *to review* the status of our XR-1 project. (All the phrases began with infinitives.)
>
> James's outfit was *wrinkled*, *mismatched*, and *dirty*. (Three adjectives describe the noun *outfit*.)
>
> The instructor complimented the student *for taking part in classroom discussions* and *for writing a superb library research paper*. (The two phrases begin with the preposition *for*.)

Parallelism is achieved in the first and third examples with phrases that are identical in form and in the second example with the same part of speech repeated throughout a series.

Another type of nonparallelism results when items are wrongfully included in a single series.

> This estimate includes the cost of constructing the driveway, foundation, building, carpeting, light fixtures, plumbing, and furnace.

This sentence appears to be referring to the cost of constructing the carpeting, light fixtures, plumbing, and furnace. The problem can be corrected by rewriting the sentence so that it includes two series.

> The estimate includes the cost of constructing the driveway, foundation, and building, as well as the cost of the carpeting, light fixtures, plumbing, and furnace.

Elements Following Correlative Conjunctions. Correlative conjunctions (pages 423–24) emphasize the ideas that they link. Nonparallelism occurs when the correlative conjunctions are followed by unlike grammatical elements. Once again, awkwardness and decreased effectiveness are the result. Here are three sentences in which the elements following the conjunctions are not parallel in structure. In each case the conjunctions are underlined once, and the elements that follow them are underlined twice.

He is <u>either</u> <u>sick</u> or <u>he is drunk</u>. (adjective, main clause)

When asked whether she would pledge a sorority, Edith replied that she <u>neither</u> <u>had the time</u> nor <u>the inclination.</u> (verb plus direct object, noun)

The play was <u>both</u> <u>well acted</u> and <u>had beautiful stage sets</u>. (adjective, verb plus direct object)

Ordinarily, repositioning one of the correlative conjunctions will eliminate the problem. Sometimes, however, one of the grammatical elements must be rewritten. Here are revised versions of the three sentences shown above.

<u>Either</u> <u>he is sick</u>, or <u>he is drunk</u>. (two main clauses)

When asked whether she would pledge a sorority, Edith replied that she had <u>neither</u> <u>the time</u> nor <u>the inclination</u>. (two nouns)

The play was <u>both</u> <u>well acted</u> and <u>beautifully staged</u>. (two past participles modified by adverbs)

The first two sentences were corrected by repositioning the first correlative conjunction; the last one was corrected by rewriting the part following the second correlative conjunction.

Exercise

Indicate whether each of the following sentences is correct (C) or non-parallel (NP), and correct the faulty sentences.

He was tall, broad-shouldered, and had red hair. (NP)
He was tall, broad-shouldered, and red-headed.

1. Edith could neither recall the purse snatcher's height nor build.
2. The shop was dark, gloomy, and dusty.
3. Uncle Solomon not only flies planes but he also fixes them.
4. Some good reasons for going to college are to gain an education, to learn independent living, and getting a better job.
5. He wishes either to major in industrial hygiene or environmental health.
6. She performs her tasks quickly, willingly, and with accuracy.
7. Professor Jensen was neither a good lecturer nor a careful grader.

8. The novel's chief character peers through a tangle of long hair, slouches along in a shambling gait, and gets into trouble constantly.
9. Joel's problem is not that he earns too little money but spending it foolishly.
10. While working for the health department, I inspected marinas, children's day camps, public water supplies, and various nuisance complaints.

Avoiding Faulty Comparisons

A faulty comparison results when a writer fails to mention one of the items being compared, omits words needed to clarify the relationship, or compares unlike items.

Failure to Mention Both Items. Writers of advertisements often produce sentences like the following.

Snapi-Krak Cereal is a better nutritional value.

Such sentences, however, have no place in formal writing because they fail to specify exactly what their writers mean. With what other cereal or cereals is Snapi-Krak being compared, for example? Mentioning the second term of a comparison eliminates guesswork and ensures that the reader receives the intended message.

Snapi-Krak Cereal is a better nutritional value than any of its competitors.

Omission of Clarifying Words. Two words, *other* and *else*, are especially likely to be omitted from comparisons. Doing so results in illogical sentences like these two examples.

Mr. Smothers, my history instructor, is more conscientious than any instructor I have had.
Grigsby has more merit badges than anyone in his scout troop.

The first sentence is illogical because Smothers is one of the writer's instructors and therefore cannot be more conscientious than any instructor the writer has had. Similarly, because Grigsby is a member of his scout troop, he cannot have more badges than anyone in the troop. Adding *other* to the first sentence and *else* to the second clears up these difficulties.

> Mr. Smothers, my history instructor, is more conscientious than any *other* instructor I have had.
> Grigsby has more merit badges than anyone *else* in his scout troop.

Another common error of omission is the failure to include the second element of the word pair *as . . . as* in sentences that make double comparisons.

> The house looked just *as* decrepit, if not more decrepit than, the barn.

The two comparisons in this sentence are *as decrepit as* and *more decrepit than*. Because of the omission of the second *as*, however, the first comparison reads as follows: "The house looked just as decrepit the barn." Supplying the missing *as* corrects this error and gives us the following sentence.

> The house looked just *as* decrepit *as*, if not more decrepit than, the barn.

Sentences of this sort are often smoother when written so that the second comparison follows the name of the second item.

> The house looked just as decrepit as the barn, if not more decrepit.

Comparison of Unlike Items. To make a sentence of comparison logical, we must compare similar items. We can compare two or more insurance policies, cereals, instructors, Boy Scouts, or buildings; but we cannot logically compare Boy Scouts and insurance policies or cereals and buildings. Nevertheless, student writers often unintentionally compare unlike items. The following sentences illustrate this error.

Beth's *photography* is like *a professional*. (The sentence compares *photography* and *professional*.)

The electronics *graduates* from Acme College get better job offers than *Apex College*. (The sentence compares *graduates* and *Apex College*.)

This problem can be corrected by changing the sentences so that things of the same kind are compared.

Beth's *photography* is like *that of a professional*.

Beth's *photography* is like *a professional's*. (The word *photography* is omitted but understood.)

The electronics *graduates* from Acme College get better job offers than do electronics *graduates* from Apex College.

Exercise

Indicate whether each of the following sentences is correct (C) or contains a faulty comparison (FC), and correct the faulty comparisons.

New hardcover novels cost much more today than they did twenty years ago. (C)

1. Compared with her sister Maxine, Sybil has a better sense of humor.
2. Unlike my job at the restaurant, I received two weeks' vacation when I worked in Grady's Department Store.
3. American business has invested much more heavily in the Far East.
4. This physics class beats anything I'm taking this term.
5. Kimberly works as hard as, if not harder than, the other trainees.
6. The students at Passwell College earn better grades than Flunkwell University.
7. The industry in Port Arthur is much more varied than Crestburg.
8. Suzanne is more talented than any dancer in her ballet troupe.
9. The offset printing process is more widely used than any other printing process.
10. Studies show that children whose parents smoke are much more prone to respiratory ailments than nonsmoking families.

Avoiding Wordiness

Wordiness results when a paper contains deadwood or gobbledygook. Such papers are long-winded, boring, and often difficult to read.

Deadwood. This term refers to words and phrases that do nothing but take up space and clutter writing. In the following passage, the deadwood is enclosed in brackets.

> Responsible parents [of today] do not allow their children [to have] absolute freedom [to do as they please], but neither do they severely restrict their children's activities. For an illustration, let's see how one set of responsible parents, the McVeys, react to their son's request for permission to attend a party at a friend's house. When he asks [his parents] whether he can attend [the party], his parents say that he may [do so] but tell him that he must be home by a particular time. [By telling their son to be home by a particular time, the parents place restrictions on him.] If he does not [pay] heed [to] the restrictions and comes home late, he is punished: [to punish him,] his parents refuse to let him go out the next time he asks.

Deleting the deadwood not only reduces the length of the passage by 30 percent—from 135 words to 94—but also increases the clarity of the writing.

The following list includes some of the more common wordy expressions and corrections for them.

Wordy Expression	Correction
absolutely essential	essential
at this point in time	at this time, now
audible to the ear	audible
combine together	combine
commute back and forth	commute
completely eliminate	eliminate
completely unanimous	unanimous
each and every	each
exactly the same	exact, same

Wordy Expression	Correction
free gift	gift
in the vicinity of	near
in the modern world of today	today
in this day and age	today
in view of the fact that	because, since
large in size	large
once again	again
personally, I believe	I believe
red in color	red
due to the fact that	because, since
final outcome	outcome
four different times	four times
four in number	four
important essentials	essentials
in my opinion, I believe	I believe
in the event that	if
refer back	refer
repeat again	repeat
round in shape	round
true facts	facts
usual custom	custom
very unique	unique
visible to the eye	visible
with the exception of	except for

Gobbledygook. Gobbledygook, a special form of wordiness, features the unnecessary use of long words and technical terms. It is usually the result of an attempt to make writing sound impressive or to conceal the lack of anything to communicate. Here are some sentences written in gobbledygook. Revised versions in plain English are given in parentheses.

> The fish exhibited a 100-percent mortality response. (All of the fish died.)
>
> Implementation of this policy will be effectuated on January 2, 1990. (The policy will take effect on January 2, 1990.)

Technical terms in writing are justified only if (1) they save words *and* (2) the reader knows their meaning. Biologists, for instance, know that *symbiotic relationship* means "a mutually beneficial relationship between two unlike organisms," and so the term poses no problems in technical journals published for biologists. It should not, however, be used in an article aimed at nontechnical readers unless it is clearly defined the first time it is used. As a general rule, technical terms should be used sparingly in articles for general audiences.

Exercise

Indicate whether each of the following sentences is correct (C) or wordy (W), and correct the wordy sentences.

It is essential that we completely eliminate this problem within a time span of two days. (W) We must eliminate this problem within two days.

1. As a rule, I am usually up and about by 7 A.M. in the morning.
2. We have been made cognizant of the fact that the experiment will be terminated in the near future.
3. After crawling over a fence and through a tunnel, the boys found themselves in a small garden.
4. At this point in time, I am planning to pursue a major in the field of environmental health.
5. Fillmore's proposal that a committee study the proposed merger was adopted unanimously.
6. Last summer I engaged in the repair of railroad cars.
7. Illumination is required to be extinguished on the premises on termination of daily activities.
8. Disturbed by the screaming jets, the animals fled into the wilderness surrounding the airport.
9. At the present time, I am preparing for a business trip that I will soon be going to make to Buffalo.
10. The sarcastic remarks that Linda delivered had the effect of causing everyone to become quite angry.

Avoiding Sexist Language

Sexist language stereotypes people according to sex. Although some masculine stereotyping does occur, most sexist language casts women in an unfavorable light, either by implying that they are less important than men or by reinforcing outdated notions about the roles they should play. Sexist language—whether used intentionally or unintentionally—has no place in any of the writing you do on or off the job nor in your speeches and discussions. You can avoid it by following these guidelines.

1. Do not unnecessarily call attention to a woman's appearance, husband, or family. Here are some examples of sexist language and their nonsexist revisions.

    Sexist: The candidate, tall and attractively dressed, made a favorable impression on everyone who interviewed her.

    Sexist: Phyllis Lord, wife of Allen Lord, manager of Delta Bank and Trust, was elected to the Senate last week.

    Sexist: Maureen Armani, who for six years successfully combined the role of teacher and mother, received Bodine College's 1989 Teacher of the Year award.

    Nonsexist: The candidate, knowledgeable and self-confident, made a favorable impression on everyone who interviewed her.

    Nonsexist: Phyllis Lord, a three-term member of the Grantville City Council, won election to the Senate last week.

    Nonsexist: Maureen Armani, an associate professor in Bodine College's mathematics department, won the school's 1989 Teacher of the Year award.

    In each revision, the offending portion has been replaced with material that bears directly on the main point of the sentence.

2. Do not use the pronouns *he*, *him*, and *himself* to refer to any antecedents except those that are clearly masculine.

    Sexist: If anyone needs a ride to the conference, I'll take *him* in my car.

Sexist: Each of the crash victims examined *himself* carefully to be sure *he* wasn't hurt.

To correct this kind of error, replace the singular antecedents and pronouns with plural ones or revamp the sentence to eliminate the pronouns.

Nonsexist: Anyone who needs a ride to the conference can ride in my car. (The sentence has been revised.)

Nonsexist: All of the crash victims examined *themselves* carefully to make sure *they* weren't hurt. (The singular antecedent and pronoun have been replaced with plural ones.)

Pages 453–55 provide additional information on avoiding sexist language.

3. Do not use occupational terms that suggest that the positions are held only by men.

Sexist	Nonsexist
chairman	chair
draftsman	drafter
fireman	fire fighter
policeman	police officer
postman	letter carrier
weatherman	weather reporter

Some writers replace the suffix *-man* with *-person* in many job titles. This practice, however, can result in awkward expressions that should be avoided.

Punctuation and Mechanics

Apostrophes

Apostrophes (') are used (1) to show possession, (2) to mark contractions (the omission of letters or numbers in a word or date), and (3) to form plurals of letters, figures, symbols, and words used in a special sense.

Possession. Ordinarily, possessive apostrophes show ownership (*John's book*). Sometimes, however, they are used to identify (*Shakespeare's plays*) or to indicate an extent of time or space (*one day's time, one mile's distance*).

Possessive apostrophes are used with nouns as well as with pronouns like *anyone, no one, everyone, someone, each other,* and *one another.* The way possession is shown depends upon how the word ends. If the noun is singular or if it is plural and does not end in an *s,* add an apostrophe followed by an *s.*

My *friend's* car was stolen. (possessive of the singular noun *friend*)

The *children's* toys were stolen. (possessive of the plural noun *children*)

Anyone's guess is as good as mine. (possessive of the singular pronoun *anyone*)

The *boss's* orders must be obeyed. (possessive of the singular noun *boss*)

When the addition of an *'s* to a singular noun ending in *s* makes its pronunciation awkward, use only the apostrophe.

Mark *Simonides'* article on the moral aspects of bioengineering has generated considerable controversy.

The addition of an *s* here would change the pronunciation of *Simonides* to the awkward *Simonideses*.

Plural nouns that end in an *s* form the possessive by adding only an apostrophe at the end.

The *workers'* lockers were moved. (possessive of the plural noun *workers*)

At times you may wish to let your reader know that two or more people own something jointly. To do so, use the possessive apostrophe with the person who is named last only. At other times, you may want to indicate individual ownership. In this case, use an apostrophe with each name.

Ben and *Martin's* project took them a month to complete. (joint ownership)

Madeline's and *Mary's* notebooks were lying on the laboratory bench. (individual ownership)

Some businesses and other organizations with names that show possession write the names without the apostrophe.

The Veterans Administration

Citizens Bank and Trust Company

Do not, however, do this in your own writing. Use an apostrophe whenever the name of a company or organization calls for one.

Although the pronouns *his, hers, whose, its, ours, yours,* and *theirs* show possession, a possessive apostrophe is never used with them.

> This car is *hers*; the other car is *theirs*. (No apostrophe is needed.)

Contractions. Contractions of words or numbers are formed by omitting one or more letters or numerals. The omission is shown by placing an apostrophe exactly where the deletion is made.

> *Isn't* our report longer than theirs? (contraction of *is not*)
> *I'm* a University of Delaware graduate, class of '76. (contraction of *I am* and *1976*)

The contraction *it's*, meaning *it is* or *it has*, presents a special problem, as it can be confused with the possessive pronoun *its*, which has no apostrophe. However, there is an easy way to tell whether you should use an apostrophe in an *its* you have written. Just expand the *its* to *it is* or, if necessary, to *it has*, and see whether the sentence still makes sense. If it does, the *its* is a contraction and needs the apostrophe. If the sentence becomes nonsense, the *its* is a possessive pronoun, and no apostrophe should be used.

Plurals. For clarity, the plurals of letters, numbers, symbols, and words used in a special sense—that is, singled out for particular attention rather than used for their meaning—are formed by adding an apostrophe and an *s*. In addition, an apostrophe is often used to form the plurals of abbreviations.

> Your *i's* look like *e's* and your *a's* look like *o's*. (plurals of letters)
> Your 2's and 3's should be spelled out. (plurals of numbers)
> Your *&'s* should be written as *and's*. (plural of symbol and word referred to as word)
> The furnace has a capacity of 250,000 *Btu's*. (plural of abbreviation)

When there is no danger of confusion, however, an *s* alone is sufficient.

> This turbine was installed in the *1960s*.
> The president gave a reception for the *VIPs*.

Exercise

Supply apostrophes where necessary to correct the following sentences.

> Arent you glad that they invited us to the party? (Aren't)

1. Both meetings will be held at Jake and Charlottes house.
2. When transcribing what you hear, you must be careful to distinguish the ors from the oars.
3. The Browns relatives from the Twin Cities are visiting them for two weeks.
4. When everybodys special, nobody is special.
5. Susans and Ryans safety suggestions won company awards.
6. I always do my laundry at Burtons Washeteria.
7. The algebraic equation included two πs and three Δs.
8. Its apparent that my car is on its last legs—or should I say wheels?
9. For pitys sake, havent you heard that expression before?
10. All persons viewpoints will be aired at the meeting.
11. James ambition is to become a civil engineer.
12. I find Euripides plots very entertaining.

Commas to Separate

Commas (,) are used more often than any other mark of punctuation. One important use of commas is to separate one sentence element from another. The elements thus separated include main clauses, items in a series, coordinate adjectives, and introductory words and word groups.

Main Clauses. When two independent clauses are connected by a coordinating conjunction (*and, but, or, nor, for, yet,* or *so*), the conjunction should be preceded by a comma.

The side of the heater cracked, *and* Elise stood staring glumly at the ruined experiment.

Alvin is majoring in electronics, *but* his sister is studying dental hygiene.

I did not authorize the expenditure, *nor* do I accept responsibility for it.

Writers sometimes omit commas between short independent clauses, but it is safer to avoid this practice because the reader may be at least temporarily confused.

No one spoke *but* the instructor appeared surprised.

No one spoke but the instructor . . . (initial confusion)

No one spoke, but the instructor appeared surprised. (confusion eliminated by comma)

Do not mistake a simple sentence with a compound predicate for a compound sentence.

Harry washed the dishes, and Doreen sliced the carrots. (compound sentence)

Harry washed the dishes and sliced the carrots (simple sentence with compound predicate)

Items in a Series. A series consists of three or more words, phrases, or clauses grouped together. Ordinarily, the items in a series are separated by commas.

Tom, Manuel, and *Roberta* earned two-year degrees in television servicing. (words in series)

He walked *through the door, down the hall*, and *into the engine room*. (phrases in series)

The employment director said *that his company had openings for chemists, that it was actively recruiting*, and *that a representative would visit the school soon*. (clauses in series)

Business writing, however, customarily omits the comma after the next-to-last item in a series.

Our chief competitors for this market are IBM, General Dynamics and Atari.

When a coordinating conjunction comes between each successive pair of items, no commas are used.

Feuding and fussing and fighting are our pastimes.

Coordinate Adjectives. Commas are used to separate coordinate adjectives—adjectives that modify the same noun or noun substitute and that can be reversed without changing the meaning of the sentence.

Sam was a sympathetic, intelligent listener.
Sam was an intelligent, sympathetic listener.

When the word order cannot be reversed, the adjectives are not coordinate, and no comma is used to separate them.

Many advanced models of computers were on display.

In this sentence, *many* and *advanced* cannot be reversed without making the sentence meaningless.

A second way of testing whether or not adjectives are coordinate is mentally to insert an *and* between them. If the meaning does not change when *and* is inserted, the adjectives are coordinate, and a comma is used to separate them.

Introductory Elements. Introductory elements separated from the the rest of the sentence by commas include words, phrases, and clauses. When an introductory element is very short and there is no chance the sentence will be misread, the comma can be omitted.

Soon I will retire.
Below, the river threaded its way through the valley.
By 1982 we expect to double our sales.
In all, the task was very difficult.

Omitting the commas from the second and the fourth sentences might temporarily confuse the reader.

With introductory elements of six or more words, commas should always be used.

> *After changing the oil and checking the tire pressure*, Albert started his journey.
>
> *Whenever she finished a laboratory report*, Pamela treated herself to a sundae.

Exercise

Supply commas as necessary to correct the following sentences. If a sentence is correct, write a C.

> In all the directions were very confusing. (In all, . . .)

1. Get your work done or I'll have to fire you.
2. Few short men ever become movie idols.
3. The rewards of hard work include financial security peace of mind and self-respect.
4. To win Mae practiced her violin three hours each day.
5. Wilma expected to attend the meeting but fell ill the day it was held.
6. In April the company will move to Tennessee.
7. When she finishes writing the report Mary will start typing it.
8. Ralph is a careful accurate worker.
9. On Saturday I'll buy Dad a birthday gift.
10. Moe jumped violently when he heard the sharp high scream.

Commas to Set Off

A second important use of commas is to set off sentence elements. These elements include nonrestrictive expressions, geographical items, dates, and various kinds of parenthetical expressions.

Nonrestrictive Expressions. A nonrestrictive expression provides added information about the person, place, or thing that it modifies. It is set off by commas from the rest of the sentence.

Here are two sentences that include nonrestrictive expressions.

The inspector, *engrossed in her work*, did not hear the fire alarm. (The nonrestrictive phrase adds information about the inspector.)

Dr. McKay, *our laboratory director*, will address the seminar. (The nonrestrictive appositive adds information about Dr. McKay.)

A nonrestrictive expression is not essential to the basic meaning of its sentence. If we delete the phrase *engrossed in her work* from our first example, we still know that the inspector didn't hear the alarm. Similarly, removing the appositive from the second example does not destroy its main idea—that Dr. McKay will address the seminar.

Restrictive expressions—which are *not* set off with commas—single out the persons, places, or things that they modify from other persons, places, or things in the same category, thus *restricting*, or limiting, the noun modified. Unlike their nonrestrictive counterparts, they are almost always essential to the main idea of the sentence. When a restrictive expression is removed, the meaning of the sentence changes, and the sentence that results may make no sense.

Anyone *running for governor in this state* must file a report on his campaign contributions within one month after the election.

Omitting the italicized material in this sentence changes its meaning entirely. The sentence now makes the absurd statement that everyone, not just candidates for governor, must report campaign contributions. Applying this meaning test will tell you whether an expression needs to be set off with commas.

Geographical Items and Dates. Geographical items include mailing addresses and locations. The following sentences show where commas are used.

I live at 2497 Jarrett Court, Westbury, New York 11590.

> Skiing at Aspen, Colorado, is my idea of a perfect way to spend a winter vacation.

Note that although commas appear after the street designation and the city and state, they are not used to set off the zip code.

Dates are punctuated by placing commas after the day of the week, the day of the month, and the year.

> On Monday, June 9, 1975, I began working for the Bennett Corporation.

With dates that omit the day of the month, you have the option of using or not using a comma between the month and year.

> In April, 1865, the Civil War ended.
> In April 1865, the Civil War ended.

Although both of these examples are correct, the second is preferable.

Parenthetical Expressions. A parenthetical expression is a word or word group that is added to a sentence to link it to the preceding sentence, gain emphasis, or clarify the meaning in some way. Like a nonrestrictive expression, it can be omitted without affecting the basic meaning of the sentence. Parenthetical expressions include the following.

> incidental, interrupting, and clarifying phrases
> names and titles of persons being addressed directly
> degree titles and abbreviations of junior and senior following a person's name
> echo questions
> adjectives that follow, rather than precede, the words they modify

The following sentences illustrate the use of commas to set off such expressions.

Leo's whole life seems taken up with sports. Randy, *on the other hand*, is totally uninterested in athletics. (phrase linking a sentence to the one before it)

He knows, *of course*, that his decision to become a free-lance writer may cause him financial hardship. (phrase adding emphasis)

Cake, *not pie*, is my favorite dessert. (a clarifying phrase)

You know, *Sally*, that your attitude is hurting your chances for promotion. (name of person being addressed directly)

Marcia Mendel, *M.D.*, is tonight's lecturer. (degree title following name)

Tom realizes, *doesn't he*, that his research report is due this Friday? (echo question)

The kittens, *playful and energetic*, chased each other wildly through the house. (adjectives out of usual order)

Exercise

Supply commas as necessary to correct the following sentences. If a sentence is correct, write a C.

I don't believe dummy that you'll ever become a ventriloquist. (I don't believe, dummy, . . .)

1. This company it is clear never intends to install pollution-control equipment.
2. His wife whom he first met on vacation works as an air-traffic controller.
3. Sherry Davis 230 Archer Boulevard Morristown Oklahoma won the grand prize.
4. The slacks not the sweaters are on sale.
5. Look Senator at these horrible figures on inflation.
6. Jens Hansen our new classmate from Norway is an expert skier.
7. Any mother who mistreats her children should lose custody of them.
8. The boss told you didn't he that you're being considered for promotion?
9. On Sunday June 15 1975 Shirley received her degree in civil engineering.
10. John Asterbilt Sr. made ten million dollars during his lifetime; John Asterbilt Jr. spent it all in two years.

Semicolons

The semicolon (;) is used to mark especially noticeable pauses in the flow of sentences. Its chief use is to separate main clauses. These clauses may have no connecting word, or they may be connected with a conjunctive adverb. In addition, semicolons are used to separate two or more series of items, items containing commas in a single series, and main clauses that contain commas and are separated by a coordinating conjunction.

Main Clauses. The following sentences illustrate the use of semicolons to separate main clauses.

> John apologized for being late; he said he had been caught in rush hour traffic. (No conjunctive adverb is used).
> Noreen didn't want to be chairperson; *however*, she agreed to accept the position. (A semicolon precedes the conjunctive adverb.)

Two or More Series of Items. With sentences that contain two or more series of items, semicolons are often used to mark the end of each series and thus reduce the chances of misreading.

> The table was cluttered with pens and pencils; newspapers, magazines, and books; and plates, cups, and saucers.

Because of the semicolons, this sentence is clearer and easier to read than it would be if only commas were used.

Comma-Containing Items within a Series. When one or more of the items within a series contain commas, the items are preferably separated by semicolons rather than commas.

> The judges of the Homecoming floats included Jerome Kirk, Dean of Men; Elwood Barnes, the basketball coach; and Elsie La Londe, the president of the student council.

Again, using semicolons improves clarity and reduces the chance that the sentence will be misread.

Independent Clauses with Commas and a Coordinating Conjunction. Ordinarily, a comma is used to separate independent clauses joined by a coordinating conjunction. However, when one or both of the clauses contain commas, a semicolon will provide clearer separation.

> The short, serious student wanted to explain the experiment; but the visitor, nervous and impatient, would not stay to listen.

Using the semicolon in a sentence like the preceding one makes it easier to see the two main divisions.

Exercise

Supply semicolons wherever they are necessary or desirable in the following sentences. If a sentence is correct, write a C.

> The meeting will start in thirty minutes meanwhile, I'll read this magazine. (The meeting will start in thirty minutes; meanwhile, I'll . . .)

1. The president of the college did not oppose vocational education, on the contrary, he strongly supported it.
2. For recreation the Smiths golf, hike, and play tennis, the Browns swim, water ski, and fish, and the Greens attend plays, movies, and concerts.
3. He wanted employees who were completely loyal, totally dedicated, and outstandingly brilliant, and so, after trying many humans, he turned to computerized robots.
4. The scouts, tired and discouraged after two days of rain, asked to go home, and the scoutmaster, yielding to their pleas, cut the trip short.
5. You have missed the last three committee meetings and executive sessions, furthermore, your reports have been consistently late.
6. The table closet contained carpenters' saws, hammers, and planes, draftmen's T-squares, drawing boards, and triangles, and machinists' calipers and micrometers.
7. Nearly all our graduates find jobs, for example, 93 percent of this year's printing technology students have found newspaper jobs.
8. Pollution is not new to the human race it destroyed the Sumerian civilization and plagued the Romans.

9. When I was a child, my favorite comedians were Curly, Larry, and
Moe of the Three Stooges, Spanky, Alfalfa, and Buckwheat of Our
Gang, and the three Marx Brothers, Groucho, Chico, and Harpo.
10. He refused to write a term paper, therefore he failed the course.

Colons, Dashes, Parentheses, and Brackets

Like commas and semicolons, colons, dashes, parentheses,
and brackets are used to separate and enclose: they clarify the relationships among the various parts of the sentences in which they
appear.

Colons. One important use of the colon (:) is to introduce
appositives, formal lists, and formal explanations when they are
preceded by material that could serve as complete sentences.

All her efforts were directed toward one goal: earning a degree
in civil engineering. (appositive)

Four occupations were represented by those in attendance: elec-
trician, carpenter, plumber, and sheet-metal worker. (formal
list)

To determine if the product is suitable, do as follows: (1) select
random samples of six-inch angle irons, (2) mount each sample in the testing machine, and (3) test for deformation tensile
strength. (formal explanation)

Unless the introductory material can stand alone, *do not* use a colon. The following sentence is incorrect because of the colon.

My courses for next semester include: algebra, economics, English, and history.

Here is how the sentence should look.

My courses for next semester include algebra, economics, English, and history.

A colon is often used instead of a comma to introduce a long,
formal quotation, particularly if the quotation consists of more
than one sentence.

The candidate arose, faced his audience, and said: "Ladies and gentlemen, we are living in troubled times. Millions of Americans are out of work, food prices are soaring, and we face critical fuel shortages. The present administration is doing nothing to solve these problems. We need new leadership."

With long quotations, the material preceding the colon may be a complete sentence or just part of one, as in our example.

Colons are also used to separate hours from minutes, titles of publications from subtitles, salutations of business letters from the body of the letters, and numbers indicating ratios.

The second show begins at 9:15 P.M. (The colon separates the hour from the minutes.)

Our textbook for this course is entitled *The Short Story: Fiction in Transition*. (The colon separates the title from the subtitle.)

To make French dressing, start by combining salad oil and wine vinegar in a 4:1 ratio. (The colon separates numbers indicating a ratio.)

Dashes. Like colons, dashes (—) are used to set off appositives, lists, and explanations, but they are employed in less formal writing.

Only one person could be guilty of such an oversight—William! (appositive)

The workroom was very sparsely equipped—a workbench, a small tool cabinet, and a single lathe. (list)

There's only one plausible reason why your level has disappeared—it was stolen. (explanation)

A sudden break in thought is generally set off by two dashes—one preceding the interrupting material and the other following it.

Her TV set—she bought it just last month, didn't she?—is at the repair shop.

Dashes also set off parenthetical expressions that contain commas.

The speaker—poised, articulate, and well informed—made a pleasing impression on her audience.

Finally, dashes are used to set off comments following a list.

A set of crescent wrenches, pliers, and a screwdriver—these are what he bought.

In typing, a dash consists of two hyphens (--), one after the other with no space between them and the words that come before and after. The dash emphasizes the material it sets off.

Parentheses. Parentheses—( )—are used to enclose numbers or letters that accompany formal listings in sentences and to set off examples and other supplementary information or comments that would interrupt the main sequence of ideas.

Each paper should contain (1) an introduction, (2) a number of paragraphs developing the thesis sentence, and (3) a conclusion.

Some vocational programs (auto service, for example) are filled months before the new semester begins.

John's first promotion came as a surprise. (He had been with the company only three months.) But his second promotion left all of us astounded.

James Watt (1736–1819) helped pioneer the development of the steam engine.

Of all the findings, only those obtained at the Hendricks site (see Table 4) offered any surprises.

Parentheses de-emphasize rather than emphasize the material they enclose. If the material in parentheses appears within a given sentence, it is not necessary to use an initial capital letter or a period even if the parenthetical material is itself a complete sentence.

The development of nuclear energy (one cannot foresee where it will lead) is a controversial issue today.

If, however, the material in parentheses takes the form of a separate sentence, punctuate it as you would a sentence. In such sentences, the closing parenthesis follows the final punctuation.

> John's first promotion came as a surprise. (He had been with the company only three months.)

If the material in parentheses appears at the end of a sentence, the closing parenthesis precedes the final punctuation.

> The development of nuclear energy is a controversial issue today (one cannot foresee where it will lead).

Brackets. Brackets—[ ]—are used with quoted material to enclose words or phrases that have been added or changed for clarity. They are also used with the word *sic* (Latin for "thus") to identify errors in the material being quoted.

> "The founder of the school [Woodbridge Ferris] also served as governor of Michigan." (The bracketed name is added to the original.)
>
> "[Margaret Mead's] years of study have made her one of the foremost experts on culturally determined behavior." (The bracketed name replaces "her" in the original.)
>
> "The accused man dennied [*sic*] all charges." (The word "dennied" is misspelled in the original.)

As the third sentence illustrates, when a writer notices an error in material being quoted, he or she inserts the word *sic*, in brackets, directly after the error. The reader who sees this knows that the error was not made by the writer but is being accurately reproduced from the original.

Exercise

Supply colons, dashes, parentheses, and brackets wherever they are necessary in the following sentences. If a sentence is correct, write a C.

> Adlai Stevenson 1900–1965 ran unsuccessfully for president in 1952 and 1956. Adlai Stevenson (1900–1965) ran . . .

1. My bus leaves for Chicago at 850 A.M.
2. The procedure for taking a blood sample requires 1 a sterile syringe, 2 a sterile cotton ball, 3 alcohol, and 4 a tourniquet.
3. He ate just four things all week hot dogs, hamburgers, peanut butter sandwiches, and chocolate cake.
4. Our own findings see Table 3 clearly support the state's conclusion that this lake is contaminated.
5. Mary writes textbooks for two reasons to gain professional recognition and to make money.
6. The report concluded with this sentence "These statistics clearly show that drunk driving is the principle sic cause of auto accidents."
7. Whitman's outburst I never dreamed he was capable of such anger stunned everyone in the office.
8. Our school has a 4 2 1 ratio of technical, business, and liberal arts students.
9. Rubber aprons, chemical workers' goggles, and hard hats all these are needed for this job.
10. "His Charles Darwin's book touched off a religious controversy that hasn't yet died." said the review.

Periods, Question Marks, and Exclamation Points

Periods, question marks, and exclamation points serve primarily to mark the ends of sentences; thus they are sometimes called *end marks*. In addition, periods may indicate abbreviations and omissions and are used in certain numerical designations, while question marks may be used to indicate uncertainty.

Periods. Periods (.) are used to end sentences that state facts, make requests that are not in the form of questions, give instructions, or ask indirect questions—that is, questions that have been rephrased to form part of a statement.

Monty works for Northgate Tool and Die Company. (Sentence states fact.)

Please lend me your protractor. (Sentence makes request.)

Do your assignment before you leave. (Sentence gives instruction.)

She asked whether I had attended last week's sales presentation. (Sentence includes indirect question as part of a statement.)

Periods also follow common abbreviations as well as a person's initials.

Mr.	B.C.	Ave.
Mrs.	A.D.	Inc.
Ms.	A.M.	etc.
Dr.	P.M.	i.e.
Jr.	c.o.d.	vs.

Harvey H. Borden, Jr., will address the Rotary Club this evening.

Today, periods are often omitted after abbreviations for the names of organizations or governmental agencies. The following are some abbreviations that are commonly written without periods.

AFL-CIO	TVA	FHA	NASA
ROTC	IBM	PTA	CAB
FDIC	CBS	NAACP	USDA
VA	FBI	CIA	NFL

If you do not know whether a particular abbreviation should be written with periods, check an up-to-date collegiate dictionary.

Periods are used to precede decimal fractions and to separate numeral designations for dollars and cents.

0.39 percent	$6.29
4.39 percent	$0.76

Question Marks. A question mark (?) is used after a whole sentence or part of a sentence that asks a direct question (one in the exact words of the person who asked it).

Will you show me how to focus this laser beam? (The whole sentence asks a question.)

Have you checked the oil? cleaned the windshield? replenished
the battery water? (A series of sentence parts ask questions.)

Mrs. Kendall—wasn't she your teacher once?—has retired after
thirty-five years of service. (An interrupting clause between
dashes asks a question.)

The inspector asked, "Why is the guard missing from this gear
box?" (A quotation asks a question.)

As noted in the preceding section, indirect questions are followed
by periods.

Exclamation Points. Exclamation points (!) are used after
words, phrases, or clauses to denote a high degree of fear, anger,
joy, or other emotion or to express an emphatic command.

William! It's been years since I've seen you!
Walter! Get back to work immediately!
Ouch! That hurts!

Don't overuse the exclamation point. If you do, it will soon fail to
produce the intended effect.

Exercise

Supply periods, question marks, or exclamation points wherever
they are necessary in the following sentences. If a sentence is correct,
write a C.

Our new neighbor, Dr Jerome Beardsley, Sr., moved here from
North Carolina. (. . . Dr. Jerome Beardsley, Sr., moved . . .)

1. If your temperature is 100° F you are running a low fever.
2. When are you scheduled to begin the project.
3. The president asked her assistant which of the district sales managers was most qualified for the position of sales director.
4. Dr. Winkler asked, "What do you plan to do this summer?"
5. Please don't dangle your arm out the car window.
6. For the love of Pete, watch what you're doing there.
7. Stepanski's Grocery Shoppe—didn't it begin as a meat market—is
   moving to its new location next week.

8. The program begins at 9 PM and lasts about an hour.
9. This year, the budget for the VA was increased just 123 percent—scarcely any gain at all.
10. While you were in New York, did you see the Statue of Liberty visit Radio City Music Hall take a carriage ride through Central Park.

Quotation Marks

Quotation marks (" ") are used to set off direct quotations, titles of shorter works and subdivisions of books, and to identify expressions used in a special sense.

Direct Quotations. A direct quotation repeats a person's written or spoken comments in his or her own words.

The placement director announced, "The Aeolian Heating and Air Conditioning Corporation's recruiter will be on campus this Thursday." (spoken comments)

"Coffee prices are expected to increase by ten cents a pound in the next three months," the first sentence of the newspaper story said.

Sally described her job as "a total bust."

As these examples show, the commas that come before direct quotations are positioned outside the quotation marks. Commas and periods that come at the end of direct quotations are positioned inside the marks. Quotations that are sentence fragments are not preceded by commas.

Titles of Shorter Works and Subdivisions of Books. Besides setting off written and spoken quotations, quotation marks also are used to denote titles of the following.

magazine articles	chapters and sections of books
essays	short poems
short stories	songs
other short pieces of prose	television and radio programs

> The article was titled "Results of Testing Willow Creek for Coliform Organisms." (article)

Do not, however, include the titles of your themes within quotation marks.

With titles, as with direct quotations, commas and periods that directly follow the quoted material are positioned inside the quotation marks. Commas that precede the quoted material are outside the quotation marks.

> Next week we will discuss Chapter 8, "Letters and Memorandums." (chapter of a book)

Expressions Used in a Special Sense. Words, letters, numerals, and symbols used in a special sense—that is, singled out for particular attention rather than used for their meaning—are sometimes set off by quotation marks.

> "Bonnets," "valves," and "lifts" are British terms for car hoods, radio tubes, and elevators.
> It's hard to tell whether this letter is a "G" or a "C."

Often, however, such expressions are printed in italics (see page 519).

Note that the commas and periods again appear inside the quotation marks.

Quotation Marks Within Quotation Marks. Occasionally, a direct quotation or the title of a shorter work will occur within a direct quotation. In such cases the inner quotation or title is set off with single quotation marks (' ').

> The witness told the court, "I heard the defendant say, 'Let's rob Peterson's Party Store.'"

Notice that the period at the end of this double quotation comes ahead of both the single mark and the double mark.

Quotation Marks that Accompany Semicolons, Colons, Exclamation Points, and Question Marks. Unlike periods and commas, semicolons and colons that come at the end of quoted material are always placed outside the quotation marks.

> He said, "I want to study drafting"; however, his placement test indicated a low aptitude for that field.

A question mark or exclamation point may be placed either inside or outside the quotation marks, depending upon what it applies to. If, for example, only the quoted part of a sentence asks a question, the question mark goes inside the quotation marks. If the entire sentence, but not the quoted material, asks a question, the question mark goes outside the quotation marks. If the entire sentence asks one question and the quoted material asks another, then the question mark goes inside the quotation marks.

> He asked, "When will your laboratory project be finished?" (The quoted material, but not the whole sentence, asks the question.)
>
> Why did Irma suddenly announce, "I've quit my job"? (The whole sentence, not the quoted material, asks the question.)
>
> Where did he get the nerve to ask, "How much money did you earn last year?" (The whole sentence and the quoted material ask separate questions.)

Exercise

Supply properly positioned quotation marks wherever they are necessary in the following sentences. If a sentence is correct, write a C.

> Tomorrow, we'll discuss the article The ABC's of Supply-Side Economics. (. . . article "The ABC's of Supply-Side Economics.")

1. Harry called the following my favorite English authors: Jane Austen, Charles Dickens, and George Orwell.
2. If you say I told you so one more time, I'll scream, Penny snapped angrily.
3. The interviewer asked the applicant, Why do you want to work for this company?
4. Sidney told everyone, I spend two hours each night studying the course; nevertheless, he could never answer his instructor's questions.

5. In Baskerville type, the bottom loop of the g is not completely closed.
6. Nova is a popular program on public television.
7. What made my father ask me, Don't you think you're acting awfully foolish?
8. The 7 in my house number isn't lined up with the other numbers.
9. Who said, A little inaccuracy sometimes saves tons of explanation?
10. Elsie called the article on genetic engineering a scientific bombshell.

Hyphens

Hyphens (-) are used to separate compound adjectives and nouns, two-word numbers and fractions, and certain prefixes and suffixes from the words with which they appear. In addition, they are employed to prevent misreadings and awkward combinations of letters or syllables.

Compound Adjectives and Nouns. Perhaps the most widespread use of hyphens is to join separate words that function as single adjectives and precede nouns. The use of these hyphenated, or compound, adjectives is very common, allowing a wide range of ideas to be expressed. Here are two typical examples of hyphenated adjectives.

The *deep-blue* sea was beautiful.
The *cane-shaped* tube measures both vacuum and pressure.

Note that the meaning of the first sentence would change if the hyphen were replaced with a comma or simply omitted. With the hyphen, we are referring to a sea that is deep blue in color. If the hyphen were replaced with a comma, we would be referring to a sea that is deep and blue. With neither a hyphen nor a comma, there would be no way to tell which is deep, the color blue or the sea itself.

When the first word of the compound is an adverb ending in *-ly* or when the compound adjective comes after the noun it modifies, the hyphen is omitted.

The *deeply* embarrassed man apologized for his comment.
The sea was *deep blue.*

In a series of two or more compound adjectives that all have the same term following the hyphen, the term following the hyphen need not be repeated throughout the series. It is often briefer and smoother to use the term only at the end of the series. However, the hyphens preceding the omitted parts are retained.

Several *six-* and *eight-cylinder* engines were overhauled yesterday.

Hyphenated nouns include such expressions as the following:

editor-in-chief	go-between
father-in-law	jack-of-all-trades

Here is a sentence with hyphenated nouns.

Denton is *editor-in-chief* of the largest newspaper in this state.

Two-Word Numbers and Fractions. Hyphens are used in two-word numbers from twenty-one to ninety-nine and in fractions when these are written out.

The company's *seventy-eighth* year saw its sales exceed $800 million.
Three-fourths of the class will receive C's.

Prefixes and Suffixes. Prefixes and suffixes are words or groups of letters attached to words to expand or change their meaning. A prefix is attached at the beginning of a word, a suffix at the end. Although most prefixes are not hyphenated, the prefixes *self-* and *all-* and the suffix *-elect* are set off with hyphens, as is the prefix *ex-* when it precedes a noun.

The founder of this magazine is a *self-made* woman.
The timing of this announcement is *all-important.*

Norbert is *president-elect* of our club.

The *ex-governor* gave a speech.

A prefix used before a term that begins with a capital letter is always hyphenated.

The *anti-CIA* speaker received little applause.

Preventing Misreadings and Awkward Combination of Letters or Syllables. Hyphens are also used to prevent misreadings of certain words that would look like other words if they were not hyphenated, as well as to prevent awkward combinations of letters or syllables between some prefixes and suffixes and their core words.

The *un-ionized* salt precipitates from the solution. (Without the hyphen, the word, meaning *not ionized*, might be misread as *unionized*.)

The worker *re-covered* the exposed pipe. (Without the hyphen, the word might be misread as *recovered*.)

The committee is determined to *de-emphasize* sports at Franklin Pierce High School. (The hyphen prevents the awkward repetition of the letter *e* in *de-emphasize*.)

Exercise

Supply hyphens wherever they are necessary in the following sentences. If a sentence is correct, write a C.

Three fourths of the directors missed the last meeting of the farmers' coop. (Three-fourths . . . co-op.)

1. The villain tried to whisper sweet nothings into the shelllike ear of the pure young maiden.
2. Wouldn't it be nice to have a six or seven figure income?
3. About one third of our work force will lose their jobs if this recession continues.
4. The transCanadian pipeline brings Alaskan oil to the United States.
5. The president's antiinflationary measures seem woefully inadequate to me.

6. I like the pea green blouse better than the one that's navy blue.
7. Two student coops will open next term.
8. Mr. Gonzales, our chairman elect, has served on the board of directors for twelve years.
9. This drawing is a recreation of the scene of the accident.
10. At the age of twenty three, Sidney was graduated from MIT with a doctorate in physics.
11. Our new neighbor, an excolonel in the army, feels that this country's military budget is inadequate.
12. Maxwell is truly a jack of all trades.

Capitalization

The first letter of any sentence, including any sentence that appears as a quotation within another sentence, is always capitalized, as is the pronoun *I*, both by itself and in contractions.

He said, "When *I* finish this job, *I*'ll watch television with you."

In addition, capitals are used with proper nouns, adjectives derived from proper nouns, certain abbreviations, personal titles preceding names, and titles of literary and artistic works.

Proper Nouns. Proper nouns refer to one particular person, group of persons, place, or thing, and their first letters are always capitalized. They includes names of the following.

persons
organizations and institutions
national, political, religious, and racial groups (but not *black* and *white*)
countries, states, cities, streets, and buildings
geographical locations and geographical features
days, holidays, and months (but not seasons)
trademarked products (and slogans that are trademarked)
languages
ships, trains, and airplanes
academic and professional degree designations and their abbreviations

The following sentences illustrate the capitalization of proper nouns.

> He attends *Ferris State University,* an institution that has pioneered in offering health-related programs.
>
> *Lolita Martinez,* our class valedictorian, was born in *Matamoras, Mexico.*
>
> Next *Monday, June* 5, I begin work as a supervisor for the *Bradley Company.*
>
> To protect the food, she covered it with *Reynolds Wrap* aluminum foil.
>
> I have a *Bachelor of Science* degree, and my brother is a *C.P.A.*

Terms such as "building," "street," and "company" are not capitalized unless they form part of a proper name. Thus, in the first sentence in the preceding list, "college" is not capitalized when it is written by itself. Similarly, the names of nonlanguage courses are not capitalized unless they are followed by a course number or begin a sentence.

> This term, *Geology 101* is my worst course, but algebra is causing me no difficulty at all.

Proper Adjectives. Adjectives created from proper nouns are called proper adjectives. Like the nouns themselves, they should be capitalized.

> Lolita Martinez, our class valedictorian, is of *Mexican* ancestry. (*Mexican* is derived from the proper noun *Mexico.*)

Certain usages of proper nouns and words derived from them have become so well established that the expressions are regarded as common nouns and written without capitals. Here are a few examples.

chinaware	plaster of paris
frankfurters	turkish towel
india ink	volt
italics	watt

Abbreviations. Abbreviations are ordinarily capitalized if the words they stand for would be capitalized; otherwise, they are not.

> Stanley Kolinski is an *FBI* agent. (*FBI* is capitalized because "Federal Bureau of Investigation" would be.)
>
> The shaft revolved at 1,500 *rpm*. (The abbreviation *rpm* is not capitalized because "revolutions per minute" would not be.)

Common exceptions include the abbreviations A.M., P.M., A.D., B.C., TV, and VCR, which are capitalized even though the words they stand for would not be capitalized.

Personal Titles. Capitalize the first letter of a personal title that immediately precedes a name. A personal title not followed by a name is ordinarily left uncapitalized unless it is used in place of the name.

> The banquet for graduating chemical technologists was addressed by *Dean* Arthur Swanson.
>
> Tell me, *Dean*, will this year's enrollment exceed last year's?
>
> The *dean* of our Special Education Division is Dr. Helen McConell.

With persons of high rank, titles used in place of names are often capitalized as a mark of respect.

> I plan to watch the President on TV tonight.
> I plan to watch the president on TV tonight.

Either of these usages is acceptable.

Titles of Literary and Artistic Works. Literary and artistic works include books, magazines, newspapers, articles, short stories, poems, reports, films, television programs, musical compositions, pictures, and sculptures.

When you write such titles, capitalize the first and last words as well as all other words except *a, an, the,* coordinating conjunctions, and prepositions with fewer than five letters.

He used a study guide, *Solving Problems in Chemistry and Physics*, when he did his homework.

For tomorrow, read the handout article "New Trends in Preparing Aluminum Alloys."

Exercise

Capitalize words or abbreviations as necessary to correct the following sentences. If a sentence is correct, write a C.

Paul gleason, one of the most prominent blacks in this city, holds a graduate degree from the wharton school of finance. (Gleason, Wharton School of Finance)

1. Each account at people's savings bank is insured by the Federal Deposit Insurance Corporation (fdic).
2. tom's family doctor referred him to dr. Leland F. Hilton, who specializes in eye surgery.
3. Negotiations for a new contract between general motors and the uaw will begin next week.
4. In our part of the country, it's not wise to manifest marxist beliefs.
5. Do you believe that the popular image of politicians has improved, senator?
6. Our office has a new xerox copying machine.
7. *the wall street journal* and *business week* keep me posted on the latest business trends.
8. This article, "after the me generation," offers a fine analysis of modern social trends.
9. Professor bacon is one of the world's most foremost shakespearean scholars.
10. We are fortunate to have as our speaker mayor jerry manders.

Abbreviations

Abbreviations are used for certain personal titles, names of organizations and agencies, Latin terms, and for scientific and technical terms. Names of persons, streets, geographical locations, days, months, and school and college courses should be spelled out.

Personal Title. *Mister, doctor,* and similar titles of address are always abbreviated when they immediately precede a name.

> *Mr.* John Williams and *Dr.* Sandra Barkon operate a small medical testing laboratory.

Junior, Senior, Esquire, and degree titles are abbreviated when they immediately follow proper names.

> The company was founded by Anthony Cappucine, *Jr.*
> The sign on the office identified its occupant as Elizabeth Williams, *M.D.*

Names of Organizations and Agencies. Some organizations or agencies are commonly referred to by their initials. Here are some typical examples.

FBI	AMA	NASA
GOP	UN	HUD

Latin Terms and Abbreviations with Dates. Certain Latin terms are always abbreviated, and other terms, mostly Latin, are abbreviated when they occur with dates or numerals.

> e.g. (*exempli gratia*: for example)
> etc. (*et cetera*: and [the] others)
> i.e. (*id est*: that is)
> vs. (*versus*: against)
> B.C. (before Christ)
> A.D. (*anno Domini*: in the year of our Lord)
> A.M. (a.m.) (*ante meridiem*: before noon)
> P.M. (p.m.) (*post meridiem*: after noon)

> I'll pick you up around 7 P.M.
> Certain diseases (e.g., measles and polio) are no longer serious childhood threats.

Scientific and Technical Terms. Science and technology make use of many terms of measurement. When these terms occur repeatedly in a single article or report, they are generally abbreviated. Whenever the meaning of the abbreviation might not be known to every reader, the term is written out the first time it is used and its abbreviation, in parentheses, put immediately after it. (This procedure can also be used with unfamiliar organizations and agencies that are mentioned repeatedly.)

The heater was a 250,000 British thermal unit (Btu) model.

Ordinarily, such an abbreviation is written without periods. However, if it has the same spelling as another word, a period is generally used after the last letter to distinguish the abbreviation from the word. Thus, *inch* is abbreviated *in.* to distinguish it from *in*, and *fig.* rather than *fig* is used for *figure*.

Exercise

In the following sentences, supply abbreviations wherever they are necessary or customarily used. If a sentence is correct, write a C.

This engine is now operating at 5,000 revolutions per minute.
(. . . 5,000 rpm.)

1. I think 8:00 *ante meridiem* is too early to begin a marketing seminar.
2. Tell me more about those noises you've been hearing, Mister Usher.
3. It's about time the Environmental Protection Agency established and enforced strict rules for toxic waste disposal.
4. Please hand me that 30 milliliter syringe.
5. Ten years ago, I sold all my stock in International Business Machines, and now I couldn't be sorrier.
6. If that pain in your chest doesn't go away, make an appointment with Doctor Abraham Goldberg, Senior.
7. Terence didn't know that 212° Fahrenheit is the same as 100° Celsius.
8. The Interstate Commerce Commission is investigating the Central States Trucking Company.

9. The expression *et cetera* should be used very sparingly in one's writing.

10. Gail Birnhausen, Master of Arts, has joined the Faculty at Grove Community College.

Numbers

Some writers use figures for numbers larger than ninety-nine and spell out numbers smaller than 100. Increasingly, however, writers in scientific and technical fields spell out numbers one through nine and use figures for all others. No matter which practice your instructor prefers, the following exceptions apply.

Numbers in a Series. Numbers in a series should be written in the same way, regardless of their size.

> We have 150 salespersons, 52 research engineers, and 7 laboratory technicians.
> Harley owns three cars, two motorboats, and one hundred and fifteen motorcycles.

Dates. In dates that include the year, figures are always used.

> January 3, 1975 (not January 3rd, 1975)

When the year is not given, the number may be spelled out or a figure may be used.

> August 5
> August fifth
> the fifth of August

Page Numbers and Addresses. Figures are used for page numbers of publications and most numbers in street addresses.

> The diagram is on page *223* of the text.
> Her photographic studio is located at *139* Powell Street.

If the name of the street is also a number, spell out the name unless it is preceded by a word like "North" or "South." The following examples are both correct.

> 175 Fifth Avenue
> 203 West 48th Street

Numbers Beginning Sentences. Any number beginning a sentence should be spelled out. If this would require too many words, the sentence should be rewritten so that the number occurs within the sentence.

> *Forty thousand* voters went to the polls.
> A crowd of *115,394* people attended the game. (If this number began the sentence, eight words, an excessive number, would be needed to write it out.)

Units of Measurement, Decimals, Percentages, Expressions of Time. In business and technical writing, figures are used for units of measurement; for decimals, percentages, and other mathematical expressions; and for expressions of time with P.M. or A.M.

> The metal is *0.315* inch thick.
> The project has been *35* percent completed.
> This constant, multiplied by *3*, gives *12.424*.
> The plant's work day starts at *9* A.M. and ends at *4:30* P.M.

Fractions, Two Consecutive Numbers. Ordinarily, fractions are spelled out unless (1) they occur in a mathematical expression or with a unit of measurement, (2) they have denominators larger than 10, or (3) they occur in a series that includes four or more fractions.

> Of the students in highway technology, three-fourths have received job offers.
> Multiply $\frac{3}{4}$ by $\frac{3}{16}$ to obtain the answer. (mathematical expression)
> A $\frac{5}{16}$-inch crescent wrench is needed for the bolt. (unit of measurement)

The new machine performs the operation in $\frac{1}{20}$th the time required by the old. (denominator larger than ten)

When the two numbers occur one immediately after the other, spell out the first one and use numerals for the second one. Exception: if the first number is larger than 100, use numerals for the first one and spell out the second one.

The parts are held together by *six* 2-inch bolts.
Hanson's Hardware sold *125 sixty-watt* light bulbs last week.

Exercise

Rewrite any incorrectly expressed numbers in the following sentences. If a sentence is correct, write a C.

We must increase the diameter of the hole by two one-hundredths of an inch. (. . . by 0.02 inch.)

1. Jay has twenty-four suits, eighty-seven shirts and 114 ties.
2. The *Directory of Publishers*, page seven, lists the address of the Dowling Company as eleven J Street, Modesto, California 95355.
3. He graduated June 8th, 1957, from Northeastern College.
4. Fifty ten-foot beams will be required for this job.
5. Lend me a one-sixteenth inch drill bit, please,
6, During the last two years, Jerry has worked 7 months in a grocery store, 3 months in a car wash, and four months as a carpenter.
7. The seminar will start promptly at ten A.M. next Thursday.
8. You can find the John Kennedy quotation on page nineteen of your text.
9. Pam isn't thrilled about her fourteen and a half percent mortgage, but at the time she got it, no better rate was available.
10. October twenty 9, 1929, the day the stockmarket crashed, is sometimes known as "Black Tuesday."

Italics

Italics are used for the titles of longer publications and of artistic works, the proper names of vehicles and vessels, foreign words and phrases, and expressions used in a special sense—that is, called to the reader's attention rather than used for their meaning. In handwritten and typed papers, use underlining to indicate italics.

Titles of Longer Publications and of Artistic Works. Italics are used to designate the titles of the following:

books	full-length movies
magazines	long musical works and poems
newspapers	plays
journals	sculptures
bulletins	paintings

Titles of articles, newspaper columns, short stories, short poems, one-act plays, and the like are set off with quotation marks.

> His paper included quotations from the *New York Times*, the *Journal of Business Education*, and a U.S. Office of Education bulletin entitled *Business School Enrollments, 1978–1988.* (newspaper, journal, bulletin)

Names of Vehicles and Vessels. Proper names of individual airplanes, ships, trains, and spacecraft are italicized (but not their model designations, such as DC-7 or Boeing 747, or abbreviations preceding them, such as S.S.).

> He flew to Oslo on the *Star of the North*. He sailed back on the *Queen Elizabeth II*. (plane, ship)

Foreign Words and Phrases. Many foreign words and phrases have made their way into English over the centuries. At any one time there are many that have not been completely absorbed, and these are italicized.

> He committed a terrible *faux pas*. (a social blunder)
> I have a strange feeling of *déjà vu*. (a sensation that something has been experienced before)

After a foreign word has been completely absorbed into the English language the italics are dropped. For example, the word *employee*, originally a French word, used to be italicized but no longer is. Collegiate dictionaries use a special symbol such as an asterisk (*) or a dagger (†) to mark words or phrases that should be italicized. Check the introductory part of your dictionary to see what symbol it uses, and italicize any items marked with the symbol.

Expressions Used in a Special Sense. Expressions used in a special sense—that is, singled out for special attention, rather than used for their meaning—include words, letters, numerals, and symbols.

> The English word *thou* is related to the German word *du*.
> My handwriting is hard to read because each *r* looks like an *s*, and each *4* looks like a *9*.
> The symbol *&* is called an ampersand.

As noted on page 506, quotation marks are sometimes used instead of italics for words, letters, numerals, and symbols used in a special sense.

Exercise

Supply italics wherever they are necessary in the following sentences. If a sentence is correct, write a C.

> Mark is a noun in the first sentence and a verb in the second.
> (*Mark* is a noun . . .)

1. Detective Holmes tried to piece together a modus operandi for the series of robberies in Pinehurst Subdivision.
2. One whole wall of our basement is lined with my father's back copies of the quarterly bulletin Business Barometer.
3. Voyager II is the second in a series of unmanned spaceships that this country will launch.
4. I mistook that M for an N; that's why I marked the word as misspelled.
5. "My Turn," a column by Felix Farnsworth, appears five days a week in the Columbia Post Gazette.
6. A copy of Van Gogh's painting Sunflowers hangs in my sister's living room.

7. Gone with the Wind, starring Clark Gable and Vivien Leigh, is my all-time favorite movie.

8. The sudden coup de main took the enemy completely by surprise.

9. The May 1980 issue of Today's Backpacker contains an article on avoiding blisters.

10. The passenger train that passes through this town is called the Peoria Pearl.

Acknowledgments (continued from page iv)

Berne, Eric. "Can People Be Judged by Their Appearance?" From *A Layman's Guide to Psychiatry and Psychoanalysis.* Copyright 1947, 1957, 1968 by Eric Berne. Reprinted by permission of Simon and Schuster, Inc.

Birmingham, Donald J. "Occupational Dermatoses: Their Recognition, Control, and Prevention." From *The Industrial Environment—Its Evaluation and Control.* Washington, D.C.: U.S. Department of Health, Education, and Welfare, 1973, pp. 503–5.

Carson, Rachel. *Silent Spring.* Boston: Houghton, 1962.

The Dow Chemical Company. Specific Gravity of Aqueous Ammonia graph. From *Aqueous Ammonia.* Midland, Michigan: The Dow Chemical Company, 1962. Data for graph from W. C. Ferguson. *Lange's Handbook of Chemistry,* 7th. ed. New York: McGraw, 1949.

Drucker, Peter. "How to Be an Employee." Reprinted from *Fortune,* May 1952.

The Eastern Company. Hi-Tensile Anchor Selection Guide table. Reprinted with permission of the Danforth Division of the Eastern Company.

Einstein, Albert. *Ideas and Opinions.* New York: Crown, 1954.

Eiseley, Loren. *The Unexpected Universe.* New York: Harcourt, 1969.

Flocon Products, Inc. Cutaway view of the Floguard Check Valve. Reprinted with permission of the designer and manufacturer, Flocon Products, Inc., Houston, Texas.

Forbis, Steven, "A Little Disk Music," *Money,* April, 1985, pp. 128–132.

Gamow, George. *One, Two, Three . . . Infinity.* New York: Viking, 1947.

Johnson, Harriet C., "House Calls Have Found a Home," *USA Today,* August 25, 1988, pp. B1–B2. Copyright 1988, USA TODAY. Excerpted with permission.

LaTarte Company, Inc. Exploded-view diagram of the belt guard assembly for the Econo-Mitre saw. Reprinted by permission of the LaTarte Company, Inc., Smith Creek, Michigan.

Physicians for Social Responsibility. "Psychological Impact of the Nuclear Threat on Children and Adolescents: 1965–1984." Reprinted by permission of Physicians for Social Responsibility.

Price, Bernie L. "Add a Skylight for Light & Air." Reprinted from *Mechanix Illustrated* magazine. Copyright 1981 by CBS Magazines.

Ramirez, Anthony, Sources of CO_2 from burning of Fossil Fuels graph. Reprinted from Anthony Ramirez, "A Warming World: What It Will Mean," *Fortune,* July 14, 1988, 102–110.

State of Michigan, Department of Treasury, Size of Michigan Income Tax Personal Exemption graph. Reprinted from *1987 Income Tax Return,* Lansing, Michigan, 1987.

U.S. Department of Agriculture, Agriculture Exports Graph. Reprinted from *1988 Agricultural Chartbook,* Washington, D.C.

U.S. Department of Agriculture, Handbook No. 673, 1988.

Wald, George. "The Origin of Life." Reprinted from *Scientific American,* Aug. 1954.

Index

Revision Symbols
for Student Papers